Misperceptions in
Foreign Policymaking

Published with a grant from the

KADOORIE FAMILY FUND

A Project of the

FUND FOR HIGHER EDUCATION

About the Book and Author

Misperceptions in Foreign Policymaking:
The Sino-Indian Conflict, 1959–1962
Yaacov Y.I. Vertzberger

This book examines the process by which government leaders perceive events and use information in making foreign policy decisions. In his case study of the Sino-Indian conflict, the author explores the attitudes that shaped India's policy toward China and traces the network of misunderstandings that led to a war unwanted by both sides. Taking into account technical, organizational, cultural, group-dynamic, and key personality variables, Dr. Vertzberger discusses the Sino-Indian conflict within a global and regional systems perspective and describes what was at stake in the conflict from the point of view of each country involved. Subsequent chapters analyze Nehru's view of India's role, the influence of national public opinion in shaping Nehru's attitudes, the perceived relationships between Sino-Indian interactions and India's relations with its neighbors, and India's evaluation of the balance of power between itself and China. One section of the book focuses on India's intelligence community and the mishandling of information that led to a failure of signaling efforts on both sides. Cultural differences between China and India, Nehru's personality and style of leadership, and the role of major organizations such as the army, various ministries, and Parliament are also assessed in terms of their impact on the conflict.

Dr. Vertzberger is lecturer in international relations at the Hebrew University in Jerusalem.

Published in cooperation with
The Harry S. Truman Research Institute
for the Advancement of Peace,
The Hebrew University of Jerusalem

Misperceptions in Foreign Policymaking: The Sino-Indian Conflict, 1959–1962

Yaacov Y.I. Vertzberger

Westview Press / Boulder, Colorado

For my parents Ester and Tuvia Vertzberger

A Westview Replica Edition

Copyright © 1984 by Westview Press, Inc.

Published in 1984 in the United States of America by
Westview Press, Inc.
5500 Central Avenue
Boulder, Colorado 80301
Frederick A. Praeger, President and Publisher

88-4218

Library of Congress Cataloging in Publication Data
Vertzberger, Yaacov.
  Misperceptions in foreign policymaking.
  (A Westview replica edition)
  Bibliography: p.
  Index included.
  1. Sino-Indian Border Dispute, 1959–1962. 2. India—Foreign relations. I. Title.
DS480.85.V43 1984   954.04   83-10206
ISBN 0-86531-970-7

Printed and bound in the United States of America.

10 9 8 7 6 5 4 3 2 1

"I do not expect, and I do not want the House to imagine that something very serious is going to happen on our frontiers. I do not at all expect that to happen." (*Prime Minister in Parliament on Sino-Indian Relations,* September 12, 1959)

"We were getting out of touch with reality in the modern world and we were living in an artificial atmosphere of our own creation. We have been shocked out of it." (Jawaharlal Nehru, *The Hindu,* October 26, 1962)

"We were like bad chess players who make moves without anticipating the opponent's moves, or expecting him to counter our move." (Brigadier J.S. Dalvi, 1969, 125)

"It was a game of Russian roulette but the highest authorities of India seemed to feel that the one shot in the cylinder was a blank. Unfortunately for them and for the country it was not so. The cylinder was fully loaded." (General J.N. Choudhuri, quoted in Maxwell, 1972, 177)

Contents

Tables and Figures

Acknowledgments

A book is a brainchild of its author but no man is an island, a fact reflected throughout the entire process from which this study emerged in its final form. When I first arrived as an undergraduate student at the Hebrew University in Jerusalem, I had the opportunity to study under Professor Ellis Joffe. It was he who introduced me to the intricacies of Chinese politics, both domestic and foreign. This he did with much skill, knowledge, and, most of all, elegance, and in a way that imprinted upon me a long-range interest in the complexities of Asian politics in general and Chinese politics in particular. In response to his constant encouragement, I eventually took up research in this field. Ultimately, he became one of my advisers for the dissertation that provided the groundwork for this book. Professor Joffe's advice, guidance, and intimate knowledge of the Chinese arena were indispensable to its writing. Critical, patient, and firm, he steered me around pitfalls and away from errors. Subsequently, he encouraged me to rewrite the dissertation in book form. For his ongoing friendship and guidance I shall always be indebted to him.

The other main influence on my intellectual development was Professor Michael Brecher, of McGill University, who pointed me toward the theory of international relations, virgin land for me until then, and demonstrated its richness and utility and the excitement of applying it to a better understanding of international politics. His enthusiasm was so inspiring that I have carried it with me ever since. As a noted scholar, also, of South Asian and in particular Indian affairs, he suggested that I take up an Indian case study, in which his advice and first-hand knowledge could be most useful. During the period in which he served as the other adviser for my dissertation, which combined my interest in theory, in China, and in India, he allowed me generous use of his private library and archives as well as free access to his time, knowledge, and wise advice. Later, he was kind enough to read an earlier draft of this study and to make important comments. His involvement with my work in general and with this project in particular I value most highly.

Professor Alexander George of Stanford University made it possible for me to stay at Stanford during the year I wrote the draft of this book. Professor George is an outstanding and versatile scholar, and his penetrating advice and support for my project made my year at Stanford most fruitful, stimulating, and memorable. For all his assistance, and for his friendship, I am most grateful.

Although my mention is necessarily brief, I would also like to thank the following people: Dr. Daniel Feferman, who was most helpful in advising me on matters relating to the application of statistical methods; Mr. Rafi Lipkin, who did the computer programming; Mr. Yoel Schleicher, an excellent research assistant, who helped in coding and other matters with his usual reliable dedication, patience, and sound judgment; and my friends Mrs. and Mr. Miriam and Maurice White, who provided me with a home away from home in Palo Alto during the year spent at Stanford University and thereby contributed more than they know to this study. The book could never have been started in the first place without the generous funding and support of the Kadoorie Family Fund for Chinese Studies (a project of the Fund for Higher Education), The Truman Institute of the Hebrew University, and its academic director, Professor Zvi Schiffrin.

I also wish to thank the following publishers and journal editors for the use of portions of my articles published by them: "India's Strategic Posture and Border War Defeat of 1962: A Case Study in Miscalculation," *The Journal of Strategic Studies,* Vol. 5, No. 3, September 1982 (published by Frank Cass, London); "India's Border Conflict With China: A Perceptual Analysis," *Journal of Contemporary History,* Vol. 17, No. 4, October 1982 (published by Sage Publications, London and Beverly Hills); "Misperception in International Politics: A Typological Framework for Analysis," *International Interactions,* Vol. 9, No. 3, October 1982 (published by Gordon and Breach, New York); and "Bureaucratic-Organizational Politics and Information Processing in a Developing State," *International Studies Quarterly,* Vol. 28, No. 1, March 1984 (published for the International Studies Association by Butterworth Scientific, Guildford).

The book would not have ended up in its current form but for my editors at Westview Press, Mr. Dean Birkenkamp and especially Ms. Christine Arden, who with great skill and diligence gave the manuscript its final literary polish and form, and Ms. Dalia Heftman, who with care and creativity prepared the graphs and tables.

Last but not least, my family was a constant source of inspiration and encouragement on the road to scholarly achievements. In particular, I would like to mention Berta and Leopold Werzberger, who followed my academic education so closely. But I owe the largest debt to my parents, who made so many sacrifices in order to fulfill what they have considered their main task of seeing to the education of their sons. To them I dedicate this book with love and respect.

Y.V.

Preface

The Rationale

Every research project has its own "trigger mechanism," the incentive that gives the researcher his first push and sustains him in the face of the inevitable difficulties and fatigue on the way to its completion.

This book grew out of my experience as an Israeli who underwent and shared the traumatic national "earthquake" of the Yom Kippur War, which may be considered a classic case of misperception and miscalculation by the Israeli leadership. There was no lack of warning information: nevertheless, the preferred interpretation—and, as a consequence, the preferred definition—of the situation was the one that fitted in with a less threatening evaluation.

My experience with the Yom Kippur War set me thinking about several questions: Was the Israeli experience unique? If it was not unique, what were the variables and dimensions relevant to misperceptions occurring in the first place, and what made them impervious to change in the face of dissonant information that should have raised serious doubts about the "conventional wisdom" in respect to the definition of the situation? In other words, What is behind the management and mismanagement of information? Misperception, miscalculations, and often surprise are nothing but the outcome of information management or processing.[1]

Behind these questions lurked the awesome possibility that there might be a strong element of determinism in the phenomenon of misperception. This possibility in turn might mean that although a social scientist could and should seek an explanation of the phenomenon, his or her chances of being able to provide some plausible and working prescriptions—to help avoid mismanagement of information—are at best slim.

The outcome of the search for answers to these questions was two-fold, consisting of a detailed theoretical analysis of the dimensions, processes, and causes of the mismangement of information as well as an in-depth analysis of a case study applying that same extensive theoretical framework. This volume's first chapter is a shortened presentation of the theoretical framework,[2] but it deals mainly with the specific case study chosen for analysis, that is, the Sino-Indian confrontation of 1959–1962. The case study is analyzed in line with the framework suggested in the opening chapter of the book. As such it also serves to test the validity and utility of the proposed theoretical framework,[3] and gives some additional insights into the research problem as is often the case with a detailed analysis of historical events. So what we have, in effect, is a research effort that combines elements of both inductive and deductive processes.[4]

This approach, termed "disciplined-configurative," was best described by H. Eckstein (1975, 100):

> Case study thus is tied into theoretical inquiry—but only partially, where theories apply or can be envisioned; passively in the main, as a receptacle for putting theories to work; and fortuitously, as a catalytic element in the unfolding of theoretical knowledge.[5]

The Case Study

Once I decided on a research strategy involving a mixed theoretical-empirical approach, a suitable case history—the Sino-Indian conflict—presented itself. It would be difficult to find an event more representative of the problem of misperception than the Sino-Indian confrontation, or more specifically, Nehru's perceptual dynamics in relation to Sino-Indian relations between 1959 and 1962.[6] The period ended abruptly with the dramatic and, for India, traumatic Chinese attack in the dawn of October 20, 1962, an attack that deprived India of more than 20,000 square km of territory, was a humiliating defeat for the Indian army, and occasioned a severe loss of face for the ruling National Congress Party and its leader both in domestic and international politics. Some even go so far as to suggest that the event was instrumental in the death of India's adored leader Jawaharlal Nehru, whose heart could not withstand the shattering of the vision, hopes, and beliefs he had held since the early 1930s.

Any investigation of perceptions and the concepts that derive from them finally comes down to an analysis on the individual level. Although organizational, social, and national variables play an important part in the formation of the individual's definition of the situation, the final product is epitomized in the individual policymaker himself. In this case, the intention is to concentrate on the man described by his biographer in the following words: "[Nehru] is the philosopher, the architect, the engineer and the voice of his country's policy towards the outside world" (Brecher, 1959, 564). He functioned officially as such from 1947 until 1964, but was already crystallizing Indian foreign policy perceptions in the pre-independence era[7] when the subject held little interest for most other leaders of the Congress

Party. This man more than any other in the Indian elite symbolized the "China policy" of the Indian government in the period under discussion.[8]

Apart from fulfilling the basic conditions of the subject of research, this particular case history had some additional advantages.

1. The time perspective. Serious deterioration in Sino-Indian relations started with the uprising in Tibet in 1959, which gives one a time perspective of twenty years, a most important asset in a historical case study.

2. Source material. There is enough source material, both primary and secondary, to make dealing with perception and information management possible.

3. Complexity. The case has enough complexity to make possible a multivariate treatment, providing a wide range of insights, implications, and relevance. And it is certainly a great intellectual challenge to the researcher.

4. Noninvolvement. Because many an analysis reflects the writer's national and personal biases,[9] it was hoped that choosing a case in which the author had no prior likes and dislikes and no personal or emotional attachment to personalities and events would contribute to a detached and objective analysis.

5. Historical importance. Nehru's China policy was of major importance within the general framework of India's foreign policy and, as such, was a reflection of Nehru's value and belief system. An in-depth analysis of the events might contribute to a better understanding of India's foreign policies during the Nehru era and to the post–Nehru policies, to the degree that their foundations were laid by Nehru.

The time span covered by the study is 1959 to 1962. It was not difficult to choose the end point. as the main preoccupation of the book lies not in the actual Sino-Indian war but in the misperceptions leading up to it, as such the surprise attack on October 20, 1962 provided a natural break. It was, however, more difficult to decide at what point to pick up the dispute. There were several possibilities: (1) October 1949, the founding of the People's Republic of China; (2) October 1950, the Chinese invasion and occupation of Tibet; (3) April 1954, the signing of the Panch Sheel Agreement symbolizing the honeymoon in relations between India and China; (4) March 1959, the escape of the Dalai Lama from Lhasa to India; or (5) August 1959, the Longju incident, which heralded the military escalation in Sino-Indian relations and the transition from verbal to physical violence[10] and also brought Indian public opinion as a relevant variable into the decisionmaking process.

The choice fell on the fourth possibility, the escape of the Dalai Lama from Lhasa, for the following reasons: the period from 1959 to 1962 was, in contrast to previous periods, the richest in events, reactions, and counterreactions, producing an abundance of data on the attitudes and conceptions of both sides. As a result, for India it was a period in which the Chinese problem provided a constant flow of information to be evaluated and in which the perceptual problems became most acute. Once 1959 was established as a point of departure, it was easier to choose between event (4) and event (5).

The Longju incident acutally took place in the context of a deterioration in relations between the two countries. Chinese suspicions were aroused when, following the rebellion in Tibet, the Chinese were vehemently attacked by certain Indian leaders[11] and the mass media. They feared that India might itself become a base for the subversive activities of the Dalai Lama's supporters. On the other hand, for a substantial part of the Indian public, Chinese behavior revealed a flagrant disregard of the 1951 agreement, which had given Tibet autonomy, and secured a prologue to a more aggressive stance against India. Thus, one must consider the Longju incident against the background of events in Tibet culminating in the escape of the Dalai Lama to India, which is the starting point for our analysis.

A Note on Sources, Methodology, and Structure

The Sino-Indian war and the events leading up to it have been dealt with extensively in the literature, a large part of which involves Indian apologetics, that is, a shifting of the blame from certain individuals or organizations to others. This type of literature helps us glimpse the interpersonal relations within the Indian political-military elite.[12] A different category of literature tries to lay the blame on Chinese "treachery"[13] while emphasizing India's, and especially Nehru's, generosity towards China and his attempts to legitimize the Chinese regime in the international arena and in forums such as the Nonaligned and Afro-Asian Conferences, and especially at the United Nations.[14]

A third kind of writing is devoted to blaming the Indian leadership for being aggressive and unyielding. Such literature promotes a sympathetic attitude toward what it considers a Chinese policy of compromise and magnanimity, based on altruism and a consistent quest for peace.[15]

Another category tries to pinpoint the "guilty" from a legal point ov view. In addition to its abundance of technical legal details, claims, and debates, this literature is overflowing with political and historical material serving to substantiate this or that claim. Here, too, of course, each side has its own advocates.[16]

The last category of studies on the subject tries to give a straight objective historical account of events, that is, without taking a position. Rather, it is up to the reader to make up his or her own mind. This literature is basically descriptive in nature.[17]

What characterizes most of the literature is the abundance of political and legal detail of varying significance, and despite the occasional contradictions, it is generally of immense descriptive value. This book, however, does not intend to be another descriptive, legal, or partisan treatise. Its principal subject is the dynamics of misperception as expressed in the attitudes, evaluations, and concepts of one particular political leader, India's Prime Minister Jawaharlal Nehru. In other words, this is an analysis of the rationale and sources of India's China policy from 1959 to 1962.

Because of the central role played by the Chinese issue in India's overall foreign policies, an analysis of the subject is also revealing with regard to the basic framework of Nehru's foreign policy—on the conceptual, organizational, and personal levels. This framework consisted of Nehru's world view and value system as applied to foreign policy, the interaction of economics and politics, the linkage of domestic and international politics, the role of organizations in shaping foreign policy, and last, but not least, the impact of personal interactions in the processes of crystallization of views and policies.

The reader must keep in mind that this is a book about India and that the Chinese side is brought in only to supplement our analysis with regard to India. This fact is also reflected in the bibliography.

The sources used vary in terms of quality and type, as the bibliography further indicates, and include both primary and secondary sources:

1. An exchange of letters between the leaders of both countries, Nehru and Chou En-lai, and between their respective foreign ministries. These were published by the Indian government as *White Papers* (*W.P.*). For the period under discussion, 1959 to 1962, the first eight volumes were used. This source will be quoted by initials, volume, and page number (e.g., *W.P.*, II, 22).
2. Nehru's speeches and answers in the Upper and Lower House debates (Lok Sabha and Rajya Sabha) during the same period of time. These were published by the Indian government in two volumes and will be referred to by volume and page number (e.g., *Par.*, I, 24).
3. Press conferences held by Nehru in the period under discussion, collected and published by the Indian government in two volumes, to be quoted by volume and page number (e.g., *Press*, I, 36).
4. Nehru's speeches at various forums, as published by the Indian government in four volumes covering the period from 1947 to 1963.
5. Nehru's classified fortnightly letters to the chief ministers in which he discussed frankly his thoughts on current affairs as well as long-term purposes. This source has not been used in earlier publications on Sino-Indian relations. The letters are quoted by number and date (e.g., *F.N.*, 5/59, May 28, 1959).

6. Collections of documents published by governmental and non-governmental organizations.
7. The *Peking Review,* an important source for the Chinese version of the historical events in question. It will be quoted by initials, date, and page (e.g., *P.R.,* Sept. 15, 1962, 24).
8. Autobiographies, biographies, and personal accounts of eye witnesses, as published in subsequent years by some of those involved.
9. Scholarly works published by Indian and Western scholars and journalists.
10. Background material provided by the widely circulated and prestigious *Times of India.*

A quantitative content analysis was performed on the *White Papers,* on Nehru's speeches and answers in Parliament, and on the *Peking Review.* A traditional historical analysis was carried out, of course, on all of this material. Throughout the process of analysis, the aim has been to rely whenever possible on double verification (qualitative and quantitative). However, in order to make the text readable to those not acquainted with the various statistical methods used, only the results and conclusions drawn from this data are presented in the text. The quantitative data itself is presented in detail in the Statistical Appendix.

As for structure, the book can roughly be divided into four parts. The first presents the theoretical framework and the general hypotheses derived from it. The second and third parts, respectively, present a description and explanation of Nehru's misperceptions and their dynamics, using the framework mentioned earlier. The fourth and last part draws the conclusion for the specific case study as well as for the general problem of management of information and evaluates the validity of the framework in light of its employment in the analysis of the case history.

Yaacov Y.I. Vertzberger

Misperceptions:
Sources and Processes—A Theory

The Critical Assumptions

This chapter presents a theory that deals with the dynamics—the sources and the processes—of misperceptions in international politics. The theory is holistic, in the sense suggested by Diesing: that is, "composed of several relatively independent loosely linked parts, rather than that of deduction from a few basic postulates. . . . When a theory is applied to a case, each section illuminates a different aspect of the case so that the whole theory together gives many-sided illuminations and guidance to case studies and comparisons" (1971, 222). The choice of a holistic approach, rather than any other, was dictated by the complex and multifaceted nature of the phenomenon of misperception in foreign policymaking. This theoretical framework, then, provides the guidelines for both describing and explaining the case study.

The process of decisionmaking can roughly be divided into three stages. In the first, information from the environment is accumulated and processed. In the second, this information serves as a basis for the evaluation of alternatives perceived by the policymaker as relevant to the situation; a particular alternative is then chosen. In the third stage, the decision is implemented. Thus, the first stage, the definition of the situation, becomes the critical one, as it forms the basis of the entire process. A distorted image of reality may engender a situation in which the decisionmaking process and its results will be far less than optimal, with all the ramifications for those involved; hence, the importance of understanding the dynamics of misperception.

Misperception as a phenomenon is not exclusive to the area of foreign policy. But the international scene and the realm of relations among nations, as we shall discover, do facilitate the creation of conditions under which misperceptions are formed and maintained. The special relevance of the subject to this specific human field of action also stems from the particularly grave implications that mis-

Figure 1.1. Environment-Decision Nexus

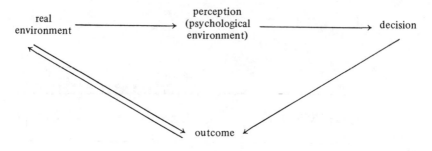

perceptions may have in the area of foreign policy, due to the high price they exact in human, material, and moral terms. This price is paid by the nation, the collective, in its entirety, in contrast to misperceptions in daily life by which the individual, or at most a few people, suffers the consequences. Moreover, in the international arena, interdependence being one of its characteristics, the implications of misperceptions go far beyond national boundaries to influence the lives of other nations as well. Thus, even if some leaders are especially adept at adopting a realistic view and perception of reality, they might still fall victim to the consequences of perceptual fallacies that occur beyond their own national borders.

In this book the term *perception* is defined as being composed of two elements: a dynamic one—the process of becoming cognizant of the environment and its evaluation; and the other, a static one—the cognitive, evaluative, and affective consciousness of the stimuli flowing from the environment—in other words, the final product of the process, namely, the image[1] formed at the end (Krech and Crutchfield, 1971).

Misperception, then, is bidimensional: it includes the process by which a distorted perception of reality is formed as well as the specific content of the distorted image. In operational terms, a misperception is seen as a gap between the real environment and the psychological one of the policymaker. In other words, we are dealing with the cognitive connections between the decisionmaker and his environment, which are at the same time the mediating factors between the environment and the decision. The relationship is shown in Fig. 1.1.

The perception of the environment influences the decision, the results of which serve as input to the change in the environment, but which are also constrained by the limitations imposed by the environment. The new environment serves as input for a new process of decisionmaking through the intervening variable of the perception, and so on.[2]

The critical assumptions at the basis of this study follow:

1. There are two realities: objective and subjective. The objective reality is a yardstick against which the perception of the policymaker can be measured and the degree of distortion and incompatibility determined.

2. Perceptual processes of political leaders are of particular interest because of their important consequences and because they are more susceptible to distortions due to the nature of leadership roles and the patterns of interaction resulting from them.[3]

3. The quality of the decision is determined to a large extent by the size of the gap between the image and reality. All else being constant, there is an inverse relationship between the quality of the decision and the size of the perceptual gap.

4. Despite what was noted in assumption 3, considering that international relations are based on interaction, the probability that a decision based on a balanced and undistorted perception will be optimal is *conditional* also on the perception of the opponent. However, a necessary, though not sufficient, condition is that the perceptual system forming the basis of the actor's decisions must be as accurate as possible.

5. The degree of inefficiency of any decisionmaking system is to a large extent a function not only of the amount of the perceptual distortion at the point of departure but also of the policymaker's ability to adjust over time.

6. No decisionmaking system is immune by nature[4] from misperceptions, and there is no such thing as absolute immunity. Thus, the process of decisionmaking in the political sphere is at best one of limited rationality.

The theoretical framework based on these assumptions and presented in this chapter deals with the presentation of a typology describing the main patterns of misperceptions and the patterns of possible adjustment. In addition, an attempt has been made to present an interdisciplinary, multivariable, integrative explanation of the phenomenon and its dynamics. The explanatory variables are the nature of the information and the rules for its processing, the personalities of the decisionmakers, organizational processes, group dynamics, and national culture. As we shall see, these variables cover the three levels of analysis of the individual, the state, and the international system. Moreover, I have attempted to state the background conditions determining the nature and direction of the influence of the above-mentioned variables on the perceptual process. Thus, it is my intention to suggest a systematic, conceptual framework that will further an understanding of the investigated phenomenon.

Two aspects should be emphasized: first, the investigated phenomenon comprises not the whole process of decisionmaking but only the stage of the flow of stimuli from the environment to the cognitive system of the policymakers, their absorption, and their processing into a consolidated definition of the situation that encourages the preference of this or that action orientation. The evaluation of the situation includes the situation's description and the environment in which the policymaker acts, the apprehended alternatives, and the possible anticipated outcomes of each alternative.

Secondly, we are not interested in situations in which erroneous conceptions are formed due to a *lack* of relevant information.[5] From an intellectual point of view, these situations are uninteresting for one concerned with the processing and managing of information. For that reason, this study, both in its theoretical and in its empirical parts, concentrates on those situations in which the misperceptions cannot be accounted for as resulting from lack of information. Specifically, the concern is with situations in which the decisionmaker in a particular political system has available information of a quantity and quality sufficient to provide a suitable image but still chooses an erroneous situation definition.

The Real and Psychological Environments: Dimensions and Content

What are the dimensions and content of the real and the psychological environments? The definition of these criteria is crucial, as the gap between the two environments has been defined as an indicator with which to test the degree of misperception.

Let us begin with the presentation of the dimensions of the real environment, keeping in mind that the term *real environment* includes the totality of conditions and factors that could be relevant to the behavior of the State and that define the constraints within which the policymaker is bound.

In general terms, one can define six dimensions that determine the framework of limitations dictated by the environment.[6]

1. The Ecological Dimension (in the narrow sense): limitations to behavior resulting from geographical, topographical, and climatic elements.

2. The Organizational Dimension: the organizational structure of the environment. This dimension deals with questions such as: How many poles has the global system? What international organizations exist? What are the areas of their activity? What is the degree of their influence? The answers to these and other questions set the limitations resulting from the organizational content of the environment.

3. The Reinforcement Dimensions (Reward and Punishment): What are the reinforcements that the environment provides for different forms of behavior? For example, is an aggressive state punished (or sanctioned) by international organizations? Or is aggression received complacently by nations not directly harmed by it? The existence or nonexistence of reinforcement may in itself act as a limitation on certain kinds of behavior.

4. The Normative Dimension: The system of values, beliefs, norms, and dominant aspirations may act as a limitation on behavior that contradicts that system. Significantly, this normative dimension may also contribute to, or be part of, the reinforcement dimension of the environment, as a factor encouraging or deterring certain kinds of behavior.

5. The Commitment Dimension: with reference to behavioral patterns to which an actor is bound by being part of or related to specific political entities. Thus, partnership within an alliance demands certain types of behavior toward the partner, and a different sort toward those outside the alliance. Membership in an organization such as the United Nations, for example, demands, at least nominally, the adoption of specific standards, and any deviation from them requires explanation or self-justification.

6. The Power Dimension: The components of power (economic, military, and so on) may determine which kinds of behavior are possible and which are not.

How the policymaker perceives these dimensions is of crucial importance, as it affects the choice of behavior and, once a policy is chosen, how it fits the set of real or illusory limitations.

The ability of the actor to respond to these limitations, that is, to change them, is dependent on the following factors:

1. The power of the actor in question. Super powers have fewer environmental limitations, and their ability to mould the environment, or parts of it, is greater than that of smaller states.

2. The nature and quality of a said behavior. The effect of large-scale war on the environment is often greater than that of diplomatic moves, in terms of changing the structure of the environmental balance of constraints.

3. The nature and quality of the various elements comprising the environment. There are some elements in the environment that are more flexible than others and that, as a result, allow for more deviations from the limitations set at a given time. There are other more rigid elements as well, which dictate very difficult or unchangeable limitations over a foreseeable period. For example, if we examine the current global system, we find that the nuclear military power balance between the two super powers dictates the limitations defined earlier as rigid, and it does not seem that they can be changed in the near future. For such change would necessitate that one of the super powers achieve a significant technological breakthrough, of a kind that would guarantee it first-strike capability and the ability to survive any counterattack. On the other hand, there is a still more flexible aspect of the nuclear nature of the global system, namely, the number of nations having a nuclear military option. That number has changed over time.

If we summarize the three factors, we could say that the implications of the reciprocal relations between the environment and the actor are a function of the actor's attributes, the attributes of his acts, and the nature of the relevant environmental attributes. An understanding of these factors is crucially important in the actor's estimation of the extent to which he can change the environment or to which he can prevent it from becoming an obstacle in the implementation of his decision and goal achievement.

The psychological environment is a reflection of reality in the policymaker's mind, but it is also functional:

> Perceiving is goal-directed behavior. The goal of perception, in its broadest sense, is the construction of a meaningful behavioral environment—an environment congruent with "reality" on the one hand and the needs and the disposition of the organism on the other (Postman and Bruner, 1948, 314).

Thus, in order for the psychological environment to perform efficiently and thereby satisfy the policymaker's basic needs, it may at times be oversimplified or distorted.

The perceptual totality is made up of two layers: one of background attributes, and the other containing the definition of the specific contents of the environment. There is an interaction and reciprocal influence within and between the layers. This interface, as we shall see, is an important source of misperceptions, as the final concept is an outcome of the mutual relations between these two layers. Moreover, the interaction between the first layer and the second necessarily dictates the nature of the dynamics in the conceptual system. This point will be enlarged upon later in our discussion.

The first layer includes the following elements:[7]

- *The spatial factor,* which determines the actor's definition of his own locale. For example, do Israeli policymakers see Israel as belonging to Asia or to Europe? Do Indian policymakers perceive India as part of the developing nations?
- *The temporal factor,* which determines how each actor sees time and its implications for his behavior. Is the passage of time perceived as neutral, as acting against, or as acting in his favor? Does he estimate that he has much time in which to make a choice or does he feel that he is pressured for time?
- *The interaction factor,* which determines the basic perception of the mutual relations between the actor and his environment, such as the extent to which the international environment is one of constant struggle, hostile or friendly, changeable or fixed. This factor, of course, determines conclusions and anticipations as to the results of alternatives modes of behavior.[8]

- *The affective factor,* which determines the feelings of the actor toward the object of perception.
- *The value factor,* which determines the hierarchy of values used to evaluate the object of perception. This hierarchy falls along a scale ranging from what is morally good to what is morally bad.[9]
- *The individual-public factor,* which determines the extent to which the individual's perception is shared by the collective to which he belongs.[10]
- *The level-of-uncertainty factor,* which determines the degree of the actor's faith in his perception, which in turn determines how resistant his perception is to change.
- *The consciousness factor,* which determines to what degree there are elements in the image of which the individual is not wholly conscious. The greater the number of such elements, the more difficult it is to prevent or correct perceptual distortion.
- *The internalization-externalization factor,* which determines whether the image is concerned with the self or with others.

There may certainly be connections and mutual influences and reinforcements among the various dimensions of the image.[11] Thus, for example, the affective factor, the estimation of a certain object as liked or disliked, may be influenced by the ethical factor. It might also be that the degree of uncertainty may be influenced by the individual-public factor, that is, by the extent to which the image is supported by the identical images of others.

As for the specific contents of the environment, it seems that the most detailed description of these, as it applies to foreign policy, was suggested by Brecher and his colleagues (1969),[12] to which we have made some additions and modifications. These included the structure and nature of the global system; the structure and nature of the immediate subsystem; the impact of other subsystems; relations with the super powers; reciprocal relations with other actors, national and transnational, state and nonstate; geographical influences;[13] military power; economic power; the structure of the actor's political system and institutions; pressure groups; competing elites, representing alternative conceptions of the totality of problems and orientations in foreign policy;[14] and the perceived legal status of the specific problem in question.

As mentioned earlier, there are reciprocal relations between the two layers. Feelings of hostility and threat toward other actors are to a large extent an outcome of the affective or ethical factors. Thus, for example, the attitude and the perception of developing nations toward multinational companies and their activities are the outcome of their view that these companies are a version of neocolonialism or economic imperialism, with the ethical and emotional connotations such as approach carries with it.

But these mutual relations are important not only on the static level, that is, such that they define the situation at every given moment, but also for the question of the dynamics of the existing perceptions in the face of dissonant information. For example, the smaller the factor of uncertainty, or the greater the faith that the existing concepts are consensual, the lower will be the willingness to change them, even in the face of dissonant information.

Misperceptions and Adaptational Processes

At the beginning of this study, perception was defined as composed of two factors—static and dynamic. The static element of misperception is measured by the size of the gap between the real environment and its perception at a given point in time, symbolically represented as T_0. The dynamic element determines what happens to misperceptions over time—in other words, in the period between T_0 and T_1. What happens to misperceptions in this time period may determine the static component of misperception—the gap between reality and the image—in the time T_1. Thus, we see how these two components complement each other.

The point of departure for this study is the misperception at a given moment. It is possible to differentiate between three categories of misperceptions:

1. *Awareness gap,* which will be defined as a gap stemming from the fact that the policymaker is totally unaware of a relevant variable in the environment. This is a purely qualitative gap, as the variable does not exist at all in the decisionmaker's cognition.

2. *Relevance gap,* which will be defined as a gap resulting from the fact that the policymaker does not see the relevance of a variable or variables pertaining to a particular decision, although they are in fact relevant. In this case, the policymaker is aware of the existence of the variable(s) in the environment. This kind of gap is on the borderline between the qualitative and quantitative; that is, the decisionmaker recognizes the variable but accords it zero importance in his cognition. Relevance gap relates not only to the lack of attention paid to relevant variables but also to the inclusion of irrelevant variables.

3. *Evaluation gap,* which will be defined as a gap resulting from the fact that the policymaker, while seeing the variable as relevant to the decision, does not evaluate its relative importance realistically within the ensemble of relevant variables. This kind of gap, then, is a purely quantitative gap.

The interaction between the different elements of information, which add up to a total picture, is a kind of kaleidoscopic process. Herein lies the reason for which misperceptions of the types described, even with regard to relatively few information items, tend to lay the ground for distortions of interpretation; that is, from among possible alternative definitions of the situation, a wrong one will be chosen.

It may happen that the policymaker will suffer from more than one type of misperception simultaneously, in relation to different variables and different issue areas. He might, for example, suffer from an awareness gap in the context of the influence of economic variables, a relevance gap in relation to the role of public opinion, and an evaluation gap as to military power. Moreover, there might be, as we shall see in the case of India, mutual support and reinforcement among the misperceptions.

The contribution of each type of misperception to a fallacious decision will be the outcome of the following:

1. The importance of the misperceived data within the ensemble of variables relevant to the decision. The greater their weight, the greater will be their influence on the quality of the decision.
2. The type of misperception. It seems that a misperception is easier to correct when there is awareness of the data, even if underevaluated, than when such awareness does not exist at all in the decisionmaker's cognition.
3. The spill-over effect. Specifically, to what extent does a misperception about a certain variable lead to misperception about other variables? This issue is related to the question of the extent to which different variables are seen as interconnected.

Attention must also be paid to the different levels and types of aggregation of occurrences where misperceptions are likely to occur, which represent the range of fallacious information processing:

1. The isolated event that occurred or did not occur. It must be remembered that in social relations the fact that something did not occur is no less important than the fact that something did occur. Even the fact of the nonoccurrence of any event is given an interpretation that is rooted in the perceptions of the individual.
2. The sequence of events. In this case, the misperception may relate to the pattern seen as emerging from a set of events.
3. Nonevents, in other words, processes that are not event-bound.
4. The ecology. This refers to misperception of the overall constraints within which the policymaker is obliged to operate and against which the isolated event or the sequence of events are evaluated and interpreted.

The four levels of aggregation are in fact interdependent in the sense that each is a necessary part of the higher levels of aggregation. Any set of events is made up of individual events. Any process is at least partly made up of patterns that are the outcome of combinations and interactions of sets of events that are nonadditive, meaning that the sum is not a simple adding up of the individual events but is more than or different from that sum due to some interaction effect. Thus, for instance, any change in the ecology is, in the long run, an outcome of a combination of the other three levels.

Consequently, misperceptions at the level of the individual event will have an impact—at the sequence-of-events or process levels—to the degree that this event was part of the others. However, it will be very difficult to predict the final degree of misperception without specific information about the relative weight of the misperceived event as well as about its exact relationship with the other components of the sequence or process.

The degree to which any particular type of misperception of any specific data-set will have a spillover effect on other present or future data-sets is dependent on (1) the perceived and objective relationship between the two data-sets, which might lead to either disjunction or conjunction of the two, and (2) the importance of the misperceived data to the overall picture that included as part of it this specific data.

The dynamic aspect of misperception, the processes of adjustment, and revision due to feedback or newly available information can be classified into three categories: (1) *maladaptation,* in which the gap(s) between the environment and its perception grows over time, (2) *nonadaptation,* in which the gap(s) between the environment and its perception remains constant over time; and (3) *positive adaptation,* in which the gap(s) between the environment and its perception diminishes over time.

It might certainly happen that different processes will take place at once. The adaptation toward certain gaps may be positive in some cases and maladaptations in others.[15] The fact that the variables that were relevant in T_o are not necessarily relevant in T_i is not an obstacle in the analysis of the process, although it seems to create a problem of comparison between the periods. What is of interest to us is this question: Has the performance of the decisionmaker improved over time,[16] as expressed by the criterion of a more precise situation evaluation? Or, in other words, What is the role of experience in improving the precision of perception?

The entire adaptation process includes four stages that are parallel, in large part, to the types of perceptual gaps mentioned earlier. These stages are (1) becoming aware of the existence of the data; (2) assigning the data to a certain issue area (economic, military, etc.); (3) evaluating the importance of the data within the issue-area; and (4) choosing between possible interpretative alternatives. Any failure in one or more of the components of the process will finally lead to one or more of the described misperceptions.

The content of these stages is influenced by the actor's response to the difficulties within his environment. This response, in turn, is expressed in his foreign policy. Thus, a number of general response patterns may be anticipated from an actor in the international arena:[17]

1. The development of attributes and behavior patterns that recognize the limitations imposed by the environment. A tendency to such a response pattern usually leads to what we have defined as positive adaptation. In such a case, the foreign policy does fulfill its role; in other words, it copes optimally with the changing international environment.

2. An attempt to escape from the existing environment to one in which the patterns of behavior and the qualities needed fit those of the actor in his present situation. Such a pattern of adaptation is not one that is realistic to an actor on the international scene, for obvious reasons. Instead, the actor may conceive of his environment as different from what it really is. Thus, an "escape" is made by means of a distorted concept of the environment, which now fits his present abilities, wishes, and anticipations. Such a pattern of response leads to nonadaptation.

3. Changing the environment. This possibility is also usually unrealistic in the short run for an actor in international politics. But quite a few delusions have been created by policymakers from the belief that they could change the environment and mould it according to their wishes. When this outcome did not materialize, they deluded themselves out of a reluctance to admit the failure of their vision and thus "escaped" from reality (see pattern 2). Similar results might also arise from the unwillingness to accept, as a given, the length of time required to remould the environment or from the creation of illusory shortcuts. This type of reaction leads to nonadaptation or even maladaptation.

We have seen, then, that there is room for distinction between different patterns of misperception, as between different possible processes of the dynamics of these misperceptions. Later on in this chapter we shall explain the above-mentioned phenomena in terms of the interaction among 5 variables: the nature of the information and the procedures of its processing; the personality factor; the organizational structure; the structure and nature of the decisionmaking group; and the societal-cultural system.

The Information and Its Processing Procedures

The Nature and Types of Information in International Relations

Information is transmitted, received, interpreted, and used by decisionmakers in the foreign policy field as in any other. However, the first explanatory variable, the nature of the information and its processing procedures, demands an understanding of the unique difficulty that exists in handling information in the political sphere. The policymaker, who is involved in information-processing, struggles with a number of critical questions, which, in the logical order of their appearance, are as follows: (1) Is what he is dealing with truly information? (2) Assuming that it is information, is it relevant to the problem? (3) Assuming that it is relevant, is it important? (4) Assuming that it is relevant and important, which of all the possible interpretations is the correct one?

For reasons to be clarified, and for reasons that are connected to the uniqueness of the international arena, each processor of information will consciously or unconsciously set himself criteria and standards of acceptability, which may range from rigid to very flexible.

Whatever the criterion, the answer given to the questions mentioned earlier may lead either to a Type 1 error or to a Type 2 error. A Type 1 error is the kind that is made when information that should have been grasped as information is rejected, that is, when it does not penetrate the cognitive system; or information that should have been considered relevant is rejected as irrelevant; or information that should have been estimated as important is dismissed as unimportant. A Type 2 error is one in which noise is perceived as meaningful information; or in which information that should have been rejected as irrelevant is seen as relevant; or in which information that should have been evaluated as unimportant is regarded as important. Referring back to question 4, each error usually implies making both a Type 1 *and* a Type 2 error simultaneously, as the rejection of the correct interpretation (Type 1) is concurrent with the adoption of an incorrect one (Type 2).[18] As will be seen, one source of error is connected with the four layers of problematics resulting from the qualities of the information and its flow: the nature of the environment, the characteristics of the information, the interaction with the information, and its transmission from one actor to another.

This special difficulty of handling information in the realm of international politics and the need to set standards of acceptability stem from the uniqueness of its basic characteristics related to those of the environment, which is the source of the information. In order to understand this, we must examine the possible components of the generalized term *information:*

- *Occurrence:* anything happening in the actor's environment or any part of it, whether it stems from a specific decision or from circumstances, or from a process, such as a change in the structure of the international system.
- *Event:* a specific behavior (including verbal behavior) stemming from a *decision* by the authorized political government of a

state or any other political organization. The government is that body that has the authority to commit the resources of the said political entity to carry out the specific behavior. From this it follows that every event is an occurrence, but not all occurrences are events. In addition, an event is limited in time and place, whereas an occurrence is not necessarily thus limited.

- *Message:* an event or happening that results from a decision of the authorized government and that has a specific, predetermined target. It should be emphasized that the message may not necessarily reach, or even be seen as a message by, the defined target.
- *Stimulus:* an event or occurrence that penetrates the cognitive system of a given actor in the system, although not all stimuli necessarily bring about active responses. Every message may become a stimulus, but not all stimuli are necessarily messages.

In other words, even given the assumption that an occurrence, event, or message becomes a stimulus, that is, penetrates the actor's cognitive system, the actor must still determine the nature of the information. Is it an occurrence, an event, or a message? This determination is crucial in terms of the answers to be given to the questions we noted earlier. But, at the same time, the determination encounters difficulties connected to certain characteristics of the international political environment:

Multiplicity of Actors. International society is a multi-actor society. This characteristic has two aspects: (1) The plurality of actors creates a large quantity of information and stimuli flowing into each actor. Often, the systems of dealing with the information cannot cope with the quantities coming in, in terms of both actual absorption and systematic decoding. To this we must add the fact that each actor participates in a number of games simultaneously and receives feedback from several sources, a factor that also contributes to the variety of the information. (2) Every major actor, whether a state or an international organization, is divided into a number of secondary actors,[19] or bureaucratic bodies, which struggle for influence over policymaking (Allison, 1969; 1971). These secondary actors contribute to an enlarging of the quantity of information; to a multiplicity of explanations given to specific bits of information fitting each actor's particular goals; and to the accumulation of noise in the system. The final result is an increased confusion of the major body dealing with the gathering and processing of the information.

Deception. The use of deception has been accepted as legitimate in international relations. The different actors try to mislead the target actors by leaking incorrect or correct but partial information to create the desired conceptions. As a result, a difficulty is created in distinguishing between three types of messages: (1) noises: insignificant signals transmitted on purpose or not, but interpreted by an actor as relevant and significant for him (Wohlstetter, 1962, 3);[20] (2) signals: statements or acts the significance of which has been decided on by explicit or implicit agreement between actors. Both sender and receiver are aware that their signals may express real or deceptive facts; and (3) indices: statements or acts the significance of which was explicitly or implicitly agreed on by both sides, but, in contrast to signals, in their substance there is some kind of proof that the facts they express must be *true*—for example, an action, the cost of which is too high to have been carried out just in order to deceive the opponent. In other words, the nature of the action is such that it is inextricably connected to the true intentions and capability of the actor who performed it (Jervis, 1970, 18).

Such difficulty in distinction could be the result of either intentional behavior on the other side[21] or the fear of one actor that his opponent does indeed intend to deceive him, even if he is not sure of this. Such fear stems from the idea that bargaining power in international politics is defined as the ability to deceive and pretend, with the hope of influencing the opponent's expectations and hence his behavior (Schelling, 1970, 23).

Uncertainty. Information is often of multiple significance and can be given various interpretations. This ambiguity could be the result of the content of the specific information or of the awareness of the actor that intentional misleading is an accepted rule of the game. This is why there is a tendency to look for additional meanings in the information and to attribute ambiguity to it even when it does not lend itself to such a view. What is more, even when the information is unambiguous, often its long-run implications—in terms of future results or the reaction it demands—are not obvious.

Secrecy. Naturally, actors in the international scene tend to keep a great deal of information required by other actors under a curtain of secrecy. The result is a lack of information classified as "sensitive" or at least the subjective feeling of such a lack.[22] On the other hand, there is a relative abundance of what is defined as routine, undesirable information. The greater the demand for the first kind and the smaller its degree of availability, the higher the "price" the consumer is willing to pay for it. One of the main components of this price rise is the lowering of the threshold of critical appraisal of the information's reliability.[23] In other words, the consumer will adopt needed information as true, even if it does not stand up to all the criteria of reliability. To this we should add the fact that difficulty in obtaining information facilitates the intentional transmission of misleading information by the opponent.[24] On the other hand, the shortage of information increases the uncertainty about what has already been gathered and processed (see the earlier section on "uncertainty).

The shortage in information stemming from secrecy enables the policymaker to legitimize the adoption of a "convenient" definition of the situation that answers his psychological-personal needs or others such as domestic or political ones, even if they are not realistic.[25] On the other hand, as it is accepted that important information is secret, increasing its availability may lower its reliability in the eyes of the consumer. An outstanding example of this was shown in October 1973 in the Israeli leadership's ignoring of Sadat's warnings that he was preparing for war.

Nonexistence of Information. Certain kinds of desired information do not exist. For example, how is it possible to find information concerning the opponent's intentions if he himself has not decided yet what his intentions are? There is always the tendency to assume that it is unlikely that important information does not exist. This problem creates similar ones to those mentioned as resulting from a shortage originating in secrecy, which are also expressed in the tendency to "invent" information based on noises or other irrelevant data.

Multiplicity and Variety of Audiences. Messages exchanged among nations have several potential audiences: local elite, local public, opponent's elite, opponent's public, elites in other countries, and world public opinion. Therefore, even when the content of any particular message itself is not ambiguous, it is often possible to find different messages, delivered on the same subject to different potential audiences, that contradict each other. In this instance, of course, we have the difficulty of choosing the message representing the true intentions of the sender.[26] And even if we assume that the message conveying the true intentions can be pinpointed, there is still the problem of implementing their content. A situation might arise in which the sender of a message finds himself, due to circumstances, having to make true precisely the message that he originally defined as being only for domestic needs. Then, because the message does exist, he can legitimately carry it out without seeming to have wished to deceive.

Source Ambiguity. One of the criteria that determines the salience and relevance of a message and its potential for becoming a stimulus is the question of who initiated it. At times it is not possible to locate the source easily, especially in those cases where the initiator and the known sender of the message are not one and the same, such as when the latter acts as a facade. This situation enables the initiator to avoid committing himself to a certain line of action and at the same time to examine his opponent's response to a certain kind of possible behavior. An acceptable tactic is to attribute a message to a third party—as if coming from there—and thus present the sender himself as having closed options, as one who cannot disengage himself from the third party's patronage. Or, conversely, the sender can present himself as one who should not be considered seriously, lacking the opportunity to take the intiative such as he is.

The awareness of these difficulties, the constant need to deal with the problems that they present in connection with the reliability of information, and the increasing challenge of making decisions that necessitate at least a minimum of reliable information create the conscious or unconscious drive to set criteria of acceptability. Without such criteria, which actually determine the margin of risk the policy-maker is prepared to undertake in relation to information involving some degree of uncertainty, and which may be unreliable, the policy-maker will find himself helpless to carry out his functions.

The Absorption of the Stimulus and Its Evaluation

The characteristics of the information and the environmental circumstances in which it is perceived or evaluated are very important in information processing. They may, in fact, be no less important than the actual content of the information. Moreover, it should be noted that the same factors often act in opposite directions in processing procedures. Although such factors may contribute to the illumination of certain information, they may also be responsible for the belittling of the importance of the information such that its impact on the final picture becomes secondary.

Basically, it can be said that there are two main categories of circumstances that determine the level of likelihood that the information will be given attention. One category is not conditional on a change in the existing threshold of attention. In other words, the question of whether the information will penetrate or not will be conditional only on the nature of the information to the extent that it stands up to the criteria of penetration set by the *existing* threshold of attention.

The second category is the one involved with changing the level of the existing threshold of attention, that is, with its raising or lowering, as a result of situational or other influences. The significance of this category is that, were there to be changes in the level of the existing threshold of attention, information that in the past succeeded in penetrating may not be able to do so in the present or in the future.

For the sake of brevity, only a small number of examples showing the difference between the two categories will be presented.[27] For example, there are two qualities in information that facilitate its penetration into the decisionmaker's cognition.[28] One is notability. The more unusual and exceptional the information, the greater its chance of being noticed. The other quality is specificity. When information concerns a long and protracted process, there is a tendency to notice at most only its beginning or end, whichever is the more specific. The process itself often does not gain the observer's attention.

Circumstances such as timing[29] can, as said, lower or raise the threshold of penetration of information. When there is a demand for certain information, the threshold for it is lowered (Triandias, 1971, 98; Jervis, 1976, 203–204; Janis and Mann, 1977, 212–214). Another example is self-confidence. When an individual already possesses information about his ability to deal with a potential threat, then the level of alertness is lowered and the threshold of penetration of information dealing with that threat rises (Janis, 1962; Lazarus, 1966, 89). On the other hand, the individual's willingness to be exposed to dissonant information grows with his confidence in his ability to deal with it. In such a case, the threshold permitting the penetration of dissonant information is lowered (Janis and Mann, 1977, 214–218).

Once the information has penetrated the cognitive system and the possibility of the creation of an awareness gap is thereby avoided, the information's characteristics and the method of its processing influence the possibility of the development of relevance and evaluation gaps. Thus, for example, a factor such as the amount of detail contained in the information has a positive influence on its evaluation in the sense that there is a tendency to attribute more reliability and insight to detailed information. On the other hand, the more uncommon the information, the lower is its influence on the judgment, as there is a tendency to view what is unusual with skepticism. Here we have an example of the sort of contradiction mentioned earlier. Despite the fact that such information gains attention more easily than nondramatic information, it is precisely its peculiarity that causes it to be underestimated in situation evaluations in general.

The context of the information in the past determines its significance and importance in the present.[30] However, information that has once penetrated into the cognitive system will penetrate a second time more easily. This means that information that has lost its objective importance will penetrate more easily despite its low significance. Moreover, once it has succeeded in penetrating the awareness, the value attributed to it in the past influences that attributed to it in the present, even if this value is no longer objectively justified.

A basic, crucial aspect of the information system, which is of vital importance in its processing, is its quantity. Two extreme situations are possible. One is a lack of information, and the other is an overload. We will not go into a detailed discussion of the problems arising from a real or imaginary lack of information. The difficulties in determining an accurate situation evaluation when there is a real lack of information are obvious. But there might be a situation in which a real lack of information is not conceived as such, when the criteria adopted by the information processor as to "how much is enough" justify determining a definition of the situation with a sufficient degree of certainty. On the other hand, there could develop a perception of a lack of sufficient information when in fact this is not justified, in the sense that more information would not add accuracy to the evaluation or the quantity of existing information is already sufficient to yield a reasonably accurate interpretation. Such a situation might encourage procrastination in decisionmaking or the production of arbitrary decisions from the assumption that, as there is not sufficient information available, all or most of the alternative interpretations and evaluations are more or less equally justified.

But the particularly interesting situation is that in which the information processor must deal with an information overload,[31] a prevalent phenomenon in international relations stemming from the plurality of players and arenas. The pressure of information above a certain threshold with which the policymaker can effectively deal might cause him to manipulate one of the following factors:

The Process of Absorbing Information from the Environment. The processor may manipulate this factor simply by ignoring any additional information or by delaying its absorption until the pressure eases. The delay is based not on choosing between the more and the less important but on when the information reached the gathering system. A different technique could involve filtering, the nonprocessing of certain categories of information according to criteria decided upon in advance such as the areas of immediate concern, the source of the information, and so on.

The Channels of Information Flow. The most common technique in this context is the division of labor among a number of bodies or organizations and, as a result, the creation of the problem of coordination among them (Allison and Halperin, 1972). An alternative technique is reduction of accessibility, that is, diminishing the number of bodies processing the information that have access to major policymakers. Thus, although this technique gives the appearance that the system is functioning and coping with all the information, in fact only a part of the information reaches the policymakers.

The Content of the Information. One possible technique in this area is routinization, or absorbing without processing—that is, operating under the assumption that the information is of a routine nature that does not add to the quality of interpretation. Another technique is approximation, or resting content with an approximate or crude interpretation of the information. And finally, there is the possibility of erroneous processing.[32] In this case, the policymaker is usually unaware of the negative results of the information overload.

The Problem to Which the Information Relates. This situation takes the form of suspension of the confrontation with the problem (George and Associates, 1975, 22–23; Janis and Mann, 1977, 86–88), in other words, neglecting or underestimating the importance of the problem to which the information relates. This suspension allows for the ignoring or nonprocessing of significant quantities of the information pertaining to it.

Three points must be made in connection with this matter. One is that the individual confronting the problem of overload does not always consciously choose the technique of handling it. Hence, there is no awareness of the resulting danger to accuracy in the processing of the information. Secondly, beyond the functional-practical need that the individual has for dealing with the problem, there is an emotional, psychological aspect to the matter. An overload of information overpowering the already overburdened decisionmaker creates a state of stress that might have negative, cognitive side effects such as reduction of the scope of attention, cognitive rigidity, or a short term perspective, which makes a correct interpretation of the information even more difficult (Holsti and George, 1975, 273).

Attention should be called to the final point, which is often overlooked. The ability to handle information overload properly, overload being usually related to role overload and/or the structure of the situation (crisis versus non-crisis), seems at least partly to be a function of biological constraints that are the source of organic limits on human behavior. Factors such as fatigue, ill health, or age and the use of related drugs decide, to a large degree, what will be the amount of information any specific individual can handle and process properly.[33] This is sometimes a self-perpetuating process: role and information overload might lead to fatigue, ill health, and the use of drugs, which, in turn, may lead to the inability to process information properly. If these conditions do not change, they can bring about a deterioration in the quality of decisionmaking, which in itself might cause stress and anxiety—hence, further negative consequences for the quality of information processing.

Interaction with the Information

Thus far we have considered the influence of the characteristics of the information on the individual's attitude toward it. But there are no less severe problems resulting from different aspects of the *interaction* between the information and its recipient. These aspects have an impact in several areas: the degree of openness to information, the degree of importance and reliability attributed to it, and cognitive conservatism in the face of dissonant information. The points we shall discuss briefly are the nature of the contact, whether direct or indirect; the degree of involvement; the preferred orientation; and the primary categorization.

The importance of the nature of the contact is a function of its implications for a number of areas. Information received through direct contact is usually perceived as being more reliable and is therefore preferred to information received through indirect channels. Moreover, direct contact with the object of an attitude has implications for the affective component of the attitude as well and, as such, creates emotional commitments that are more difficult than otherwise to change (Triandis, 1971, 67). Thus, the tendency toward cognitive conservatism is enhanced. This issue is especially important in the contact between people of different cultures, which is often the case in foreign policy. The actual contact influences both self-perception and perception of the opponent; therefore, when a conflict of interests occurs, a more positive self-stereotype is created (Triandis and Vassiliou, 1967) and hence a feeling of self-righteousness, which makes empathy with the opponent and an understanding of his thought processes more difficult. On the other hand, there are indications (Kelman, 1975, 98) that a positive, active, direct contact with the representatives of a different nation might bring about a change in perception and evaluation of intentions in a positive direction, though not necessarily in line with the objective content of the specific information. It is no wonder, then, that certain "successful" summit meetings have served as a source of self-delusion or a means of deception due to the friendly direct interaction that became the main input for evaluation, at the same time leading to a rejection of contradictory, even if reliable, information. Just as importantly, direct contact may increase the sense of personal involvement, a subject to be discussed shortly.

The degree of involvement, defined as the degree to which the information processor sees himself responsible for an issue and/or personally influenced by it, has a number of important implications. First, it determines what type of information will be included in the areas of interest and attention, and the threshold for alertness to this type of information is thus lowered. Secondly, the actions and behaviors of the other side are regarded as a function of the personal implications they would have (Jones and Decharms, 1957). Thus, involvement immediately becomes a factor influencing the interpretation of information content and the importance attributed to it. Furthermore, there is a tendency for the creation of an inverse relationship between personal involvement and the effectiveness of dissonant information (Apsler and Sears, 1968). As a result, in situations with a high degree of personal involvement, the search for selective information intensifies.[34]

An additional means of evaluation and judgment available to the individual is the preferred orientation, for example, toward the source of the message, the content of the message, the target of the message, or any combination of these criteria.

Orientation Toward the Source. Judgment on the information is passed on the basis of the evaluation of the identified source of the message. Herein, then, lies the first obstacle, as earlier discussed— namely, the difficulties often encountered in international relations in identifying the source of a message. In the case of an orientation toward the source, such a high degree of identification with the sender may be created that the content of the message becomes identified with the individual's attitude toward the communicator (Kelman and Eagly, 1974). Thus, a message that seems reliable can be rejected purely on the basis of the low reliability of the sender (Johnson and Scileppi, 1969). Three patterns of orientation toward the source of a message can be located in all: (1) orientation toward the source resulting from the source's personality; (2) orientation toward the source resulting from factors that are not an essential part of the source but that emanate from his location in the social system;[35] and (3) orientation toward the source resulting from a preference for the source on the basis of identification with his value system and positions.[36]

The matter thus far discussed has significance for two categories of information. One category is the information arriving at the processing system from the external environment, from what is defined as an opponent or the other player. The second category of information is the kind that comes from within the decisionmaking system and goes to another part of it. In other words, we are speaking of information that, after having arrived from the "outside" world, is given different interpretations by different bureaucratic bodies competing for the "ear" of the chief policymaker. In this context, the orientation of the policymaker toward the source could be crucial in choosing between the alternative interpretations and definitions of the situation presented to him. This is an example of a choice that is made not on a functional basis but on the basis of a criterion that is not necessarily relevant to the decision. Moreover, such an orientation encourages those competing for the leader's attention to develop techniques that attract his attention toward a particular source, such as adopting positions similar to his own—in other words, techniques that arouse confidence in the source rather than in the essence of the information. In that instance, the content becomes secondary.

Orientation Toward the Content of the Message. For an individual possessing this orientation, the judgment and evaluation criteria include two factors. One is the order of presentation of the arguments, an order that includes elements such as presentation of the threat and then the promise, or presentation of the areas of agreement before the areas of disagreement, and so on. The second is the essence of the contents, which includes such elements as the degree of hedonism, of concreteness, and of anxiety that the message contains (Triandis, 1971, 95; 187–190). This phenomenon allows for the manipulation of the message by "cosmetic" treatment to its structure without the receiver being aware of it. The policymaker's close advisors, who know his weaknesses and preferences in this area, can influence his reaction to the message by manipulating the way it is presented to him.

In sum, an orientation toward the content of the message causes the recipient to separate the content from the source, which does not allow him to see the message in its full context. In addition, a tendency is created to accept or reject the message on the basis not of its essential content but rather on that of the "decoration."

Orientation Toward the Target. The target of a message can also be a criterion of judgment. As already noted, due to the plurality of political audiences in international relations, messages may be meant for various destinations. Thus, when the necessity to evaluate the importance or reliability of a message arises, there is a tendency to decide on the basis of the target of the message: Was it a speech directed at public opinion outside the State, or a message meant for the domestic public, or what? This criterion in itself does not relate to content or to the message's general background, and thus evaluations made on its basis alone can contribute to perceptual distortion.

Combination of Criteria. A different, more complex kind of criterion for interpretation is one that combines two or more of the above-mentioned types; that is, it is based both on the source and on the content, or on source, content, and target. Although there is no doubt that this is an optimal criterion, as compared to the other single-variable kinds, it may cause several difficulties.

Should all three criteria be given equal weight in the combined criterion? If so, where two of the three criteria point in a particular direction, then that direction should be considered as the correct evaluation. The dilemma in this case arises when each criterion points in a different direction. It would seem that in such ambiguous situations there will be a strong incentive for the decisionmaker to choose from among rivaling interpretations on the basis of arbitrary rather than analytic criteria.

Should any of the three criteria be given more weight, or should any order of priorities be set up? Here there is a danger that preference will be attached indiscriminately and that the information processor may lack the ability to handle adequately the complexity of a process involving the combining of three differently weighted dimensions into one single outcome (thereby coming up with a single weighted average) and yet not be aware of his inadequacy in this matter.

Finally, a very important point must be emphasized. We must not think that background factors, such as the source of the message, are unimportant in the formation of a situation evaluation. On the contrary, one should always be careful to examine whether the background factors are correct, properly weighted, and relevant to the specific information and situation. It is sometimes the case that the external criteria are chosen[37] and used mainly to make it easier for the information consumer to absorb and employ it according to his own needs.

Last but not least is the factor of primary categorization of the information and its influence on the process of judgment. The importance attributed to the process of primary categorization in the theory of information processing (Triandis *et al.,* 1968, 38–39) does not require further elaboration. But it is especially interesting in terms of its relevance in the area of foreign policy decisionmaking. Brecher, in an exhaustive study dealing with the major decisions of Israel's foreign policy (1974, 573), determined that "Most strikingly the evidence suggests that while it is valid to define issue-areas objectively, that is, by the content of the decision, the analytically significant dimension of the issue-area concept for understanding the behavior of states is not the reality definition but, rather, the way decision-makers *perceive* the issue."

In other words, an error in the primary definition and classification will have a great if not fatal influence on the degree of accuracy of the final product of information processing. This basic definition could be influenced by the same factors mentioned earlier, such as orientation, involvement, and so on, which do not necessarily help in making judgments and evaluations more accurate. Moreover, when information from the environment starts to flow into the body that is assigned to gather it, the decision about who is responsible for the gathering of a certain kind of information and who might be its possible consumer is defined in advance, and usually is part of a basic, predefined, permanent set of procedures (SOPs). The mere fact that a specific organization is responsible for gathering a particular type of information, and the knowledge that this body gathers information pertaining only to certain specific issue-areas, predefines the information in the eyes of its consumer as being relevant particularly to those specific areas. An additional aspect of the problem is that when the collectors of information and its processors must decide which of the decisionmakers is the main consumer of that information, in other words, to whom it should be sent, then the classification of the information decides in advance which policymaker will receive it. These two aspects point to the fact that the categorization into issue-areas is of great significance, as it is the first step in image formation—by giving a title to the information, that is, defining it as economic, military, and so on, and by determining who should receive it in full, who in part, and who not at all.[38] And what is no less important, the classification determines to a large extent the expectations as to the issue-areas for which the information has significance, while ignoring the possible relevance the information may have for other issue-areas.

Transmission of Information

One of the more difficult problems of judging and evaluating information in international relations emerges from the process of transmitting information from one actor to another. The dynamics of the signaling system and its characteristics[39] may contribute to the formation of distorted perceptions even when the sender does not mean to mislead the target. Two categories of failures that could arise from the signaling systems should be noted: (1) Failures resulting from the fact that the signals of actor A, which were meant to convey

Figure 1.2. Possible Combinations of Errors in Encoding and Decoding Signals

Actor A

		encoding error	decoding error
Actor B	encoding error	encoding error / encoding error	encoding error / decoding error
	decoding error	decoding error / encoding error	decoding error / decoding error

his intentions to player B, were unsuitable. Such errors are encoding errors.[40] (2) Failures resulting from a situation in which the signals were suitable but the target for some reason misinterpreted them. These sorts of error are known as decoding errors. The blame for the perceptual fallacies in this case must rest with the target.[41]

Countries that wish to maintain an efficient and functioning signaling system must be aware of the various combinational possibilities among encoding and decoding errors. The matrix in Figure 1.2 presents the patterns of these possible combinations.

1. Both actors make encoding errors. This may point to the fact that each actor is unable to empathize with the other's thought processes. The result is a lack of efficient communication between the two sides.
2. Actor A usually performs encoding errors, that is, misunderstands his opponent's thought patterns. Actor B usually makes decoding errors; that is, he has a weakness in absorbing or interpreting information, which is not necessarily connected to a lack of empathy. In such a case, one should check to see whether actor A is not making intentional attempts to mislead, or whether he has changed the traditional meanings of his signals or is employing new signals without managing to bring these new meanings or signals to his rival's knowledge.
3. Actor A usually makes errors of decoding and actor B makes errors of encoding (see possibility 2).
4. Both actors make errors in their decoding. This means either that each is attempting to mislead the other or that each has changed the meaning of his signals or had added new signals to the code, without having clarified this to his opponent and without being aware himself that his opponent is unaware of the changes.[42]

Errors of encoding and decoding, as earlier noted, may lead to misperception of signals and their meanings.[43] The main fallacies that can be caused by encoding errors are as follows:

1. The transmitter of the signals assumes that the recipient will understand him. The recipient, however, may not have the necessary prior information and background knowledge to do so. The sender then interprets the target's moves as a response to his signal, thus attributing to the opponent's acts irrelevant meanings. This phenomenon is prevalent in international relations and especially grave when one of the actors changes the traditional meanings or adds new signals to his interpretation system.

2. As the sender tries to transmit a certain message, he is often unaware that the same signal may also express information contradictory to what he is trying to convey.[44]

3. When one actor is not trying to hide his images and intentions, he assumes that the other side also perceives them accurately (Jervis, 1969). The sender in such a case does not distinguish between likelihood and certainty. Moreover, the other side may distrust his opponent and interpret the lack of an attempt to disguise his intentions as an attempt to mislead, in itself due to the tradition of secrecy in foreign policy.

4. A special problem is the use of time as an indicator. When state A sends a signal meant to test how state B will respond to a particular move (in order to decide whether it is worthwhile to proceed with the policy hinted at in the signal), it determines in advance what the maximum time allotted for response should be. This means that if within the expected time span state B does not respond at all or at least not negatively, a positive interpretation will be indicated; that is, state B probably does not object to the policy suggested. But time is often evaluated incorrectly for various reasons: the signal's content may allow for reactions unpredicted by the signaler, in which case the target actor might need more time than anticipated to choose among alternatives. The fact, then, that a response is not received in the time allotted may create a false impression related to the sender's time calculations, which are then attributed to the receiver.

5. As the international scene is blessed with a multiplicity of actors and each is involved simultaneously in a number of games, actors often cannot transmit their messages explicitly to specific opponents for fear that the messages will be intercepted by other actors for whom they are not intended—an outcome that would have a negative impact on other games.

The main fallacies that can be caused by decoding errors are as follows:

1. The distinction between signals and indices raises a number of difficulties. (a) An action that in the past had a high price attached to it such that one could regard it as an index, might, as a result of a reevaluation of the cost-benefit relationship, receive a new value.

Thus, at present it may serve as a signal at most (Jervis, 1970, 52). (b) An actor may notice that his opponent perceives a certain action of his as an index. If so, the index becomes a candidate for manipulation and a means for misleading the opponent. The cost-benefit ratio of the action has changed, since we must add to the benefits that of misleading the enemy.

2. Evaluating a move of the opponent as an index due to the assumption that its price would be too high to use only for fraudulent purposes presupposes two things, neither of which is necessarily true: (a) that the opponent uses a cost-benefit analysis, in other words, that he is rational; and (b) that if he makes cost benefits and calculations, they must be correct.[45]

3. When the time span of thinking on the conflict is different for the two sides, distortion in signal perceptions may result. One actor's move could be considered as an index due to its perceived high price for the actor who has the shorter time perspective of the conflict, although in practice this might actually be of a lower price to the actor who has a longer time perspective of the conflict—given that what is not worthwhile for the short term may certainly be worthwhile in long-term calculations.

4. There are early steps necessary for a certain action to take place. On the one hand, taking such steps creates an opening for the action to happen, but this does not mean that it will *necessarily* happen. There is, however, a tendency to perceive such steps as if they predicted the occurrence of the action with certainty.

5. The tendency to exaggerate the degree of coordination in the opponent's decisionmaking system (Jervis, 1969) may lead to a perception of every step of every bureaucrat in the rival camp as an expression of its overall policy, even if many such are not in fact major factors in policymaking. The result is that noises are interpreted as signals.

6. Noises can interfere with the attention and the reception of signals. However, at times, what were noises over a long period may become signals or even indices but continue to go unnoticed. This means that the information-gathering system has not updated its definitions. Thus, for example, a military maneuver that takes place regularly may be perceived as a noise. In a certain year, however, it could change into a signal; yet, because the action had for so long been seen as noise without that image being made conditional on the circumstantial framework, it becomes a perceptual fallacy, as what should be evaluated as noise with only conditional probability is perceived as such with an unconditional probability.

7. There is a tendency to regard actions as indices and words as signals, thus ignoring the committing power of words, which raises their price—at times intolerably.[46]

8. It is difficult to distinguish between caution and fear on the part of the opponent, as the external signs of both may be identical.

A display of caution might be regarded as fear by an opponent who, because of that, may be tempted to take the very steps that the other side was trying to avoid by means of his cautious actions.

9. The repeated use of any signal or its use toward a great many actors might create the perception that the signal should not be treated seriously: (a) The fact that the signal was repeated many times but its content was not carried out may point to a lack of seriousness of intention. But it might also be that, precisely because the move hinted at has not been executed until then, the sender will finally have to carry it out in order to gain back credibility in the eyes of his opponent. (b) It is assumed to be impossible for the signaling actor to carry out what is hinted at in his signal toward all the actors who received the signal. And if he should carry it out toward only one of them, it is further believed that this would happen to some other actor or, at least, that the risk is low. Thus, the perceived likelihood that the move will be made diminishes as a function of the number of actors who received the signal. In any case, whereas such thinking is valid in terms of objective probability, it is not necessarily so in terms of subjective probability, which is the more relevant approach in assessing the potential behavior of the signaling actor.

The Need for Evaluation Criteria

The main point taken up in this discussion is that criteria that are external to the content of the information might—unjustifiably— have a great influence on the perception of the information content; the definition of its importance; and the question of whether all the information will gain the attention of, and be able to penetrate, the policymaker's cognitive system. The need to develop an "external" set of criteria is a function of the characteristics of information in international relations, which make its processing on content basis alone very difficult. For this reason, such criteria serve an important purpose.

These criteria are an important link in the series of evaluative rules necessary to the person dealing with the information. They are necessary at both the conscious and unconscious levels, in that they serve to control a confusing and complex web of information in the surrounding world—information that, in the event of an error, could mislead such a person or even threaten his status.[47] These criteria transform the treatment of information and its decoding into a simple and relatively easy procedure that, in addition, minimizes psychological stress. But the price extracted for this convenience to the information consumer is sometimes paid in terms of the loss of vital information that, having been disregarded, fails to become a stimulus, and in terms of inaccurate evaluations and interpretations of stimuli.

This explanation is in line with both the schemata theory (Axelrod, 1973; Reed, 1973, 26–32) and the cybernetic paradigm (Steinbruner,

1974). These theories differ from analytic or rationalist paradigms, which assume that when new information arrives it is integrated into the recipient's causal models of reality and that, on the basis of this information, a process of adaptation of the models, their updating, and their refinement takes place. It is assumed by the rationalist paradigm that there is a process of perfect learning in which all information is examined and in which relevant conclusions are drawn, immediately integrated into the existing perceptual system, and utilized as the basis of any future analysis (Stein and Tanter, 1980, 27–47, 63–77).

In contrast to the analytic approach, the cybernetic paradigm assumes that the individual has a system of predetermined evaluation procedures. In this context, the process of adaptation becomes a mechanism that sifts all information for which the standard operating procedures (SOPs) are not programmed. The process of adaptation is minimal, and there is a clear tendency to ignore information that requires significant change in existing perceptions.

The schemata theory takes this claim even further in suggesting that at the evaluative stage of the information the individual makes use of a predetermined schemata that facilitates his finding a *satisficing* interpretation rather than an optimal one for the information at hand. The schemata includes a series of procedures and steps according to which the information will be interpreted, with the object not of reaching maximum compatibility between the information and the schemata but a *satisficing* correlation between them.

Although we can understand the psychological need and the practical advantages of using these shortcut judgment and evaluation procedures, we cannot ignore the fact that these advantages are truly beneficial only if the result is an accurate interpretation of the extant information. If not, there has not only been a failure in the present, but seeds of future misinterpretations have been sown as well—and this is the real price paid for the short-term relief acquired.

Personality as a Source of Misperception

Beliefs, Values, and Stereotypes

The second explanatory variable set is the individual's personality, a term I use in its broadest sense to include the structure and content of the belief system, values, and attitudes of the individual, as well as his unique personality traits.

The individual's belief system represents all the beliefs, hypotheses, and expectations that he is convinced are valid at a given moment in time. Parallel to the system of beliefs is the system of disbelief, which includes all the beliefs, hypotheses, and expectations that the individual believes to be invalid at a given point in time (Rokeach,

1960, 33). In other words, the individual locates the information coming to him on a scale between belief and disbelief and thus the belief system takes on a central role in the processing of information, given that "in order to function every individual requires during the course of his development a set of beliefs and personal constructs about the physical and social environment. These beliefs provide him with a relatively coherent way of organizing and making sense of what would otherwise be a confusing and overwhelming array of signals and cues picked up from the environment by his senses" (George and Associates, 1975, 30).

The belief system, as opposed to attitudes, which will be examined later, is more general in content and usually includes principles and general ideas relating to the nature of the environment that comprises the policymaker's field of action. Within the entire belief system, what has been defined as the operational code[48] (especially its philosophical part) plays a major role in political information processing (George, 1969; 1978b, 11–14). The sets of beliefs underlying this type of information processing deal with basic assumptions about the nature of the political world and the place and role of the individual in it, and with the most effective means by which to realize goals. As such, the operational code has "diagnostic propensities that extend or restrict the scope of search and evaluation, and that influences [the policymaker's] diagnosis of the situation in certain directions" (George, 1978b, 15).

The attributes and role of the belief system as a whole, and especially the interdependence of those core beliefs that comprise the operational code, make the belief system a possible source of information manipulation. This is due, in the first place, to the fact that the importance and relevance attached to information is largely determined by its location on the belief-disbelief continuum. The more information is perceived by the policymaker as closer to the disbelief pole, the less its importance in the situation evaluation, and vice versa. Moreover, information that is in itself not evaluated along the belief-disbelief continuum, but is conceived to be related only to beliefs, assumptions, or expectations closer to the pole of belief, will be regarded as having greater relevance to the general situation evaluation. A different aspect is concerned with the degree of flexibility or rigidity of the belief system; that is, when a certain item of information has been defined as belonging to the "truth" sphere, to what extent is there a readiness to change the definition and reclassify it as false and vice versa, or to what extent does the belief system tend to adapt itself to new information? It appears that when the beliefs of another actor are close to those that one has adopted, there is a tendency to see them as closer than they really are; conversely, when they do not fit the accepted belief system, they are conceived as being more different and contradictory than they actually are (Sherif and Sherif, 1967; Atkins *et al.,* 1967). This means that in such a case, evaluation or relevance gaps might develop, resulting from an unrealistic evaluation of the behavior and goals of the opponent; and from there it is but a short step to the conception of an illusory compatibility between opposing interests or to one of noncompatibility between essentially common interests.

A number of other structural characteristics of the belief system have implications for adaptational ability and for the possible development of distortions. First, the greater the differentiation between, and insulation of, different beliefs, the greater the possibility of contradictory beliefs coexisting simultaneously (Rokeach, 1956). In other words, the less systemically the beliefs are organized, the higher the probability that this contradiction will go undetected—thus providing the basis for assimilating contradictory pieces of data without proper attention to the significance of the contradictions.

Another important characteristic is the degree of centrality of a belief, as measured by the dependence of other beliefs on it (Rokeach, 1968, 5). The centrality of any single belief influences its degree of resistance to change: the greater the centrality, the greater the rigidity. On the other hand, making a change in a central belief might lead to a chain reaction of changes in all the beliefs dependent on it. Hence, information connected to beliefs comprising the operational code, thereby possibly forcing the policymaker to institute changes in it—especially in the operational code beliefs relating to the nature of the political life and the image of the opponent—is liable to be manipulated and distorted, because of the centrality of such beliefs.

Although the individual's system of beliefs answers the question "What is available?" the policymaker's value system and ideologies determine what is desirable. The value system defines the beliefs about desirable behavior, objects, and situations along a continuum of relative importance (Rokeach, 1973, 5). The importance of the ideologies and value system lies in their function as criteria for the evaluation of information and the classification of objects and situations into desirable and undesirable categories. This classification has implications for the perception of the information related to the different objects and situations—which have been defined as desirable or undesirable—mainly due to the inclination for consistency. An object that has been defined as negative according to ideological-ethical criteria[49] tends to be evaluated, along with all the information associated with it, not in terms of its objective content, but negatively. The implications with regard to misperceptions are clear.

A second aspect of the value system is that perception of the desirable is often confused in the policymaker's mind with perception of the available, resulting in what is known as wishful thinking. Naturally, this phenomenon depends on the importance accorded by the policymaker to specific values.[50]

A third aspect of the value system is the degree of rigidity in conceptions rooted in values. The relative permanence of the value system and the commitment to it often causes inflexibility, as a change in a conception demands a change in values. Thus, information that contradicts such conceptions must either be ignored or distorted in some way.

The significance of attaching values to specific objects is broken down as follows:

1. There is an increased sensitivity to stimuli that are compatible with one's values; in other words, the threshold of penetration for such information is lower.

2. Stimuli that contradict the value system tend to be ignored; that is, the threshold of penetration for such information is higher.

3. There is a tendency to create "illusory" bridges between certain kinds of information and the value system, even when quite un-justified.[51] The immediate implications of judgment and evaluations made according to irrelevant criteria are distortions in the evaluation of information, distortions that can create a convenient background for a relevance gap.

4. There is a tendency to create information artificially, in order to justify the adoption or maintenance of values important to the individual.

5. The fact that ideology and practice are not always identical— in other words, the fact that a contradiction sometimes exists between the values the individual believes in and those according to which he must act in reality—forces him to explain his behavior in a way that distorts its true meaning in the process of avoiding cognitive dissonance.

A certain type of belief or value of special importance in this sphere is the stereotype. A stereotype is a simplistic, unsophisticated perception of an object, which can be either descriptive or normative. A number of characteristics of stereotypes make them a threat to the accuracy of perception.

1. The fact that the same stereotype often has different meanings and connotations in different contexts[52] creates a situation in which the same phenomenon can easily receive contradictory explanations.

2. Stereotypes are characterized by a large degree of absolutism. As a result, once a particular trait is attributed to a collective as a whole, there is a tendency to attribute the same trait to every individual in the collective without exception.[53] If a certain nation is perceived as aggressive, then the expectation is that all its policymakers will possess the same quality—hence, the tendency to explain and perceive the verbal and actual behavior of all policymakers in the same terms (that is, without making distinctions between individuals) even when this perception is not objectively justified.

3. An image consisting of stereotypes emphasizes the uniqueness in motives and behavior of its holder or its object. As a result, both

the self-perception and the perception of others' behavior serve to justify the sharp distinction each actor draws between himself and others, a distinction that is not necessarily realistic.

4. Stereotypes arising from simplification create simplified and unreal causal attributions. Consequently, unsuitable explanations may be given to events, and unrealistic expectations may be created. The main danger of such attributes is that expectations dictate behavior and thus may turn out to be self-fulfilling prophecies.

The Impact of Function and Structure of Attitudes

The encounter between beliefs, values, and specific information in relation to an object or situation is expressed in the total set of attitudes that the policymaker develops. Such a set of attitudes, termed the cognitive map, affects the defined content and the subject matter of the process of information selection and interpretation.

The term *attitude* is defined for our purposes as the formation of an "idea" having both affective and cognitive dimensions that create an inclination to prefer a certain category of actions toward specific categories of objects and social situations, or some combination thereof.[54] It follows, then, that an attitude is the result of a judgmental-evaluative process, which includes three factors: a cognitive component, an affective component, and an action orientation.

Attitudes fulfill an important role in easing the individual's adjustment to his complex environment and instilling order in the selection of relevant response categories to the situations and objects that he confronts, in relation to which information pours in. The choice of response to situations and objects might become a process of standard operating procedures as, from the moment that the object is classified in a certain category, a reaction may be chosen with no need of reconsideration. But the action orientation factor determines not how the individual will actually respond, but what his behavioral intentions are. It should be emphasized that there is not always a correlation between intentions and actions. (The significance of this fact and its contribution to possible perceptual distortions will be discussed in detail.) Moreover, it should be remembered that any particular attitude is not an isolated component in the individual's cognitive map. Rather, (1) it is part of a continuum of attitudes on the specific subject with which it is dealing; (2) it is a part of a system of attitudes relating to the issue under discussion (for example, foreign policy); (3) it is part of the totality of attitudes that comprises the cognitive system; and (4) it is connected to the individual's system of values and beliefs and reflects at least part of them. As such, attitude influences and is influenced by the individual's other attitudes on the same subject and belonging to the same issue-area— influenced, in fact, by his entire system of attitudes, beliefs, and values. Thus, an attitude rooted in misperception becomes a candidate for a potentially much wider distortion than is merited by the actual issue with which it is directly concerned; in other words, there is a "distortional bonus" or spillover effect. On the other hand, any attitude is potentially the conveyer of a misperception originating in other fallacious attitudes.

Because the individual's cognitive map is functional, it may display a tendency toward the distortion of information or toward the ignoring of feedbacks that would necessitate a change in attitudes that is perceived to render those attitudes dysfunctional in serving their instrumental, knowledge, value-expression, or ego-defense functions (Katz, 1960). Hence, information content may become subservient to the functional needs served by existing attitudes.

The individual's set of attitudes is composed of individual attitudes that fill the aforementioned functions. The quantitative balance among the different kinds of functions is a result of the needs of the individual, which are, in turn, the outcome of his personal traits or pragmatic necessities, such as his given circumstances and role at any point in time. For example, a large percentage of the attitudes of an individual lacking in self-confidence is involved with ego defense. On the other hand, an individual in the midst of a political power struggle might adopt a greater number of attitudes that serve him instrumentally in that particular struggle. It should also be remembered that not every attitude has a single role; more often each one fulfills several functions at once. The more functions a particular attitude has, the more difficult it is to change, despite contradictory information flowing in from the outside world. The attitude, due to a plurality of functions, becomes more and more central; as such, it also becomes more rigid and more apt to fall victim to nonadaptation or maladaptation processes as a vehicle for the entrenchment of misperceptions.

A second relevant aspect in relation to the cognitive map is the structure of the system of attitudes.

Degree of Openness or Closedness. The cognitive component of an attitude set is defined as closed when its owner sees its characterization as fully covering the specific subject matter. The more closed a cognitive component is perceived to be, and to the degree that the individual does not think he needs additional information, the fewer the changes that can be wrought upon it, even by new information. Thus, the actual decision as to the completeness of the characterization becomes a determining criterion that prevents the necessity of relating to certain other kinds of information.

Degree of Sophistication. What is the number of categories that the holder of the attitudes uses in order to characterize an object that is the predicate of his attitude? The less the sophistication, the more defined in black and white terms will the conception be, leaving less room for doubt. The more complex the cognitive system, the more the individual is capable of confronting information that demands new or more subtle distinctions[55] (Bieri, 1966; Scott, 1963; 1965, 87; Suedfeld and Tetlock, 1977).

Degree of Differentiation Between the Different Characterizations. This involves the degree to which the different characterizations are perceived to be causally interconnected (if . . . then) and the extent to which different characterizations are conceived as contradictory. These two factors have implications for the degree to which a characterization of a situation or object by the policymaker leads to a series of additional characterizations that do not necessarily result from the original information.

The Breadth of the Classification Categories. A category is defined as broader in direct proportion to the number of event types the individual includes within it.[56] The broader the categories, the less likely it is that contradictory information will require a change of attitude; the narrower the category, the greater will be the pressure for a change in attitude (Eagly, 1969).

The third significant factor that ties attitudes into the process of interpretation is that relating to the essence of the relevant attitudes. The important aspects in this context are as follows:

Degree of Systemization. The more systemized are the attitudes of the individual in the different areas and subjects, the more difficulties are likely to appear in the digestion of the dissonant information. Or, as Scott (1958, 10) characterized it: (a) "Mutual dependence of elements within the system on one another; (b) 'Boundedness' of the system in the sense that the rate or intensity of interaction of the component elements with each other is greater than their interaction with outside elements; (c) Tendency towards self-maintenance and resistance to incursion or alteration by outside forces." This is the case because there is a greater chance that such information may require trade-offs among values, a situation that is preferably avoided (Jervis, 1976, 128–142; George and Associates, 1975, 17–18), and, with reference to point (c) above, also because the effectiveness of the feedback from the environment is limited.

Degree of Centrality. Centrality is measured by the extent to which other attitudes depend on a particular attitude as well as the degree to which the policymaker's ego is involved. Naturally, an attitude that has many others depending on and deriving from it is one that involves the ego of the policymaker, due to the necessary commitment it demands, and its centrality may thus become a cause of inflexibility.

Degree of Generality. The more general an attitude, the more difficult it is to change, as by nature it is more central. Moreover, its generality facilitates the manipulation of dissonant information.

Degree of Emotional Intensity. The greater the emotional intensity of an attitude, the greater its resistance to dissonant information, as it is more difficult to change attitudes having an emotional basis than those having an intellectual one.

Degree of Consistency. Individuals have a basic need to maintain the balance of the cognitive system (Heider, 1958; Festinger, 1957; Rosenberg, 1960; Adelman, 1973; Zajonc, 1960; Osgood, 1960; Class, 1968). We can describe this balance on three levels: first, there is a balance within the attitudes—among the cognitive, emotional, and action components, "Individual will tends to act as to balance the maximum number of triads" (Insko and Schopler, 1971, 33); second, there is a balance among attitudes, mainly an attempt to avoid the creation of cognitive dissonance (Festinger, 1957, 1964); and finally, on the most general level, there is the attempt to prevent the creation of an imbalance in the cognitive entirety—that is, among different attitudes, beliefs, and values. The need for balance increases the tendency of a balanced cognitive system to remain stable (Burnstein, 1967; Scott, 1969), either by ignoring information or by manipulating it. Most of the tactics used by individuals to protect themselves from the results of imbalance are connected in some way to the increasing rigidity of the existing system of attitudes and beliefs, or to its interpretation in such a way that new information can be distorted or not attributed to the relevant areas.[57] A situation of consistency creates a sense of satisfaction and psychological well-being that "satisfies" the individual's criteria for a harmonious and pleasing definition of reality.

From the inherent need for balance, several conclusions as to possible distortions may be drawn: (1) There is an attempt to create a balanced cognitive system despite the fact that reality is neither consistent nor balanced. (2) Causal connections are created when they do not necessarily exist,[58] such as the assumption that a player described by negative character traits has hostile intentions and, as such, poses a threat. Of course, such a conclusion is not always realistic, as the player's characterizations do not necessarily imply his actual intentions or his actual activity.

(3) There is a danger in the creation of a "domino" of distortions when the cognitive system is conceived as one and its components are integrally interconnected, or when a central attitude is anchored in a misperception.

Object-Situation Relations. The fact that an inclusive attitude is some sort of integration of attitude-toward-situation and attitude-toward-object (Rokeach, 1966) creates the problem of making the attitude-toward-object compatible with the changing situations—that is, in order to give suitable weight in the general account both to the situation and to the object. The interaction between these two variables determines the preferred reaction. This interaction has several implications: (1) The policymaker who determines his overall attitude by his attitude toward a situation is in danger of overpragmatization and of producing evaluations that are merely circumstantial. (2) The policymaker who determines his inclusive attitudes only on the basis of the characterizations of an object, when the characterizations are closed ones and perceived as complete, tends to conservatism and to nonadaptation to new situations and changes in his environment. (3) The policymaker who accords equal importance to attitude-toward-objects and to attitude-toward-situations may be deficient in two areas. First, his approach is mechanical, in that it determines criteria by such principles as 50:50 chance. This equation, it is true, is easily grasped, but one doubts whether it reflects reality, which is not so easily and smoothly divisible. Second, in those cases in which attitude-toward-situation is positive and at the same time attitude-toward-object is negative, or vice versa, the individual will have difficulty in arriving at an inclusive attitude due to the effect of mutual cancellation. The final attitude will be either arbitrary or unrealistic, or it will tend toward avoidance of the problem such that the individual ignores it or refuses to take a stand.

It is impossible to summarize the discussion of the impact of the attitude system without noting that the different elements that characterize them might be interrelated. Therefore, we must see the entirety of functions, structure, and essence as an *interactional* system. Thus, for example, in an individual whose need for ego-defense is the most prominent drive, it may be assumed that the attitudes serving that function will be the most central within the whole attitude set. It follows that a change resulting from dissonant information is most likely to occur if it touches on more than one aspect of the characteristics of the attitude system as analyzed earlier.

Interaction Between Attitudes and Actual Behavior

One of the difficult problems involved in the relations of the individual with his environment is the connection between his attitudes, especially those made known to others, and his actions in reality. This problem is even more acute in relations between nations, due to the characteristics unique to international communications that we have discussed earlier, as well as to the high price that might be extracted as a result of unduly underestimating or overestimating the causal connections between attitude and action. This is at the same time a problem of the individual decisionmaker with himself, that is, a problem connected with self-image; and, as such, it is one that demands of the policymaker self-justification of his behavior in light of his known attitudes.

The policymaker who must develop expectations concerning the behavior of other players acts as a "naive scientist" and evolves a causal model (Kelley, 1967, 208) that connects the attitudes of the other players with his future behavior, or serves as a criterion to which his present behavior is compared and according to which conclusions are drawn as to his credibility. Heuristically, we can distinguish three such types of model, and we should hasten to emphasize that we do not claim that the policymaker necessarily adopts any one of them globally:

1. The Model of a One-to-One Relationship Between Attitude and Action. The policymaker assumes that one can predict anticipated behavior from knowledge of the opponent's attitudes. If these are not known, it is possible to predict attitudes from past behavior. The attitudes that are noted from past behavior become the basis for evaluating behavior in the future.

2. The Model of a Complete Lack of Correlation. The policymaker assumes that it is impossible to predict the opponent's behavior on the basis of his known attitudes. If there is no information about his attitudes, it is not possible to conclude them from past behavior. Such a model expresses a lack of confidence in the sincerity or ability,[59] of the opponent to realize his attitudes.

3. The Model of Selectivity. The policymaker assumes that at times it is possible to predict anticipated behavior from attitudes and at other times it is not possible to do so. The difficulty he faces, then, is to decide when there is and when there is not a relevant connection. Here, certain subjective needs may come into play, such as cognitive convenience, historical memory, value system, and so on.

Some distinctions are necessary at this point. First, policymakers do not adopt the same models for all the actors and subjects with whom they come into contact.[60] Second, models 1 and 2 are such that the policymaker gives an unequivocal preference to his attitude-toward-object over attitude-toward-situation, which creates the problems we have already mentioned. Third, in the framework of models 1 and 2, the policymaker will prefer to handle dissonant information, that is, behavior that does not fit his expectations, through manipulation of the causal linkage between the attitude and the behavior, such as attributing it to accident.[61]

We have already discussed the policymaker's tendency to prefer simple models to complex ones that may nevertheless give a more accurate picture of reality. This is the source of the oft-noted preference for models that assume a noncomplex causal relationship, that is, a one-to-one relationship or complete lack of correlation. In other words, there is created in advance a preference to expect or interpret actions so as to suit the aforementioned causal models; in the case in which the model of complete compatibility is adopted, there will be a tendency to interpret every action as an intention to realize known attitudes, or as their expression. And in the case in which the model of noncompatibility is adopted, there will be an expectation of actions that contradict the known attitudes. Hence, behaviors that are compatible with known attitudes will be left out of the scope of expectations about the probable behavior of the other actors, and when such behaviors occur they have to be explained away even at the cost of misinterpreting them so that the general model that provides the basis of expectations can survive intact.

A second problem concerns the extent to which the conception of the other side's attitudes is really accurate. Even in those cases in which attitudes are actually related on a one-to-one basis with actions, there may be distortions as to the expectations of the other side's actions if the attitudes are misunderstood. In other words, a chain of distortions is formed that is a result of distortion in the perception of attitudes.

A third problem stems from the fact that at times a certain attitude may justify any of a number of dissimilar reactions. By the same token, even when the attitude is accurately perceived, it may be that the different perceptions of the two sides of what should be the proper behavior resulting from it will lead to inaccurate expectations of anticipated actions.

A fourth problem is related to the model of selectivity. When the criteria according to which selection is determined are subjective— that is, when the determination as to whether there is a one-to-one connection is based on subjective criteria—it is clear that misconceptions may occur that will be expressed in unrealistic expectations.

The subject of correlation between attitudes and actions is equally important in the context of the policymaker's self-perception. There is a definite preference for a self-image that fits model 1. As one scholar put it: "It may be that the training in our society leads the layman to expect attitude-behavior consistency. This expectation is particularly strong as it applies to public officials" (Wicker, 1971, 141).

There is generally a need for the actor to perceive his behavior as reflecting and compatible with his attitudes,[62] whether that need results from the public's expectations, from the accepted values and norms, or from mental reasons—namely, the need for consistency as part of the individual's general psychological makeup. Such a need is prominent in an especially problematic area of international relations—the conflict between moral values and the pragmatic behavior required to achieve what is regarded as the national interest. This problem is especially difficult for those leaders who have a special commitment to morality in politics, such as Woodrow Wilson, Nehru, or Jimmy Carter. The need for a self-perception that shows consistency between attitude and behavior, which is at times strong enough to bring about a distortion of the perception of self-behavior, invites a discrepancy between the actor's self-image and the perception of that actor by the other actors in the international arena. Moreover, when for any reasons the actor cannot perform an act that is congruent with his attitudes, he may commit a symbolic act that is. The danger in this lies in the fact that the symbolic act may be perceived by him as a congruent act, with all the resulting implications.

Another possibility open to the actor in such a situation is to commit referent acts—that is, behaviors that relate to the attitude but are not congruent with it. Again, there is the danger that an illusion of a congruent act will be created.

An additional problem involved with referent acts arises when various acts are a necessary but not sufficient condition for other acts to be performed. The problem is caused by the fact that the opponent might get the impression that a given referent act sets a precedent after which the anticipated act will take place rather than a substitute act, which is actually all that is in the actor's power to perform.

Another way to deal with the problem of incompatibility between attitude and action is *not* by giving an incorrect interpretation to an act that has already been performed, but by pre-empting the need to respond with incompatible overt behavior. This could be accomplished by giving an erroneous interpretation of reality, so that the need for that reaction will be avoided. Alternatively, there is a possibility, especially in cases of moral dissonance, to explain any deviation as an exceptional case, and so on.[63] The difficulty here is that one has a tendency to judge one's own behavior and that of others by different criteria. Thus, although an actor might be willing to accept such an exceptional-case explanation pertaining to himself, he is not necessarily ready to do so in relation to others and is more likely to see the latter instance as an attempt at fraud. As a result, a noncompatibility is created between the significance attributed by each side to attitude-behavior discrepancy related to their mutual relations.

Rules of Prediction and Attribution of Causality

Beliefs, values, and attitudes supply the groundwork necessary for the policymaker, who gropes in a maze of uncertainty as to the shape of the present and the future and who searches for manageable formulae through certain rules of judgment and evaluation for predicting outcomes and attributing causality. The need for such rules increases when he has to choose among alternatives that might have different outcomes, a situation that in turn necessitates deciding between various interpretations of a situation. These rules also serve to define causal connections[64] between his own behavior and its results or the other actor's characteristics as he sees them and the anticipated behavior to which they might lead; in other words, they help him "peep" into the future. Three heuristic rules that may serve this purpose were suggested by Tversky and Kahneman (1974); we shall see that each one opens up the possibility for its own typical misperceptions,[65] just as the actual process of choosing the preferred rule might be fallacious.

The first such rule is that of *representativeness*. An individual considers it very likely that a certain object A belongs to some category of B objects, or that A is the outcome of B the more A is conceived as similar to, or more reminiscent of, B. In other words, this rule explains that the classification of information into different categories—which is the first stage of perception, the consideration of causal processes, or anticipation as to possible developments— results from the rule of representativeness, which is a principle that equates input with output; and the greater the similarity, the more authoritative the inference process seems to be. One example of this is the belief that the giving of economic aid by nation A to nation B will render nation B dependent on nation A, as the term *receive* is perceived to be related to *depend*. Such an expectation may lead to the operational conclusion that one of the most reliable ways to acquire political influence is by giving economic aid. Another example is the connection of the terms *radical regime* with *identification with the USSR,* which leads to the conclusion that radical regimes would voluntarily serve Soviet interests and thus automatically become a threat to U.S. interests. This rule may, of course, contain typical fallacies. For example, a successful outcome in a certain situation is often attributed to the success of a specific move that preceded it, on the assumption that if event A *preceded* event B, then A *caused* B. Here the representativeness is expressed in the linear time line between the events. The fallacy is in perceiving a temporal connection as proof of a causal one, which, of course, has no objective justification. Another common misperception occurs when there is a high degree of representativeness that leads to a high level of faith in the predicted result, even when there is an awareness of factors limiting the accuracy of the prediction. This stems from the fact that the representativeness becomes so central in the thought process that all the limiting elements, such as the lack of sufficient information, its inaccuracy, or the unique aspects of the specific situation, seem marginal.

The second rule is that of *availability.* This rule states that an individual evaluates the likelihood of a certain event or the evolution of a series of developments on the basis of the availability of data. Hence, the greater number of similar events a policymaker can recall from the past, or the greater the ease with which he can conjure up certain developments, the higher will be his expectations of the occurrence of an event or the development of a chain of events. The implications for the situation evaluation in which anticipation plays an important part are clear. Thus, for example, an evaluation that a certain action is doomed to fail might depend on the ease and speed with which the policymaker may imagine the various difficulties to be encountered.

This rule may lead to still other fallacies, such as the fact that policymakers tend to rely on a small sample of similar historical events and to assume that if a certain political process happened a specific number of times, it will surely happen again. Even though the sample he draws on may be too small, its advantage lies in its

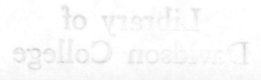

availability. Moreover, there is an ignoring of the fact that available analogies are not necessarily the most suitable ones for the information being compared, and that a certain analogy may be available not necessarily because it is the most suitable but for other reasons irrelevant to the matter with which the information is concerned (Jervis, 1976, 239–279). Another misperception proceeds from the assumption that an associative connection between two events leads to the conclusion that both events happened at the same time more often than they actually did, or that there is indeed a basic substantive connection between the two events. This misperception can withstand even contradictory evidence; for example, Suez and the route to India remain entwined in the British mind, even though the British Empire no longer exists. Another misperception related to this rule is that lack of imagination and of the ability to imagine certain types of difficulty might lower the subjective evaluation of the threat involved, even if the objective evaluation would have warranted the granting of a higher value to that threat.

The third rule is one of *base rate*. This rule states that a point of departure must be defined and then constantly adapted to changing data. The point of departure is defined at times by the way the problem itself is defined or presented. But a point of departure can also be an ideology or a system of values that dictates anticipations, rules of behavior, and a world view. Naturally, the degree of suitability of this point of departure to the changing reality will depend on its constant updating on the basis of changing circumstances.

The existence of a master plan or an ideology presenting a plan of action causes the policymaker's subjective evaluations of the plan's chance of success to increase. The existence of a plan or ideology gives a feeling of power and control over the situation, which is not always justified. Moreover, the evaluation of the successful outcome of a plan, the success of which depends on the execution of a series of preceding actions, is seen as higher than is warranted, due to the continuous nature of the plan.[66] An example of such a misconception was the high evaluation that the Soviet leadership gave in the 1960s to its chances of acquiring influence in the Third World, which was based on a Communist ideology that determined a series of events that would result in the development of symbiotic relationship between the USSR and the Third World. This ideology did not take into account the fact that there was also a chance that one of the predicted events might not materialize, thus weakening the entire chain. Furthermore, the anchoring trend is often strong; that is, feedback does not necessarily update the point of departure (Tversky and Kahneman, 1974, 1128).

In situations of uncertainty, there is a pragmatic process of alternative or inclusive usage by the policymaker of all three rules, depending on the policymaker's conception of the available information and applying the rule that he thinks is relevant, according to the type of information at hand or to the desirable results as far as definition of the situation is concerned, such as a positive evaluation of himself, his policies, or nation. These rules, which were meant to facilitate the policymaker's dealing with complexity and uncertainty, thus threaten his accuracy of perception (Nisbett and Ross, 1980).

The first danger is that the policymaker may choose the wrong rule for the information he has. The problem stems from the fact that at times he has no choice but to find some way of overcoming the uncertainty, and to do so he must make a decision. In such a case, the relevant question is whether he chooses the right rule of decision (in those cases in which more than one rule can be used). A second difficulty lies in the time span. With time, the rule that formed the basis of the perception tends to be forgotten, and the existing concept becomes a basis for additional concepts that are based on an arbitrary rule of decision imposed by force of circumstance. The fact that now there is already new information that could clarify the uncertainty without requiring one of the decision rules does not help, as the previous concepts continue to be accepted as given, without re-examination of their current justification.

Personality Traits

In this chapter we have pointed to some patterns of cognitive structure and organization that have potential implications for the accuracy of perceptions and the degree of their rigidity. It seems that there are a number of personality traits that, more than others, encourage and are related to the development of these structures and patterns.[67] This cluster of personality traits[68] is either one of the causes of the above-described phenomena or at least a symptom of their existence.[69]

Authoritarianism. A number of the symptoms connected with this trait[70] are directly related to the way in which the individual handles difficulties involved with information processing: (1) A tendency toward stereotypification, the significance of which has been discussed earlier; (2) intolerance of ambivalence (Sidonius, 1978; Budner, 1962), a mental need for unequivocal explanations and interpretations, even if the information itself does not lend itself to same or if contradictory information exists. This need might lead to the ignoring of information or its distortion in a way that will prevent its ambivalent interpretation. Such a process may also occur when the new information itself is unequivocal but threatens to create ambivalence in the information already existing in the system; (3) rigidity, that is, the disregarding of connections between various beliefs and concepts. In such a setup there is a tendency to consider information as relevant only to a certain issue-area without seeing its overflow into other areas; (4) ethnocentrism, which leads to a biased negative judgment of other actors and a positive one of the self; a (5) a tendency to rely on sources according to their authority rather than their reliability.

Dogmatism. The trait that relates to the organization of beliefs, ideas, opinions, and concepts into a relatively closed cognitive system. This trait is accompanied by certain symptoms: (1) making sharper distinctions between the belief and non-belief systems, so that the difference between what the individual believes in and what he rejects is conceived to be greater than it actually is; (2) the tendency to ignore information that threatens the closed system of beliefs (Rokeach, 1954); and (3) the inclination to remember information that fits the individual's beliefs and views (Kleck and Wheaton, 1967).

Tendency toward Concreteness. This trait is connected with the development of a simple cognitive structure in which information is characterized by a number of limited categories. Such a cognitive system is also related to a pronounced need for cognitive consistency and the adoption of stereotypes.

Introversion and Extroversion. The introverted type tends to submit reality to his subjective psychological needs (Eysenck, 1954, 267). His attitudes are more resistant to change. On the other hand, the extrovert, because of mental needs conditioned to the response of the social system in which he operates, is more vulnerable to the adoption of misperception resulting from social pressure.[71]

Self-esteem. Self-esteem leads, on the one hand, to openness in the absorption of new information (the individual is confident enough of his ability to deal with it). On the other hand, it leads to overconfidence in the existing set of beliefs and attitudes, even in the face of dissonant information, whereas an individual with a lower opinion of himself would be more open to change once new information was absorbed (Block and Petersen, 1955; Janis, 1954; McClosky, 1967).

Although there might be other personal traits that may be relevant to our case, those mentioned above are the most obvious and important.

The Group and Organization as Sources of Misperception

Group Structure and Stratification

Decisionmaking and information processing in foreign policy are usually not the affairs of one person only. These processes are undertaken by professional organizations, and major decisions are often made within the framework of a small group composed of central cabinet members, their advisors, and others. The question is, then, how the interaction between individuals in the group and the organization, and how the characteristics of the relevant decision-making group and organization, affect the selection and evaluation of information, the degree of openness to dissonant information, and the processes of adaptation. Although we are speaking of two separate variables, the group and the organization, at times the dividing line between them is very fine. A great deal of what we have to say from here on applies to the organization as much as to the group, which is why we have included both variables under the same section heading.

The fact that the individual is part of a group might contribute to his preference for a certain definition of the situation because of the following calculations in which he might indulge.

1. Who in the group is to benefit and who will lose by the focusing of the group's attention on the new interpretation? Whose power and importance will increase? And is it profitable—in those cases in which there is a general consensus in the group—to raise an issue that might cause the disintegration of the convenient consensual framework? Is it worthwhile to create conflict with powerful members of the group? And as for the leader of the group, should he put his leadership to the test if one of his suggested interpretations conflicts with the interests and concepts of any other policymaker in the group?[72]

2. What is the significance of each of the alternative interpretations to the importance of the subject with which the information deals, and, by extension, what is the amount of group energy and time needed for the subject? What are the implications in terms of other issues that the group is considering at the same time, regarding the time and energy that it will be possible to devote to them?

3. How will the answers to the questions in section 1 and 2 affect the emotional relations among group members? Being part of the group enhances the desire to be liked, or at least not to be rejected by other group members. The presentation of interpretations that might harm the delicate tissue of common percepts is undesirable. Generally, such a tissue is woven with much effort over a prolonged period, and it forms part of the emotional basis of the relations among group members as well as the sense of each member of his acceptance by the others. Hence, a natural tendency to avoid offense is promoted, even at the price of distorted perceptions.

The nature of the shared perceptions, how they are created, and the degree to which they reflect group needs rather than the essence of the information all determined the degree of reality and functionality of group concepts. The greater the functionality of the concepts, that is, their role in bolstering group cohesion, the greater will be the chance of perceptual distortion of all three kinds: awareness, relevance, and evaluation.

It should be remembered that the group or organization is composed of individuals who have different roles within it. Consequently, they also have different sensitivities to the information arriving from the environment. The information is perceived by them chiefly in terms of its perceivable connection with those issues with which they are mostly preoccupied[73] (Simon, 1976, 210–212; Jervis, 1976, 206–211).

As a result, two basic situations are possible. One occurs when information coming in is perceived as lacking significance for the topics with which the particular member of the group is dealing. Of course, in such a case the group member will tend to accept the interpretation offered by the rest of the group or dictated by the chief policymaker. The other situation is one in which the information is conceived as relevant to the subjects preoccupying the policymaker. Here, different interpretations are possible, stemming from the different realms of interest.

When there is such a clash in the group between contradicting perceptions and situation evaluations, and if the differing perceptions lead to similar operational conclusions, it is likely that the group will continue to contain conflicting perceptions without the need arising for a perceptual consensus; the *operational consensus,* which is the important one to the group, is achieved despite the dissimilarity of the situation evaluations of different group members. Moreover, a positive feedback from the operational decision in this case serves as an assurance and justification of essentially differing concepts.

On the other hand, when such a conflict between perceptions leads to different operational conclusions, one of the following outcomes may occur: the central policymaker, if he has the power, decides on the basis of his preference; or a majority in favor of one of the interpretations is formed, thereby imposing the decision on the minority. The decision is then accepted because loyalty to the group means accepting the majority rule.[74]

The third possibility is that there is no way to decide between conflicting perceptions due to the balance of power in the decision-making group. But because there is, after all, a need to reach a decision, and because a decision demands some mutually accepted perceptual basis for its formation, a compromise is reached. The compromise may take several forms.

A Compromise over Content. As a substitute for the conflicting situation evaluations, a third evaluation is adopted that is so formulated as to contain elements from the conflicting original ones. Of course, this does not really reflect the substance of the information; rather, it is the fruit of the balance of power in the decisionmaking group.

Compromise in Time. One side in the dispute is willing to yield and accept the other's perception with the understanding that, should a similar situation arise in future, the other side will forfeit its stand as a gesture of gratitude. In such a case, both the present perceptions and any future ones are determined on the basis of some rate of exchange and not on that of the content of the information.

Interperceptual Compromise. A compromise of this type is possible when a dispute simultaneously involving more than one perception takes place. In such a case, it may be that each side will relinquish what seems to it the less important evaluation and on that issue adopt the other side's interpretation. Again, the result is determined not on the basis of the information content but on that of some exchange ratio.

Once a perception has been accepted, it acquires a life of its own. In particular, those policymakers who were not party to the perception-creation process tend to see the compromise perception as having a firm objective basis originating in information and not as a result of irrelevant and tactical needs. Such a perception then forms the basis for the evaluation of new information, and for new decisions, resulting from the concepts described earlier. This kind of dynamic is what makes fallacious perceptual processes of the kind described dangerous, given their contaminating effect and because they acquire a life of their own.

We have mentioned the influence of role on the kind of information in which the policymaker is interested and on its interpretation in a way that fits his area of interest. But the situation may be even more complex in those cases in which he has several roles that require different emphases and attention spans. This situation might cause conflict, as "when the role expectations placed upon him are incompatible, making it impossible to confirm both sets of expectations" (Thomas, 1968, 709). This is a frequent problem for national decisionmakers in foreign policy whose roles in the national arena (such as protecting national interests) contradict their roles in the international system (preserving world peace, for example).

The situation could prove even more difficult when there is a contradiction between the decisionmaker's own perception of what his role entails and others' expectations of same (Levinson, 1959). His colleagues in the decisionmaking group or the citizenry of his country might, for example, have a different concept of what his job entails or a different notion as to how the contradictions between his roles on the national and international scenes should be resolved.[75]

Such a situation can create stress (Kahn et al., 1964), which, as already mentioned, might have adverse effects on the individual's ability to deal with information and, furthermore, may cause him to ignore information pointing up such contradictions, to lessen its importance, or to interpret it in such a way as to dismiss the conflict even if this calls for distortion. The stratification and division of roles and functions in the group also determine the degree of responsibility each policymaker as an individual, and the group in general, has for the successes or failures resulting from the definition of the situation finally adopted. The greater the need the policymaker has to prepare for himself an "insurance policy" against possible failure, the more he may be inclined to adopt the group's evaluations. Moreover, group pressure to accept a group conception has the advantage of diminishing the possibility of cognitive dissonance, as the individual can claim "no choice" legitimacy or insist that the majority is usually right.

Finally, the structure of stratification in the group or organization is based both on functional division of labor, which is, in effect, an expression of formal power, and on the informal status stemming from the personal relations within the group, such as close personal relations with the chief policymaker—namely, the president or the prime minister. This stratification determines the ability of each member of the group to deviate from basic shared perceptions.[76] if the information available to him so indicates. On the other hand, status in the group, which expresses itself in gaining the maximum attention of the decisionmaking members, encourages acceptance of the conventional wisdom, both because status enhances self-confidence and cognitive conservatism and because other group members are apprehensive of contradicting the status holder.

Types of Group-Inspired Compliance

Group membership might encourage conformism, the causes of which we have enumerated. Conformism can be classified into four types:

Compliance Conformism. In this situation, the individual who adopts the group's attitudes and concepts does so only for instrumental reasons arising from compliance—to win a reward or to avoid punishment by the group leader or members. The probable outcome of this kind of conformism is increased alertness to information or to interpretations that support the concepts of the group and its leader, as compared with decreased attentiveness to dissonant information and interpretations. The reason is that only the first type of conformism serves the instrumental goals of compliance, that is, gaining some reward or avoiding punishment. At the extreme, the individual may be involved in distorting either information or its interpretation in order to please. This phenomenon can be expected in a decisionmaking group with a rigid hierarchical structure and a highly authoritative leader.

Identification Conformism. In this situation, the attractiveness of the central policymaker is the basis of the group members' willingness to accept his concepts and situation evaluations. In such a case, the pleasure is in the actual act of conforming and not necessarily in the reward or punishment that follows. The act of conforming gives the member a sense of identification with an admirable person—the leader. This is particularly true for a group with a charismatic leader. Yet conformism of this type carries with it dangers similar to those associated with compliance conformism. In both situations, the source of information and the guidelines to interpretations of that information are related to the central policymaker, so that any change in perception must come from him. And yet a change in his concepts can come about only as a result of suitable information, of which he might be deprived due to the group members' conformism.

Internalization Conformism. In this case, the group member adopts the group's concepts because they are in line with his own value system or beliefs, or because he regards conformism to the majority view as a value in itself. The source of such a concept could be, as earlier noted, his personal values, or it could stem from cultural values. The difficulty in changing such perceptions and the degree of openness to dissonant information depends on the totality of factors relating to the personality variable.[77]

Combined Conformism. This kind of conformism stems from a combination of two or all three of the types previously described. Certain policymakers conform to the group's definition of a situation because it suits their values and beliefs, causes them pleasure as they identify with the group's leader, and also brings them instrumental benefits.

The conformism encountered in a group is usually not homogeneous. Indeed, the conformism of each member might have different sources: identification, compliance, internalization, or a combination thereof. It is to be expected that the nature of the conformism will be influenced by the method of choosing the members of the decision-making group. Thus, for example, an individual who has been brought into the group on a functional basis, because of his role in a relevant organization (e.g., foreign ministry or ministry of defense), or because of his relevant knowledge of a subject or his political status (e.g., a powerful position in the ruling party), will tend toward compliance conformism. The personality of the policymaker must also be considered in this context. The degree of *need* for conformism may stem from personal traits such as extroversion, a tendency toward submissiveness, or intolerance of ambivalence. The type of conformism adopted might also be influenced by the functions fulfilled for the individual by the relevant attitudes. Thus, for example, compliance conformism may well serve the function of ego defense by permitting avoidance of rejection by the group.

The frequent interaction of group members and the drive toward conformity that such interaction brings about increase the cognitive similarity among the members, which, in turn, gives rise to further interaction and thus creates a closed circle of interaction, increased cognitive similarity, preference for further interaction with the same individuals, and so on. The extreme expression of group conformity is "groupthink," a term coined by the social psychologist, Irving Janis, to refer to a situation in which all the group members think like one person. The conditions promoting groupthink are defined by Janis as follows:

1. A high degree of group cohesion, which might stem, for example, from a common background.
2. The isolation of the decisionmaking group from expert judgment; for example, if the issue is classified as secret, experts have no access to it.
3. The application of pressure by the group leader to have his preferred definition evaluation or solution accepted.

Groupthink has a number of symptoms:

1. An atmosphere of overoptimism prevails, thus encouraging the taking of unwarranted risks.
2. The group collectively attempts to rationalize its evaluations in order to ignore those items of information that "threaten" the evaluations.
3. The group profoundly believes in its own righteousness, a belief that contributes to a complimentary self-perception.
4. The opponent is conceived in stereotypic terms, the perceptions of the opponent are negative, and the opponent is regarded as extremely evil and stupid (the stupidity of the opponent also serves as a justification for overoptimism).
5. Direct pressure is brought to bear on deviating group members.
6. Each group member acts as his own censor, in order to reduce his doubts as to the accuracy of the evaluations accepted by the group.
7. As a result, a shared illusion is created about a group consensus.
8. Some group members appoint themselves responsible for the "protection" of the group from dissonant information (Janis, 1972, 197–206).

The negative implications of these symptoms, in terms of both the accuracy of the perceptual framework adopted by the group and the possibility of its adjustment to reality, is obvious.

The Impact of Organizational Membership

The individual who is a member of a decisionmaking group, such as the cabinet, is usually an important member of some organization (he may hold a ministerial portfolio, for example, or be a senior army man). This raises the question of the distinction between the peer group and the reference group. The former is the group to which the individual physically and formally belongs at a given moment, whereas the latter is that group to which the individual looks as a source of norms, judgment, evaluation, rules, and basic conceptions. As such, the reference group determines the judgment rules and criteria that the individual uses and regards as right and proper for the evaluation of incoming information, as well as the degree of acceptance that any particular interpretation will enjoy (Kelley, 1965).

There is no problem as long as the peer and reference groups are congruent—either physically, by being one and the same group, or cognitively, by having the same values, beliefs, and judgmental criteria. The problem arises when there is no such congruence, when the reference group employs criteria for judgment and evaluation different from that of the peer group, resulting at times in different interpretations of the same information. To what extent and under what conditions is the influence of the reference group important, and when is it dominant? One can determine a number of relevant conditions:

- The importance of the reference group increases the closer its beliefs and everything it represents are to the personal values and beliefs of the given policymaker. Obviously, under such circumstances the individual's tendency to respond to what is represented by the reference group and to conceive his environment in those terms increases.
- The time span during which the individual belongs to the reference group is also of great importance. The longer the time spent in the peer group, the smaller becomes the influence of the reference group.
- Another important factor is the degree of perceived permanence. If the individual's presence in the peer group is seen by him as relatively permanent, then he will pay less attention to the reference group, and its importance as a rule provider will diminish. On the other hand, if the policymaker assumes that his presence in that decisionmaking group is temporary, or ad hoc, the reference group will play a more important part in his reasoning and definition of the situation.
- The balance of power, and not necessarily the formal one, between the reference and peer groups also plays an important role in this context. When the peer group has more real power than does the reference group and can, as a result, impose a pyramidic hierarchy of loyalties, the importance of the reference group as a source of criteria for situation evaluations diminishes.

The interaction among these conditions determines the ability of the peer group to dictate conformism to its own beliefs despite the differing perspectives brought to the group by its members. But the policymaker is not always happy with the conformism imposed upon him. At times, he may feel guilty for not representing properly the views he was supposed to represent. To prevent such a situation from arising, he may take one of two courses of action: he may either try to reach an advance agreement with the group about a perceptual compromise, so that he will not feel guilt later on; or, if he does not succeed in that, he might attempt to find information and interpretations of that information that will support the peer group evaluation he has perforce adopted. Thus, he can rationalize that his conformism was, in fact, a move toward overcoming parochialism.

The policymakers with whom we are concerned in this study have a "professional" pride in their appointments to the organization and group to which they belong, and which give meaning and content to their roles. They tend to see the future of the nation as being in the hands of this decisionmaking group and to identify any success of the state with that of their particular group or themselves. This is why the individual's level of aspiration in relation to his group, or that of the group in toto, is of such importance. The level of aspiration is defined (Zander, 1971, 180) as the level of *quality* of performance expected of the group or organization in the future. This quality is measured in terms of the perceived success of the group's decisions and actions. The more an individual identifies himself with the organization, the more his level of aspiration will increase in importance;[78] thus, his level of aspiration becomes more closely connected with his positive self-perception, and pressure is created to assess past actions in a positive light without any regard to the question of whether they were really successful. As a result, the impact of negative feedback meant to inform about past mistakes and to correct present perceptions and future expectations is reduced.

The lack of feedback, of course, encourages the phenomenon of positive overestimation, and this phenomenon receives further impetus from the tendency toward conformism, so that a shared evaluation is slowly created as to the level of performance of the organization or group. The process of "mutual back-slapping" creates confidence and raises the threshold for the penetration of dissonant information that might disturb that confidence. Moreover, the more exaggerated is the positive perception of the past level of performance, the more the optimism as to the group's ability to succeed in the future is exaggerated. This optimism, as earlier noted, often has little basis in reality and encourages the dismissal of warning information pointing to dangers, threats, and other difficulties.

The Organization and Group as Subcultures

Every organization or group represents a coherent system of values, beliefs, behavioral ethos, and myth—the results of its history. The older the group or organization, the more obvious these factors are. This totality of factors forms the framework that organizes and channels the conceptual process of each organization member as an individual and creates the particular subculture of the organization.

The totality described actually forms the set of motives that dictates the objectives of the organization and thus defines the relations of the organization with its environment (Thompson and McEwen, 1969). By dictating these objectives, this system of motives determines the framework within which the incoming information will be treated, as it is dealt with in terms of the causal connection between it and the organization's goals. In other words, when an organization evaluates incoming information, it asks itself the following questions: To what extent does the information or its interpretatioin point to an increase or decrease in the likelihood that the organization will succeed in achieving its declared objectives? If the answer is negative, the next question would be: What can we do with this information in order to cancel the negative effect? If the answer is positive, the question would be: What can be done to increase the effect of the information such that the positive potential is used to the utmost? The information, then, becomes instrumental in the working out of the relations between the organization or group and its environment, in such a way that the maximum benefit will come to them, or that at least a minimum amount of damage will be done to the organization or to its members (Allison 1969, 1971; Halperin, 1974). The treatment of the information could thus become instrumental rather than substance oriented. Thus, it is possible that an organization that injects information into the decisionmaking group, and has members represented in it, can prevent dissonant information from contributing to an improved evaluation if this evaluation conflicts with its own concepts and motives.

This problem is even more serious from the standpoint of the difficulties the adaptation process may encounter, given these two characteristics of distortion: (1) the impossibility of verbally defining some of the cultural characteristics of the organization, and (2) the intolerable price of admitting the existence and the impact of such factors as parochialism in the organizational culture.

In relation to the difficulties of verbal definitions of the culture of the organization, Katz and Kahn (1966, 66) stated: "Though the subculture of the organisation provides the frame of reference within which its members interpret activities and events, the members will not be able to verbalise in any precise fashion this frame. They will be clear about the judgement they make, but not about the basic standards or frames they employ in reaching a judgement." When the criteria of classification and evaluation of information are not recognized, the motivation for re-evaluating the information is reduced. And even if there is such a motivation, a proper evaluation is made difficult when the sources of the mistaken evaluation are impossible to locate. This difficulty results from the inability to define the rules according to which the evaluation is made, given that the process is cybernetic or cognitive rather than analytic.

As for the intolerable price of a clear and definite statement of vested organizational interest; an organization or its members will not admit that some of their actions are motivated by parochial thinking, that is, by their own narrow interests—in part, certainly, out of fear that the organization, upon such an admission, might be punished, by, say, a reduction in its authority or even by dissolution. There are also moral reasons preventing such an admission, in that social norms declare that the purpose of a social organization is to serve the society that formed it. Under such conditions, when neither the organization as such, nor the individual members, will admit even to themselves the motives that determine the interpretations they give to incoming information, the processes of adjustment and adaptation cannot, of course, take place.

It should be further noted in this context that the term *subculture* can refer to both formal and informal organizations, and can cut across even national boundaries. In this sense, it is possible to speak of world elites such as the subculture of foreign ministers. The individual can be a member of a number of subcultures simultaneously, but this standing might be a source of inner conflict to him, requiring adjustment.[79]

Societal Sources of Misperception

The Impact of Social Characteristics

The last variable to be discussed is the national society. Interaction between policymakers of two national entities involves an encounter not only between personalities and organizations, but also between different cultural and social systems, each dictating different conceptual frameworks forming the basis of beliefs, expectations, values, moods, and styles of thought. These systems and frameworks determine large areas of the national self-perception, the national perception of other nations, and the interaction between the two. They also act as a limitation on what the policymaker perceives as a legitimate and acceptable range of alternative interpretations.

Two social characteristics of central importance in the context of our discussion are the age of the society and its level of development. The "national age" is important for several reasons. First, the age of basic national concepts determines their degree of embeddedness in the national consciousness and in the individual consciousness of each of the policymakers. Older images and concepts are more difficult to eradicate, even if they no longer fit the new reality, and consequently it is more difficult to change other images arising from and conditioned by them.

Second, the age of the state also determines the content of its historical heritage. The older the nation, the richer its history in the sense that images exist relating to a greater number of areas, there are ready-made historical analogies to a larger number of situations, and hence there are more issues in connection with which the national leader's freedom to conceptualize is curtailed and for which the historical heritage determines the general perceptual framework.

As noted earlier, an additional central characteristic is the level of national development. This factor determines the degree of institutionalization of the political process and hence the possibility of externalizing the policymaker's personal preferences and psychological needs in response to incoming information. Moreover, under conditions of a low level of development and of institutionalization of the political process, differentiation between the political and the personal and social spheres is narrowed, as is the differentiation between roles (Pye, 1961). This finding has negative implications for the processing of information, as interpretation becomes subservient to the significance of the information for personal and social relations, and its power to influence by its objective content is reduced. In addition, the problem of internal contradictions in the individual's cognitive system arising from the need to fulfill several roles at once becomes more frequent.

The breadth of the social strata from which the decisionmakers are recruited, as well as their attributes, determine the degree of homogeneity in terms of background and education. In developing nations where this stratum is rather narrow, as a result of the social structures and tradition, the decisionmaking group is often highly homogeneous. When this characteristic is added to a lack of differentiation between the political and personal spheres mentioned earlier, there is a greater likelihood of the development of groupthink with all its implications for and inherent dangers to the accuracy of perception.

In those states where domestic problems seem insoluble and are a dubious source of political success, there is a growing tendency on the part of policymakers to turn their main attention to foreign policy. International politics are perceived as a relatively more structured area, easier to manipulate. Thus, an illusion of success is relatively easily projected by the policymakers, especially since the criteria for success in foreign policy is very vague and elusive.

The above-mentioned characteristics are also influenced by the question of national age and the related breadth of national political experience. Characteristics such as the degree of distinction and differentiation between different functions, and the breadth of the strata from which policymakers might be recruited, are not static factors. Their dynamics are to some degree the result of the process of maturation of the national society and state.

The National Culture as a Conceptual Framework

The national culture conditions the policymaker's style of thinking and attitude toward information, and it determines the categories that will be set up to classify the information. The same activities may create different perceptual interpretations in different cultures: similar stereotypes may have different connotations, which is why affective reactions to certain stereotypes may be quite different.[80] The evaluation of the same objects will differ in cultures representing various systems of values and beliefs. Thus, the classification of information into categories and the connections between them are different from one culture to another (Triandis, 1964), as a function both of the historical experience and the accepted system of societal values and beliefs.

The basis of interaction among humans is speech, the use of language. Even in the contact between members of different cultures, the preferred basis for judgment and evaluation is language (Jacobson *et al.*, 1960). But the preference for this means of communication might also be a source of misconception, resulting from the nature of language itself. The meaning of words is perceived similarly by the parties to communication only if they have the same cultural and historical background with which to give the words their full symbolic values, as is expressed in a "tacit agreement" (Katz, 1960; Ogden and Richards, 1972, Ch. X).

Every language is the expression of a particular world view, representing cultural patterns that are different from those of other languages, and through which phenomena are examined and interpreted, their importance assessed, and decisions made as to what should and what should not be noticed. In other words, language is not only an instrument of communication but a tool for thought as well (Whorfe, 1956, 252).

These two characteristics of language—as a framework for thought and as a means of communication—are the cause of the problematical nature of language in relation to perception. First, given that a native tongue does form a framework for conception in the communication process between two policymakers, when at least one is not using his mother tongue he nevertheless thinks in that language, and thus an illusion of mutual understanding may be created by the use of similar terminology with different connotations. Then, when reality belies that illusion, a mutual feeling of deception may occur, and hence the way to mistrust is opened.

An additional problem might arise, such as the change in the connotations of the different terminologies as a result of the ongoing national experience. The dynamic of the process is not always conscious. Furthermore, words have different emotional impacts in different cultures, thus leading to different interpretations of emotive words, such as "sister state" or "brotherly solidarity."

Another major cultural factor is the national historical heritage. Its power to impose patterns of perception increases in proportion to the historical consciousness of the state; the greater the importance attributed to national history, the more ambiguous is the information that the policymaker must tackle. As a result, there is a growing need for a key that will enable the policymaker to interpret the information unequivocally, and one such key is the historical analogy.

There are several types of historical analogy. The first distinction to be made is between macro-historical and micro-historical analogies. The macro-historical kind are generalized and declarative, such as "history proves that the strong destroy the weak" or "there is historical justice that sees to it that aggressors are punished and that proves that aggression does not pay off." An analogy of this type is usually based on a philosophical-historical national sentiment, which is not always based on fact; rather, it is formed by the national impression of the direct national history or the histories of other nations that bear indirectly but strongly on the nation's history.

Micro-historical analogies are of the kind that relate to specific situations. Thus, a state that was never attacked from the north will tend to regard that direction as an unlikely one for attack. Such analogies are based only on events from the direct national history. They serve mainly to handle tactical problems. Although the first type form the basis for the general orientation of foreign policy, they also make up the background for the use of the second type of analogy.

Analogies create a number of problems in relation to information processing. First, historical events unimportant in themselves may become, through a macro-historical perspective (such as the victory of David over Goliath), symbols loaded with emotional meaning and hence powerful tools of evaluation. Second, history is full of analogies with conflicting meanings that, on the one hand, create the possibility of justifying different and even contradictory evaluations and, on the other hand, create the need to explain either the information or the history away so that the contradictions will disappear. In the process, all cognitive doubt and dissonance are done away with, once an analogy has been chosen as a basis for evaluation or interpretation of information.

A last problem is related to the relative rigidity of perceptions and expectations having historical analogies as their basis, as opposed to those for which the basis is analytical. It seems that concepts of the first kind are more durable in the face of dissonant information, unless the information also arouses an historical analogy having more power than that elicited by the original information.

Another issue of importance is that of the national styles expressed in abstract versus pragmatic thinking, or in an associative versus analytic response to environmental information (Hoffmann, 1968b; Glenn *et al.*, 1970). A culture of abstract thinking that tries to see every event as part of a much wider phenomenon, or, at the other extreme, a pragmatic culture that tries to see every event in itself without reference to symbolic significance or historical precedence is the fruit of a national-ethical tradition that finds its expression also in the language—in the wealth of the adjectives and emotional and cognitive connotations that the adjective carries, and in the symbols that the language contains. A culture that encourages an associative reaction and evaluation attributes importance to elements that enhance associative reactions, such as emotional evaluations or simplistic and approachable historical analogies. A culture that encourages analytic reactions and sees these as an important value will tend to minimize the importance of emotional factors and encourage evaluations of every situation in rational terms. An encounter between such different cultures and styles of thought inevitably leads to mutual misunderstandings and misperceptions.

National Conceptions of Belonging, Role, and Status

National self-perception is focused on three concepts: (1) the concept of belonging: To which group of nations does the state see itself belonging? (2) the concept of role: What role does it perceive for itself in the international arena? and (3) the concept of status: What status does the state think it deserves? These concepts are important in that they determine the state's expectations in its relations with other actors in the system, and thus form a framework for the evaluation of information pertaining both to its behavior and to the reaction of other actors to it.

First, most states belong to several groups at one and the same time. A nation can be simultaneously part of the developing, Asian, and Socialist countries, and so on. But because this group belonging determines the expectations that any specific state entertains about its group members, as well as the expectations of the other members in the group toward it, a problem may arise when "membership" in several groups at once creates conflicting expectations. One of the main techniques for settling such conflicting expectations is to explain them away as nonconflicting ones, while other nations may regard these contradictions as serious enough to need resolution. This need finds expression in the other nations' behavior toward the particular state, which it may misunderstand. Second, a situation may arise in which there is a lack of correlation between the expectations of the state belonging to a particular bloc of states and the expectations and perceptions of other bloc members as to the commitments arising from that membership. Third, at times a state perceives itself as belonging to a certain bloc and, as a result, develops expectations about the attitude and behavior of other states toward it. But the other members in the bloc may have a different conception of that particular nation; they may not even consider it as belonging to their bloc. Their ensuing behavior often causes the particular nation to feel deceived. It does not understand the reactions of other states toward it, whereas the other members do not understand why the particular state expected any other kind of behavior.

The concept of the international role is defined thus: "A national role conception includes the policy-makers' own definition of the general kind of decisions, commitment, rules and actions suitable to their states and of the functions, if any, their state should perform on a continuing basis in the international system or in subordinate regional systems" (Holsti, 1970, 245–246).

There are a number of potential perceptual problems associated with any particular state's role conception:

- Because a number of nations play multiple roles at the same time, a gap is often created between the perception of the role player as to the legitimacy of a multirole position and the other actors in the system who may regard a multirole game as an expression of hypocrisy and hence as nonlegitimate. But, as the role player himself does not perceive such a contradiction, he may have difficulty in perceiving the negative light in which other actors in the system regard his actions.
- When an actor adopts a certain role perception, this has in it an element of interaction insofar as it involves other actors toward whom the role perception will operationally be directed. Two basic misperceptions are possible as a result: (1) An erroneous evaluation may be made about the willingness of other actors to play the roles assigned to them in such a way that our role player is able to play the role he assigned to himself (e.g., if the role of leader is to be played, somebody must also be found to play the follower); and (2) Even if the other actors are ready to accept the role concept in a general way, there might be a lack of compatibility between the specific expectation of the role as seen by the actor himself and the other actors in the international arena.
- In those cases in which an actor refuses to take on a specific role, or in which other countries try to impose a certain role perception on an actor, a situation may arise in which the actor's self-perception contradicts the way in which other actors see him, without his being aware of it, as, according to his self-perception, it is not his role. On the other hand, the other actors interpret his actions in light of that role. Their expectations of his behavior and reactions are a result of the role they have attributed to him.

The concept of the status of the state is connected to that of role perception, as status perception determines to some extent what roles a certain state believes it is able to play and should play. The status perception of each state may become a source of misperception:

- The great importance attributed by nations to their status makes them ignore or repress information that points to a possibility that their own perceived status is much higher than that accorded them by other nations.[81] As a result, they attribute an unrealistic role concept to themselves.
- Contradictions may arise when the historical heritage bequeaths rigid status concepts that do not correspond to changes in a state's relative power over a period of time.
- As different cultures determined different values as indications of status, differences in perception may occur among nations as to their status. This phenomenon finds clear expression in the eternal struggle in human history over status among nations that perceive it to be a natural outcome of physical strength and those that regard it as resulting from spiritual power.
- When attributed status is higher than deserved status, the state tends to adopt the unrealistic status and the related expectations as an expression of its real power.

The General Theoretical Framework

The process described and the misconceptions that result from it raise serious doubts as to the ability of foreign policy to serve as an aid to society and state in adjusting to the changes occurring in the external and internal environment,[82] for such an ability is conditional on an accurate perception of changes in the environment. If the perceptual process is defective, foreign policy, rather than serving the purposes it aims at, tends to serve subjective needs and conceptions of actors who are not in tune with reality. It is therefore, overoptimistic to rely on the magical belief that a distorted perception of the environment is eventually corrected by feedback processes.

It should also be noted that past perceptions serve as important information inputs, both on the factual and interpretative levels, and thus they become a central factor in the formation of present and future perceptions; that is, they become the point of departure for the whole process. As a result, a closed circle can emerge in which misperceptions form the basis of additional misperceptions, thus increasing their own importance and so forming a vicious circle. In this event, the described perceptual system is a circular one, which, although fed from external input, is also a self-nourishing system.

Three systems of perceptual channeling have been pointed out— the technical, the psychological, and the social. But it is suggested that the influence of these channeling factors is not static; rather, such influence requires proper arousal preconditions, which set the whole system in motion. Such conditions follow:

1. The degree of uncertainty involved in the issue;
2. The degree of importance and complexity attributed to it;
3. The degree of personal involvement and responsibility that the policymakers feel toward the problem; and
4. The stress and anxiety under which the policy-makers operate.

These conditions may create or accentuate a need or dependence on extrarational and nonanalytical rules, patterns, and norms for information processing.

A number of general propositions emerge from the theoretical framework, a model of which is presented in Figure 1.3:

The Channelling Proposition. The degree of accuracy of the perception of the real environment at every point in time and the effectiveness of feedback processes may be channeled by technical, psychological, and social factors with little relationship to the essential content of the information. Such channeling systems are defined in this context in terms of five major variables: the system of information handling, that is, the nature of the information and the rules of its processing; the societal cultural system; the organizational structure; the structure of the decisionmaking group; and the personality of the individual.

The Cumulative Proposition. With the passage of time, the cumulative influence of misperceptions creates a structure of distortions, which build up layer upon layer and make adjustment difficult. This process also stems from the fact that accumulation breeds commitment, on the part of the policymaker, to the distorted conceptual system. As a result, attempts to impose change on it may have a boomerang effect and only strengthen it, as commitment increases its centrality and vice versa. Thus, feedback processes are not necessarily effective in the area of correcting perceptual distortions (see also the following proposition).

The Ripple Proposition. Misperceptions follow the ripple principle. A misperception in one area may cause misperceptions in other areas, just as a stone thrown into a pool creates spreading ripples. The extent of the spreading of misperceptions is a function of the extent to which the policymaker perceives the different issues as interrelated. This phenomenon also stems from the fact that some of the variables causing it are "globalistic" in nature (i.e., cognitive and social systems) and are not necessarily specific to a certain issue or situation.

The Point of Departure Proposition. There is a connection between the misperception at T_0 and the following process of adaptation. When a process of adaptation takes place, its power and direction are influenced by the gap at the point of departure:

- A process of maladaptation ("C") will tend to be connected with an awareness gap ("1") as its point of departure;
- A process of nonadaptation (B) may be connected with either a relevance gap (2) or an evaluation gap (3);

Figure 1.3. Model: The Dynamics of Misperception

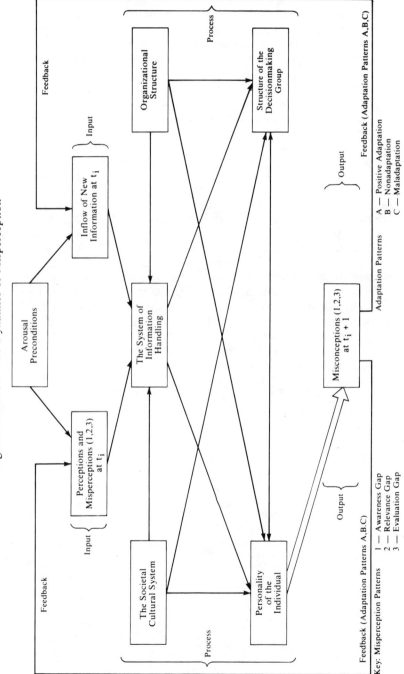

- A process of positive adaptation (A) will tend to be connected to the point of departure of an evaluation gap (3);
- Even when a process of adaptation does take place where the point of departure was an awareness gap (1), there will not be full adaptation but rather the awareness gap will tend to become a relevance gap (2) or evaluation gap (3);
- When a process of adaptation takes place following the point of departure of a relevance gap (2), there will be only partial adaptation, although the relevance gap will then tend to become an evaluation gap (3).

The Pendulum Proposition. If misperceptions lead to mistaken decisions (or behavior), the consequence is not necessarily correction of the misperceptions; instead, preference may be given to views diametrically opposed to the original concepts. The explanation of this hypothesis is that the cumulative process of distortion leads to an "explosion" resulting from the increasing contradiction between perception and reality. When the wrong decision is fatal, and there is no way to "escape" from recognizing the misperception, there is an immediate need to adopt substitute concepts. The simplest way to do so is to take up those that are diametrically opposed to the ones that failed and that, as such, are the most easily available to the perceiver's mind. These concepts are easily accessible and, as such, satisfy the policymaker, for they stand out against the background of the failure of rival concepts. Thus, when one country adopts a "good faith" model in its relations with another, and is later disappointed, the model does not become more balanced; rather, the immediate reaction is to adopt an extreme "bad faith" model.

2
The Issue

Sino-Indian Relations, 1949–1962: A Brief Historical Survey[1]

In July 1914 an agreement to determine the border between Tibet, which then enjoyed de facto independence of distant Peking, and British India was signed at Simla. The line was called the "McMahon line" after its creator. Although Tibetan representatives signed the agreement, the Chinese only initialed it; they refused to ratify it, fearing that such an action would be interpreted as Chinese recognition of the sovereignty of Tibet, which China saw as a vassal state.

The following years were to be difficult for China, shaken as it was by a Japanese war and occupation, civil war, and extreme political polarization while under the leadership of a corrupt and weak government. Tibet's status as a de facto independent state suited British geo-strategic interests in maintaining a buffer state between themselves and Tsarist (later Soviet) Russia and China. The McMahon line thus became the de facto boundary between British India and Tibet, despite its nonratification by Peking.

In December 1949 India became the second nation, after Burma, to recognize Communist China and declared its friendly intentions toward the new regime. India's sympathetic attitude was received with conspicuous coldness and indifference; the new regime in Peking was still preoccupied with consolidating its internal position. There were still pockets of resistance by Kuomintang supporters; various sectors of the population objected to the new domestic policies; and the tremendous tasks undertaken by the government—the establishment of a strong centralist regime, the exercise of effective control over all the territories that were considered part of the great Chinese Empire, and the changing of the whole socioeconomic structure—had yet to be realized.

In October 1950 the Chinese took a practical step toward imposing their authority on territories that they defined as traditionally Chinese. The People's Liberation Army entered Tibet from Sinkiang, crossing on its way the western corner of the Aksai Chin area, which is part of Ladakh in the western sector of the Sino-Indian boundary. Within a few years, the Chinese were to build a road in the same area connecting Sinkiang with Tibet; this road was to become one of the major bones of contention in the dispute. The Chinese take-over of Tibet and the demand for sovereignty over an area that had not been under effective Chinese control since the beginning of the century, and that was accepted by the British and their Indian successors as under Chinese suzerainty, aroused thunderous indignation in India.

The right wing of the Congress Party, under the leadership of Sardar Vallabhbhai Patel, Home Minister and Nehru's copartner in the duumvirate that actually ruled India, demanded an uncompromising stand on the Chinese action; in Patel's own words, in a letter to Nehru of November 7, 1950: "The final action of the Chinese, in my judgement, is a little short of perfidy."[2] Nevertheless, the official reaction, decided on chiefly by Jawaharlal Nehru, V.K. Krishna Menon, and India's ambassador to Peking, K.M. Panikkar, was very restrained and cautiously formulated,[3] disregarding even moral claims. Moreover, India refused to represent Tibet on the matter at the United Nations. It was through India's mediation, however, that the Seventeen Points Agreement of May 1951 was finally reached. The agreement acknowledged China's sovereignty over Tibet but, at the same time, in sections three and four, ensured Tibet's autonomy and the preservation of its existing social and economic order. Section five ensured the status of the Dalai Lama.[4] The agreement also removed the first stumbling block in the relations between the two countries, at least in the short run.

The outbreak of the Korean War and China's involvement in it allowed Nehru to prove his friendship toward China in a series of steps: he objected to the labeling of China as an aggressor and condemned the United States for bringing the Seventh Fleet into the Taiwan strait and for signing a separate peace treaty with Japan; he criticized the U.S. attitude on the Indochina issue and expressed support for the Vietminh. India played an active role in the termination of the war in Korea and later also at the Geneva Conference of 1954, which dealt with the Indochina problem.

But the peak of Sino-Indian friendship was the signing of the Panch Sheel Agreement in April 1954,[5] the title of which was "Agreement between India and China on trade and intercourse between *Tibet region of China* [author's italics] and India." This agreement regulated India's status and rights in Tibet, after having given up the special status inherited from British India. But the main importance of the agreement lay in the five principles that were to guide the relations between the two countries: (1) Mutual respect for each other's territorial integrity, (2) Mutual nonaggression, (3) Mutual noninterference in each other's internal affairs, (4) Equality and mutual benefits, and (5) Peaceful coexistence.

In 1955 India initiated the invitation to China to attend the Bandung Conference, at which the Indian delegation took the Chinese representatives under its wing and Nehru introduced Chou En-lai to the other members. But within a short while, Chou En-lai actually became the focus of the conference and "stole the show" from Nehru.

Shortly after the signing of the Panch Sheel Agreement, several nonviolent border incidents occurred and the question of the Sino-Indian frontier was reopened. These incidents were kept from the Indian public at the time and were known only to Nehru and his close advisors.[6]

In September 1957 the Indian government discovered that China had built a road connecting Sinkiang with Tibet through the north-western border sector on the Aksai Chin plain, an area to which both India and China were to lay claim. On October 18, 1958 the Indian government protested to the Chinese government against the violation of its territorial sovereignty (*W.P.,* I, 26–27).

In March 1959 a full-scale popular rising took place in Tibet following attempts to bring about its Sinicization, in what seemed to be a contradiction of the Seventeen Points Agreement in the matter of preserving Tibet's political, economic, and cultural autonomy. India refused to give the rebels military or diplomatic support. On March 31 Tibet's spiritual and temporal ruler, the Dalai Lama, crossed the border into India where he received political asylum. His dramatic escape brought the matter to public attention, and enraged public opinion demanded a firm Indian stance. A propaganda war broke out between the two countries, in which Peking blamed India for interfering in China's internal affairs. Nehru's position became increasingly difficult. On the one hand, he had to consider Parliament and public indignation, yet, on the other, he had no wish to provoke Peking.

A border incident in August in the eastern sector at Longju and another in October in the western sector at the Kongka Pass, in which the Indian army suffered a number of casualties, turned the pressure of public opinion, the media, and opposition members of Parliament into a public furor. Nehru, obliged to take a firm declaratory stand and to prove that he had not forfeited Indian interests, made public his current exchange of letters with the Chinese government.

Simultaneously, in September 1959, the Chinese declared invalid the existing boundary in the eastern, central, and western sectors (*W.P.,* II, 27–33). In April 1960 Chou En-lai came to New Delhi for talks with Nehru, but the only result was the establishment of a joint committee whose task was to work out the territorial claims of both sides. The committee's work ended in deadlock: the Chinese claimed the McMahon line to be illegal, whereas in the western sector a border had never officially been drawn. India, on the other hand, claimed that the border between it and China was clearly defined on the basis of valid agreements, tradition, geography, and de facto control.

The relations between the two nations became increasingly strained. By mid-1961 the Chinese already occupied about 20,000 square km of territory, regarded by India as its own. The Indian government, as a precondition to any significant negotiations, demanded a return to the earlier status quo ante. The Chinese did not agree. In Tibet they began preparing for a military confrontation quite openly. Their well-equipped, well-trained military forces, with well-organized communications and logistic systems, were concentrated against the Indian army, which was deficient in all these areas. Against this background, India continued to pursue its "Forward Policy," which consisted of active patrolling and the establishment of military outposts in territories claimed or occupied by the Chinese, so long as any direct encounter with Chinese troops was avoided.

The 1954 agreement expired and was not renewed. The Forward Policy became increasingly provocative to the Chinese. A series of declarations and unfortunate slips of the tongue by Nehru, continuing attacks in Parliament and in the press demanding a tougher Indian reaction, and the exchange of letters (the language of which became increasingly aggressive and hard-lined) created an atmosphere of impending crisis. On September 8, 1962 Chinese forces crossed the Thag La Ridge in the eastern sector, thereby—according to the Indian definition—crossing the McMahon line south. On September 20 a serious incident broke out in the eastern sector, and at dawn on October 20 Chinese forces opened a simultaneous offensive in the eastern and western sectors. On November 16 they launched the second offensive. The defeat of the Indian army was complete. On November 21, 1962 the Chinese declared a unilateral retreat in the east beyond the McMahon line and in the west, forming a defense line that enabled them to secure the strategic road from Sinkiang to Tibet that was so essential.

The Centrality of the Chinese Issue in Indian Foreign Policy

The preceding historical survey shows the great importance of the Chinese issue in Indian foreign policy. The aim of this book will be to show that the subect was so central as to arouse in Indian policymakers the entire complex of cognitive-perceptual problems and conflicts, and to demand their resolution.

Nehru himself testified to the centrality of the Chinese issue when he said:

> the situation that has arisen on our borders is of such historical significance from a long-term point of view. India and China, these two great countries, for the first time face each other on a long border which is a live border, and even if we are friends, even then, we have a live and dangerous border; if we are not friends, then it is worse. (*Par.*, I, 288–289)

The Chinese issue was already a major factor for Indian policymakers at the beginning of the 1950s. For Nehru and the left wing of the ruling National Congress Party, it became a channel through which to externalize their political, moral, and social values. Nehru's China policy enabled him to prove his independence of the West and his devotion to the cause of Asian solidarity, even at the price of confrontation with the United States, which, since 1949 and especially after the Chinese intervention in Korea, considered China to be the "black sheep" in the family of nations—a typical expression of the Communist danger and a potentially explosive combination of un-limited human resources and an aggressive Marxist ideology.

Furthermore, the Chinese issue evoked deep emotional reactions in those who favored cultural, political, and economic ties, and who thought in terms of a symbiotic link between the two Asian powers, as was expressed in the motto "Hindi Chini Bhai Bhai," or "The Chinese and Indians are brothers." The problem aroused the same degree of sensitivity and heated reactions in the right wing of the Congress and other parties in India, as it touched on some basic issues—namely, the territorial issues that for young nations are of particular consequence. Territory and territorial sovereignty constitute the most tangible evidence of independence and boundaries of na-tionalist self-determination. The Chinese threat was also seen as jeopardizing India's standing as the leader of Asia, an issue that involved the question of national pride, also a very sensitive topic for newly created states. By the end of the 1950s, these factors had made the Chinese problem a central one, not only for policymakers but for the entire Indian public, a fact that further exacerbated an already emotion-laden problem.

Thus far, and as will be seen in the following analysis, it seems that the China problem was so pervasive as to have influenced the entire range of foreign and domestic policies. This influence was not always of a consistent intensity, but it was always there. Again, as we shall see, Nehru was aware of this and took account of it in his reasoning. He understood that any decision he made in relation to the China policy would affect the strategic-defensive and diplomatic-political situations and the economic-industrial growth of the country. Consequently, the results of such decisions were felt in all the major areas of state involvement.

The China issue was also significant at the organizational-insti-tutional level. The subject's far-reaching implications made it the focus of legitimate interest and involvement for different organizations, politicians, and bureaucrats, as well as an instrument of rebuttal in the interorganizational and interpersonal struggles within the Indian political system—all, of course, under the banner of national interest, which, as stated, had rival interpretations. Thus, for example, the China problem became an issue in the rivalry between the Ministry of Defense and the Army, and between the Ministries of Defense and Finance; moreover, on the personal level it fed the animosities between the minister of defense, Krishna Menon, and the finance minister, Morarji Desai, and among the CGS, Lieutenant General B.M. Kaul, and Lieutenant General Umrao Singh, Commander of the 33rd Corps, to mention only a few.[7]

The intensified emotionalism of the issue and the increasing polarization of public opinion gave minor events a greater significance than they should have had; it made attitudes rigid and concessions much less likely than could be expected on the basis of a less emotional assessment. Decisions concerning the Chinese problem were, consequently, complex and multifaceted. Their implementation was dependent on the goodwill and interpretation given them by organizations and rival personalities and was difficult to control at the executive level. The moment a decision was taken, it was almost impossible to retract or cancel the decision outright. The complexity and wide range of the implications of such decisions caused long-term effects and trends that were not easily reversible.

Clearly, even without going into detail, the problem of China was not just another issue in India's foreign policy.[8] The judgment of one of the foremost scholars in this area is succinct: "All of India's policy was an extension of Nehru's political personality; but no part of it was more markedly associated with him personally than India's friendship with China" (Maxwell, 1972, 121)—so much so that one of his friends remarked the day of his death, "He died the day the Chinese crossed our border" (Moraes, 1964, 116).

Definition of the Problem by the Chinese
and Indian Leaderships

Earlier on, the point was made that the first phase in any perceptual process is deciding the categories into which to classify the information. These categories serve policymakers as yardsticks for relating to the problem and, as such, also serve as a basis and framework for interpreting the information, as a means of separating the important from the unimportant, and as a criterion for the assignment of the problem to the organization or persons whose skills or experience are particularly relevant. These same people, as compared to those whose skills do not seem relevant to the problem, will be more readily listened to by policymakers even if their suggestions are not necessarily adopted. In the struggle for the policymaker's ear, the winner is predetermined by the basic definition of the problem, such that the intra- and interorganizational and interpersonal competition occurs at the initial stage.

As in every political dispute between states, there are at least two sides; thus, different basic definitions may be formulated, either of the problem itself or in the evaluation of the relative importance of its characteristics.[9] Ignorance of such possible incongruence of conceptions might also bring about failures in encoding and decoding of signals.

In the Sino-Indian dispute, six definitions or dimensions of the ⟵ problem as apprehended by both sides can be determined:

1. *The legal definition,* which saw the dispute as emerging from and chiefly revolving around legal technicalities such as the legality of the Simla Conference and its ensuing agreements; the criteria for determining ownership of territory; and the de facto occupation, historical rights, geographical markings, and so on. The sides argued a great deal directly and indirectly[10] about this factor and saw it as one of the major characteristics of the dispute; it finally led to the appointment of the Joint Committee, which was to settle, or at least to clarify, the mutual legal claims.

2. *The teritorial definition,* which saw the problem in terms of the occupation of a particular territory or geographical location. It was not necessarily connected with the legal problem or the strategic value of the territory, but was seen simply as unwillingness to give up a piece of land considered to belong to the nation. The determination not to give up any piece of Aksai Chin, which was worthless to India, is a good example, as is the series of border incidents over tiny territories or villages, which Nehru himself saw as absurd (*Par.,* I, 118).[11]

3. *The strategic definition,* accepted by both sides, which saw the problem as having strategic-security significance to India (*Par.,* I, 397) and to China. The main anxiety of China had to do with preventing a situation in which it would have to fight on two fronts simultaneously (*P.R.,* July 27, 1962, 13).

4. *The national honor definition,* which, in seeing the Sino-Indian dispute in emotional terms, brought a deep sentimental element into the problem, significantly limited Nehru's maneuverability, and turned the problem into a "zero sum game." National honor for one side seemed to be the denial of it for the other: "There are some things which no nation can tolerate. Any attack on its *honour,* on its integrity . . . you cannot barter these things, your self-respect and honour" (*Par.,* I, 193) or, in the Chinese version: "The days when the Chinese people could be bossed around are gone forever" (*P.R.,* Sept. 15 1959, 3).

5. *The international status struggle definition,* in which the desire to play a role in international politics was seen as mutual. As the dispute progressed, it became increasingly an expression of a struggle for status in the Asian and international arenas. Any concessions by either side were seen as a loss of face and thus as leading to an inferior position and to less influence in world politics. Nehru perceived this struggle for status as a reason for India's problems with both

Table 2.1. The Indian and Chinese Definitions of the Problem

	Legal	Territorial	Strategic	National Honor	International Status	Ideological-Political
India						
Total	23	20	9	15	7	41
Percentage of all expression	20%	17.39%	7.82%	13.04%	6.08%	35.65%
China						
Total	30	22	2	3	2	31
Percentage of all expression	33.33%	24.44%	2.22%	3.33%	2.22%	34.44%

Sources: Content analysis for Nehru from two volumes of Parliamentary debates (*Prime Minister On Sino-Indian Relations: In Parliament).* Content analysis for China from *Peking Review,* 1959–1962. (For a list of articles see bibliography.)

Note: Inter-coder Reliability for the Indian documents is 91.4% and for the Chinese documents, 88.2%.

China and Pakistan (*Par.,* I, 315–316). China, on the other hand, repeated that it was a great power, and yet everything was being done to make China lose face and to deny general recognition to its new regime (*P.R.,* Dec. 15, 1961, 13–14).

6. *The ideological and political definition,* in which the broadest view of the problem was seen as part of the network of political and ideological relations on the international scene—bilateral, regional, and global. For example, already in September 1959 high officials told the Soviet representative in Peking that India had initiated the border dispute in order "to oppose *Communism* and China" (*P.R.,* Nov. 8, 1963, 19).

Nehru, in his turn, repeatedly stated that China's aggression toward India on the bilateral territorial issue was only secondary in importance to the wider Asian issue, a problem that might have had global implications, and that India was obliged to think in those broad terms and not to isolate the problem as a territorial-military one alone (*Par.,* II, 64–65).

From Table 2.1, the following conclusions can be drawn as to Nehru's conceptions:

1. Nehru saw the problem not only as a border dispute in a wider political context pertaining both to overall Sino-Indian relations and to the entire Asian subsystem, but also as inseparable from global events. This conclusion likewise emerges from the analysis of Nehru's psychological environment, in which the geo-strategic factor is only third in importance.[12]

2. The central issues of the problem per se were seen by Nehru as territorial and technical-legal, which, connected as they were to issues of national honor, made them emotionally loaded.
3. The status aspect and, what is more important, the strategic-security aspects, were not central to Nehru's thinking (only 7.82% of the definitions see the problem as strategic).
4. Considering the previous conclusions listed, the military, both as an organization and as a group of individuals, was usually given only a minor say in the assessment of the situation. On the other hand, organizations and individuals thought to be capable of wide-ranging political-diplomatic thinking and treatment of the problem were the ones listened to.[13] Of importance also were organizations and individuals who could provide advice on the legal or territorial aspects of the Sino-Indian conflict, such as the precise location of a border, historically based evidence, and so on.
5. The view that the problem involved national honor, though less important than other dimensions, gave public opinion a growing degree of influence with policymakers.
6. The various definitions indicate that the Sino-Indian problem was seen as being influenced by and as having an impact on both internal and external environmental factors, although the significance of the political aspect gave extra weight to the latter.
7. Because the problem was basically defined as political, Nehru favored moves and solutions that were considered unlikely to provoke the Chinese militarily.[14] This preference on Nehru's part was another reason for which the military did not play a larger role in the evaluation and definition of the situation throughout most of the period.

On the Chinese side, the following conclusions can be drawn:

1. The most important dimension of the problem, as for the Indians, was political. In other words, it was conceived not only as a border dispute but as having broad political and ideological implications as well.
2. The legal aspect was just as central but will be better understood in light of the Chinese world view in which the legal and political aspects are closely related.[15]
3. In comparison with India, the problem of national honor was a relatively minor one for the Chinese. Emotional reasons therefore played a relatively small part on the Chinese side.
4. The strategic aspect was also of relatively minor importance to China. Its leadership did not see the border dispute with India as a major strategic threat.

5. Territorial considerations carried considerable weight, though less than the political ones, and were related to and reinforced by the legal aspect. The difference between India and China in the significance given to the territorial factors as such is also expressed in the analysis of the Chinese psychological environment, in which the territorial factor is second in importance among the four main aspects.[16]

A comparison of the two sets of conclusions suggests that the sources of problems lay in the perceptual process and in the evaluation of the situation on both sides. The fact that India and China saw the problem chiefly as ideological-political and had at the same time essentially different political and ideological systems and concepts created difficulties in communication and mutual understanding. The removal of the dispute from its local context and its placement in a broader political and ideological medium led to misconceptions of the relevance and evaluation types.

Second, the somewhat reckless behavior of both sides is explained by the fact that neither regarded the strategic problem as central. Actions that under different circumstances would have been regarded as provocative and would have been avoided for fear of retaliation were not so regarded in this case. Similarly, the threshold of caution in the assessment of the rival's reaction was heightened,[17] leading to an evaluation gap. The price was eventually paid by India, the weaker side of the equation.

Third, India's concern for its national honor led to a hardening of positions and reinforced dangerous processes, which further aggravated the situation.

Against this background, we shall proceed in the following chapters with a detailed discussion of each of the cognitive components perceived by Nehru as relevant. In the process, we shall see how realistic these perceptions actually were.

Conclusions

When two nations deal with one another, more often than not there exist at least some differences in the way in which each defines a problem. The definition of the problem determines several matters, such as the expectation of a possible acceptable solution, the degree of threat inherent in the issue, basic policy orientation, and which individuals or organizations will be of relevance in the ongoing process of evaluating the situation and prescribing alternatives for behavior.

In the Sino-Indian case, the two most outstanding features of the definition of the situation were as follows:

1. Nehru was unaware that, although both India and China defined the problem as political in nature, that is, as having repercussions

beyond the narrow bilateral aspect, their two separate political definitions rested, as we shall see in the coming chapters, on two quite different basic sets of assumptions. Over time we find no change in this awareness gap, which led Nehru to the conclusion that some common denominator could be found without having to change India's basic positions.

2. Nehru gave a low evaluation to the strategic threat inherent in the problem. This evaluation gap underwent only very minor adaptations over time and was in part responsible for the fact that the nonpoliticized army officers as individuals, and the army as an organization, had but little to say in the overall definition of the situation. It also supported the conclusion that India would stick to its unrelenting position and, later, to its reckless Forward Policy without running the risk of a Sino-Indian war.

3
The Global International Environment

India Within the Global System

One of the most basic premises in Nehru's world view was that India's present and future situation should be evaluated in light of not only its immediate surroundings, but mainly the events and developments in the global system at large. In fact, he saw India's future as conditioned by the turbulences in the global arena. It is not surprising, then, that already in the early stages of the escalation of the Sino-Indian dispute he declared:

> Now, I should like this House to consider our problem [with China] in that large context of the world. We never forget the world, we are too closely knit to it to separate ourselves, and in the world today the major thing that is happening is this approach of the leaders of rival countries trying to find a way out, trying to go ahead with disarmament and solve or lessen the tension which exists. (*Par.*, I, 315)

In December 1961 he reconfirmed in Parliament that "these things [the border conflict and global situation] are connected with each other. We cannot isolate them" (*Par.*, II, 50).

Nehru viewed the global system as an arena of constant and dangerous confrontation between East and West, in which the Third World nations, the nonaligned bloc, and especially India had a special role to play as moderators. To maintain their position as an island of sanity in a world that could annihilate itself through sheer ineptitude or aggression, it was important to have a united nonaligned front, even if it did not necessarily lead to the creation of a third rigid bloc in the pattern of the prevailing power balance (Nehru, 1964, 361–362; *F.N.*, 3/61, June 27, 1961).

Nehru saw the existence of a bloc of nonaligned nations led by India as a matter of interest also to the two super powers and especially to the West, which had in the past shown reservations toward nonalignment in general and toward its leaders in particular

(*Par.*, I, 182). The arguments in favor of the creation of a nonaligned bloc had first crystallized, according to Nehru, at the Bandung Conference in 1955. The fruitful outcome of India's role in the settlement of the Korean crisis and the solution to the Indochina question presented at the Geneva Conference in 1954 gave impetus to the concept of Third World power. This power had gained momentum in proportion to the escalation of the nuclear armaments race and to the deepening of the conflict between the two major powers and their need for a third force that, aided by international organizations such as the United Nations could serve as a moderating influence to prevent a nuclear holocaust (Nehru, 1964, 362). There was thus a coincidence of interest among the major powers and the nonaligned nations; the solution of the latters' specific problems had to be subservient to the resolution of the central issue, that of saving the world from itself. In a speech in November 1957, Nehru expressed this position most succinctly: "We in India have grave problems to face. But I am overwhelmed by the thought of the crisis in civilisation which the world is facing today, the like of which it has not known ever before. . . . Our Earth has become too small for the new weapons of the atomic age. . . . There are enough weapons of mass destruction already to put an end to life on Earth" (Nehru, 1964, 308).

This deep anxiety for the fate of the world was accompanied by Nehru's search for good omens that might indicate that the two main protagonists were adopting his attitude. Nehru did indeed find positive signs, although progress in the desired direction was not linear. There were temporary relapses that, if not immediately arrested, might have caused a general regression resulting in a holocaust. Nehru was convinced that it was his duty not to add to existing tensions with yet another dispute that might deprive him and India, morally and politically, of the essential role of world mental-balance keeper. It is for this reason, when the suggestion was made to bomb Chinese positions in retaliation for the incident in the Kongka Pass in October 1959, that Nehru reacted by warning: "let us realise in all consciousness that such a conflict, such a war between India and China, will be bad, terribly bad, a tragedy of the deepest kind—a tragedy for us, a tragedy for China too and a tragedy for Asia and the world" (*Par.*, I, 204).

Nehru perceived super-power recognition of India's chosen role in several developments. Since 1953 there had been a vast improvement in Soviet-Indian relations. In Stalin's successors Nehru found goodwill and appreciation of the nonalignment policy, which, viewed in the past as supportive of the West, was now seen by the USSR as second best only to actually joining the Soviet bloc. At least it did not enhance Western power as Pakistan had done by joining both the Central Treaty Organization (CENTO) and the Southeast Asia Treaty Organization (SEATO).

A similar attitude seemed gradually to evolve in the United States, where John Foster Dulles denounced nonalignment as an immoral, hypocritical, and extortionist stance. "Sitting on the fence" was worse than, or at least as bad as, joining the Soviet side. In 1959 what Nehru regarded as a victory for common sense occurred in the United States: President Dwight D. Eisenhower visited India in December, U.S. aid to India was increased, and in 1961 President John F. Kennedy sent a congratulatory message to the Nonaligned Conference in Belgrade.

Nehru also perceived, with a sense of personal satisfaction, a real breakthrough in the relations between the two super powers themselves, symbolized by the Camp David Summit where the spirit of Camp David was born:

Our policy has been boosted tremendously by what has happened in Europe and America . . . because of these significant developments which have taken place in the last few months—Mr. Khrushchev's going to America and President Eisenhower's going, in future, to Moscow and all that is around it and the probability of a summit conference coming. . . . You could not boost our policy more." (*Press,* I, 52)

The international system seemed to be advancing, though somewhat haltingly, from an era of rigid polarization to one of looser bipolarity or even to a balance-of-power system. Within the "bloc" framework there was increasing maneuverability for member states that began to see positive options resulting from the loosening of the blocs. The thaw in the cold war had been gaining momentum since the Twentieth Soviet Communist Party Congress in 1956, at which Nikita Khrushchev had pronounced his de-Stalinization policy, marking the beginning of an era of peaceful coexistence and competition. Nehru saw India as having contributed directly to this state of affairs with the signing of the Panch Sheel Agreement with China in 1954, which had introduced the five principles of peaceful coexistence that were seen as a guide and a basis for an alternative to the cold war.[1] Of course, this notion held more than a grain of boastfulness, as the same principles were already written into the United Nations Charter.

The changes in the relations between the super powers were felt in regional conflicts. There were encouraging signs of cooperation between them, which diffused local flash points. In 1956 they worked together both in the United Nations and elsewhere to bring about a return to the status quo ante in the Middle East following the Sinai Campaign and to prevent what seemed blatant neo-Imperialism. The Lebanese crisis of 1958, which threatened the delicate and complex relations in the Middle East, was also resolved by a return to the status quo ante; moreover, in this crisis India's unique position on the international political scene was emphasized when Khrushchev suggested convening a five-power meeting including India (but not

China). The first Congo crisis in 1960 seemed at the time to have been kept under control thanks to the intervention of UN forces, and it looked as if real attempts were being made to achieve disarmament. An agreement was made to hold a disarmament conference in Geneva on March 15, 1960. The decolonization process continued, and the influence of the Afro-Asian bloc, which included many new nations in international forums, constantly grew.

In all of those areas of concern to Nehru as a leader with a global perspective, things seemed to be developing in the desired direction. Of course, there were setbacks, such as the cancellation of the Paris Summit due to the U-2 incident, Khrushchev's attack on Dag Hammarskjold at the beginning of 1961 over UN activities in the Congo, the lack of progress in the Geneva disarmament talks, and the escalation of the Indochina conflict in the early 1960s. Yet although these incidents aroused in Nehru a deep concern that they might bring about a regression in the generally positive process of advancement, all in all he remained cautiously optimistic about international developments.[2]

It seemed to Nehru that the major powers had undertaken to prevent local wars for fear that they might develop into global confrontations; indeed, the larger the countries in question, the greater did the danger seem: "local wars do not take place, are not likely to take place, between two great countries without developing into big wars and the big wars without developing possibly—not certainly—into a world war" (*Par.*, I, 279).

It was only a short step from this idea to the conclusion that a military confrontation between China and India would inevitably lead to a nuclear war (*Par.*, II, 61; 114). This was especially true in view of India's status as a rising power, in view of China's power, which was amply demonstrated in Korea and in the effectiveness of a strong centralist regime such as China had not experienced for decades, and in view of the tremendous potential of these two states. It is no wonder, then, that Nehru reached the definitive conclusion on the basis of his assumptions, as expressed in December 1961 in the Upper House in answer to a suggestion that policing action be taken against China, that "war between India and China would be one of the major disasters of the world . . . for it will mean world war. It will mean war which will be indefinite. We would not be able to limit it in time, because it will not be possible for China to defeat us and it will be impossible for us to march up to Peking across Tibet" (*Par.*, II, 62).

This being the case, the major powers were supposed to have a mutual interest in preventing any confrontation between India and China (*F.N.*, 11/59, Dec. 15, 1959). But even if the worst were to happen, despite efforts to prevent it, Nehru still felt India to be safe, for he tended to understand and interpret the vague statements made by Khrushchev and U.S. leaders from Eisenhower to Kennedy as tacit obligations to stand by India in the event of a clash with China.[3]

India's prestige and influence in the international system in the late 1950s and early 1960s were at their peak. India's perceived political and moral power were seen by Nehru as promising protection from any hostile neighbor. Who would dare to enrage public opinion in both the Western and the Third Worlds (*Par.*, I, 398) or displease the United Nations, which, under the leadership of the tough and dynamic Hammarskjold and with the support of the emerging states, had begun to develop political and, to some extent, military muscle and to play a more active role in international affairs, and in which India played a major role? China seemed the least likely candidate to take such a risk: it had not yet been accepted into the United Nations, and common wisdom held that this acceptance was essential to it;[4] its most effective and active supporter there was India (*Par.*, II, 139).[5]

The global approach to regional problems, that is, the concept of a symbiotic linkage between India's local conflicts and the global situation, was basic to Nehru's thinking and evaluation of the immediate and future developments in Sino-Indian relations. An over-time quantitative analysis did, indeed, find in his perceptions a correlation of .515 between Sino-Indian bilateral relations and the global situation.[6] Nehru was constantly explaining this view to this critics, who attacked both his China policy and his foreign policy in general, that is, his nonaligned orientation.[7] Nehru's globalism finally brought him to the verge of absurdity in overassessing the importance of global events relative to immediate problems of India's own foreign policy, at a time of growing tension on the Sino-Indian frontier.[8]

The operational expression of Nehru's political and moral values, and of his assessment of the structure of the global system as earlier presented, was his adoption of the nonalignment policy. As was already suggested, this policy had a strong active dimension known as "positive neutralism." In a speech he made as early as 1949, during a visit to the United States, Nehru explained to his listeners that it was India's duty, right, and fate to be actively involved in the international scene: "Our geography, our history, the present events, all drag us into a wider picture" (Nehru, 1954, 117).

The idea of nonalignment became Nehru's most cherished and irreversible notion. It seemed to him an ideal solution for Third World nations that had achieved independence with such efforts in the post–World War II period. Its main object was to preserve their independence and prevent their submission to super-power interests. Keeping out of white man's conflicts would keep them from committing immoral violence, which was nonproductive for their short- and long-term socioeconomic development. The policy was to have enabled them to receive aid from both super powers: they were sought after by both sides and yet were allies of none. There was also an element of cultural-ideological pride in this stance, as Nehru pointed out in one of his speeches at the Bandung Conference in 1955: "We are not copies of Europeans or Americans or Russians. . . . It would not be credible for our dignity and new freedom if we were camp followers of America or Russia or any other country of Europe" (Nehru, 1958, 291).

Nonalignment thus became the basis for a kind of new political culture unrelated to either Western or Communist ideologies; at the same time, it gave those nations adhering to it a basis for the assumptions that they could prevent the countries still holding opposing ideologies—the cold war warriors—from dragging the world into a nuclear holocaust in which all would perish.

This attitude tended to see neutralism as a universal truth unshakable by circumstances, and it was given credit for every success of India's foreign policy (Levi, 1968, 93). It was seen as putting power into the hands of the weak so that even the super powers would have to bow to it. In the Nonaligned Conference in Belgrade in September 1961, Nehru said: "The power of nations assembled here is not military power or economic power; nevertheless it is power. Call it moral force. It does make a difference obviously what we in our combined wisdom feel and think about this issue of war and peace" (Nehru, 1964, 362). Thus, nonalignment was transformed from a tactic adaptable to changing reality into an objective truth independent of circumstances. It also became an ideal political tool for a conceptual system that interpreted and predicted all bilateral events through the macro-perspective of the global system. This approach to nonalignment called for active intervention on the global level as essential to deterring regional conflict. But, as we shall see, Nehru's "globalistic" interpretations of current events and future developments and the basic political orientation of nonalignment suffered from a series of theoretical and practical misperceptions and misconceptions.

Nehru's first assumption was that the nuclear era had created a situation of mutual deterrence that, ironically, had made local confrontations doubly dangerous: if they got out of hand, they could force the major powers into a nuclear confrontation. This danger, according to Nehru, was an automatic deterrent against the possibility of large-scale violence in the Sino-Indian dispute, which, even if likely, would immediately be stopped by the super powers. But he had not learned the lessons of recent history.

First, regional wars or crises do occur and do not necessarily involve nuclear confrontation. Wars limited in time and scope may continue for quite a while without involving both super powers, as was shown in the Korean war, the Middle East and Berlin crises, and the Indochina conflict, even though they all took place in areas defined as crucial to the major powers' interests. On the contrary, those countries involved exhibited an impressive ability to avoid crossing the critical line in the process of dealing with the issues.

Second, the assumption that crisis management is possible only up to the actual outbreak of violence and not afterwards, when the situation assumes its own dynamics, has been proven to be false. Chinese behavior in the period between October 20 and November 21, 1962 taught Nehru, who saw himself as at least one of the most outstanding diplomats on the international scene, an interesting lesson in the management of crises after they have erupted into violence. But, all the same, it is puzzling as to why he had not learned the lessons of the Indochina and Korean conflicts with which he had had first-hand experience in the past. This omission points to some faults in Nehru's basic assumptions, as will be shown.

Third, it is difficult to understand the universalism of the assumption that any regional confrontation, be it in the most remote regions, might bring in its wake a nuclear escalation, even when two emerging powers are involved. And it is definitely not clear as to why this should happen as a consequence of a conflict in the Himalayas, where geographic and topographic conditions obviously limit the conflict in terms of time, space, and scope.

Fourth, if a danger of escalation did exist, it would be more logical, according to Nehru's own premises, to assume that the major world powers would keep out of a violent clash. If so, why should they be relied upon to intervene on behalf of India?[9] Nehru should have learned from the first Congo crisis that even when the super powers were on the same side of a conflict, they were sooner or later at odds with each other and therefore might prefer not to be involved in the first place.

A second assumption that cannot really be justified was that the existence of the Third World bloc, with India in a position of leadership, was in the interest of both major powers. On the contrary, the United States and the Soviet Union, despite the lip service they paid to nonalignment, conceived of it only as the least of evils, preferable to having a country join the other camp. It was optimism bordering on vanity to assume that the super powers would permit any nation, even India, or its leader—be it Nehru—to interfere actively in their relations and dictate terms to them.

And certainly there was no room to suppose that the super powers would permit the United Nations, given its varied and many participants, its lack of real effectiveness, and its stance as a main theater of the cold war, to play an independent role in world affairs. Nehru should have learned from his own experience that the United Nations succeeded in its role only when and if it suited the super powers or at least was not in contradiction to their interests. India's position in the United Nations and in the Third World did not guarantee it a dual-power umbrella in the event of a regional war.

It is even more difficult to understand the idea that India was protected by its status in the Third World, that no nation could afford to offend such an abstract body as Third World public opinion. Behind this idea, in all probability, were some unstated and unjustified suppositions.[10] One assumption was that the Third World would act concertedly and virtually support one side—the Indian side, of course; a second was that all Third World nations interpreted events in the global arena in the same way, the Indian way; and a third was that all would prefer to take a common stand on the issues, above and beyond their narrow nationalistic interests.

These unstated assumptions were not based on facts. Nehru had already been prevented from playing the part of the sole Third World leader at Bandung. Ambitious politicians from other nations such as Burma and Egypt were competing for the role. Chou En-lai, too, introduced to the conference by Nehru himself, upstaged him. And the more prestigious the Third World bloc became, the more ambitious did several leaders of small nations in it become. And the greater the eagerness for the crown of leadership, the less was India's effectiveness and the greater the anticipation of other countries to see it tripped up and its leadership position undermined.

The idea of homogeneity of attitudes in the Third World also soon proved a fallacy. Even in the nonaligned world, opinions were divided as to both the particular content and the significance of nonalignment for specific policies on the concrete issues facing those states. The Congo crisis of 1960 pointed up how far this group was from being homogeneous in perceptions or action.

An additional problem was Nehru's misunderstanding of the rules of the international system. Nehru, who objected to such terms as *balance of power* for moral reasons, had actually adopted the assumption that the international system was becoming another classic instance of a balance-of-power system in which the Third World would play the balancer's role. What he did not fully understand was that the international system remained, despite a certain loosening, a bipolar system. He also failed to grasp that even in the balance-of-power system the balancer, having a significant power base itself, might tip the scales to one side or the other. In a system in which the sides were dependent on a third power to keep the balance, any involvement of the third power in a military confrontation that could shake its position would cause the major powers to hasten to its aid to prevent that outcome. However, India (or, for that matter, the Third World) never was in that position; it had little to offer except moral power, which, in international politics, is not a salable commodity.[11]

Furthermore, in the modern international system, one of the basic, essential components of the balance of power is nuclear technology, which characterizes the system. In fact, neither India nor any of the

Third World nations, even if they had joined one of the major blocs, could have brought about any radical changes in the basic component of the balance—that is, the nuclear balance. Thus, even the threat of India's strength being sapped, or of the collapse of the neutralist bloc, was not enough to bring the super powers into the confrontation between India and China.

Nehru's confidence in the support of the super powers as being unconditional was utterly mistaken. That support was only a function of circumstances, convenient for the powers in question in a certain constellation. The temporary success of nonalignment was not an expression of its standing as a universal truth. To a certain extent, it was a successful policy, so long as it did not harm the essential interests of any major player on the international scene. But that was a far cry from the assumption that it brought about a major change in international values or guaranteed protection to a nation claiming those values. Nehru did not see this at all.

The faith that Nehru had in nonalignment as the optimal policy and in the importance of the global environment was based partly and unconsciously on the conviction that Chinese conceptions and evaluations were similar or at least close to his own on two central issues: the relationship between the global and regional spheres and the imminent danger of a nuclear war.[12] Actually, although Nehru saw bilateral problems as a dependent variable of the global situation, the Chinese leadership gave local events no less emphasis than global ones and could conceive of the possibility that, under certain circumstances, in certain areas, regional political developments could go against the global trend of the times. In such situations, those regions might even become the avant garde, which would change the face of the global system in the future; and certainly in the short-term view, regional events could be separated form global ones. Neither did China see the danger of regional conflcits carrying the entire world into war. These different viewpoints led to different evaluations both of specific events and of general trends in the international system by Chinese and Indian leaders. Consequently, the Chinese did not see nonalignment as positive under all circumstances or that its adherents enjoyed unconditional immunity.[13]

The discussion thus far shows that globalism in Nehru's world view led to a series of faulty evaluations and orientations and created optimism as to the unlikelihood of regional wars, especially those in which India might become involved. It was the same globalism that formed the basis of the faith that India's bilateral interests were protected by the sheer effort it put into solving global problems. It automatically distorted Nehru's assessment of the relative importance of the Chinese problem in relation to others in terms of the level of threat it represented, all this while resting on faulty assumptions that were never brought into the open, of which he was unaware, and by which he was misled. His failure to appreciate the level of threat resulted in his confidence in the maneuverability and daring that India could afford within the framework of nonalignment without earning the severe penalty of war and defeat.

India and the Super Powers

Nehru's globalistic conceptual framework demanded intensive interaction with the super powers, so as to give prominence to India's relations with the United States and the USSR. His perceptions on the subject were ambivalent. On the one hand, he saw India as their coequal; on the other, he took for granted India's need for political and economic aid to achieve its own goals, but that, too, without kowtowing to the givers.

Nehru, committed as he was to socialism in his world view, did not find Communist society and the Soviet Union as a Communist state untenable. On the contrary, although he did not agree with the regime's handling of internal affairs, he preferred the Socialist values in principle to U.S.-type Capitalism, which he rejected out of hand. Realizing also the tension between India's designated role as mediator and peacemaker on the one hand and its dependence on external massive economic and military aid on the other, Nehru tried, from the moment of India's independence, to approach the USSR. Until 1953 these attempts were one-sided. Stalin was contemptuous of Indian society and of India's national movement's leaders. Neither did his Nonalignment Policy make him more acceptable to Stalin. At the peak of the cold war, all those who did not join forces with the USSR were regarded as enemies. Furthermore, India's joining of the British Commonwealth in 1949 marked Nehru in Stalin's eyes as a camp follower of the West. The Soviet press and media described Nehru and Gandhi as the inheritors of, and successors to, British Imperialism, and the policy of nonviolent resistance as a means of achieving independence was scorned (Ray, 1969). But, despite this hostility, Nehru did not change his attitude toward the USSR.

Nehru was rewarded for his patience when Stalin died. His successors in the Kremlin changed their policy toward the nonaligned nations and toward India in particular. At this time their goal was to encourage as many countries as possible not to take any stand in the global conflict as the best alternative to actually joining or supporting the Soviet bloc. Within the framework of this strategy, Nehru had a major role to play. The strategy gained additional momentum with Khrushchev's rise to power in 1955. Both Nehru and Mahatma Gandhi were now recognized as progressive,[14] as were Nehru's domestic and foreign policies. Nehru's satisfaction with this state of affairs grew following the Twentieth Congress of the Communist Party of the Soviet Union (CPSU) and the de-Stalinization process that resulted. It seemed as if the Soviet Union was progressing toward internal liberalization and a constructive role in world affairs, aiming to contribute to the moulding of a new world order in accordance with Nehru's ideas (*F.N.*, 4/57, July 15, 1957).

Nehru saw a vindication of his view in the Soviet Union's agreement to sign a peace treaty with Austria in 1955 and in the dismantling of the Cominform in 1956. This was proof enough of the sincerity of Communist leaders when they spoke of adopting a policy of peaceful coexistence. Nehru was especially pleased with the instructions given by Moscow to Communist parties in democratic countries, stating that the parliamentary way and participation in the "democratic game" was the only path to power. What is more, starting in 1955, the USSR took a firm stand in supporting India on its central foreign policy issue—namely, Kashmir. In 1957 for the first time the USSR vetoed at the Security Council a resolution to hold a referendum in Kashmir. This stance was all the more significant against the background of Pakistan's joining of the Western alliances and receipt of modern Western arms.

As of 1959 one could state the five main points characterizing Nehru's thinking on the USSR as follows:

1. The Bolshevik revolution had made a deep impression on Nehru and created in his mind an emotional and intellectual link between Soviet Communism and the Indian national movement. The Soviet Union, which had no imperialist past and having a strongly anti-imperialist ideology, was seen as a natural ally against Western neo-Imperialism, perceived to be the result of the West's refusal to accept the right of former colonies to self-determination. Such an alliance between the USSR and India was to rest on mutual interests and on their shared ideology (Nehru, 1958, 303).

2. The Soviet Union, being a Socialist nation, was nonaggressive and a pursuer of peace; as Nehru put it, "I do not think there is any country which is more anxious for peace than the Soviet Union" (*Par.*, I, 215). He saw the arms race and the Warsaw Pact as imposed on the USSR by Western imperialist and capitalist behavior. If only the West would leave the USSR alone, it would preoccupy itself with internal growth and stop what seemed to be expansionism but was really nothing more than a defensive reflex, the source of which was distant and recent memories of Western invasions.

3. In light of points made in the preceding two paragraphs, it was a foregone conclusion that India had nothing to fear from the Soviet Union, as it had long given up the imperialist ambitions of Tsarist Russia. But in order to assuage Soviet fears of being encircled from the south—via India—Nehru proposed to adopt a policy of explicit friendship toward the USSR and clear resistance to any Western attempt to threaten the Communist regime. Only in this way would India be an acceptable intermediary to both sides.

4. The Soviet Union was seen as a source of unconditional military and economic aid to India, in contrast to Western aid, which always

came with strings attached. The ability to diversify sources was essential to a country as dependent on foreign aid as India.[15]

5. Ties of friendship with the Soviet Union were important in order to preserve good relations with China. Since the Soviet Union was the leader of the Communist bloc, hostile relations could lead to the exertion of pressure on India's northern border. Later, when the dispute with China grew worse, Nehru claimed to critics that his nonalignment policy was the only thing that prevented Soviet support for China, and that the USSR was the only country able to restrain China[16] (Stein, 1969, 122).

Nehru thought that his policies toward the USSR bore fruit in the China issue. Following the Longju incident, the USSR took a neutral position. On September 9 it published a statement[17] that was defined by Nehru himself as "a very fair unusual statement for the Soviet Government" (Ray, 1973, 82). On another occasion in Parliament, he declared similarly: "this House knows the very close relations that the Soviet Government has naturally with the Chinese Government. The issue of that statement [on the Longju incident] itself shows that the Soviet Government is taking a calm and more or less objective or dispassionate view of the situation considering everything" (*Par.,* I, 156). Khrushchev himself, during his visit to India in February 1960, told journalists that if India ever needed help all it had to do was shout as "we are near, just over the mountains." On that visit he was not short on praise for India. In a speech made before the Indian Parliament, he expressed support for almost every one of Nehru's most cherished notions: disarmament, anti-Imperialism, the dismantling of blocs and alliances, peace, and especially India's moral contribution to the international environment. As he said: "The principles of 'Pancha Shila' have forced their way in history owing, in a considerable measure, to the efforts of peace-loving India."[18]

Nehru and Menon, who concluded that Soviet friendship was vitally important for their China policy, decided to preserve Soviet goodwill at any price. Nehru's agreement to meet Chou En-lai in April was in no small measure due to his desire to accede to Khrushchev's insistence on such a meeting, despite the acute criticism his agreement aroused in the press and in Parliament, so much so that he was forced to draw a distinction between a meeting and actual negotiations. The Indian leadership was aware that the Soviet position, although defined as neutral, was biased toward India. A proof of this they saw in the Soviet agreement to sell India equipment for road building in a disputed area of the Himalayas and, at a later stage, in their willingness to equip the Indian air force with transport planes and helicopters, which were to solve the problem of India's logistic inferiority in the Himalayas. They also realized that this was the first time the Soviet Union had not taken a one-sided stand in favor of a Communist state in a dispute with a non-Communist one, which was a distinct departure from "proletarian internationalism."

The Soviet position became increasingly pro-Indian as time went on. Khrushchev's visit brought in its wake an increase in Soviet economic aid, while at the same time aid to China almost ceased. In August 1960, the 1,300 Soviet technicians in China were withdrawn, causing great disruption of civilian and military industries. A stream of high-ranking delegations from all fields, political-military, economic and cultural, flowed between the USSR and India.[19]

Between 1959 and 1962 not a year went by without the signing of new agreements or the expansion and extension of existing ones. Trade between the two countries grew significantly.[20] In the period from 1955/56 to 1961/62, imports from the Soviet Union grew fourfold from 0.9% to 3.7% of total Indian imports, and the Soviet share of Indian exports grew from 0.5% to 4.9%, or ten times[21] (Sebastian, 1975, 173).

In February 1961 an Indian scientific delegation visited the USSR to discuss the possibility of nuclear cooperation for peaceful purposes. At the beginning of October 1962 India and the USSR signed an agreement stating that the latter would assist India in the development of nuclear energy, including delivery of natural uranium, enriched uranium, uranium 235 and plutonium for research, as well as in the mining of uranium ore (Ray, 1973, 203–204). Against the background of the cancellation in 1959 of all nuclear aid agreements between China and the USSR, the Chineese reaction is understandable. The climax was the signing of an agreement to supply Mig fighters to the Indian air force and to establish an aeronautics industry in India to enable it to manufacture such planes itself. The discussions on the subject had already begun in May 1962 with Pakistan's purchase of twelve F-104 fighters from the United States. In July an agreement was signed for the Soviet supply of engines for fighter planes to be manufactured in India. At the beginning of October contracts were signed for the supply of two Mig 21 squadrons and the setting up of an Indian aeronautics industry for production of the same plane. This necessitated a complete change in the orientation of the Indian air force (Graham, 1964). Up to that time only the logistic arm of the force had Soviet-produced planes, but now the fighting arm of the service was also to become dependent on Soviet equipment and technology.

The Soviet Union also put pressure on the Chinese leadership to make political concessions to India, for it was in Chinese policy that Khrushchev saw the greatest obstacle to India's ties with the Socialist bloc. Eisenhower's visit to India in 1959 followed on the heels of the Kongka Pass incident. In the Soviet view, China was damaging world Communist interests by putting narrow nationalistic considerations above those of world Communism. Chinese behavior threatened to torpedo the plan in which the Soviets designated India a leader of the "Peace Zone," which was to be composed of nonaligned states ruled by national bourgeois elements but in the long run bound to convert to Socialism. And indeed, at various Communist conferences, such as in Bucharest in June 1960 and in Moscow in November of that year, the USSR attacked the Chinese position in the Sino-Indian dispute as irresponsible and even claimed that it was a contradiction in terms for a Communist country to fight for territory. As an example, Moscow cited the settlement of its border dispute with Iran in the 1920s, in which the Russians had agreed to concessions so as not to be forced into a military confrontation (*P.R.*, Nov. 8, 1963).[22]

Nehru was not unaware of Soviet pressures on the Chinese to settle the dispute on conditions agreeable to India. These efforts were well known to the Communist Party of India (CPI). Nehru was also conscious of the growing rift between the USSR and China, but did not see it as very significant: "[W]e must not exaggerate it [the importance of the Sino-Soviet rift] as both those countries have to rely on one another a great deal and cannot afford to break" (*F.N.*, 9/59, Oct. 26, 1959). Basically, he continued to believe that the Soviet Union, as leader of the Communist bloc, would succeed in keeping China under control, and he probably saw in the results of the Moscow Conference in 1960 evidence of Soviet dominance of the Communist world (Menon, 1963, 279).

Confidence in the Soviets' ultimate control of the Communist camp in case of an emergency fed Nehru's belief that, in light of its importance to the USSR and their close ties,[23] India was protected from a massive Chinese attack. It also led him to trust in the Soviet Union's evaluation of the Chinese intentions and degree of threat; as Krishna Menon, the minister of defense, put it: "So far as I know, the Soviets did not regard the Chinese as a threat to India. Unfortunately for us, and I think for China, they went on thinking like this rather too long" (Brecher, 1968, 169).[24] This was despite the fact that it was obvious that Chinese moves during the dispute were a complete surprise to them.[25]

Nehru made a grave error in relating the Soviet-Indian relationship to the Sino-Indian one. The Soviet position and Soviet-Indian cooperation were actually more of an obstacle to India than a help. One reason for this was that Nehru did not in the least comprehend the breadth and depth of the Sino-Soviet conflict[26] and its implications and, as a result, underestimated the gravity of the Chinese assessment of the situation.

The Chinese saw Soviet "neutrality" as a priori biased in India's favor: "although assuming a facade of neutrality, [Moscow] actually favoured India and condemned China" (*P.R.*, Nov. 8, 1963, 19). In a meeting between Mao Tse-tung and Khrushchev in October 1959, Khrushchev spoke harshly to Mao about the Sino-Indian border dispute and rejected the claim that India had been the initiator of border incidents. At the Bucharest Conference in June 1960, there was a bitter exchange between Khrushchev and Peng Chen, the Chinese representative. China saw in Soviet behavior a betrayal of the principle of Communist solidarity, or in the current terminology, "Proletarian Internationalism" (*P.R.*, Nov. 8, 1963, 18–19; Zagoria, 1962, 245; Sen Gupta, 1970, 168–170).

The Soviet position in this dispute was so important to the Chinese that they spared no effort to get the Russians to change their views and conducted a campaign on various levels. On the ideological front, they published pamphlets describing India's reactionary social structure and its condemnable domestic and foreign policies (*P.R.*, May 12, 1959; Sept. 15, 1959; Dec. 15, 1961), thus exposing it as a country not worthy of support of a leader of the Communist bloc.

Through personal contact with Soviet diplomatic representatives in Peking and in talks with Khrushchev, Chinese leaders tried to convince the Russians that India had initiated the conflict as an anti-Chinese and anti-Communist move.[27] On the interparty level, they tried to muster the support of Communist bloc nations at forums such as the conferences of Bucharest, Moscow, and Hanoi, both through discussion of the Indian problem and as part of a general discussion on the policy toward Third World nations. Finally, they chose to bring direct pressure to bear by increasing tensions on the Sino-Soviet border, beginning in 1960, and with verbal attacks, covert and overt, in the Chinese and Albanian press.[28]

One reason the issue assumed such importance was that it exposed deep divisions of opinion and perceptions in both the ideological and practical spheres. On the ideological side, the Chinese saw in Soviet "neutrality" following the Longju incident, on the eve of Khrushchev's visit to President Eisenhower at Camp David, the beginning of U.S.-Soviet, anti-Chinese collusion, of which India was the focus. The Chinese had already begun to resent this process in 1956 when the ideological debate between China and the USSR commenced, against the background of China's objection to a policy of compromise and peaceful coexistence. This was related to Mao's faith that the Communist camp had reached a turning point in which it could, by means of daring policies, change the balance of power in the world using the "excellent revolutionary situation." Their approach was the complete antithesis to that of Khrushchev: they rejected any attempt at disarmament and detente; they refused to accept the common anxiety over a possible nuclear war and the evaluation that this weapon technology changed the essence of East-West relations and defined nuclear weapons as a paper tiger; and they rejected the fear that revolutionary regional war would lead to a world war if the Socialist camp, meaning the USSR, should dare to use the nuclear umbrella to prevent Capitalist interference in revolutionary wars (Hinton, 1966, 126–144; 1972, 96–107).

Soviet policies toward India reflected precisely the basic element of Khrushchev's foreign policy, and thus the dispute with India became a focus for the exposition of opposing Chinese views.[29] Moreover, from a Chinese point of view, the Congress Party was a classic bourgeois party, and the massive Soviet aid, according to their concepts, was preventing the development of a real revolutionary movement in India. This "face" of the Congress Party was revealed in its foreign policy positions during the Tibet uprising and in the adoption of frontier policies inherited from British Imperialism (*P.R.*, Nov. 2, 1962). Domestically, the Chinese saw in the dissolution of the Communist government at Kerala in July 1959 proof of the uselessness of trying to advance the revolution by parliamentary means. They rejected out of hand the Soviet concept of a national democratic state ruled by a coalition of anti-Imperialist parties (including the national bourgeoisie after it had freed itself from Imperialism), as seemed to be the case in India and which justified the Soviet reliance on aid rather than force. The Chinese thought that continuing Soviet economic aid to Afro-Asian states merely strengthened the bourgeois elements in them and prevented progress toward revolution, as was the real case with India. They thought that priority in aid should be given to the underdeveloped states in the Communist bloc, and that the radical elements in the developing countries should be supported, without dictating to them how to achieve power and without tying in that question with the problem of Capitalist-Socialist bloc relations. An important polemical article signifying a turning point in the Sino-Soviet debate, and published on the anniversary of Lenin's death under the title *Long Live Leninism*, stated: "Whether the transition will be carried out through armed uprising or by peaceful means is a question that is fundamentally separate from that of peaceful co-existence between Socialist and Capitalist countries; it is an internal affair of each country, one to be determined only by the relation of classes in that country in a given period, a matter to be decided only by the Communists of that country themselves" (*P.R.*, April 26, 1960, 19).[30]

On the level of specific interests, it may be assumed that the more support the Soviets gave Indian positions on the border question, the more analogies policymakers in China drew between the Sino-Soviet border issue and the Sino-Indian one (*P.R.*, May 12, 1959, 14).[31] The Sino-Soviet border, like the Sino-Indian border, was an inheritance of Imperialism, which had imposed unequal treaties on the Chinese. The Soviets, like the Indians, had refused to negotiate on the problem of the entire border and agreed only to discuss slight border alterations. Now two additional factors entered the picture: the ideological differences between the USSR and India seemed to have diminished, as we have seen, whereas, from 1958, the frontier dispute between China and Russia grew, and in 1960 border incidents broke out between them (Hinton, 1972, 211).[32]

In addition to the historical, ideological, and timing analogies, the Chinese might have drawn an analogy from the ethno-political aspects of the two border disputes—the great similarity between the Tibet and Sinkiang situations geographically and politically.[33]

Topographically, Sinkiang and Tibet border on each other and are not easily accessible. Mountain ranges separate them from the rest of China. Ethnically, the Han race was the minority in both provinces, and the local population, both in religion and culture, is closer to the population on the other side of the border than to that of the mother country. India and the USSR, respectively, had a significant influence on the economies of Tibet and Sinkiang (especially in its western parts), where both had their respective representatives. Tibet and Sinkiang both had traditions, of which the Chinese were acutely aware, of attempts to break away with the support of British-India and Soviet Russia, respectively.[34] These regions were of strategic importance and experienced periods of unrest and uprisings due to "Sinicization" and attempts to integrate into the Chinese state, and also as the result of the economic difficulties resulting from the "Great Leap Forward." The unrest was accompanied in both areas by the escape of tens of thousands of refugees across the border.[35]

Against the background of these striking similarities between the two situations, and in light of the Chinese perceptions of the similarity of ideas and identity of interests between the USSR and India, it is not surprising that the Chinese saw the frontier dispute with India as part of a conspiracy to which India, Taiwan, Japan, the United States, and the USSR were partners. This collaboration seemed to the Chinese to be the source of India's reckless policy and belief in immunity: "They [Indian imperialists] thought that with the backing of the imperialists and the support of the Soviet leaders they had nothing to fear"[36] (*P.R.,* Nov. 8, 1963, 22). Thus, it is feasible to assume that Chinese hostility and apprehensions deepened with the growing military dimension of Soviet-Indian relations, especially after June 1962, when the agreement concerning the modernization of the fighting arm of the Indian air force was signed. It looked as if the time had come to put India, and through it, the Soviet Union, in its place. In this complex political situation, any concession to India might have been interpreted as a confession of weakness and might have set a precedent in the Sino-Soviet dispute as well. As a result, a settlement according to Indian conditions, whether procedural or substantial, became impossible. And the fact that India was a major power made Chinese concessions even more unlikely: whereas giving up territory to a small country like Nepal, Burma, Afghanistan, or Mongolia could be seen as magnanimity, yielding to a power could be read only as weakness.

On the tactical level, it might have been that the Mig contract created a convenient pretext for propaganda purposes, for China to expose what it defined as Soviet Revisionism and to force the USSR's hand. An attack on India would have forced the Russians to take a stand. A pro-Indian stand would put the USSR clearly in the U.S. camp and an anti-Indian reaction would have damaged Soviet-Indian relations (Floyd, 1964, 159).

Nehru, who, as we have indicated, was aware of the Sino-Soviet disagreements,[37] did not grasp its complicated implications for the Sino-Indian issue. He did not perceive that the factors he thought guaranteed India's protection (such as being a big state and having special relations with the USSR) actually provoked rather than deterred the Chinese. This lack of insight stands out in a contradiction of which he himself was not aware. On the one hand, he expected the USSR to restrain China, and on the other, he was somewhat pleased with the differences of opinion between the two Communist giants, not realizing that as the Sino-Soviet conflict deepened, it was used by China to challenge Soviet leadership of the Socialist bloc[38] and its right to dictate policies and terms to China. The Soviet ability to protect India from a Chinese attack became much weaker as a result. India became a pawn on the Sino-Soviet chessboard without Nehru ever quite realizing it. It was no accident that the Chinese leadership emphasized the fact that the bulk of Soviet aid to India for the years 1955–1963 had, in fact, come since 1960 (*P.R.*, Nov. 8, 1963, 25), the year when Sino-Indian relations began to deteriorate and when the rift in Sino-Soviet relations grievously deteriorated.

The other major factor that reinforced Nehru's certitude that India's relations with China would not lead to war was its relations with the United States. The year 1959 was the turning point. U.S.-Indian relations had always been ambivalent, as was reflected in the image each had of the other. On the one hand, the United States from 1939 on continuously pressured the British to give India independence, and when they did, the new nation was warmly congratulated by the United States. But, as the United States' attention at the end of the 1940s and beginning of the 1950s was focused on Europe and East Asia, its interest in India was limited. Soviet hostility toward India until 1953 also contributed to the lack of interest, as there was no fear that India would become another cold war satellite. Even when Soviet hostility disappeared, the United States did not take much notice or make a positive approach toward India, chiefly because of Dulles's impatience with the nonaligned fence-sitters, led, among others, by Nehru, who tried to make political fortunes from the ideological struggle between Communism and Democracy. Dulles saw Nehru as a hypocrite preaching conciliation, whereas he himself, immediately upon gaining independence, engaged in a war with a neighbor. His support of China's application for UN membership and the expulsion of Taiwan and his objections to condemning China as an aggressor in Korea and to the "Pactomania" policy did not endear him to Dulles, to say the least.

From the Indian point of view, matters looked similar. On the one hand, Nehru greatly appreciated and admired the basic U.S. principles of justice, freedom, equality, and democracy as they appear in the United States' constitution. They were his principles, too. On the other hand, Nehru the Socialist abhorred U.S. capitalism, which in Nehru's eyes made the United States a natural successor to the traditional imperialist powers. To him the cold war was a continuation of the old struggle for power among European nations, only now it was the United States and its allies that were trying to dominate the international scene. For that purpose the Communist bogeyman was invented, a name given to what was actually the legitimate nationalism of countries like China and the USSR, which, after generations of tyranny, had succeeded in establishing Socialist regimes. And if there were deviations from absolute democracy, he saw this to a large extent as the result of Western military pressure, which might have been moderated if only the West would stop trying to topple Communist regimes.[39]

Nehru's visit to Washington in 1949 and his meetings with President Harry S. Truman and Dean Acheson (then Secretary of State) left him with the impression that the United States was determined, in order to contain Communism, to dominate the international system and to inherit the role of Britain and France (Jain, 1969). He saw Washington's behavior toward China as vengeful and provocative, an attempt to prevent another major power, with a nobler and much longer history than that of the United States, from taking its rightful place in the family of nations. Dulles's frigid attitude toward non-alignment, and especially toward India, was explained as intolerance toward any nation willing to play an independent role. Nehru saw the U.S. objection to China's joining the UN and the Security Council as a wish to retain Western dominance over these important international bodies, since the only Third World nation that had a permanent seat and a right of veto, Taiwan, was nothing but a weak Western puppet.

A change was perceptible in 1956 following Nehru's visit to the United States and the trust that grew up between him and Eisenhower. In the years 1957 to 1958, when India was faced with an economic and food crisis, the United States signed an agreement to supply 16 million tons of wheat and 1 million tons of rice to India for four years, on excellent terms. The signing of a mutual defense agreement between Pakistan and the United States in 1959, in keeping with the Eisenhower doctrine, did not hurt this rapprochement, as Eisenhower promised Nehru that only the agreements already signed would be honored and that no new arms would be supplied to Pakistan.[40] The mutual thaw culminated in Eisenhower's visit to India in December 1959, during which hundreds of thousands turned out to welcome the U.S. President. In the Nehru-Eisenhower talks, considerable U.S.

economic aid was promised. But Nehru did not ask for U.S. military aid, both because he feared that it would be conditional on concessions to Pakistan on the Kashmir issue,[41] and because it would imply admitting that the nonalignment policy had been a mistake and that the United States was right in warning him against China's aggressive intentions. The Chinese problem was discussed, however, and observers concluded from Eisenhower's public statement in his speech to the two houses of Parliament and in other forums, in which he used the sentence, "We who are free must support one another," that the United States would be ready to come to India's aid if the need arose (*New York Times,* Dec. 12, 1959, 10; Dec. 14, 1959, 1).

John F. Kennedy's accession to power further enhanced Nehru's perceptions of the United States, and his anticipation of an improvement in U.S.-Indian relations skyrocketed. Kennedy was known to be deeply sympathetic toward India and, as a member of the Senate, had acted energetically to enlarge U.S. aid to India. His new ambassador to India, the brilliant economist John Kenneth Galbraith, was known to be especially sympathetic and appreciative of that country's needs (Galbraith, 1969). Other friends of India held key posts in the Kennedy administration: Chester Bowles was Under Secretary of State; Phillip Talbot, Assistant Secretary of State on Middle Eastern and South Asian affairs; Adlai Stevenson, ambassador to the United Nations; Averell Harriman, ambassador at large and later Assistant Secretary of State on Far Eastern Affairs; and Walt Rostow, Assistant to the Special Advisor to the President on National Security.

On the practical level, Kennedy demonstrated a very warm attitude toward the nonaligned nations. U.S. aid to India was expanded. Thus, for example, in the years 1961 to 1962 India received $400 million in aid;[42] the United States was interested in India's development and saw it as a competitive and alternative model to the one presented by China. On the matter of the border dispute with China, the United States supported India unconditionally. Addressing a press conference, the Secretary of State declared: "We, of course, support the Indian view with respect to their northern borders. Those borders have been well established in law, if not, in every locality, demarcated exactly on the ground. But the McMahon Line generally is something that the rest of the world has accepted" (*New York Times,* Dec. 9, 1961, 6). In November 1961 Nehru visited Washington and met with Kennedy for a series of talks in which various matters were discussed. Although there was a temporary cooling in relations between India and the United States following India's invasion of Goa[43] in December 1961, Henry Kissinger's mission and Jacqueline Kennedy's visit, which came in January 1962, mended the fences.

It seemed as if India's international position was better than it had ever been. Both the United States and the Soviet Union competed for its favors. It received economic and military aid from both powers.

Nehru spent much of his time in discussion about the world's future and the major problems of the international system, and the world's leaders listened. This strengthened his conviction that no country, however powerful, would dare attack India. And, indeed, it seems that both the United States and the USSR reached the conclusion that there was no chance of China attacking India[44] (*New York Times*, Oct. 18, 1962, 1).

But that is not the way things seemed to the Chinese. U.S. expressions of friendship toward India and its definition of India as an alternative model to China in Asia deepened Peking's hostility toward what seemed an attempt to increase China's isolation through U.S.-Soviet collusion via India. On the ideological level, the Chinese saw India's growing economic dependence on the United States since 1959 as evidence that, despite Indian pretensions, its economy was still colonial as well as dependent on imperialist countries and their willingness to invest in it. According to Chinese calculations, India, in the years 1959 to 1961, had received aid or promises of aid from the United States to the tune of $4,100 million, whereas in the twelve preceding years it had received only $1,900 million, coming mostly following the failure of the April 1960 talks between Nehru and Chou En-lai, for which it was a reward, as they thought: "Who pays the piper calls the tune. . . . Thus it appears that the anti-Chinese campaign in India grows in direct proportion to the amount of U.S. 'aid' " (*P.R.*, Dec. 15, 1961, 12).[45]

What Nehru saw as an achievement of economic diplomacy was viewed by the Chinese as an expression of dependence and political camp-following, behind which stood their main enemy power. The Chinese evaluation of U.S.-Chinese relations was that they reflected basically a strategic confrontation, as was expressed in Taiwan, Korea, and Indochina, although the United States was capable of making tactical concessions as a result of local weaknesses and treachery (Whiting, 1975, 35–36). This is why the U.S. adoption of India as an alternative model to China was a good enough reason to make Peking wish to put India in its place and to diminish its status in an Asian struggle for prestige and influence where it enjoyed the support of two major powers.

This basic difference in perception is made clearer by the following content analysis. Whereas for China we find a correlation of .487 between its perceptions of China–super power relations and Sino-Indian relations, we find only a relatively weak correlation (.123) between Nehru's perception of Indo–super power relations and Sino-Indian relations. The reason was that for the Chinese the issues were *inherently* linked, as earlier noted, whereas for Nehru they were linked only *indirectly*, that is, by ensuring India's immunity but not substantively.[46]

In other words, what Nehru considered an important source of political power and military immunity was actually perceived as a threat to China, which had no choice but to act against it decisively, immediately, and firmly. From the Chinese point of view, the Sino-Indian conflict had already advanced beyond the narrow bilateral stage to one in which much more complex and important stakes hung in the balance. Nehru, who did not realize this, and who did not see the linkage perceived by the Chinese, was a victim both of relevance and perceptual awareness gaps.

India's Regional Roles and Activities

From the discussion thus far, it is clear that for moral and practical reasons India assumed that it had an active role to play in Asia, Africa, and the Middle East. The following assumptions formed the basis of that belief:

- Geographical determinism: "Look at the map. If you have to consider any question affecting the Middle East, India inevitably comes into the picture. If you have to consider any questions concerning Southeast Asia, you cannot do so without India. So also with the Far East" (Nehru, 1949, 235).
- Sub-systems that had become the focus of international conflicts since Europe's relative quiescence should not be left to simmer, for they might deteriorate from regional conflicts into global nuclear confrontations. India's presence, therefore, was required in all other areas, to preserve India's national interests on the one hand and for altruistic reasons on the other. And India was, indeed, involved in all the turbulent regions in the 1950s and the beginning of the 1960s from Southeast Asia through the Middle East and to Africa. Thus, for instance, it had the second largest contingent in the UN armed forces in the Congo.
- The process of decolonization, which India was especially keen to hasten, and which was a principle that Nehru preached from every possible rostrum, necessitated Indian activity in the African and Asian subsystems. At issue was the question of how to aid the new states politically and economically and so prevent their becoming camp-followers of either bloc, and how to deal with problems such as South Africa and apartheid as part of a campaign against colonialism in all its forms (Nehru, 1964, 364).
- India wanted to serve as the model for new nations to follow, a model that was neither Communist nor Capitalist, but Social Democratic (Nehru, 1962, 38–39). And the chances were good: most of the new nations declared themselves in one way or another as Socialist and Democratic, and rejected formal commitment to any of the power blocs, or at least paid lip service to the need to remain nonaligned. As for the relations between the new nations and their neighbors, India preached the appli-

cation of the Panch Sheel principles of peaceful coexistence, even between countries whose social and political structures differed in every way, as Sino-Indian relations were supposed to exemplify. The success of the new nations in thus regulating their own affairs would lessen the possibility of major power interference in bilateral conflicts and their exploitation in the inter-power struggles, and generally limit Soviet and U.S. influence—especially that of the United States, which representing neo-colonialism, was deemed more dangerous.

- India's success in the achievement of these goals would be its main source of prestige and influence based on a new moral-ethical, rather than crude, military power (*Par.,* I, 246–247), and this would also serve as a basis for the transformation of values in the international system. This approach was identical to, or rather an extension of, the political teachings of Nehru's revered teacher Gandhi. The advantage of such power is that it achieves the desired results without the use of violence or force, as had been the case in India's struggle for independence. India's political and moral prestige was seen as its main guarantee of security.[47]

And last but not least was the idea that most of these assumptions, if not all, were acceptable to most of the actors in the various subsystems, whether they were neighbors of India or not. Nehru thought they were particularly applicable to the Asian subsystem, which was the leading one of his period, as it was one of the first to achieve independence. And as the nations in the area had rich cultural and poltiical histories, they were better equipped to deal with the problems that came with independence and to serve as models and examples to those nations still under foreign rule or those that had just won freedom in Africa, Asia, and the Middle East.

Nehru's optimism concerning the concerted political goals of Asian nations resulted from his basic assumption that Asia was a unity; the notion of Asian solidarity was based on the heritage of colonial subjugation and on the existence of a common Asian culture that was unique and different from Western culture. Nehru's trips to China and Southeast Asia in 1939 and 1948 made a deep impression on him and strengthened his conception of the Asian common cause. At the Delhi Conference on Asian Relations in 1947, in which 243 delegations representing 31 nations took part, he emphasized the special role designated to Asia in post–World War II international affairs. In Asia, he claimed, there was rivalry but not hostility. It was the model of peaceful competition, and the 1954 Sino-Indian agreements were an example of this. Thus, Asia had a role to play and a contribution to make to the international system.

It follows that Nehru saw involvement in Asian problems and in their solution as vital. Failure to solve these problems would be a severe blow to the idea of Asian solidarity and to the exemplary nature of inter-Asian relations. Success or failure in this area was tightly intertwined with relations between the two leading Asian nations—China and India—which had first established the Panch Sheel Agreement and its principles. Also for this reason, a failure of that agreement or a reevaluation of it by either of the two signatories would constitute a threat to a basic assumption in Nehru's foreign policy.

Nehru's error was fundamental. As with many myths, that of Asian solidarity had a grain of truth. All Asian nations had shared the fate of being exploited by European societies. Then again, it is difficult to find cultural homogeneity in Asia. The differences between Chinese, Indian, and Islamic cultures in Asia are no less basic than those between them and Western culture. Not only are they different, but the Chinese and Islamic cultures looked down on Hinduism; moreover, there has been a tradition of struggle for dominance in Asia among all three that has never been resolved. Chinese culture became principally a mainland culture, whereas the Hindus gained a foothold and influence particularly in maritime Asia. Thus, it happened that "What should have been regarded essentially as hopes were interpreted [by Nehru] as 'facts' in this philosophy of Asianism" (Gokhale, 1976, 113). Furthermore, Nehru should have realized that if his assumptions were correct an increase in India's prestige, as a result of its activities on the international scene, had to come at the expense of other nations in Asia that saw themselves as equally legitimate candidates for leadership. It was precisely this prestige, which was supposed to protect India from threats, that provoked them. The mere objection of nations such as Pakistan and Indonesia, not to mention China, to a secondary role in Asia, was enough to "kill" the notion of Asianism, and resulted in at least one other conceptual interpretation of events in Asia, and especially in Southeast Asia, in a way not only different from, but also dangerous to, India.

It seems that Nehru forgot his own words: "Never forget that the basic challenge in Southeast Asia is between India and China. That challenge runs along the spine of Asia"[48] (Moraes, 1973, 221); he also forgot that there was a protracted history of rivalry between China and India for influence in Southeast Asia. India's diplomatic success as an intermediary in Korea and later in Indochina must have suppressed the fact that India had earned this success not through power but because it was acceptable to all sides, being a threat to none of the protagonists, including China.

Caught up in the enthusiasm of his rejection of the traditional power play, Nehru assumed that the disputants would be interested in Indian neutral activity even at the price of damaging their own interests. In this connection, India's position as chairman of the International Committee for Indochina[49] was viewed with great reservations by China.

At the end of the 1950s, a change came over India's position on the Indochina question,[50] and in 1959 to 1961, regarding a series of central issues raised in the committee, India took a position in complete opposition to the North Vietnamese, who were aggressively supported by China. The point in question was the unification of Vietnam. India was apprehensive of the Pandora box situation that might follow in the wake of such an attempt.[51] North Vietnam had renewed its subversive activities in South Vietnam in 1959, and South Vietnam had complained to the committee. North Vietnam simultaneously complained about the presence of U.S. experts and the supply of U.S. military aid to South Vietnam. On all of these issues the position of the North Vietnamese was rejected. Its enraged representatives reacted in private by asking whether India's position had something to do with the Sino-Indian dispute (Sardesai, 1968, 202). On Nehru's visit to Washington in 1961, Kennedy showed him documented evidence indicating North Vietnamese subversive activities and violations of Sections 16 and 17 of the Geneva Agreement. North Vietnam rejected the committee's report out of hand, even though one of its clauses affirmed what they had been claiming all along, that there was an active military pact between the United States and South Vietnam (Sardesai, 1968, 207–208).

Thus, the report, which Nehru saw as neutral and unbiased, seemed to the Chinese to express India's growing dependence on the West. China saw the border dispute with India as part of the complex of Sino-Indian relations in Asia; to the Chinese it went hand in hand with Nehru's political alliance with Marshall Tito in the nonaligned movement. Because the Chinese leadership considered Tito to be the symbol of modern Revisionism, this political alliance was proof that China had been correct in its estimation of Nehru's hypocrisy and of his regime, which had become reactionary and a facade for the United States and the West in Asia. Speaking of the Belgrade Conference, they stated: "at the conference of non-aligned countries last year, Nehru took the lead in opposing the anti-imperialist, anti-colonialist stand taken by the heads of the majority of the countries attending" (*P.R.*, Nov. 16, 1962, 6). This was also their view on India's African policy (*P.R.*, Nov. 2, 1962, 17). So the prestige that should have protected India actually turned into a threat and, when added to its display of "muscle" in its Forward Policy, became one more reason for the Chinese to put India in its place so as to diminish its importance to the West as a leader of the Asian and other subsystems. China was aided in this effort by the fact that, despite India's prestige in Asia as a nation that had made major economic progress, there were growing reservations about its selfishness: relative to its ability, India supplied less economic aid to needy countries than did China (Moorthy, 1961).

The concept of political homogeneity was especially strong in relation to the South Asian subcontinent that Nehru regarded to a certain extent as Indian. The desire for its political Indianization had manifested itself in one way or another since India's independence (Muni, 1975). The fact that most of the population of the subcontinent, including Ceylon, had a common Anglo-Western political culture made this type of thinking only natural and a remaking of all the nations of the subcontinent in India's image a vital aim from the strategic, political, economic, and moral points of view.

This approach was reversed, however, only when military circumstances demanded friendly relations with India's neighbors for strategic reasons. It was, of course, a mistake in judgment: on the one hand, it sharpened India's neighbors' interest in maintaining Sino-India tension, as this gave them greater power of maneuverability against India themselves. It also encouraged China to enlarge the scope of the dispute by threatening the political homogeneity of the subcontinent with India as its core. This Peking did by promoting such ideas as the Himalayan Federation, which was to be a political bloc independent of India and capable of autonomous political action not necessarily in line with the concept of an Indian subcontinent.

We now see that in evaluation, concept, and actions concerning the different sub-systems, and especially as they pertained to Asia, Nehru overemphasized those concepts that encouraged his sense of invulnerability and that led, as a result, to a daringly active orientation in bilateral relations with China. At the same time, he isolated issues from their broader contexts, not realizing that his rivals were linking issues (Indochina with India-China) and that within the Chinese conceptual system a negative interpretation could be given to Indian activity within and beyond Asia (*P.R.,* Nov. 2, 1962). What Nehru conceived of as a positive, ethical activity imbuing him with moral power was seen by China as part of the overall struggle for naked power, not necessarily moral.

Conclusions

Nehru, man of vision and wide horizons, looked at events in India's immeidate environment through the macro-perspective of the global international environment, *as perceived by him.* This globalistic approach contributed to his downfall, as far as realistic attitudes and evaluations of the threat inherent in the Sino-Indian conflict were concerned. More specifically, as a result of our analysis, we can present in a nutshell his basic perceptions and conceptions and their dynamics.

- That the Chinese issue is secondary to global problems, so India must concentrate its attention on the more important area. This conception was an evaluation gap that did not undergo any process of adaptation over time.
- That war between India and China would almost necessarily lead to world war, especially given that, within the existing international system, conflict management is not possible once hostilities break out. Under the circumstances, the super powers would intervene to prevent *any* large-scale war between India and China. This, of course, was a case of turning a blind eye to the lessons of current history, as earlier pointed out. But even worse, there was no adaptation process that might have afforded a chance of changing these mistaken expectations.

Such evaluations were supported by the following conceptions:

- That India's tremendous prestige in the international arena as the mediator between the two camps and as leader of the Third World—especially in the United Nations, in which India is the main supporter of China—ensures India's immunity. This conception was, of course, a gross overestimation of the importance of these factors, revealing unawareness of the fact that neither the Third World in general, nor India in particular, could play the role of balancer in the contemporary international system and that their deterrent effect was therefore minimal.
- That the Soviet Union is the unquestionable leader of the Communist bloc and that the Sino-Soviet dispute is not a central issue, although some kind of disagreement exists. So, under these conditions the Soviet Union is *able* and *willing* to restrain China as far as India is concerned. This conception was, of course, a demonstration of Nehru's perceptual blindness relating to the USSR's actual ability to handle China and an evaluation gap with regard to the depth of the rift in the Communist bloc.
- As for the other super power, Nehru made the mistake of overestimating the ability of the United States and its interest in preventing a Chinese victory over India in order to keep Chinese influence in Asia as low as possible.
- Lastly, his belief in "one Asia" having more common than conflicting interests led him to reject any information concerning the possibility of war between the two major pillars that constituted Asianism.

In all of these conceptions, we basically see no substantive change in the light of incoming information, although Nehru adhered stubbornly to views that more often than not had no real basis; in particular, he stuck to his belief in the immunity of India and the very low probability of a major Chinese threat. Thus he saw no reason to initiate major changes in India's China policy, except toward a tougher position.

4

The Regional Environment

Geo-strategic and Geo-political Conceptions and Premises

Indian policymakers, including Nehru, were guided by a series of geo-strategic and geo-political concepts and assumptions that influenced their assessment of future threats and their political expectations and goals in relation to India's powerful and less powerful neighbors. A general discussion of these concepts follows. A more specific and detailed analysis is presented in the subsequent chapters dealing with India's bilateral relations with its neighbors and an evaluation of its power.

Much of independent India's geo-strategic thinking was inherited from the British Raj, although in some areas it led to different policy conclusions due to real-politik or ideological preferences; yet there was still a strong element of continuity in geo-strategic concepts and premises on both the regional and bilateral levels.

The first assumption was, and remains, that India's size and geographic location make it a relevant, even essential, factor in the influence and control of the Middle East, Southeast Asia, East Asia, East Africa and, of course, South Asia. Its ports are important to any power seeking to dominate the major navigational routes in the Indian Ocean. The British regarded their rule in India as vital, a key to the Empire, and the defense of the passage to India became a permanent issue in British geo-strategic thinking. Indian policymakers adopted the same attitude (Nehru, 1949, 235). Assuming that none of the major powers could afford to let a rival, or a rival's ally, take Britain's place, they concluded that India would be protected by mutual deterrence. This was, incidentally, also one of the rationalizations behind India's nonalignment policy; choosing one side could be considered a threat to the opposing power and lead to repercussions that would make the price of partisanship too costly.

The second British assumption was that the main overland threat to India was from the northwest, the traditional land invasion route, as the Himalayas prevented any effective military action from the north or northeast. Politically, this meant that the Pathan tribes were seen as a relatively mild danger, the main threat coming from the potential expansionist goals of Tsarist, and later Soviet, Russia. This approach viewed the control of Kashmir as crucial for the defense of the subcontinent. The Indian national movement tended to minimize the potential dangers from the Pathans and Russia, and saw in this threat-perception a part of the dynamics of British imperialist policy: first build a large army and then find an occupation for it by creating imaginary threats. But the confrontation with Pakistan, which began immediately after India's independence, encouraged it to adopt its own version of the northwestern enemy. Naturally, it was convenient, a habit almost, to adopt British strategic conceptions that seemed especially relevant in that the dispute with Pakistan revolved around Kashmir, and it was easy to explain Kashmir's importance to the defense of India. Giving up what would later be defined as Kashmir's northern part, Aksai Chin, to China might also set a precedent in the whole question of Kashmir and relations with Pakistan (Lamb, 1971; Lamb, 1973, 93), thus increasing the threat to India's security. So British tradition was upheld, to such an extent that when the question of the border arose, what came to mind was the northwestern border, or as one scholar noted: "To guard the northwest became a habit" (Chopra, 1969, 219).

Third, according to the British conception, the defense of the land area of the subcontinent was based on two defense lines that could be called the external and internal defense lines. Tibet formed the subcontinent's external line, as a natural buffer between Britain and Russia in the north and northeast, just as Afghanistan did in the northwest. An agreement in 1907 between Britain and Russia sanctioned this notion. In it the two sides agreed not to violate Tibet's sovereignty and to avoid interference in its internal affairs: "Subject to the above stipulation, Russia [is] to recognize that, by reason of its geographical position, Great Britain has a special interest in seeing that the external relations of Thibet are not disturbed by any other power."[1]

The areas and principalities of the North-East Frontier Agency (NEFA), Bhutan, Sikkim, Nepal, and Kashmir were to serve as an internal defense line. Although this strategy necessitated some form of British political domination over them, the British were satisfied with a symbolic presence in the northeastern border area. Britain enabled the groups living there, which were ethically and religiously akin to the Tibetans, to preserve their character and did not interfere in their lives or tax them to any real extent.

Bhutan and Sikkim were tied to Britain by special agreements that, although promising nominal independence, gave Britain an overriding influence in matters of foreign policy and security. There were British representatives permanently placed in the two principalities. Nepal, on the other hand, did keep its independence, but it also had a British representative to ensure that it would not turn north toward Russia or China and would not initiate independent positions in foreign policy that might deviate from the definition of British interests. In Kashmir itself, Britain demonstrated a regular presence and made certain that its ruler was a docile ally.

Britain's effectiveness in doing this with a minimal show of force was due to three factors: the power and prestige of the Empire, which deterred in advance any attempt to disturb the status quo; the relative lack of Russian interest in South Asia, especially considering the price of confronting the British Empire; and the weakness of the Chinese Empire.

This British approach was based on the distinction between political and specific boundaries, or between what we would today call the Empire's security boundaries and the actual borders. The territorial considerations were not emotional but political, which is why the question of where the border actually ran was of minor significance, except in locations of strategic importance. This position was clearly expressed by Sir Henry McMahon, who distinguished between *frontier* and *boundary*. The first could signify any wide strip of land the special location of which made it a barrier between two countries, whereas the latter was a specifically defined line delimited verbally in an agreement or, in a series of demarcations, on the ground itself.

Once independent India accepted the logic of two defense lines, it had to adopt all that this implied: Tibet as a buffer zone and Sikkim and Bhutan as essential for mutual defense. The loss of Sikkim, for example, would significantly weaken the defense of the northeastern boundary, as Sikkim was essential to the defense of Bhutan and Bhutan contained a number of major Himalayan passes that were open all year round (Wilcox, 1968, 427). The importance of Nepal was due to its topographical structure, which declined from north to south. This meant that an invasion through Nepal's northern border with Tibet would allow a relatively easy infiltration into India. As a result, the defense of Nepal's border with Tibet was defined as strategically crucial for India's defense. In a debate in the Rajya Sabha in December 1950, Nehru said:

> The Himalayas lie mostly on the northern border of Nepal. We cannot allow that barrier to be penetrated because it is also the principal barrier to India. Therefore, much as we appreciate the independence of Nepal, we cannot allow anything to go wrong in Nepal or permit that barrier to be crossed or weakened, because that would be a risk to our own security. (Nehru, 1954, 176)

Until the end of the 1950s, Nehru himself saw no serious problem regarding India's political dominance in the Hill States, nor any Chinese threat to it. This was in no small measure due to the belief that throughout history Chinese expansion was directed toward Southeast Asia and not into the subcontinent, and, indeed, the Indian and Chinese cultures had clashed in Southeast Asia throughout history.

Thus, it happened that the Indian leadership adopted the British geo-strategic ideas without special reservations, believing that what was good for the British would be good and true for independent India, as had been proved historically. So great was the lack of insight and reevaluation in this matter that until the Longju incident in 1959 the NEFA sector was under the supervision of the Indian Ministry of External Affairs (MEA), as it has been under the British. In mid-1954 the MEA took under its authority the border sector between Tibet and Ladakh as well, and was responsible for the organization and establishment of checkposts there. Only after the Longju incident was the whole border area with China put under military control and responsibility.

The other geo-strategic aspect of the dispute was its specific physical features. The dispute covered a border 2,000 miles long that could be divided into three sectors. In the central sector, the length of the disputed border was 400 miles and the area under dispute was 400 square miles. Differences of opinion over this area were slight. The main problems lay with the western and eastern sectors.

In the western sector, the length of the border was 1,000 miles and the area under dispute, 15,000 square miles. There were two problems. One was the question of sovereignty over Aksai Chin, and the other was concerned with the location of the border between Tibet and Ladakh. Ladakh had been a part of Tibet until the tenth century, when it became independent. It returned to Tibetan domination in the nineteenth century. In 1841, the governor of Kashmir, Gulab Singh, tried, under British inspiration, to conquer Ladakh but failed in the military confrontation, largely due to weather conditions on the Tibetan plateau. The agreement between Gulab Singh and the leaders of Tibet spoke of the "old recognized borders" without interpreting what they were.[2] This vague situation continued even after India had gained its independence. Until 1954 no border was marked on Indian maps for this area, and only in 1958 did the Indian government present formal claims over it. Yet in 1959 Nehru could still declare that although the eastern border was clearly marked, the western sector was not and, as he said, "nobody knew what was happening" about the location of the border. Moreover, Nehru saw no importance in Aksai Chin where, as he said, "not even a blade of grass grows," a claim that enraged the opposition who saw it as an encouragement to the Chinese to claim the area (*Par.,* I, 104; 134–135; 281). The difficult and inaccessible terrain of the area was the reason for which India's published boundary map for the western sector did not match the actual physical features on the ground. In fact, Indian patrols did not reach Aksai Chin, and the most forward Indian outpost was located in Chusul.[3]

The situation in the eastern sector was different. There the border was 700 miles long and the territory under dispute, 32,000 square miles (the entire area of the NEFA). A point of departure did exist—the McMahon line decided on at the Simla Conference—but the Chinese repudiated it for political and ideological reasons (which will be discussed further on), their basic approach being that "the entire Sino-Indian boundary, whether in its western, middle or eastern sector, has not been delimited" (*W.P.*, III, 64). The Indian approach claimed that "This boundary throughout has been fixed and well known for centuries" (*W.P.*, III, 82). Their readiness to compromise can be summarized in Nehru's declaration: "But having accepted broadly the McMahon Line, I am prepared to discuss any interpretation of the McMahon Line; minor interpretations here and there . . . whether this hill is there or this little bit is on that side or on this side, on the facts, on the maps, on the evidence available" (*Par.*, I, 119). In this area, the Indian government had been taking a unilateral initiative since the early 1950s. As early as 1950 Nehru had decided that the McMahon line was the natural boundary between India and China. The watershed line seemed ideally suited to be a boundary,[4] and in the years 1949 to 1951, after the takeover of the Tawang Tract, the de facto adjustment between the delimitation of the McMahon line on Indian maps and that on the ground was complete. Although the Indian army did not boast a regular massive presence in the area, this was not a source of worry for Indian policymakers as the Himalayas were considered impassable[5] for an invading army. The Himalayas and the Plateau of Tibet are the highest areas in the world. Weather conditions are rough virtually throughout the year, the area is poor in transportation routes on both the Indian and Chinese sides, and most of the mountain passes are snowbound for a great part of the year. There did not seem to be a Chinese Hannibal prepared to cross them and descend to the Assam plains and the Ganges and Indus river basins. In 1950 Nehru said that the Himalayas were such an effective defense line that even an airborne fleet could not cross them.[6] From the topography in this area he also concluded that in a military confrontation no external power could prove a useful ally, as "The type of aid that one gets from abroad is machines and in these mountain areas those machines do not reach" (*Par.*, I, 253).

The topographical isolation of the eastern sector from both India and Tibet had created an ethnic problem as well. The population there was culturally neither Tibetan nor Hindi, although it bore a greater resemblance to the former; even the British penetration of the area had come rather late, in the 1940s. Thus, Indian efforts to "digest" the area became even more difficult and increased its sensitivity; political stability and the prevention of any military flare-ups were essential. In the western sector, in Ladakh, there was a cultural problem arising from both historical and topographical conditions. The area was the meeting point of three cultures—the Hindi, the Tibetan, and the Islamic (through Kashmir). This made delimitation of the border according to ethnic-cultural criteria difficult, to say the least. Furthermore, the use of such criteria in territorial negotiations might have added fuel to Pakistan's religious-cultural claim on Kashmir. Thus, the ethnic-cultural factors also served to tie in the Sino-Indian and the Sino-Pakistani disputes.

Indian geo-strategic and geo-political assumptions and perceptions on the regional and the local-topographical levels abounded in misperceptions. First and foremost was Nehru's thinking in terms of "total war." He did not believe that a limited war between China and India was possibale. But even if we assume that in an outbreak of such a war India would enjoy maximum protection from the deterrent strength of both super powers, who would not tolerate the idea of a successor to the British in the subcontinent, there was still no reason to suppose that they would intervene in a local war where there was no danger of one belligerent taking over the entire subcontinent. Furthermore, it was precisely the possibility, which Nehru feared, of a local conflict deteriorating into a nuclear war that would make the super powers wary of interference. What is more, even if one or both super powers should risk intervention in a local limited war, the topographical features of the Himalayas would make such an intervention ineffective according to Nehru's own evaluation, as we have seen. And if the powers should not intervene, then India's assumption of immunity was baseless. So, one way or another, there was a contradiction in Nehru's thinking. But, as we shall see, he managed to maintain contradictory assumptions, without being aware of that fact.

Why Nehru believed that a limited war without the intervention of the super powers was possible in the northwestern area—Kashmir—but impossible in the northeastern sector was a second puzzle. Was it because of the sizes of India and China? Why was a confrontation with Pakistan, an ally of the United States, perceived as possible without apprehension of U.S. intervention? Was it not that Nehru took for granted that neither power could get involved in a situation that might involve the other? If so, why was the Sino-Indian affair not seen in that way? The contradictions continued.

Third, how could India accept the double-defense-line thesis without there being present at least two of the three conditions that had made the concept a success under the British Raj? (1) India did not have the power or prestige of the Empire that had succeeded in guaranteeing the de facto independence of Tibet and obtaining the total dependence of the Hill States, preventing any other foreign actor from infiltrating them; and (2) China was no longer the giant with feet of clay, but a state with an efficient centralist regime, keen on boasting effective control of all areas considered its own. When China's physical presence in Tibet extended to the edge of the Tibetan plateau, India's internal defense line became China's external one, thus making the Himalayan principalities a possible issue of Sino-Indian friction. Moreover, independent India, out of nationally motivated chauvinism, felt the need to demonstrate its sovereignty over its entire area, including the NEFA; consequently, the buffer zones disappeared and an exact definition of the boundary became imperative.

The secretary general of the MEA, Sir G.S. Bajpai, was right in demanding in 1950 that the issue be openly dealt with and a definite agreement with the Chinese reached; Nehru was wrong in resting content[7] with Chinese silence when he made his statements about the northeastern boundaries of India, and with the fact that the subject was not raised in the Sino-Indian negotiations of 1954.[8] Indeed, in 1960, the Chinese were to claim: "It is both illogical and inconceivable to argue that an outstanding issue will automatically cease to exist merely because it is not mentioned during certain negotiations" (*W.P.,* IV, 10). This was especially true in light of the fact that for China the Western conception of boundaries, that is, their actual demarcation, was historically an anathema. They had marked boundaries in the past under duress when, in the nineteenth and twentieth centuries, the regime in Peking could not withstand Tsarist Russia or the British Empire (Lamb, 1970). The Chinese tended to see the idea of boundary more in the sense of frontier. So, modern China, after 1949, had to start afresh as far as border demarcation was concerned. And this is certainly true of the western sector where there was not even a point of departure to start with, unlike the eastern sector.

Fourth, it is difficult to understand how Nehru did not see that there was a basic contradiction between his definition of himself as having a common anti-Imperialist past with the Chinese and his actions in adopting an "imperialist" strategy that aroused bleak memories and hence objections in the Chinese. The McMahon line had been negotiated with a weak and humiliated Chinese state. It is no wonder, then, that Chou En-lai emphasized in a letter to Asian and African heads of state, on November 15, 1962 that "The Indian government, however, inherited the British imperialists' covetous desires towards the Tibet region of China and persisted in regarding Tibet as India's sphere of influence, or sought to transform it into a buffer zone between China and India."[9] To them, British policy was adoptable only in toto.

Lastly, the idea of geographical determinism preventing the infiltration of any army through a natural barrier is very strange, especially for a man so otherwise aware of the technological significance of the twentieth century. Did Nehru not see that topography, just as it can be an obstacle, can also be a jumping board?[10] There is always someone more efficient in overcoming the difficulties presented by topography, as was indeed proven by the events of October 1962, when Tibet and the Himalayas became forward bases of Chinese military might.

Nehru, who mechanically adopted British geo-strategic and geo-political concepts, made grave errors both in incorrectly estimating the Chinese reaction to them and in his reliance on topographical immunity. He was not aware of the geo-political contradictions arising from his globalistic thinking, nor of the irrelevance of at least several concepts in the light of India's changed situation as an independent state in a new era facing a different enemy.[11]

Perception of the Linkage Between the Sino-Indian and Indo-Pakistani Disputes

The relations between India and China, like every other major problem of Indian foreign policy, were linked to the Pakistan issue. The inter-communal riots that broke out soon after partition of the subcontinent and the granting of independence to the two nations, the flight of vast numbers of refugees to both countries, and the Kashmir War in 1948–1949 deepened the original rift and caused the two countries to regard each other with intense distrust. From the Indian point of view, Pakistan had completely rejected the concept of a pluralistic secular state in culture and religion, diametrically opposed to the two-nation thesis adopted by the leaders of Pakistan, just as India's secularism was the antithesis of the Pakistani theocratic state. These factors, and the appraisal that Pakistan was not satisfied with the existing balance of power between India and itself, contributed to the feeling among Indian policymakers and the public that Pakistan, for ideological and practical reasons, was trying to cause the disintegration of the Indian Federation into a host of weak states characterized by their separate dominant cultures and ethnic groups. This was the source of the belief that granting independence to Kashmir or its annexation to Pakistan, whether by referendum or as a result of a military defeat or political pressures, would set a precedent for the dismantling of the federation.

To this apprehension we must add the ideological and budgetary constraints caused by economic necessities that limited the size of the army. The combination of these restrictions with an acute sense of danger created by the Indo-Pakistani dispute led to the turning of all available military resources toward the west and northwest, which resulted in a strategy of *political* defense of the 2,000 mile border with China and a *military* and *political* defense of the border with Pakistan. This trend grew when Pakistan joined SEATO and CENTO in 1954 and 1955, respectively, and became a recipient of what seemed in the subcontinent massive and modern military aid. The fear continued to haunt India even when its relations with the

West improved, and was substantiated for Nehru when, in March 1959, a further agreement was signed by the United States and Pakistan on defense and security cooperation and when, in a meeting between Ayub Khan and President Kennedy in July 1961, a further supply of arms was promised to Pakistan.

A special dimension was added to the issue by the fact that the main partners to these treaties with Pakistan were the former co-lonialists—Britain and France—and their successor, the United States, nations strongly suspected by Nehru of having adopted neo-colonialist attitudes. Nehru's hostility toward Pakistan grew, together with his foreboding that it was a puppet in the hands of colonial powers, enjoying powerful military and political backing. The rise to power of Ayub Khan in 1958 increased India's animosity. In the specific context of Indo-Pakistan relations, a dictatorship seemed especially dangerous. Nehru's meeting with Ayub Khan in September 1960 emphasized the great gap in mentality and outlook between the two (Blinkenberg, 1972, 228) and strengthened Nehru's feeling, which he had expressed in the past, that there could be no accord with Pakistan for the foreseeable future; thus, Ayub Khan's suggestion, since 1959, of a joint defense agreement was perceived not as a conciliatory gesture but as a cunning move by a shrewd enemy. To agree would have meant a betrayal of both practical interests and the moral concepts that were the basis of India's foreign policy: (1) Ayub Khan himself admitted that the treaty was aimed also against the USSR and Afghanistan, two countries with whom India had excellent re-lations. (2) The treaty stood in complete opposition to Nehru's ideological objection to military defense treaties. (3) Ayub Khan demanded the settlement of the Kashmir question on terms favorable to Pakistan. (4) A joint defense treaty with Pakistan meant for Nehru an indirect affiliation with the Western pacts of SEATO and CENTO, of which Pakistan was a member (*Par.,* I, 291), and the abandonment of nonalignment, his most cherished idea. As Nehru strongly put it: "the moment we give up the idea of non-alignment, we lose every anchor that we hold on to and we simply drift" (*Par.,* I, 42).

For these reasons, it seemed to Nehru that in a treaty with Pakistan, Ayub Khan and his country would reap all the benefits.

India's action orientation demanded a concentration of attention on the Pakistani threat, which had wide political and ideological, as well as territorial, implications. To ensure such attention, it was necessary to isolate the Pakistan problem from other border issues. At the same time, it was necessary to find allies to support India's policy, and Afghanistan and especially the USSR effectively filled the bill.

But Ayub Khan thought otherwise. When his hoped-for defense pact with India did not materialize and he realized that it probably never would, being aware that India enjoyed the unalloyed support of the USSR on the question of Kashmir, he decided that the next Pakistani move should be to exploit the Sino-Indian border dispute in order to win over a major power to support Pakistan's position. China, due to its geographic location and because the only other candidate, the United States, was out of the question, was the obvious target. Late in 1960 Ayub Khan invited the Chinese to discuss the question of the delimitation of their border; in June 1961 China agreed in principle; and on October 12, 1962, a week before the Chinese invasion of India talks commenced on the delimitation of the border between Azad Kashmir and Sinkiang.

To Nehru, Ayub Khan's move and the positive Chinese reaction came as something of a surprise. His hope that the two border disputes could be kept separate collapsed together with his belief that China recognized India's sovereignty over Kashmir (*W.P.*, VI, 97), for the origin of which it is difficult to account. And, indeed, the Chinese reacted by asking: "When did the Chinese government accept without any reservation the position that Kashmir is under Indian sovereignty?" (*W.P.*, VI, 99). This is yet another example of Nehru's wishful thinking in relation to China, which, contrary to the USSR, had taken a balanced view of the Indo-Pakistani dispute since the mid-1950s. In 1955, the year Sino-Indian relations were at their peak, Chinese leaders sent a message to the Pakistani leadership in which they reiterated that there was no conflict of interests between China and Pakistan, whereas "this position did not apply to Indo-Chinese relations, in which a definite conflict of interests could be expected in the near future" (quoted by Williams, 1962, 120; Choudhury, 1975, 152–153). The Indian assumption that there was a basic ideological and political conflict between China and Pakistan (*Par.*, II, 136) proved false. This notion was based on Pakistan's partnership in Western military pacts that were essentially anti-Chinese, on Pakistan being a Western camp follower, and on the fact that it had been created out of the severance of an Islamic religious population from a secular state, which might encourage separatist elements in Islamic Sinkiang. But this evaluation chose to ignore Pakistan's constant emphasis on the anti-Indian, rather than anti-Chinese, character of its Western alliances. The Indian government did not see that it was precisely the unrest in Sinkiang and the USSR's attempt to exploit it that brought the Chinese closer to the Muslim world in which Pakistan played an important role; moreover, it ignored the fact that for the Chinese, who were afraid of being encircled from the south by the USSR through its penetration of India, ties with Pakistan, despite the political and ideological differences, were a necessity of real-politik.

Things became more and more complex. A territorial concession to China was impossible because it might have set a precedent[12] with regard to Kashmir. It might have been interpreted by Pakistan as weakness, thus bringing about an increase in military pressure. Such a concession might also have lead to internal difficulties in Kashmir, as it could have provoked the Kashmir elite whose support, as passive as it was, India needed.

Despite this state of affairs, the Chinese-Pakistani link was still seen mainly as a Chinese political maneuver (*W.P.,* VI, 97) but one that made the danger of an Indian military confrontation *with Pakistan* more acute, as China's support could cause Pakistan to take adventurous steps; therefore, until October 20, 1962 Menon personally did not allow the tranfer of a single soldier from the border with Pakistan to that with China. The Pakistan phobia was so developed that in August 1962 Menon was convinced that Pakistan was about to attack, although he had no proof and despite the fact that India's diplomatic representative there firmly rejected the notion (Nayar, 1973). Military units stationed in Ladakh were positioned facing the south toward Pakistan rather than the north toward China. This preoccupation with Pakistan finds expression, for example, in May 1962 when Nehru mentioned the anticipated active threat of a second tribal invasion organized by Pakistani authorities, which might have led to an all-out war between India and Pakistan (Nehru, 1964, 298–299). In September 1962 Nehru spoke about the threat from Pakistan in terms of "invasion." In the same breath, he described the Chinese threat only in terms of "tension" and "petty conflicts" (*F.N.,* 2/62, Sept. 3, 1962).

As the Pakistan issue focused military attention on the northwest, and because of India's military constraints, only a low military profile, or a political defense of the Chinese border, was possible. Pakistan's aggressive intentions were overestimated, whereas China's capabilities and intentions were underestimated. On the other hand, the linking of the Chinese and Pakistani issues, and the implications of this, further restricted India's political maneuverability and made political defense of the Chinese border more difficult. Yet, although in practice the tactical steps taken were not in harmony with sober political action and were backed only by hollow power, the political defense strategy did not change.

The Hill States in India's Political Thinking

As with other aspects of Indian foreign and defense policies, those concerning the Himalayan principalities of Nepal, Bhutan, and Sikkim were patterned after the British-India government. In broad terms, the policy was aimed at Indian political, military, and economic dominance of these areas as a strategic necessity for the protection of India's northern border, as we have already seen in the discussion of the geo-strategic aspects of the dispute. But the specific nature of this political phenomenon differed from one principality to another and was conditioned by several factors: (a) precedents set in British days that emerged later in agreements signed between India and each of the states; (b) precedents set by the objective circumstances such as size, location, and ethnic composition of each state; (c) precedents set by the specific internal and external conditions; and (d) precedents set by the way in which local leaderships perceived their countries' maneuverability under these conditions.

The largest and most important of the principalities was Nepal, which had maintained its independence and uniqueness even under British rule of the subcontinent. But the fear of invasion from both north and south was ever present. The apprehension of Chinese intentions was related to historical memories of conflict with Imperial China—the 1792 war following Nepal's attempts to take over Tibet, and the subsequent defeat, which had led to a vague Chinese suzerainty over Nepal.

The perception of a southern threat was the result of the memory of the nineteenth-century attempt to expand southward after the northern route had been blocked. It, too, ended in defeat in 1816, at the hands of the British, who thenceforth included Nepal within their own sphere of influence. Britain, however, avoided interference in Nepal's internal affairs and only dictated foreign policy.

The British refrained from annexing Nepal to British India as they were interested in maintaining it as a buffer state, and, indeed, in 1923 they signed an agreement recognizing Nepal as a sovereign state. Thus, its independence was preserved and, as a result of British support, it held on to special rights in Tibet at the expense of its weak neighbor—Imperial, and later Republican, China.

Following the changes in the subcontinent that began in the mid-1940s and the preparation for Britain's exit, Nepalese leaders, who were fervent nationalists, understood that if they wished to continue to retain their independence, they would have to change their isolationist policy to a more open one, increasing outside connections in order to counterbalance India's economic and military dominance, with its political implications. In practice, Nepal abandoned its isolationist policy in 1946, although it formalized the move only in 1948 when it established diplomatic relations with the United States. It requested membership of the United Nations the following year.

In July 1950 a friendship treaty was signed between India and Nepal in which India repeated the British policy of 1923. The agreement, which recognized Nepal's independence, states in section 1: "The two governments agree mutually to acknowledge and respect the complete sovereignty, territorial integrity and independence of each other."[13] But a few months later, Communist China took control of Tibet, thus creating a direct contact between China and the mountain principalities; Nehru declared his northern border policy, which adopted the McMahon line as India's border line in the northeast; internal upheavals occurred in Nepal following the revolution directed against the ruling Rana family encouraged by India for ideological-political reasons;[14] and Nepal now feared that its fate would be similar to that of Tibet. Chinese leaders including Mao had spoken of Nepal as part of China's historical heritage. Tibet had at times been described as a palm whose five fingers were Ladakh, Nepal, Bhutan, Sikkim, and the NEFA. Against this background Nehru's doctrine, [15] which saw the Himalayas to the north of Nepal as India's security boundary, declared that India reserved the right to intervene militarily in the event of any invasion, to maintain a military presence in Nepal, and even to interfere in Nepalese politics in order to preserve internal stability. In other words, India refused to give up its absolute dominance over Nepal: "no other country can have as intimate a relationship with Nepal as ours is" (Nehru, 1954, 175).

And India did indeed act in that spirit. "The New Delhi Compromise" brought King Tribhuvan and the Nepalese Congress Party to power, and 1951 marked the beginning of the period of "special relations"[16] that lasted until 1956. In that year Indian radio operators were posted along Nepal's border with China to report on happenings in the area. In 1952 an Indian military delegation was sent to reorganize the Nepalese army from a poorly trained and equipped 25,000-man force into a smaller but more efficient one of 6,000 men (Rose, 1971, 197). The bureaucracy, too, was reorganized by Indian advisors, and key personalities from Nepal made frequent pilgrimages to New Delhi.

It used to be said that "when Nehru caught a cold, Koirala [the Nepalese Prime Minister] sneezed." In foreign policy Nepal made certain of receiving India's blessing for every move it made, especially in the Chinese context. Following India's "advice," Nepal did not rush into ties with China before 1954. Then the Panch Sheel Agreement opened the way for change, and India could no longer prevent a normalization of relations between Nepal and China. But both China and Nepal were still cautious, and China in that period dealt with all issues concerning Nepal through India (Panikkar, 1955, 171).

King Mahendra's rise to power in March 1955 and the growing resistance in Nepal to the increased Indian presence there brought the beginning of change in both the form and substance of Nepalese foreign policy and a transition from the special relations with India to a more even-handed stance. Due to both China's and Nepal's caution, it was at first a slow process.[17] In 1956 China began providing economic and technical aid.[18] Nepal agreed to concede its special privileges in Tibet, although traditional arrangements of border trading, pasture, and pilgrimages without passports were maintained. In 1957 Chou En-lai visited Nepal for the first time, and the Chinese media began emphasizing the ethnic and cultural affinity between the Chinese and Nepalese populations, referring especially to the population in northern Nepal, which was Mongol in origin and Buddhist in culture. King Mahendra frequently changed his prime ministers, sometimes appointing pro-Chinese and at other times pro-Indian prime ministers, depending on his evaluation of foreign policy needs. During the entire period of 1957–1959, China displayed goodwill toward India, kept it informed of its moves toward Nepal, and refused to send Chinese experts to Nepal. Nor did the Chinese press dwell on the increasing hostility between Nepal and India (Sinha, 1970). Chinese policy then indicated recognition of Nepal as being within the Indian sphere of influence, while at the same time the possibility of alternative options remained open.

The uprising in Tibet and the escape of the Dalai Lama clouded Nepal's relations with China for a time and aroused anxiety in Nepal over its security.[19] As a result, Nehru and King Mahendra held consultations on the possibility of reinforcing Nepalese positions along the Chinese border. The border incidents between China and India in August and October of 1959 brought Mahendra to the conclusion that the Chinese did not consider their relations with India as important as they had been in the past, and the most effective way to protect Nepal would be, therefore, to develop closer ties with China as quickly as possible, even at the expense of relations with India—all this without taking a definite stand on the Sino-Indian dispute. At the same time, China initiated a series of conciliatory steps toward Nepal—to assuage its fears—on matters concerning trade and freedom of movement between Nepal and Tibet. These steps encouraged King Mahendra to assume that he had appreciated the situation correctly and, furthermore, that the new Sino-Indian relations lessened his dependence on India and allowed him greater political maneuverability—this in spite of the fact that economically Nepal remained almost totally dependent on India.[20]

The new circumstances also enabled King Mahendra to make sweeping internal changes such as the disbanding of the National Assembly and the Nepalese Congress Party in December 1960, steps that the Indian government had to swallow and which significantly diminished its influence in Nepal. In August 1960 the Indian government had no choice but to sign an economic agreement that cancelled the link between the Nepalese and Indian rupees, and to agree to the establishment of a Chinese embassy in Katmandu and the arrival of a Chinese aid delegation there.

Matters were going speedily ahead in other areas close to home for India. In 1960 talks were begun on settling the Sino-Nepalese border dispute, and in March 1961 a temporary boundary agreement was signed between the two governments that contained a section establishing a 20-kilometer buffer zone on each side of the border, just as the Chinese had suggested for the Sino-Indian border but which India had rejected. In October 1961 all disagreements were settled and a treaty was finally signed. The agreement contained two principles important to India: one was that the watershed line at the convergence of the borders of India, Tibet, Nepal, and Sikkim would serve as a border line; and the other was that it was accepted that the border with Tibet would remain the traditional one and that it was not necessary to redefine it except in specific areas of disagreement. This was a principle that India had vainly tried to convince China to accept in their own dispute. In addition, an agreement of importance to Indian strategic policies was signed concerning a road to connect Katmandu with Tibet, construction of which began in 1962. This agreement had a special significance in light of the rumors (dating from 1960) about the construction of transportation routes connecting the mountain passes of the Sino-Nepalese border with Tibet's traffic routes (Dai, 1963).[21] It would create the possibility of outflanking Indian military posts in the northeastern sector and to the length of the Sino-Sikkim-Bhutan borders.[22] Relations between India and Nepal deteriorated sharply as a result,[23] and in September 1962 India applied economic sanctions against Nepal and encouraged subversive activity on the part of the Nepalese Congress Party. The Chinese foreign minister responded on October 4 by declaring that in the event of an attack Nepal could count on China's support.

I have dwelt at some length on this trilateral relationship because of its complexity and in order to clarify the background to Nehru's perception of it. Before Nehru's very eyes, India's status in the most important of the Hill States was declining, a state that was crucially important in his geo-strategic thinking. The situation had deteriorated from the Chinese recognition of India's special status in Nepal at Nehru's 1954 talks in Peking (Rowland, 1967, 148), which China maintained until 1959, to a policy that stood in overt opposition to India's crucial interests. It diminished India's political influence in Nepal and could even lead to a direct strategic threat to India via the construction of a road from Tibet to Nepal, which would break the barrier of the Himalayas and expose India's northern border to a possible outflanking movement.

In this situation there were implications for the two smaller principalities, whose independence was even more tenuous than that of Nepal. The precedent could cause Bhutan and Sikkim to attempt to break away from Indian influence, especially when China suggested the establishment of a Himalayan Federation. This meant, from Nehru's point of view, that India must not under any circumstances show weakness, that is, make concessions in its relationship with China. If the Hill States were to break away from India, the strategic principles on which the defense of the northern border was based would be completely undermined.

Nehru's fears appeared to be well founded. Indian-Bhutanese and Indian-Sikkimese relations were based on agreements signed in 1949 with Bhutan and in 1950 with Sikkim that perpetuated the status conceived and realized by the British.[24] Section 2 of the treaty with

Bhutan states that "The Government of India undertakes to exercise no interference in the internal administration of Bhutan. On its part the Government of Bhutan agrees to be guided by the advice of the Government of India in its external relations."

Quite different is the agreement signed between India and Sikkim in 1950, section 2 of which states that "Sikkim shall continue to be a protectorate of India and subject to the provision of this treaty shall enjoy autonomy in regards to its internal affairs." Section 3 states that "The Government of India will be responsible for the defence and territorial integrity of Sikkim. It shall have the right to take such measures as it considers necessary for the defence of Sikkim or the security of India. . . . In particular, the Government of India shall have the right to station troops anywhere within Sikkim." Despite the difference in the agreements, the common denominator is India's responsibility for the foreign policies of both Bhutan and Sikkim. On this basis, India demanded that "the questions relating to the northern boudaries of Sikkim and Bhutan have to be considered at the same time as the boundary between India and China" (*W.P.,* IV, 100).

But China, claiming that it "has always respected the proper relations between them [Sikkim and Bhutan] and India" (*W.P.,* II, 30), rejected India's demand. The term *proper relations* is hardly equivalent to India's idea of dominance. And the Chinese emphasized their view in practice. In the 1960 talks between Nehru and Chou En-lai, the latter refused to discuss the Sino-Bhutanese border question, and late in 1960 the Chinese publicly rejected the concept that the Tibet-Sikkim and Tibet-Bhutan borders were part of the Sino-Indian boundary.[25]

These developments were seen as a challenge to India's special status in an area traditionally under its influence; the strategic implications were obvious. Sikkim controlled the Chumby Valley, which contained two important Himalayan passes—Jelep Nathu and Patra—to which the Indian army had built a road. Sikkim was considered essential for the defense of Bhutan as, until the construction of a road from India to Bhutan, the only route passed through Tibet and Sikkim. Bhutan, on the other hand, was crucial for the defense of the Siliguri Corridor and the northeastern sector. As early as 1908 a letter sent by the British India Government stated: "The Chinese should not be allowed to get a footing in Bhutan and thereby bring into being a North Eastern Frontier question" (quoted by Poulouse, 1971, 197), especially considering the ethnic unrest permeating the northeastern border in those years.

The anxiety over India's political and strategic status in Bhutan and Sikkim had an historical and ethnic basis, too. Within these two states there emerged political bodies that had a great deal of autonomy but of which the cultural and government patterns were similar to those of Tibet. Central elements of their populations had a deep religious affinity with Tibet[26] and close trade relations with Lhasa. The rulers of Sikkim had arrived from Tibet in the sixteenth century. Ethnically, they belonged to the Bhuties, who, although making up only 25% of Sikkim's population, inhabited the border area with Tibet, whereas the larger ethnic group of Sikkim (70%), originating from Nepal and preferring the warmer climate, lived in the south. In Bhutan, too, there was a large minority of Nepalese immigrants, about a third of the population, that was economically and politically underprivileged. The conflict of interests in the populations of the two principalities offered an opportunity for political exploitation by China (Rose, 1961).[27] Nehru was especially concerned about the growing nationalism in Bhutan, which called for the expansion of this principality's international ties. Propagators of this stand claimed that Bhutan had to consult with India but was under no obligation to take its advice. This was significant in the light of Chinese attempts to create direct links with the Bhutanese leadership and their suggestion that their border dispute be settled through direct negotiations,[28] which was put out simultaneously with proclamations about the liberation of Bhutan and the publication of maps that showed parts of it as belonging to China (Belfiglio, 1972, 682–683). Indian apprehensions found expression in foreign policy[29] in the continuous pressure exerted on Bhutan for some kind of mutual security arrangement and the construction of a road linking it with India, which would obviate passage through Sikkim and the Chumby Valley and for which a Chinese permit was needed. The rebellion in Tibet, the masses of refugees streaming from there to Bhutan, and the tales of terror that they brought with them, together with the increased Indian pressure, finally brought about the signing in 1961 of the agreement for the construction of the desired road and for the training of the Royal Bhutanese Army by Indian officers (Rose, 1974, 195–197).

But even this success[30] did not set Nehru's mind to rest. The influence of India in the Himalayan states arose from its strength but also from the expectations of the ruling elites that it could prevent a repetition of the Tibet takeover in the principalities. A concession to China, which might be interpreted as weakness, would challenge India's ability to meet the expectations of the principalities' leadership and might result in greater Chinese involvement or in a change from an Indian orientation to a neutral or worse, a pro-Chinese, one. Nepal's policy, by which it hoped to guarantee both national security and greater political maneuverability, including less dependence on India, was very tempting to the leadership of the other Hill States. The nightmare of Indian policymakers was that their country would be surrounded by hostile, or at least unfriendly, states—Pakistan on the west; China, Nepal,[31] Bhutan, and Sikkim in the north; and East Pakistan in the east. A master plan to isolate India in South Asia— seen as remote but not impossible—was economically, politically, militarily, and ideologically intolerable.[32] One way to prevent it was to convince those nations that could still be influenced, that is, the Hill States, that it was not worthwhile, and the way to achieve this seemed to be through a display of firmness in the struggle with the main rival for influence on the subcontinent, China.

The strategic conception that political domination of these states was a necessary condition for the defense of India was pursued with a fanaticism incompatible with other assumptions. For one thing, it contradicted the idea that India was not seriously threatened from the north. If that were true, and if India had no imperialist ambitions disguised as defense strategies toward the Hill states, there was no reason to worry about Chinese influence in Nepal, Sikkim, and Bhutan. Moreover, even if there was apprehension of a potential threat from the north, the existing Indian presence there would not suffice to form an effective defense anyway, as the small nations' forces were much too small to hold back a Chinese invasion. Moreover, the Indian army, as we shall see later, could not get sufficient reinforcements to the border areas of the Himalayas quickly enough— not even to the NEFA and certainly not to Bhutan, which in those days was not even connected to India by a passage road (not to mention the fact that the establishment of a massive defense line in this border area required a military and economic effort that was beyond India's capability or willingness in the period under discussion).

It may be assumed that the small states were meant to serve as a kind of "trip wire" to signal a warning to India about any aggressive intentions on the part of China. And yet if China had wanted to launch a sudden attack, as indeed it did, it could have done so through its own border with India, not involving the principalities at all.

It appears, then, that India, divested of its former British colonial military power, inherited a concept of a northern buffer zone that might have been justified before the Chinese entered Tibet but now had little basis in reality. The problem became even more acute after March 1959, although terms such as *buffer states* and *buffer zone* as well as the map of the area created an illusion of security and led to such hollow declarations as the one made in the Upper House in December 1959: "Apart from the obvious responsibility of defending India and Indian territory, our responsibility undoubtedly extends to the neighbouring countries, Sikkim, Bhutan and Nepal. We have to stand by them, whatever the consequences" (Nehru, 1964, 270).

Furthermore, when Sino-Indian relations began to deteriorate, there was no reason to suppose that the Chinese would tolerate an Indian zone of influence in the Himalayas as, in their view, with regard to Tibet, India was interfering in an internal Chinese matter; it looked as if India was applying different standards to itself and China.

Against this background, it is difficult to comprehend the arrogant behavior of India in Nepal. Nehru should have known from his experience in the international arena that a confrontation between two powers creates greater maneuverability for the small nations involved. And certainly Nepal's behavior was predictable given the nationalistic sentiments pervading the subcontinent at the time. Nehru's paternalism and his assurances of defense,[33] which were not even always asked for, boomeranged.[34] An editorial in the *Times of India* on December 6, 1961 explicitly but vainly criticized this policy: "Too much has been said about the 'ancient ties' between the two countries and not enough attention has been paid to the need to promote a two-way traffic of sympathetic understanding." If so, why was Nehru caught off guard and offended by the ungratefulness of Nepal and the fostering of a negative bias against India by Nepal? What is more, was not Nepal on a regional level doing exactly what India had tried to do in its foreign policy on a global scale—that is, exploit the balance of powers system in favor of its particular national interest?

On examining Nehru's policy toward the Hill States, we cannot but be struck by the incompatibility of his strategic concepts and India's circumstances. Unawareness of this incompatibility led to a regional foreign policy that neglected an examination of Nepal's political options and, later, to an unyielding action orientation toward China, which was intended to demonstrate India's power to the Hill States.

Conclusions

Nehru's views on the South Asian region were littered with misperceptions, which supported a low Chinese threat evaluation. These could be summed up in short as follows:

1. South Asia is so important strategically to both super powers that they could not afford a Chinese invasion of India. What is more, the topographical conditions are such as to make a large-scale Chinese attack impractical. Nehru was unable to reevaluate these key misperceptions, which reinforced his belief in India's immunity.

2. These errors derived from his assumption that the British Raj defense policy (the "double-defense-line" concept) was still valid. This relevance gap in the face of changing circumstances was in part responsible for a policy that gave a low priority to the growth of military power and did not change despite dissonant information.

3. The major threat was perceived to be that presented by Pakistan. This error led to the view that India should concentrate its limited military resources against Pakistan. The thaw in relations between China and Pakistan was interpreted as bound to make Pakistan even more dangerous to India and thus reinforced the policy of concentrating military attention on the Pakistani border.

4. As far as India's relations with the Hill States were concerned, Nehru's perception was that the Sino-Indian conflict did not change

the dependence of *any* of these states on India. This erroneous evaluation ignored the fact that the conflict afforded the largest and strategically most important of these states—Nepal—the maneuverability to lessen its dependence on India. Only belatedly did Nehru understand that Chinese recognition of India's dominance in these states was not unconditional but dependent on Sino-Indian relations. Not fully understanding this, he maintained that India's political presence in the Hill States, which represented the double-defense-line concept, ensured India's defense, despite the worsening conflict with China.

These misperceptions led in operational terms to the assumptions that (a) India could keep to its stubborn position regarding the border conflict with China, because China could be discounted as a major military threat; (b) the main threat to India was and remained Pakistan, and that was where India should concentrate its military attention; and (c) India's influence in the Hill States was assured as long as it could prove that it was able to stand up to China's challenge. All this increased India's self-assuredness and reinforced its inflexibility in the face of what, as we shall see, was a militarily superior rival.

The Internal Environment

Assessments of Relative Economic and Military Power

"I have no fear of China, great, and powerful as that country is" (*F.N.*, 7/59, Oct. 1, 1959). This statement of Nehru's accurately reflects his basic evaluation of the power relations between India and China up to October 20, 1962, when events belied it and made a mockery of his consequent unjustified policies.

India's assessment of its strength relative to that of China was based on several assumptions:

1. A full-scale war between China and India was only a very remote possibility; it could not end decisively because of their size and power and, therefore, would be damaging rather than beneficial to the interests of both countries (*Par.*, II, 123).

2. Although unable to prevent Chinese infiltration into Indian territory altogether, given the length of the border and the difficult terrain, the Indian army could contain an all-out attack:[1]

> at no time since our independence, and of course before it, were our defence forces in better condition, in finer fettle and with a background of far greater industrial production in the country to help them than today. I am not boasting about them or comparing them to other countries, but I am quite confident that our defence forces are well capable of looking after our security.[2] (*Par.*, I, 189)

3. Considering the external constraints deriving from China's economic and political dependence on the USSR[3] and internal problems relating to the economic and political crisis that had affected even the army, it was unlikely that China would dare to initiate a major attack against India.

4. This being the case, if in spite of all diplomatic efforts and India's avoidance of military provocation Chinese expansionist plans were not deterred and the status quo ante not reestablished, a more daring policy could be pursued by India with full confidence in the army's ability to cope with any possible Chinese reaction, including a major attack.

What were Nehru's perceptions and what were the misconceptions involved? These are the topics we shall be dealing with here, beginning with an analysis of Nehru's evaluation of his rival, China.

One cannot say that Nehru was unaware of the increasing hostility toward India on the part of China, or that he rejected the possibility of a war between China and India out of hand. He became aware of the hostility especially after the uprising in Tibet, and in light of what seemed to him a growing objection to India's globalistic foreign policy, which supported detente between the United States and USSR and was approved by them. He also mentioned more than once that, historically, periods of strong government and increasing strength had always tempted Chinese leaders to expand. In other words, the Chinese militancy in the dispute with India did not in itself surprise him, but seemed under the circumstances bound to be of a limited nature. Nehru took this position in Parliament both before and after the Kongka Pass incident (*Par.,* I, 155; 183). If there was to be a Sino-India confrontation on a wide scale, it would not take place in the forseeable future, as the Chinese would not willfully desire a confrontation with India. Even as late as 1962, Nehru continued to express this sentiment: "I think we are strong enough to resist and to prevent anybody coming, and I do not think that it can arise because of the world situation apart from our strength and many other reasons" (*Par.,* II, 119).[4]

This assumption was supported by two notions. The first was that the Chinese political and economic crisis, which occurred as a result of its Great Leap Forward, had made Chinese leaders more militant in trying to externalize internal tensions, but at the same time it prevented China from going beyond a limited confrontation.

From his revolutionary experience, Mao had reached the conclusion that methods that had been successful in the past would work in the present. The basis of those methods was a reliance on China's most plentiful resource, the human factor, and only its full utilization could advance the economy at an unprecedented rate in both the industrial and agricultural sectors. The Great Leap Forward was begun in 1957 and reached its peak late in 1958. But this novel experiment proved an economic disaster. The economic and organizational difficulties were accompanied by three years of drought, and 1959–1962 were years of national crisis. The years between 1958 and 1962 saw a decline of 19% in the per capita GNP and a decline of 20% in the overall GNP. In absolute terms, the GNP went down from $74.50 per capita in 1958 to $59.50 in 1962. The decline in the overall GNP was about $7.2 billion (Eckstein, 1972, 111). This resulted in hunger, epidemics, and sharp protests against the Communist regime.[5] But, even more serious, the Great Leap Forward brought about deep divisions of opinion in the top echelons of the Chinese Communist Party. Mao was severely criticized. Leading the opposition was P'eng

Te-huai, the minister of defense.[6] At the Lushan Conference held in July–August of 1959, he declared openly that Mao's economic policy was irresponsible. The power struggle ended in Mao's victory and led to the deposition of the defence minister and the chief of staff and the appointment of two new men—Lin Piao as minister of defense and General Lo Jui-ching, who had been mainly involved with public security and lacked experience in the field—as the new chief of staff. Several high officers were also dismissed. The new appointments were typically political and pointed to the victory of the "reds" over the "professionals" even in the army.

The politico-economic crisis in China was known in the West. In an article by Joseph Alsop in July 1962 in a journal on Chinese affairs, the author prophesied the fall of the Chinese Communist regime or at least a drastic change in its nature. He saw a peasants' revolt, not unknown in China's long history, as probable,[7] stating that: "The truth of the matter is that we now confront a mountain of evidence, all pointing to the conclusion that communist China has somehow been caught in a remorselessly descending spiral. If such a spiral cannot be reversed—and it has not been reversed in the past three years—then some sort of breaking point must logically, indeed unavoidably, be reached as the spiral continues downwards" (Alsop, 1962, 22).[8] At any rate it is clear that the Indian leadership was aware of the difficult situation. At a meeting of infantry commanders in 1962 Lieutenant General B.M. Kaul, the army chief of general staff, presented the view that the Chinese were enmeshed in a series of internal economic and political problems and that both the nation's and the army's morale were low (Dalvi, 1969, 406).

It does seem that the Indian army had information pointing to unrest and low morale in the Chinese army. In late 1961 Tibetan rebels, laying an ambush for a Chinese military convoy, seized a batch of Chinese political-military documents[9] relating to the period of January 1 to August 26, 1961. Containing evidence of increasing difficulties in the Chinese army, they were passed on to Taipei and to Washington, D.C.;[10] considering the United States' support and encouragement of India and its unbending stand vis-à-vis the Chinese, it can be assumed that they were also turned over to Indian intelligence.[11] These documents dealt with the bitterness felt by Chinese soldiers in response to reports from their families describing hunger and rough treatment at the hands of the cadres. One document describes a conversation between a soldier and a political commissar in which the soldier said: "At present what the peasants eat in the villages is even worse than what dogs ate in the past. At that time dogs ate chaff and grain. Now the people are too hungry to work and pigs are too hungry to stand up"; when these comments were rejected by the commissar, he added: "To whom should I listen? I should listen to my superior, but I should also listen to my mother"

(Cheng, 1966, 13). There were a number of desertions by soldiers who returned home to help their families. Other documents deal with the decline in the will to fight, epidemics in the army due to the low quality of the food (Cheng, 1966, 43–45; 295–301); and, the most critical from a military point of view, the decrease in the soldier's fitness. In a report on one of the armored units in the Hanking area, it was said: "The tank sub-unit of the 0100th Army Unit had had meat only twice in their meals from the Spring Festival (February) until the May 1st Festival. . . . Because their food does not have enough nutrition for them the drivers of tanks are losing their physical energy. Many times when a man has driven a tank for more than an hour he becomes dizzy or nauseated" (Cheng, 1966, 584).

Prominent among the economic and political difficulties was the major military threat to China from Taiwan and the United States. This threat was clearly expressed in the 1958 crisis following Communist China's attempt to take control of Quemoy and Matsu as a first step toward the complete liberation of Taiwan, an attempt that failed as a result of Washington's active aid to Taiwan, and was distinguished by the lack of Soviet support for China. The subsequent years were years of tension in the Taiwan strait; they climaxed in 1962 following a series of aggressive statements made by Chiang Kai-shek, which were accompanied by visits from such dignitaries as Averill Harriman and Allen Dulles to Taiwan in the first half of 1962, and the appointment of Admiral Allen Kirk, widely experienced in amphibious operations from World War II, as the U.S. Ambassador to Taiwan (Hinton, 1966, 270–272). China had to reinforce its units facing the Taiwanese shore, and an acute sense of foreboding was felt among Chinese policymakers (Liao and Whiting, 1973). In July 1962 the crisis atmosphere diminished following President Kennedy's conciliatory statement about the defensive nature of U.S. commitments to Taiwan and the renewal of talks in Warsaw. But despite all this, tension continued in the Taiwan strait. These factors brought Nehru to the conclusion that under the prevailing conditions China could not afford to open a second front on India's northern border. Nehru juxtaposed China's political, military, and economic weakness against India's international political strength. But, both economically and militarily, his judgments caused him to take unjustified risks.

On the economic front, despite the difficulties at the beginning of the 1960s, Nehru was cautiously optimistic. India's First Five-Year Plan (1951–1956) enjoyed an unprecedented success; helped by favorable climatic conditions, the rises in national and per capita income were promising.

In contrast, the Second Five-Year Plan (1956–1960), which focused on the industrial sector and neglected agriculture, met with many setbacks. The investment in the public sector was smaller than anticipated; expectations of self-sufficiency in food production proved unrealistic; natural disasters and a bad harvest in 1957–1958 forced India to import grain. Its trade conditions worsened; the prices of imported products rose while export prices failed to keep up. As a result, India was caught in a foreign currency crisis and had to appeal for foreign aid and loans. The rate of population growth exceeded the forecast, and national and per capita incomes rose by much less than hoped for, although there was no recession on the scale of an economic crisis as there was in China. Against that background, in 1961 the Third Five-Year Plan was introduced, focusing again on the agricultural sector (Edwards, 1973, 263; Myrdal, 1968, 272–282). Despite the problems, compared with the Chinese economy this was a period of economic growth for India, though more modest than expected, particularly in the agricultural sector (Bhattacharya, 1974; Frankel, 1978, 216).

But the Chinese viewed it otherwise. To them, India's increasing dependence on foreign aid[12] stood in complete contrast to their own approach of self-reliance[13] and, with the United States as the main source of aid, contradicted nonalignment. India, as they saw it, was not only not advancing toward Socialism, it was rapidly regressing: Capitalism was becoming a rampant social factor and Indian society was becoming increasingly feudal. The result was perceived to be an aggressive attitude on the border question. The failure of the Second Five-Year Plan, combined with the socal regression, was causing widespread unrest in India, which proved a threat to the ruling Congress Party and necessitated the invention of the Chinese scarecrow to maintain it in power (*P.R.,* Dec. 15, 1961, 12).

The Chinese and Indian socioeconomic models became even more competitive as one economy, that of China, was in the midst of a crisis indicating its failure, whereas the other, that of India, although not spectacularly successful, looked as though, with the correcting of past mistakes, it might make significant achievements. Despite the difficulties ahead, Nehru was fairly optimistic in assuming that the worst was behind India as it was approaching the "take-off" stage (*Par.,* I, 235) and that it could thus achieve the socioeconomic goals it set for itself, at the same time serving as a model to other developing countries (Karanjia, 1960, 45–55).

One of the basic conditions underlying India's achievment of the economic goals set forth and Nehru's proof of the superiority of the Indian model was the assurance that all resources be concentrated on economic development, especially industrialization, and not deflected to unproductive areas. To this was added the further claim of an inseparable link between India's Five-Year Plans and the country's defense, repeated in the following thesis:[14] "we have laboured through Five Year Plans and the like, to build up the prosperity of this country as well as its strength because the two are allied. You cannot separate them" (*Par.,* I, 235).[15]

The building up of economic capability was especially important in a prolonged dispute, as the Sino-Indian one promised to be. Due to the acute shortage of foreign exchange,[16] it was impossible to plan wide-scale acquisitions for the renovation and enlargement of the Indian army, despite the constant pressures brought to bear by the chiefs of the armed forces to modernize it and by their complaints about budgetary restrictions.[17] When it seemed to them that Menon, the minister of defense, was not putting their case to Nehru, they did not hesitate to approach him directly, though in vain. Nehru was of the opinion that India could not afford to spend a fortune in foreign exchange to buy military equipment at market prices; nor could it, for political reasons—that is, for nonalignment—pay for arms in political currency. There was therefore only one solution, and that was to make do with local production. But that could be at best only a long-term plan. Furthermore, in the area of domestic manufacture, too, India tended in the direction of heavy armament or "status industry" production, whereas immediate needs, like the manufacture of small automatic arms, were put off. At the same time, there was one short-term problem that Nehru as a nationalistic leader could not ignore, and that, as defined by his rivals, was the creeping annexation of Indian territory by its northern neighbor. Nehru sought a policy that, on the one hand, would be active and bring results, and, on the other, would not mean a full-scale war; and one that, contrary to the claims of his political rivals, would show that the army could take on assignments despite the economic and political limitations on its acquisition needs. The Forward Policy seemed to fulfill those needs.[18]

Nehru, in Parliament and in other forums, insisted that there was no room for worry. The army was improving its performance and capabilities. He was proud of the extent of road building—especially in the eastern sector, which was more defensible (*Par.*, I, 397). In August 1961 he declared in Parliament that in the previous two years the balance of power had been changing in India's favor (*Par.*, II, 21). On that subject he received regular appeasing information from the minister of defense, but also from the chief of general staff (CGS), Lieutenant General Kaul. He rejected any criticism of the Indian soldier's equipment and decided that even though it did not reach the level of that of that of U.S. soldiers, it definitely fulfilled requirements (*Par.*, I, 262). Nehru was especially pleased with the growth in the logistic capabilities of the Indian air force. In October 1960, ten helicopters, twenty-four IL-14 cargo planes, and eight AN-12 cargo planes were purchased. In 1961 another thirteen Bell Helicopters were purchased. At the beginning of 1962, eight additional AN-12s and sixteen MI-4 helicopters were ordered, despite the dissatisfaction of the air force with the performance of the Soviet helicopters in the Himalayan heights (17,000 feet). In June 1962, twenty-nine U.S. Fairchild cargo planes were acquired, and in October

1962, an agreement was signed with the USSR that included the supply of two Mig squadrons and the establishment of an Indian aircraft industry to produce Soviet Migs.[19]

It is no wonder, then, that, considering his confidence in the ability of the Indian army as opposed to the Chinese army's weakness and his belief that the Chinese leadership would not take any extreme military steps against India, Nehru was reinforced in his decision not to make concessions and to go ahead with an active Forward Policy.[20] The policy entailed patrolling and establishing positions in territory claimed by China as well as showing a presence and preventing a creeping take-over by Chinese forces of territory claimed as Indian: "This must be done without getting involved in a clash with the Chinese, unless this becomes necessary in self-defence."[21] Later, in October 1962, he went so far as to instruct the army to evict Chinese forces that crossed the McMahon line on September 8, 1962.

Various events reinforced Nehru's conviction that he had assessed the situation correctly. The Indian army's success in taking over Goa, in which he challenged a "power" like Portugal and provoked the United States and NATO, was proof of its efficiency and India's well-established status in the international arena, which protected it from external dangers. Further evidence of this was seen in a number of bilateral confrontations in which Chinese forces retreated or did not retaliate, the most prominent of them occurring in July 1962 in the Galwan Valley in the western sector: the Chinese army surrounded an Indian position but finally retreated when the Indian forces stood firm, threatening to retaliate against other Chinese positions in the western sector. This policy seemed to be successful as a calculated risk, or as Nehru put it in Parliament: "We have taken the risk and we have moved forward, and we have stopped effectively their further march" (*Par.*, II, 113). The reliability of the deterrent effectiveness of the army and China's political and military weakness seemed thus proven.[22] So far did Nehru's confidence shoot up that while his commanders in the field were begging for additional trained units for operational activity on the northern border, Nehru, in February 1961, sent a brigade of five elite battalions to the Congo (5,650 soldiers) as part off the United Nations Emergency Force.[23]

Against this optimistic evaluation of the relative power of the Indian army and the exaggeration of the impact of internal burdens on the Chinese leadership, what in fact was the reality? Table 5.1 examines the defense budget for the years 1959–1962.

The increase in the defense budget over time was very slow: there was a lack of proportion between need and the rate of investment in defense. In light of this fact, it is unclear as to what lay at the basis of Nehru's assumption at the end of 1961 that there was a marked improvement in the army's capability. Although between 1959 and 1961 the defense budget had grown somewhat, its proportion in

Table 5.1. India's Defense Budget, 1959–1962

Year	Budget (in thousand $)	Defense Budget as % of GNP	% Growth from Previous Year	% of Government Expenditure
1959	583,700	2.01	–	22.0
1960	558,600	1.86	–4.31	21.1
1961	587,900	1.87	5.24	21.1
1962	688,200	2.07	17.06*	27.7

Sources: Adapted from Kavic, 1967, 221; Wilcox, 1964, 129.
*Mostly due to the aircraft purchase deal.

the GNP, which had risen by 8.5% in the same period, declined. Even in 1962, after the Mig deal with the USSR had been signed, the portion of the defense budget in the GNP rose by only 0.06% relative to 1959. The only significant changes in this period were investments in the logistic branch of the air force. The multiplicity of sources of acquisition, however, led to a situation in which the Indian air force in October 1962 had thirty types of planes and severe problems in training technical manpower. At the time of the Chinese attack in October 1962, a large part of the air force was grounded due to a lack of spare parts (Kavic, 1967, 114). As it was assumed that a full-scale war would not break out in the Himalayas, and because conditions there dictated the need for a logistic arm of the air force that could parachute equipment and supplies to isolated posts, the air force was not built or trained to give close support to ground forces.

As a result of the deaf ear turned to the budgetary needs of the army,[24] at the end of 1961 there were in the western sector, instead of the five regular battalions called for, only one regular battalion and two militia battalions, with almost no artillery. As a result, in the summer of 1961, the Indian army maintained in the western sector a series of military posts and positions that, for the most part, except in the Damchuk area, did not even reach the border line claimed by the Chinese as theirs. On the other hand, the Chinese in the western sector had a network of roads and a military force the size of a division, including armored elements. In a letter of April 1961 to the minister of defence, the Indian CGS wrote: "As things stand today it has to be accepted that, should the Chinese wish to carry out strong incursions into our territory at selected points, we are not in a position to prevent them from doing so" (Mankekar, 1968, 146). Along the northern border, the ratio of forces was five to one in favor of the Chinese,[25] whose units were concentrated together, whereas those of the Indian army were scattered over a wide area with hardly any communications or manageable supply routes between them. There were units that could receive supplies only from the air and were dependent on the weather and the pilot's ability to make their drops accurately; ground conditions made the retrieval of supplies inaccurately dropped almost impossible. The air force was thus under constant pressure to overestimate its transport ability. Field officers in the Eastern Command suggested concentrating Indian forces at potential invasion points in the eastern sector.[26] This action would have solved a large number of logistical problems and would have forced the Chinese to fight where India chose to fight. Moreover, sitting on the McMahon line itself allowed maneuver only backward, unless India wished to invade Tibet. But this suggestion, which was both tactically and strategically wise, was not possible politically: the politicians in New Delhi thought it essential to demonstrate a military presence in the entire area.

From a logistic point of view, the army was unable to supply its soldiers with suitable personal equipment and provisions for Himalayan conditions. The Indian soldier was issued a rifle dating from World War I. In 1962 the army lacked 60,000 automatic rifles, 700 anti-tank weapons, at least 2,000 light mortars, artillery ammunition, 5,000 communication sets, 36,000 radio batteries, and 2,000 light trucks. Two tank regiments were paralyzed due to lack of spare parts (Maxwell, 1972, 246).

The level of training and the morale were also in a deplorable state: "The Indian Army was by and large a plain army, trained and equipped accordingly. Its traditional frontier wars had been in the north-west amongst the comparatively low open plains and slopes of the north-west frontier" (Khera, 1968, 157–158). As early as the beginning of the 1950s, army commanders thought that they should prepare for the possibility of an attack from the north, and plans were made to issue a volume dealing with the tactics, strategies, organization, and equipment of the Chinese infantry. Nehru, however, shelved the idea from fear of seeming to provoke China. At the end of 1960, General K.S. Thimayya went to Switzerland to observe the training procedures, organization, and equipment of Alpine divisions. On his return he proposed the establishment of a number of mountain divisions to be supported by a motorized force whose regular base would be at the foot of the Himalayas. This suggestion was rejected by Nehru and Menon on the grounds that Indian could not take on unjustified expenditures. There were few officers trained in mountainous combat—specialization in that area did not bring advancement—as a confrontation with China seemed unlikely. The army in general was suffering from low morale resulting from its neglect by the political echelon. Pay was low and a severe shortage of officers was evident (Kavic, 1967, 96–101). Relations between the senior officers and the minister of defense were strained due to the latter's personality and the contempt with which he regarded the senior officers in general.[27] Appointments were often made on the basis of personal loyalty rather than qualifications. The position of CGS, and later that of the commander of the Fourth Corps, which was meant to take the main brunt of fighting in the northeastern sector, was given in 1961 to Lieutenant General Kaul, a political officer with very little combat experience and who, on his part, appointed his faithful followers, fast known as "Kaul's boys," to a series of key posts at army headquarters. He was closely associated with Nehru, and his appointment was made in the hope of stilling criticism of the politicians. The chief of army staff (COAS) since 1961 was an undistinguished officer, General P.N. Thapar, who posed no threat to the domineering defense minister; he was expected to do faithfully as he was told, unlike his strong-minded predecessor, General K.S. Thimayya, with whom Menon had had many clashes. Tension increased between the senior staff officers and the senior field officers, who felt that the former as well as the politicians were using them as cannnon fodder to further their personal ambitions. When General Daulat Singh, commander of the western sector, pointed out in a letter of August 1962 that the Forward Policy would result in a catastrophe, he was told that it had proven itself as a successful obstacle to Chinese expansionist ambitions (Maxwell, 1972, 271–272).

Nehru, who had a superficial acquaintance with the disputed area, was impressed by the maps shown him by senior army men, on which the dozens of new positions established as part of the Forward Policy had been marked. On the map the terrain did not look as forbidding as in reality, nor did the weather leave its impact. Distances on maps are measured by miles, but in the Himalayas they are measured by days. It was no wonder that Nehru fell victim to his own illusions; even Lieutenant General Kaul, who was a professional military man, was surprised to discover the actual conditions. When he arrived in the northeastern sector after his appointment as commander of the Fourth Corps on October 3, 1962, he made an exhaustive survey of his scattered troops and came to a new evaluation of the Indian army's chances of success, which seemed far less optimistic than they had appeared at his headquarters in New Delhi (Kaul, 1967, 265–384).

On the Chinese side during this period, estimates of China's defense expenditures (1955–1958) show that while declining in terms of its share of total expenditure, they were in fact growing in absolute terms, after shrinking from 6,500 million yuans to 5,000 milliion yuans. In 1959 the defense budget grew to 5,800 million yuans and remained at that level in 1960 (Grossman, 1969, 230). Taking into account the initial quantitative and qualitative military advantage China had over India and the trends in India's military expenditure, as earlier discussed, this advantage was, if anything, not decreasing.

Facing Indian forces in Tibet was an army of about 125,000 men, and later 140,000–150,000,[28] fully equipped with heavy supporting weapons and trained for combat in the arduous conditions of the Himalayas. This army had an effective intelligence network that reported every movement of the Indian army, a well-organized logistics system including a network of roads and freight to the actual combat zone,[29] and front-line food and ammunition storages at Leh, Maramang, and Dzona Dzong. The Chinese army in Tibet had an efficient communications system, including telephone lines to the front; some of its units had combat experience, and all had undergone indoctrination on the subject of the Sino-Indian dispute (Whiting, 1975, 93; Dalvi, 1969, 153–154).

The myth of the Indian soldier's superiority dated back to another time, to the impressive performance of Indian troops in the British army in local conflicts and both world wars (Mason, 1974; Longer, 1974). But considering the obtuse strategy with which it had to cope, its numerical disadvantage, the poor quality of its equipment and its unsuitability, the lack of combat training for the climate and thin atmosphere of the Himalayas, the Indian army stood very little chance against the well-trained, properly equipped Chinese forces commanded by battle-experienced officers,[30] no matter how rich their tradition and fighting spirit. The historian in Nehru overshadowed the realist in his assessment of the field of battle.

The deductions made from the previously mentioned documents on the state of Chinese army morale unfortunately proved irrelevant. Attempts in China to deal with and overcome the problems encountered by Chinese troops were as many and as impressive as the defects and failures. The standard of living was improved and injustices were rectified through better food, vacations, visits, talks with commanders, and so on—a situation that stands in marked contrast to the lack of consideration and passivity shown by the senior headquarters officers in New Delhi toward the plight of the Indian soldiers, who were serving under intolerable conditions without suitable equipment or food.

An additional myth, which did not stand the test of reality, was that of the impressive performance by the Indian army at the taking of Goa. In terms of planning, logistics, even secrecy, Goa was a failure. Lieutenant General Kaul, who was the army quartermaster during the operation, describes the enormous difficulties he had in acquiring 490 rifles, 240 submachine guns, and 400 pairs of shoes (Kaul, 1967, 298) for an army of half a million men. The secret of the success at Goa lay in the insignificance and passivity of the opposition rather than in courageous fighting or brilliant planning and leadership.

The faith that Chinese passivity was an expression of the Indian army's deterrent power in local confrontations during the implementation of the Forward Policy proved unfounded. In fact, considering our earlier description of power relations, it was really the result of

Chinese tolerance and last-minute attempts to reach an agreement[31] as the Chinese warned India: "We must tell the Indian authorities in all seriousness that they had better not miscalculate. If the Indian authroities insist on gambling despite the risk, then it is certain that they will gain absolutely nothing but will simply be picking up a rock only to drop it on their own feet" (*P.R.*, July 27, 1962, 14). The Chinese made it clear that they fully understood the internal logic of the Forward Policy and that their lack of reaction was not weakness but self-control (*P.R.*, July 27, 1962, 12). If they had reacted immediately and sharply, the situation might not have deteriorated into war as it did. Against this background the definition of Brigadier Dalvi, a victim of the false evaluation,[32] is appropriate: "We believed in planning for the best case, and limited the enemy's potential to suit us" (Dalvi, 1969, 123).[33]

The Chinese leadership, aware of the West's great interest in its internal crisis and apprehensive that the West might try to take advantage of its weakness,[34] continued to take firm stands in its foreign policy. It is therefore unclear as to why Nehru should have thought that China's internal weakness would lead to concessions in the face of India's daring policies. On the contrary, it was China's weakness that prevented it from yielding to a state it considered at best a second-rate power, and it certainly would not make concessions to a nation championed by the United States as an alternative model to China in Asia. Furthermore, the Maoists feared that "capitula-tionism" would be exploited by domestic opponents—namely, the Liu Shao-ch'i group (Gurtov and Hwang, 1980, 136–137).

In addition, it seems that Indian intelligence and Nehru himself did not correctly evaluate the developments in China in terms of their influence on the economic, military, or political systems. In reaction to Alsop's article, an expert on Chinese economy, Alexander Eckstein, had already warned against drawing conclusions on the basis of incomplete information: "In approaching this problem it is essential to bear in mind that our information concerning the general economic situation in China and the trends in industrial and agri-cultural production is quite poor since 1957, and most particularly since 1959. None of us, and probably not even the Chinese Communist authorities, know how much food was actually produced on the Mainland in 1958–62" (Eckstein, 1962, 19–20). What is more, despite China's domestic situation, which had deteriorated economically and politically, the regime managed to distribute the economic burden fairly equally and to soften the blow so that its rule was never seriously challenged. It should also be remembered that in the first half of 1962, when the Indian army was becoming increasingly bold, the economic crisis in China had already moved past its peak and a good 1962 harvest was anticipated that would solve a large part of the food shortage.

On the political level, although Mao's status was damaged by the events of 1959, such events indicated just how strong his hold over the party really was. His ability to oust his minister of defense and the chief of staff and to appoint loyal followers instead was an impressive show of strength. The appointment of Lin Piao to the post of minister of defense should have been of concern to India, considering the circumstances of his appointment. His first major assignment was to rally the army around Mao's leadership once again, and, if necessary, to use the army against the opposition. What better way to test an army than through a limited war with India? It can thus be assumed that the ministry of defense in China was a source of militance against India (Jayaux, 1968). Lin Piao himself, like Mao, tended to resolve political problems by military means when the balance pointed in China's favor; the blow would descend suddenly after meticulous preparations over a relatively long period.[35] This personal style and the fact that Lin Piao was a fanatic nationalist almost to the point of xenophobia (Robinson, 1970, 1109–1111), in contrast to Chou En-lai, should have lit a red light with Indian policymakers and warned them that rivalry, and certainly provocative military moves, would finally lead to a clash.

The situation took on special significance with the meeting of the Tenth Plenum of the Eighth Central Committee of the Chinese Communist Party in September 1962. The session adopted Mao's ideological line and emphasized the importance of class war while condemning international revisionism. Joffe (1975, 53–57) claims that, in reality, the line implemented by Liu Shao-ch'i continued to contradict this policy. However, defense was in the hands of Lin Piao, an ardent Maoist; moreover, the internal consensus in the years 1959–1962 reflected, in theory at least, Mao's rigid ideological line, as was evident in China's defense policy. This consensus on China's defense policy probably occurred as a result of the failure of Chou En-lai's moderate line in the face of Nehru's stubborn adherence to his tough line. At that point Chou En-lai could not, and probably did not want to, provoke a confrontation with Mao and Lin Piao on the subject of a limited war that would be supported by the ideological consensus of the Tenth Plenum and that seemed to be only moderately risky. India was not a serious military rival, and the results of limited war with India promised political and ideological gains and the dispatch of a military nuisance.

Even the Chinese preoccupation with the problem of Taiwan was no guarantee of security for India. By July 1962 the Chinese had begun preparations to prevent the formation of two military fronts.[36] They agreed to a U.S. proposal to reopen the Warsaw talks and softened their previously harsh tone toward the United States, Japan, and Taiwan. On the other hand, they began to increase significantly their hostile outbursts against India, outbursts that had been very noticeable since the beginning of 1962.[37] Moreover, India's reliance on the Taiwan problem probably only strengthened its misgivings about the link between Taiwan, the United States, and New Delhi, a claim that was brought up more than once in the Tibetan context. Nehru's condemnation of the international inter-state rivalry, side by side with his use of existing tensions between the USSR and the United States and Taiwan and China to further Indian political and territorial interests, was seen as hypocrisy.

Suspicion against India grew when India was no longer satisfied with the status quo in the northeastern sector and demanded, in addition, that the border run always across the highest range along the watershed line, even if it was north of the McMahon line. Such a claim had geo-strategic logic, particularly in terms of a military confrontation—or, in other words, for someone with dishonest intentions. That is probably why the Chinese crossed the Thag La Ridge, a controlling feature of that part of the border.

Nehru was gravely in error in his unrealistic assessment of the balance of military power and especially regarding the capability of the Indian army. His misperception increased with time. The less favorable to India was the balance of power, the more Nehru overestimated it. Eventually a process of maladaptation set in.[38] Nehru failed to adapt to information that the Chinese tried to get through to him or that arrived via Indian intelligence. Thus, the evaluation of an Indian observer is understandable: "It is now clear that the 1962 debacle was more a failure in intelligence assessment than a failure in intelligence collection and reporting" (Subrahamanyam, 1970b, 437).

The misconception of the balance of power and of the enemy's intentions, as well as the combination of the dynamics of maladaptation and nonadaptation, contributed significantly to Nehru's unrealistically low threat perception.

Perception of Domestic Politics

Since its independence, the Indian political system had followed the British party system, but it was essentially a dominant one-party system. From the very first elections in 1951–1952, the National Congress Party completely dominated the Upper (Lok Sabha) and the Lower (Rajya Sabha) Houses. This was not a new phenomenon, as the party had dominated the political scene since its inception in 1885. It was a centrist, nationally organized party, the leadership of which came from an elite usually belonging to the English-educated upper castes. Actually, the Congress Party "contributed" a fair number of leaders to the opposition.[39] It maintained its dominance because it was identified with the struggle for independence. The names of its leaders, Gandhi and Nehru, were almost synonymous with India itself, and its ideology had a universal appeal.[40]

Table 5.2. Election Results in the Lower House, 1951–1962

Party	1951–1952 Elections			1957 Elections			1962 Elections		
	% of Voters	No. of Seats	% of Total Seats	% of Voters	No. of Seats	% of Total Seats	% of Voters	No. of Seats	% of Total Seats
Congress Party[a]	45.0	364	74.4	47.78	371	75.1	44.72	361	72.6
Jana Sangh	3.1	3	0.6	5.93	4	0.8	6.44	14	2.8
Swatantra[b]	–	–	–	–	–	–	7.89	18	3.6
Communist Party of India	3.3	16	3.3	8.92	27	5.5	9.96	29	5.9
Socialist parties	16.4	21	4.3	10.41	19	3.8	9.33	18	3.6
Other parties[c]	16.4	44	9.0	7.57	34	6.9	9.39	37	7.5
Independents	15.8	41	8.4	19.39	39	7.9	12.27	20	4.0
Total	100.0	489	100.0	100.0	494	100.0	100.0	497	100.0

Source: Adapted from Palmer, 1975, 35.

Notes: The incompatibility between the percentage of voters for a certain party and its number of seats is due to the single-member constituency system. Decimals have been rounded upwards.

[a] Only the Congress Party had candidates in every one of the states of the Federation.
[b] The Swatantra Party appeared on the political scene in 1959 and first participated in elections in 1962.
[c] The "other parties" are local rather than national.

The Congress Party's control of the national political system found full expression on both national and state levels. Table 5.2 presents the national aspect.

The standing of the Congress Party in the various states comprising the Indian Federation can be seen in Table 5.3.

An analysis of the data in the preceding tables shows that in the 1957 elections the Congress Party maintained its majority in Parliament. In the elections of 1962 there was a slight drop in its representation, but it still held an absolute majority with over 70% of the House members as in the past. On the local level, despite the fact that in 1957 most states registered an increase for the Congress Party compared to 1951–1952 and that 1962 showed a slight decline in its strength, the Congress Party maintained its superiority. On the local level, however, its representation in state assemblies was in most cases under 50%.

Under these circumstances, it is understandable that the party leaders wielded enormous power and that Parliament was relatively unimportant in decisionmaking. Although one cannot doubt Nehru's

Table 5.3. Congress Party Achievements in State Elections, 1951–1962

State	1951–1952 Elections		1957 Elections		1962 Elections	
	% of Seats	% of Voters	% of Seats	% of Voters	% of Seats	% of Voters
Andhra Pradesh	34.33	31.51	61.75	41.72	59.00	47.25
Assam*	72.38	43.91	67.62	52.35	75.24	48.25
Bihar*	74.13	41.92	66.04	41.91	58.18	41.35
Gujarat	90.38	55.93	74.24	56.40	73.38	50.84
Haryana	83.60	40.31	70.91	45.85	57.41	40.42
Kerala	38.28	35.75	34.13	37.85	50.00	34.42
Madhya Pradesh	76.56	44.53	80.56	49.83	49.31	38.54
Madras	47.83	38.41	73.66	45.34	67.48	46.14
Maharashtra	80.79	47.14	51.52	45.31	81.44	51.23
Mysore	77.10	51.28	72.60	52.08	66.35	50.22
Orissa	47.86	38.85	40.00	38.26	58.57	43.28
Punjab	53.64	30.73	82.56	48.51	56.98	45.74
Rajastan	53.68	39.71	67.61	45.13	50.00	39.98
Uttar Pradesh*	90.70	47.93	66.52	42.42	57.90	36.33
West Bengal*	61.75	38.42	60.32	46.14	62.30	47.29

Source: Kothari, 1970, 174.
*State bordering China.

democratic orientation, Parliament was no more than a forum for intellectual debate or for the legitimization of political and strategic decisions already made by Nehru himself or with his colleagues in the Congress Party and the cabinet. The impotence of Parliament was especially noticeable in the area of foreign policy, which had always been a marginal issue in Indian politics and in which Nehru's single-mindedness had been most evident since the death of Sardar Patel in 1951. Patel had been Nehru's only serious rival and had formed with him what was known as a duumvirate, but even in his time Nehru had assumed responsibility for matters of foreign policy and defense. Nehru's obsession with foreign policy had begun in the 1920s when, during the struggle for independence, he was the only one who took a profound and consistent interest in the subject and in his writings had developed a comprehensive foreign policy conception. Now, under the conditions arising from the structure of the electoral and parliamentary systems, issues of foreign policy and defense became even further removed from the opposition. In these matters, Parliament generally functioned as no more than a rubber stamp.

The Tibetan issue provoked a violent political storm in India and a crushing attack by most factions of the opposition against Nehru's cautious and moderate stance. Leading the attack was Jayaprakash

Narayan, a highly respected elderly politician with great public influence. He condemned Nehru's position as cowardly and immoral and demanded that India take the initiative and raise the matter at the United Nations, a view that Nehru completely rejected.[41] As the Sino-Indian dispute escalated, the attacks of the opposition became more bitter.[42] They aroused a sympathetic echo in the right wing of the Congress Party as well. Although on a personal level Nehru was not spared and came under fire, to a great extent the main target was Krishna Menon, the minister of defense,[43] who was considered by some to be a crypto-Communist. His inability to communicate with his senior officers surfaced following the resignation of the Chief of Army Staff (COAS), General Thimayya, at the end of 1959. The affair was raised in Parliament, although under Nehru's pressure General Thimayya remained in office. The attacks on Menon also pointed to the fact that although Nehru saw the problem as one of foreign policy in the main, the opposition considered it to be a major defense and security problem; as one member of Parliament, Mahanty, stated in the first stages of the parliamentary debate: "We are not concerned with the foreign policy matter. We are concerned more with the defence matter" (*Par.,* I, 127). Out of step with the other opposition parties in this respect was the Communist Party of India, which in principle agreed with Nehru's basic views on the dispute, although not always with his tactics.

But before examining Nehru's perception of the threat to his position in terms of the internal Indian political system, I should like to survey the general positions of the main opposition parties in some detail.

The Socialist Party (PSP) opposed Nehru's moderate approach to the Tibetan question and demanded positive action. It rejected the 1954 agreement, which recognized China's status in Tibet, and did not confirm Chinese recognition of India's borders as India envisioned them. Party leaders demanded a firm and uncompromising attitude toward China. Its prominent men were Asoka Mehta, Acharya Kripalani (who retired from the party in 1960) and Jayaprakash Narayan, party leader until the mid-1950s who then retired, as he claimed, from political life altogether. Between the 1957 and 1962 elections, the Socialist Party was the third largest party in India.

The Swatantra Party, founded in 1959, was a Capitalist-conservative party with a strong anti-Communist orientation. In foreign policy it supported cooperation with the West and with Pakistan to defend the subcontinent. Its leaders, such as Rajagopalachari, demanded the elimination of the nonalignment policy and were close in their world view to that of the right wing of the Congress Party.[44] This party took part in elections for the first time in 1962; in view of the failure of the Second Five-Year Plan and the slow progress of the third, Nehru feared its potential success.[45] In reality, it became the third largest party, with eighteen members of Parliament, or 3.6% of all members of the Lower House.

The third important party was the Jana Sangh, a Hindu nationalist party that opposed Nehru's foreign policy. At the party's Eighth Congress at Nagpur in 1960, a resolution was passed to the effect that the government had failed to repel Chinese aggression and was oblivious to its inherent dangers: "In short, India's China policy has been a complete and dismal disaster" (quoted by Kishore, 1969, 98). Throughout the years 1951 to 1962, the party grew in strength. It increased its parliamentary membership from three in the 1951 election to fourteen in 1962. Its achievements were even more impressive on the local level in several states.[46]

All three parties were at odds with Nehru's China policy. Primarily, they saw the need for India to take a firmer stand in the dispute with China over Tibet and the border issue. Various suggestions of military retaliation were made, such as bombing from the air. In addition, the parties rebuked Nehru for his reluctance to accept massive military aid from the West for fear of affecting nonalignment, by pointing out that nonalignment was irrelevant in this matter and that Nehru's government had not proved that it could rally support for the Indian cause in the Third World. Furthermore, they expressed their complete lack of confidence in Nehru's loyal protégé, Krishna Menon, and demands were made that Nehru take the defense portfolio himself. Later, following King Mahendra's coup, they criticized the deterioration of relations with Nepal, which caused that state to approach China, and warned against India's growing isolation and the resulting strategic threat looming ahead.

But the most important opposition party, both in terms of seats in Parliament and of the threat it was seen to pose to the political system, was the Communist Party of India. Its adherence to a doctrine of a violent road to power during the 1940s was still vividly remembered by India's leaders. As mentioned, one of Patel's greatest fears, expressed in a letter to Nehru of November 1950, was that China's invasion of Tibet would give the Communists a logistic backyard that they had not enjoyed in the past. In the 1957 election, they emerged as the main opposition party with twenty-seven seats and in 1962 improved their position further with twenty-nine seats. From 1951 to 1962 the party's star was on the rise, whereas the power of the other Socialist parties seemed to be declining: between 1951/1952 and 1962 they lost seats, going from twenty-one to eighteen; their percentages of votes also fell from 16.4% of all voters to 9.33%, whereas the Communist Party captured three times as many votes, a faster rate of growth than any other party in India.

This state of affairs caused the party's representatives in Parliament to feel that in order to maintain its political momentum, and despite the fact that the adversary was a Communist country, it should adopt a nationalist line regarding the border dispute. True, on the Tibetan issue these representatives had taken a pro-Chinese stand, but now they could claim that the situation was different since India's territorial integrity was at stake. In September 1959 a split occurred between the nationalist and conservative factions of the party, with the secretary general taking a middle path. These developments were in actual fact a reflection and outgrowth of the drastic change undergone by the party in the mid-1950s, when the USSR called on Communist parties to accept the parliamentary road to power in place of violence.[47] The formalization of this attitude can be found in the Congress of Amritsar, where a new Party Constitution was ratified, stating: "The Communist Party of India strives to achieve full democracy and Socialism by peaceful means" (quoted by Varkey, 1974, 11). This was diametrically opposed to the "Calcutta Thesis" of 1948, which had rejected the idea of a united front with Nehru and had called for a violent revolution. The failure of rural and urban guerrilla violence led to the adoption of parliamentary procedure as a *tactic*. In 1956 the party, which was confused by the Panch Sheel Agreement and the Soviet-Indian thaw, adopted the conception that in foreign policy Nehru was already on the right track, whereas in domestic matters the party's aim should be to cooperate with the Socialist opposition parties to speed up the process of radicalization already beginning.

As a result of Chinese behavior and the need to explain this behavior to its electorate, the party emphasized both in Parliament and at meetings of its regional committees that Socialist nations such as China would not act aggressively. It made a clear distinction between events in Tibet, where reactionary landowners were acting against the interests of the people and the Chinese State, and the relations between China and India in general (Nizami, 1971, 241–242). It was stressed that the border dispute was only a local matter the likes of which had been known before among Socialist states. The party secretary, upon his return from talks with the Chinese leadership, quoted Mao as saying: "The stream of Indian-Chinese friendship could never dry up but would keep flowing, strong and serene."

Three factions developed within the party: the Nationalist trend, members of which comprised most of the party representatives in Parliament, as well as the leaders of the party in states such as Kerala and Maharashtra, and who supported Nehru's foreign policy; the Internationalist trend, which demanded acceptance of the Calcutta declaration of November 1959 recognizing both the Mcmahon line and the political and adminstrative reality, that is, China's actual possession of parts of Aksai Chin. This trend, at whose head stood B.T. Ranadive, party secretary in the 1940s, and the main strength of which lay in West Bengal and Punjab, claimed that further support of the government position would only strengthen its reactionary tendencies; and, finally, the central trend, with party Secretary Ajoy

Ghosh as its leader, which took a pragmatic view, changing according to circumstances and the need to keep the party united.[48]

Even then, at the end of the 1950s and the beginning of the 1960s, the Communist Party's position differed from that of other opposition parties. China was not accused by it of aggression or blamed for the Kongka Pass incident of October 1959. Nor did it demand China's immediate and unconditional evacuation of the territory it had occupied. The party sharply criticized the "warmongers" among the opposition who demanded a firmer Indian stand, and it was the only opposition party to support the Nehru–Chou En-lai meeting, which was to take place in Arpil 1960. Thus, in their action orientation the Communists were very close to Nehru's own position.

The Nationalist trend in the party was reinforced in its position by the Soviet leadership. A Soviet delegation to the Party's Sixth Congress, headed by Mihail Suslov, succeeded in April 1961 in getting adopted the line suggested by S.A. Dange, the leader of the Nationalist trend (Van Eeckelen, 1964, 184).

The party's Nationalist position paid off. In the 1962 election, in which one of the major issues was the government's position on the Sino-Indian question, the party's strength increased. During the campaign, it even went so far as to support Congress Party candidates thought of as "progressive" in districts where it had no candidate of its own. The Communist member of Parliament, Dange, who was appointed party chairman after the death of Secretary Ghosh, declared at a mass rally on the eve of the election that it was less important that he be elected than Krishna Menon (Varkey, 1974, 165). This support of government policy continued at the party's National Council in 1962, where Nehru was praised for his attempts to reach a settlement. The crossing of the Thag La Ridge and Chinese negotiations with Pakistan provoked a sharp response from Dange, who said that when a Socialist state showed signs of becoming too adventurous, it was the duty of other Socialist states to restrain it, even by force.

An informal axis with a clear majority, the Congress Party and the Communist Party against the others, formed in Parliament. Hence, the question is raised as to why Nehru thought it advisable to adopt an apologetic tone in the parliamentary debates on the Chinese question. Why did Nehru, who considered himself a brilliant diplomat, agree to reveal his exchange of letters and talks with the Chinese government, and how did this revelation express itself in bilateral Sino-Indian relations?

The answer to these questions lies, I believe, in an understanding of Nehru's perception of the threat to his status on the one hand, and to his world view on the other, from the parliamentary opposition and extra-parliamentary opposition such as various pressure groups.

The strongest pressure group was the right wing of the Congress Party itself. There had been a continuous struggle between right and left within the party ever since independence. The right wing had not been particularly successful until the surfacing of the border dispute with China. The internal opposition to Nehru's policy in the Congress Party was represented in Parliament by an impressive array of influential dignitaries, headed by Pant, the home minister; Morarji Desai, the minister of finance; S.K. Patil, the minister of food and agriculture; and to a certain extent, even Jagjivan Ram, the minister of railways. These men and their supporters, the backbenchers, saw in the dispute an opportunity to attack foreign policy on the basis of national defense and Nehru himself via the unpopular Menon, who had no political base of his own. Nehru saw in the attacks on his foreign policy by this elite a covert blow against his domestic policies[49] due to the close link he perceived between the two, and he feared the creation of a coalition between the right wing of his own party and those opposition parties whose economic world views were close, such as the Swatantra. Thus, Nehru's China policy became a testing ground for both foreign and domestic policies; as he said: "The critics of that foreign policy, you will find—the major critics— are critics of our domestic policy also. They are tied up—the two things—and I can understand it" (*Par.,* I, 252). At all costs, he had to prevent an alignment between the right wing of his party and the opposition,[50] and this he attempted to do by convincing his rivals that he was taking an unbending position on the Chinese issue. The matter was so pressing that at the time of Chou En-lai's visit in April 1960, Nehru had no choice but to have him meet G.B. Pant and M. Desai[51] to persuade them that he was not making secret concessions. Nehru's fear for his position was so great that he rejected the package deal, proposed by Chou En-lai, to recognize the McMahon line in return for Indian recognition of Chinese sovereignty over parts of Aksai Chin, saying: "If I give them that I shall no longer be Prime Minister of India. I will not do it" (Maxwell, 1972, 166).

It was not only his political status that Nehru saw as endangered. The things he cared about most, his personal charisma, the adoration of the masses, and his ability to influence them and create ties of affection and trust between themselves and him, which was one of his most important emotional-personal assets, also hung in the balance. The press, too, by failing to distinguish between fact and fiction, acted as a very powerful pressure group, arousing anti-Chinese and chauvinistic public feelings through an ongoing and dramatic coverage of events along the borders: "I think our newspapers sometimes rather exaggerate rumours which they get in Kalimpong Bazaar, in Kathmandu Bazaar or some other bazaar" (*Par.,* I, 265). To prevent the erosion of his charisma, Nehru felt that he had to prove that he was not giving up Indian territory and, after he was attacked in the press and in Parliament for not telling the people the truth, that he had nothing to hide in his policy.[52] He tried to provide this proof by making public the correspondence between the Indian and Chinese governments. The first White Paper was laid before Parliament on September 7, 1959.

In the 1962 elections, which Nehru saw as a personal test on both the political-ideological and emotional levels (*Par.,* II, 35–36), an additional pressure group demanded consideration. Although difficult to define exactly, it comprised the northern Indian states, bordering on Tibet: Assam, West Bengal, Bihar, and Uttar Pradesh.[53]

Bihar and Uttar Pradesh were (and are) the largest states in the Indian Federation and as such had especially heavy political clout. It should also be remembered that the most important bastion of the Congress Party lay in North India and that Nehru's and Pant's political base was Uttar Pradesh, the largest state. In Bihar, and especially in Uttar Pradesh, the party was on the decline. Whereas in the 1951/52 elections in Uttar Pradesh 90.7% of the voters voted for the Congress Party, in 1957 only 66.52% did so. In the northern states, the border problem was also an acute emotional issue. Because they had absorbed the stream of refugees from Tibet in 1959, as a result of their proximity, they were particularly aware of the Chinese military threat and of their vulnerability to economic problems resulting from the drastic decline in trade with Tibet following the revolt and the deterioration of Sino-Indian relations.[54] Between April and June 1959, for example, the amount of trade between India and Tibet declined from 8,198,000 rupees to 2,682,000 rupees (*Par.,* I, 76).

A pressure group existed on the bureaucratic level as well. It was composed of the senior officials of the Ministry of External Affairs (MEA) and a number of the senior staff officers at army headquarters in New Delhi, who demanded a stiffer attitude toward China. This group persuaded Nehru that China would be reluctant to react to India's Forward Policy, and that the army was capable of handling Chinese forces if need be. There was, in opposition to these views, a group of senior officers who thought that the Indian army was far from ready to tackle the Chinese army and that any policy leading to a confrontation in the short term should be avoided.[55] Their influence, however, was minor.[56]

In addition, there were the activities of ethnic groups in North India where the government had not yet succeeded in enforcing law and order. In 1960 a settlement was reached with the Nagas about the establishment of the Naga State. But Nehru was not convinced that the arrangement would satisfy the more extreme elements (*Press,* I, 13). He was apprehensive about the prospect that the worsening relations with China could lead to that country's involvement with, and support of, the irredentist groups,[57] a situation that Patel had warned against as early as 1950.[58] A hint of such a possibility was apparent in a polemical article published in China in May 1959, which contained a response to Nehru's statement that India's reaction to events in Tibet was an outcome of its historical, emotional, and ethnic ties with that nation. The Chinese commented: "This kind of logic is fraught with obvious dangers, because if such logic can stand, then when Tibet has taken the road of democracy and Socialism, the road of strength and prosperity, could not a 'People's Committee to Support Assam' and a 'Committee for Uttar Pradesh Affairs' be set up to interfere in the affairs of India's state of Assam or Uttar Pradesh under the pretexts of ancient religious and cultural links?" (*P.R.,* May 12, 1959, 13). The problem was intensified by internal unrest pervading Assam in the northeast due to the language question, which caused Nehru a great deal of anxiety.

The lobbying from all sides kept Nehru in constant fear of losing control. He was afraid, furthermore, that the atmosphere of cold war surrounding the militancy and clamor against China on the part of Parliament and the press, the mass demonstrations taking place in the large cities following events in Tibet, and the subsequent border incidents brought to public knowledge would seriously damage relations between the two countries. He was also aware of possible misunderstandings arising from the Chinese view of Indian democratic processes (*Par.,* I, 53–54). Chou En-lai's strong response to Nehru in a letter of September 8 gave cause for concern: "Many political figures and propaganda organs in India have seized the occasion to make a great deal of anti-Chinese utterances, some even openly advocating provocative actions of an even larger scale, such as bombarding Chinese territory" (*W.P.,* II, 32). Nehru's anxiety increased when it seemed that the Chinese government believed that the Indian government had initiated the wave of anti-Chinese protest and that the very style of the protest itself expressed the government's sentiments and intentions. In his answer to Chou En-lai, Nehru took care to deny any such allegation firmly: "to allege that the Government of India built up pressure on China in any manner is a complete misreading of the facts of the situation. It is also based on complete misunderstanding of the constitutional procedures under which the Government, Parliament and the press function in India" (*W.P.,* II, 44).

These fears weighed on Nehru to such an extent that he repeatedly called on members of Parliament and the media to take a more moderate view, yet not to sacrifice major issues on the altar of trivialities, thereby avoiding the creation of an atmosphere of suspicion and distrust from which there could be no return. Following a demonstration in which Mao's picture was pelted with eggs and tomatoes and that led to a stinging rebuke from the Chinese Embassy in New Delhi (*W.P.,* I, 70), which claimed that the government was not doing its best to curb such phenomena and actually secretly condoned them, Nehru vehemently condemned the vulgar tone of the public protest (*Par.,* I, 33).

Nehru was faced with a difficult dilemma. On the one hand, he was aware at a very early stage of the enormous damage being done to Sino-Indian relations by the press and its impact on the public mood (*F.N.*, 8/59, Oct. 16, 1959) and thus begged the press "to help in preventing people getting excited" (*Press*, I, 46). On the other hand, for ethical reasons, he could not restrict press freedom, particularly after the Chinese issue had become a nationally sensitive issue, and he began to fear that he would lose touch with the people. And so, ironically, with the doubtful claim that the press was not anti-Chinese but pro-Indian, Nehru was obliged to defend the very pressure group that was in no small measure sabotaging his attempts to temper the Sino-Indian dispute (*W.P.*, V, 159).

Nehru then found himself in a situation in which, despite his personal charisma and the dominance of his party,[59] he was concerned about the possible erosion of his unique emotional and political standing in the eyes of the Indian public and thus reluctantly succumbed to various pressure groups. His largest concession was to agree to the publication of the correspondence between the two governments, in his belief that this action would regain the confidence of the people and that he could meet and combat the resultant difficulties with his usual political and diplomatic skills.

This concession increased the power of the legislative branch of the government at the expense of the executive branch, thereby narrowing Nehru's options considerably. Moreover, as the concession had not been decided upon in cooperation with the government of China and because it went against all diplomatic customs and rules, it raised doubts as to the Indian government's discretion and served for the Chinese as an indicator of the great power wielded by anti-Chinese elements in Indian society. It also devalued Nehru's promises of accepting the status quo in Tibet as a fait accompli.

An additional factor to be considered was that the correspondents now had to remember that their letters were no longer confined to governments but would be scrutinized by the public at both the local and international levels. Considering the political systems of China and India, it was clear that most of the resulting limitations and disadvantages accrued to Nehru. The language of the documents became tougher and less flexible, and it was almost impossible to retract statements made with an eye for the public's direction. The open debate and Nehru's need to respond (in Parliament and at press conferences) to matters discussed in the letters brought with them ill-considered statements rashly made.[60] Without realizing it, Nehru became the hostage of the opposition, within the Congress Party and the parliamentary opposition outside his party, the media, and public opinion. As a result, his position became increasingly inflexible, overrun with rationalizations. India's major policymaker inadvertently became the spokesman of the opposition and public opinion in India, paying only lip service to the need to meet and talk with the other side.

Under the circumstances, it was a serious error to hold the 1960 talks in New Delhi instead of Rangoon, as suggested by Chou En-lai. The constant hostile pressure of the hawkish faction of the Congress Party, the opposition, the press, and the public in New Delhi made it impossible to hold constructive discussions. Nehru's maneuverability was so restricted that he could not take the simple and essential step of returning his ambassador to Peking; moreover, to K.P.S. Menon's suggestion[61] that he appoint an ambassador, he answered that at the time (just before the 1962 elections) he could not take the chance (Menon, 1963).

It is interesting to note that, although it is doubtful whether Nehru realized how serious his problem was, the Chinese were aware of his loss of maneuverability. At the beginning of 1959, China still distinguished between Nehru and other political leaders in India, saying: "Prime Minister Nehru is different from many persons who obviously bear ill-will towards China. He disagrees somewhat with us on the Tibet question. But in general he advocates Sino-Indian friendship" (*P.R.,* May 12, 1959, 15). But this distinction gradually disappeared following the failure of the 1960 talks, and Nehru himself came under fire for his policies. A polemical article published a few days after the Chinese attack explained by stating: "the class nature and economic status of the Indian big *bourgeoisie* and big landlords determine that the Nehru government depends on and serves imperialism more and more" (*P.R.,* Nov. 2, 1962, 15).[62]

The results of the 1962 elections, which the Chinese followed closely,[63] deepened their distrust. Parties such as the Jana Sangh and the Swatantra gained in power, calling for a firmer attitude in dealing with the Chinese, and the Chinese saw the Congress Party as responsible for the rise of feudal elements (*P.R.,* Mar. 23, 1962, 11). At the same time, they watched with pleasure the defeat of several men who were outstanding in their negative attitude toward China, such as Asoka Mehta, one of the leaders of the Praja Socialist Party (PSP); A.B. Vajpayee, a Jana Sangh leader; J.B. Kripalani, an independent who was supported by the PSP, Swatantra, and Jana Sangh; and even Dange, a leader of the nationalist faction of the Communist Party. They were pleased at the election of Menon in Bombay (where he defeated Kripalani), indicating that there was still a spark of hope for India.

For Nehru, as was already pointed out, the surge of conservatism was a source of great worry. Menon, his right-hand man, in order to beat Kripalani at his own game, had adopted a fierce campaign line on the Chinese problem. Thus, slowly, due to internal, partially emotional pressures, Nehru hardened his position against China. But he did not see that according to Chinese ideology the interrelationship between foreign and domestic policies was crucial, nor that the behavior of his government could be explained in these terms: "With any country, a given foreign policy is necessarily the continuation of a given domestic policy" (*P.R.,* Nov. 2, 1962, 17). And if to Nehru the election results reflected the will of the people for a stronger stand on the issue of China, to the Chinese government it looked like a distortion of the will of the people and an expression of "the relative strength of various classes in India today" (*P.R.,* Mar. 23, 1962, 12).[64]

In the face of growing opposition, Nehru tried desperately to gain legitimacy for his China policy. He tried to make public opinion and Parliament realize that his policy was consistent both with national interests and India's traditional moral values, and that the means he was using to achieve his objectives were the proper ones. This was easy for Nehru given his special position as the "expert" on foreign policy. The cognitive legitimacy of his policy rested largely on his projected image of past successes and experience and on his reputation as one of the leading diplomats in international politics.

As for moral legitimacy,[65] Nehru relied on the fact that he was Gandhi's closest disciple, the man chosen by this saintly figure for leadership. He spared no effort to remind the public again and again of his relationship with Gandhi, in public debates and interviews relating to his China policy.

However, on the intrapersonal level the desirability of the policy and the means used were problematic in that both involved contradictions among some of Nehru's core values and beliefs. For this reason, he was forced to perform a cognitive balancing act in the hope of eliminating such contradictions.

Moreover, because of India's unique position in world affairs— and Nehru's position in particular—Nehru tried to gain legitimacy for his China policy not only from the Indian public but also from his other constituencies, including the international community at large. Thus, contradictions between what was considered legitimate by the Indian public and that of international public opinion were bound to come to the fore, and these inconvenient contradictions could be handled only by means of a value trade-off. As with many other aspects of the situation, here, too, a realistic definition and trade-off seem to have been too painful to execute.

Nehru, although correct in his assessments of the dangers posed by the militancy of political opponents and pressure groups, fed such danger himself by granting concessions and believing that he could stop himself from going too far. Partially motivated by emotional-egotistical drives, he allowed himself, by degrees, to be led by public opinion. His overestimation of his ability to control the opposition if he gave in to it to some extent was disappointed without his being aware of it. He was even less conscious of the degree of hostility this failure generated on the Chinese side and of how this misinterpretation was finally transformed into a perception of very real threat. Perhaps his decision to take a less flexible stand on China stemmed partially from the support of the Communist Party, which also rejected as unlikely the idea of a full-scale war with China. China, however, identified most of the Indian Communist Party leadership as camp-followers of the USSR and did not bring the party up to date on its intentions.

Thus, a situation was created in which Nehru accurately saw the relevance of Indian domestic power relations to his Chinese policy but misjudged and overevaluated the relative operative strength of his rivals. Certainly after the death of Pant there was no political leader in India (in or out of the Congress Party) who could threaten Nehru's position. But by that time Nehru was a prisoner of the same public he was supposed to be leading.[66] The dominant perceptual gap in this situation was an evaluation gap that grew as Nehru's control of the situation diminished. The combination of the evaluation gap with a process of maladaptation led to an unawareness of the severity with which the Chinese leadership viewed the domestic developments in India and their relevance to the Sino-Indian dispute.

Conclusions

Two major internal environmental factors loomed large in Nehru's misperceptions. The first was his evaluation of India's military might relative to that of China. His misperceptions on this issue were two-fold:

1. Nehru believed that China was so concerned with the U.S.-Taiwanese threat that it could not afford a second front. This evaluation gap, with regard to the impact of the Taiwanese threat, was not corrected over time and brought about the underevaluation of Chinese warnings regarding their possible reactions to India's Forward Policy.
2. Nehru was oblivious to the relative weakness of the Indian army, to the inadequacy of its logistics, numbers, and training, and to the impact of all of these factors on its ability to carry out India's Forward Policy in the face of a massive Chinese military reaction. This perceptual blindness, which became even more serious over time and reached ridiculous proportions, strengthened the misperception that war between China and India was impossible since neither side could win a decisive military victory.

The second aspect of the internal environment had to do with domestic politics. Here, too, Nehru's misperceptions were two-fold:

1. Nehru exaggerated the power of the opposition within his party and other opposition circles, assuming that this power might endanger his personal and political stature.
2. Given that assumption, he adopted a policy of conceding to opposition demands on the China issue, at the same time exaggerating his ability to maintain maneuverability and freedom of decision.

This evaluation of the domestic political scene was part of Nehru's perceptual framework up to the outbreak of the war. He failed to realize that he had become entangled in his own web as a result and had reached a point of no return. This failure was related also to his misperceptions regarding the balance of power. He assumed, on the basis of the perceived adequacy of Indian military power, that conceding opposition demands would not involve too great a danger of Chinese military reaction.

6

The Bilateral Environment

Legal Perceptions

It is not my intention to discuss the legal aspects of the Sino-Indian dispute or to take a stand on them.[1] But they are relevant to our discussion insofar as the Sino-Indian conflict represented a collision between two essentially different patterns of legal thought. Legal claims were crucial in the crystallization of Nehru's position. After the Indian team on the Sino-Indian joint committee on the subject had presented its findings, Nehru concluded that the reliability and superiority of India's legal claims in the eastern and western sectors were beyond any doubt:[2] "it appears to us, and I should imagine to any impartial reader, that the Chinese case had little substance, while our case was established beyond any possibility of doubt" (*Par.,* II, 7). This conclusion calls for an examination of (a) the extent to which there was symmetry, or a lack of it, between India and China in their basic perceptions concerning international law and the dispute; (b) the extent to which there was a similarity, or lack of it, in the evaluation of the relevance of legal claims as a basis for a solution to the problem; and (c) how far the basic legal claims, insofar as they were different, influenced the evaluation of the situation, the sense of self-righteousness, and the feeling of injustice on the part of the enemy.

Indian legal claims can be divided into a number of categories:

1. Claims concerning the question of agreements not ratified by the central government of China, such as the Simla Agreement, which was ratified only by the Tibetan government.
2. Claims dealing with the question of what constitutes tacit acquiescence. For example, if the activities and declarations of one side, in this case India, concerning the subject of sovereignty over a disputed area were not met with verbal objection from the other side, in this case China, does this signify an admission of recognition on the part of China? From the Indian point of view, China's silence following Nehru's

statement in 1950 that the McMahon line constituted India's northwestern border, and the fact that the topic was not brought up in the 1954 and 1956 talks, was open to interpretation as a tacit agreement (*W.P.*, I, 48).
3. Claims concerning historical rights over territories or the accepted traditional border, or the exercise of de facto control over a disputed area.
4. Claims based on the idea of a natural borders. These were claims that had a topographical basis and held that the border line should follow the features of the terrain, such as the watershed line, mountain ridges, and so on.
5. Claims dealing with the problem of the extent to which changes of regimes legitimize the cancellation of agreements. The Indian view, of course, was that changes of regime did not justify the cancellation of existing treaties.
6. Claims connected to the issue of the extent to which changes in objective conditions, existing during the signing of the agreement, could raise questions regarding its legality in the present—in this particular case, the change in China's international position from a weak state to a power able to assert itself.

The Indian government relied on agreements and documents supporting its claim[3] that the boundary in the eastern, central, and western sectors, between China and India, as defined by it, was the recognized and permanent border (Sharma, 1965, 1971, 1–52).[4]

The Chinese for their part declared the McMahon line to be illegitimate and the other portion of the border in the central and western sectors as never having been defined, both sufficient reasons to make a completely new agreement (*W.P.*, III, 64).[5] China rejected India's claim of historical rights or de facto possession rights, especially in the western sector where India did not learn of the construction of a road between Tibet and Sinkiang until late 1957—thus contradicting Indian claims that it had effective control in the area (*W.P.*, III, 53). The Chinese refuted the claim that the Tibetan government was free to sign treaties at any time, as that kind of admission would have legitimized the Dalai Lama's argument that China's takeover of Tibet was the conquest of an independent state. As for their silence on the boundary issues, the Chinese did not think this could be taken as tacit agreement. It really stemmed, they explained, from the fact that "conditions were not yet ripe for the settlement [of the border dispute] and the Chinese side, on its part, had had no time to study the question" (*W.P.*, I, 53). In addition, to facilitate the solution of the Tibet question, they thought it wise not to confuse two separate issues (*W.P.*, III, 72).

It seems, then, that there were important legalistic disagreements between the two countries. The Indian government, both in content

Table 6.1. Evidence for Chinese and Indian Territorial Claims —
A Quantitative Analysis

Type of Evidence	Western Sector		Middle Sector		Eastern Sector		Total	
	India	China	India	China	India	China	India	China
Legal/contractual basis	23		44		47		114	47*
Traditional basis	51 }	66	89 }	41	40 }	91	180 }	198
De facto control	108 }		146 }		82 }		336 }	

Source: Adapted from Bhat, 1967, 92.
* There is no breakdown for China.

and according to the statistical analysis of the quantity of evidence supplied by both sides, saw its position as the stronger one.

As can be seen from Table 6.1, the amount of evidence supporting India's claim was signficantly greater than that for the Chinese. Altogether, the Indian government presented 630 proof items as against 245 of China's. India's case seemed to be proven beyond a shadow of doubt, and Nehru was convinced that India had justice on its side; for Nehru, a lawyer by training, this fact had great significance and strengthened his decision not to retract from the precondition that he had already set in 1959, namely, that any negotiations would have to be preceded by a Chinese return to the status quo ante: "An agreement about the observance of the status quo would, therefore, be meaningless as the factors concerning the status quo are themselves disputed" (*W.P.,* III, 49).

But, from the Chinese point of view, the purely legalistic arguments were of minor significance; evidence of this lay in the fact that in the debate over the western sector the Chinese team presented a very sloppy set of legal claims (Woodman, 1970; Fisher *et al.,* 1963, 126). China's consent to the establishment of the joint committee, as well as their reference to it as progress in the Sino-Indian negotiations, was merely a tactical step designed to project a certain image in Asia and the Third World, that of a nation preferring to negotiate, and was also aimed at convincing the Indian government of Peking's readiness to talk.

This attitude was an outcome of Communist China's general approach to international law, which Nehru probably did not understand. There were three basic Chinese theoretical positions on the content and nature of the international legal system. One saw it as universal and applicable to all nations without regard to government. The second divided the legal system into two separate entities: one applying only to relations among Socialist states and the other only to capitalist and imperialist nations in their relations to Socialist states. The third concept held that Socialist countries had an essentially different outlook from other nations in the system. Thus, in a period of peaceful coexistence, a number of legal systems could operate simultaneously.

On the practical level, the Chinese thought that one should distinguish between secondary and vital national interests. In the area of secondary interests, such as the protection of diplomats or the treatment of prisoners of war, international law was *universal*. However, on issues of national import—such as territorial matters—international law was only *instrumental* in achieving the aims of the state. Therefore, international law was binding only to the extent that could be inferred from the balance of power in the area (Christol, 1968).

Thus, although the West regarded the body of international law as a universal and indivisible entity, to be applied without distinctions between actors or type of national interests, from the Chinese standpoint the rules of international law were created to serve the foreign policy of a given state, and their application depended on circumstances arising from ideological and utilitarian criteria. One origin of this view was the idea that international law really served a capitalist-imperialist world order. The People's Republic of China—as it had not been a partner to its creation before 1949 and was not accepted by the United Nations, where membership itself required the adoption of the international legal code—did not see itself bound to fulfill its tenets (Chiu, 1966, 1972a; 1972b; Hsiung, 1972a; 1972b). Thus, even when Communist China recognized international law, it could not be taken for granted that international law would lead to behavior similar to that customary in the Western world. In other words, the application of principles such as those of the Panch Sheel Agreement were not universal in time and place but dependent on ideological circumstances and the attributes of the actors.

Maoist doctrine distinguished between a number of types of non-Socialist states: the national, the capitalist, and the imperialist. Until the end of the 1950s, India was seen as belonging to the first kind, those nations that rejected Imperialism from a true motive of self-protection and the maintenance of world peace and for which the principles of peaceful coexistence were applicable in terms of relations with China.

But this was not the case with imperialist states or their allies. At the end of the 1950s Nehru, as we have seen, was thought to be advocating a reactionary domestic and foreign policy and to be in the process of becoming the servant of Imperialism, the bourgeoisie, and feudalism. Thus, the privilege that India had acquired as an ally in the struggle against U.S. Imperialism, to have the principles of coexistence applied in its relations with China, was no longer justified. India was becoming increasingly dependent on U.S. aid, and its position on Tibet damaged what was described as China's legitimate rights, including its prerogative to exercise its full sovereignty over its own territory.[6] A content analysis of the Chinese perception of the nature of the Indian state showed that "imperialist" comprised up to 15.9% of all the characteristics applied to it.[7]

The Chinese also gleaned Nehru's "imperialist" attitude from his interpretation of the term *autonomous region*. According to the Chinese constitution, an autonomous region was merely one in which most of the population consisted of non-Chinese minorities. Nehru understood this to be a kind of protectorate, perhaps in the manner of Sikkim, which handled its own domestic affairs[8] but consulted the representatives of the central government.[9] The Chinese, however, attached limited significance to the term, as they bluntly put it in May 1959: "True, Tibet is not a province but an autonomous region of the People's Republic of China, with greater powers and functions than a province as laid down in the Constitution and by law; but it is definitely not a protectorate—neither a Chinese protectorate, nor an Indian protectorate, nor a joint Chinese-Indian protectorate, nor a so-called buffer state between China and India" (*P.R.,* May 12, 1959, 14).

From this point of view,[10] India had made a step in the right direction when in the 1954 agreement it gave up its special rights—its imperialist inheritance—in Tibet. The Tibetan revolt, however, revealed its "true face," and its hypocrisy was properly exposed by its position on the border dispute. Here, on the most basic issue, that of the legality of borders set by former imperialist powers, India adopted an unreasonable approach. The Chinese thought that "Treaties can be classified into equal treaties and unequal treaties and the latter undermine the most fundamental principles of international law—such as sovereignty; therefore they are illegal and void, and states have the right to abrogate this type of treaty at any time."[11] The boundaries, then, must be given new legitimacy and authority through renegotiation between the People's Republic and its relevant neighbor, "taking into consideration the historical background and present actualities" (*P.R.,* May 3, 1960, 24). It could very well happen that the new agreements would settle on borders geographically identical to the previous ones or would require just as many concessions on the part of China as on that of India, but these borders would be new in terms of their symbolic significance, achieved from a position of equality and dignity.

For China the border question symbolized a period in its diplomatic history that could be erased only by a concrete act of renewed negotiations on territorial injustices committed in the past. The Indian approach, which rejected any new negotiation in favor of mere minor corrections, was seen as identifying with the colonial past and tending to continue in the same pattern. It follows that future Indian behavior was anticipated accordingly and Chinese evaluations of

Indian actions—even conciliatory ones—were negative. This perception carried special weight in the years when ideology played an
important part in Chinese domestic and foreign policies.[12]

As he did not understand the Chinese border conception, Nehru
made another error, and that was in seeing the treaties with Burma
and Nepal as precedents for the Sino-Indian border (*Press*, II, 26;
W.P., V, 24). On the surface, it seemed as if the Burma agreement
of 1960, which settled on the McMahon line as the legitimate border,[13]
was a victory for India, too—that is, a concession on China's part.
From the Chinese point of view, however, it was not an admission
that the Chinese maps needed amending to suit maps left over from
the British but, once the principle was accepted that borders inherited
from the British Empire were not legal, that China was willing to
be generous.[14] The same applied to the recognition of the Nepal-
Tibet border in the 1960 agreement based on the adoption of the
"watershed line," a principle that India was eager to have applied
in its own border dispute with China. These were precedents that
reinforced Nehru's conviction that the Chinese would finally accept
his position on the border question. At the same time, his confidence
in the righteousness of the Indian position grew as did his emotional
commitment and reluctance to change any of his attitudes. But, of
course, the interpretation that he gave to these treaties was mistaken,
and the Chinese media made that absolutely clear: "the Indian side
went so far as to allege that the Sino-Burmese and Sino-Nepalese
boundary treaties, which were signed in accordance with the Five
Principles of Peaceful Co-existence and through friendly consultations,
support the Indian position with regard to the boundary. . . . The
Chinese [side] expressed its great surprise and regret at such assertions
of the Indian side which ignored the minimum courtesy and the
facts, and sternly refuted them" (*P.R.*, May 4, 1962, 20).

Nehru, the Western lawyer, did not comprehend a system that
regarded the law as subservient to political aims. This explains his
puzzlement over the selective application of the Five Principles policy
as expressed in the letter of the foreign secretary to the Chinese
ambassador in New Delhi as early as 1959: "From the statement
made on behalf of the People's Government of China, it appears
that, according to them, the Panch Sheel or the Five Principles of
Peaceful Co-existence may or may not be applied, according to
convenience or circumstances. This is an approach with which the
Government of India is not in agreement. They have proclaimed and
adhered to these Principles as matters of basic policy and not of
opportunism" (*W.P.*, I, 78). In the same way, Nehru did not understand
the emotional and ideological importance for the Chinese leadership
of rejecting formally those boundaries so uncomfortably reminiscent
of the decadent period of the Middle Kingdom and the need of these
leaders to find an expression for the historical turnabout that had

taken place in China. Thus, the question of whether Nehru was justified or not on the legal level and according to Western legal criteria was not really relevant and was of no benefit in his bilateral relations with China. Furthermore, the stubborn adherence to his legal claims and his ignoring of the Chinese political-legal concept destroyed the minimal ideological-political common denominator between the two countries that China saw as a basic condition for peaceful coexistence. On the other hand, if China expected its treaties with Nepal and Burma to propel Nehru into drawing the appropriate conclusions, then it failed: the Indian leadership drew the opposite conclusions.

Perceptions of Reciprocal Relations

India had been the second non-Communist state, after Burma, to recognize the Communist regime in China. However, tension developed in relations between the two countries after the Chinese "liberation" of Tibet in 1950, although this cooling off did not last long. Friendship with China was one of the main goals of Nehru's foreign policy for ideological, emotional, and practical political reasons, and as he said: "I have always thought that it is important, even essential if you like, that these two countries of Asia, India and China, should have friendly and as far as possible co-operative relations" (*Par.,* I, 115). When the Seventeen Points agreement concerning Tibet was signed, Nehru saw the issue as settled and recognized the legitimacy of Chinese control over Tibet. India expressed its goodwill toward China by being one of its chief and consistent supporters in the matter of its application for membership of the United Nations; by refusing to vote for the declaration of China as an aggressor following its involvement in the Korean War and seeing Chinese interests there as legitimate; by refusing to join a conference to sign a peace agreement with Japan from which China was excluded; by taking the position it did in the Geneva Conference in 1954; by signing the Panch Sheel Agreement in 1954 in which India relinquished its special rights in Tibet; and by initiating the invitation to China to attend the Bandung Conference. The attitude of senior Indian policymakers helped to foster positive public opinion toward China. Even so, this approach was not adopted en masse by senior officials and top-ranking military officers. Bajpai, the MEA's Secretary-General at the time, demanded that the matter of the northern border by brought up openly in negotiations with the Chinese, arguing that China's non-reaction to Nehru's claim in November 1950 that the McMahon line was India's indisputable legitimate boundary was not sufficient, despite Nehru's insistence that there was a tacit acceptance.[15] But the right wing of the Congress Party had, since the death of Patel, lacked a leader with enough power and influence to shake up the system of concepts and action orientations set up by Nehru and his loyal supporters, such as Menon, Panikkar, Mullik, and others. Nehru's conception of Communist China's society, and of the condition and goals of its foreign policy in relation to Indian foreign policies, persisted even when relations between the two countries began to deteriorate.

There were three basic components to Nehru's and his advisor's perceptions about China: paternalism, romanticism, and the sense that in principle there was an affinity and mutual need between the two nations.

The left wing of the Congress Party, with Nehru and Menon at its head, was thrilled by the Chinese revolution. And on the surface it did, indeed, seem as if there were a great similarity between the two societies. They both had enormous populations and territories, two resources that, if properly utilized, could achieve for each side the status of a super power. In both countries the population was mostly rural and very poor and was governed by a small elite that held possession of the bulk of the nation's capital. This situation called for sweeping social and economic reforms, and the leaders in both societies preferred Socialism as a basis. China and India had a very rich cultural past and enjoyed political and cultural influence far beyond their geographical borders. They both had recently suffered humiliation and subjugation at the hands of colonial oppressors, both had struggled for freedom, and they seemed to share a tradition of reciprocal religious and cultural relations.

Nehru repeatedly emphasized the ties between the two countries, already established in the year 67 A.D.; the 2,000 years of friendship that had endured ever since (*Par.,* I, 115); the constant exchange of visitors; and the adoption of Buddhism in China. In his book *The Discovery of India,* which discusses the centuries-long connection between China and India and its renewal against the background of their common struggle for independence in modern times,[16] Nehru wrote: "And now the wheel of fate has turned full circle and again India and China look toward each other and past memories crowd in their minds: again pilgrims of a new kind cross or fly over the mountains that separate them, bring their message of cheer and goodwill and creating fresh bonds of a friendship that will endure" (Nehru, 1951, 178). India's great poet Rabindranath Tagore contributed to this romantic image of Sino-Indian relations. Admired and honored by Nehru (his daughter studied at the poet's school), Tagore himself believed in Asian solidarity and took a number of trips to the Far East. In 1924 he traveled to China and Japan, returning convinced of the cultural and political affinity between the two countries and charmed by the Chinese people and culture. In the 1930s he held long talks with Nehru on this subject, thus reinforcing Nehru's notion of close affinity between India and China.

India's first ambassador to Communist China, K.M. Panikkar, also had a great influence on Nehru's geo-political thinking; he was a typical Sinophile, as well as an opportunist who knew exactly what Nehru wished to hear.[17] The Chinese Socialist revolution, which in a short time had succeeded in radically changing the socioeconomic structure of China and achieving important goals in agriculture and industry, interested and excited Nehru. In Peking, Panikkar reported that the regime there was not Communist in the usual sense of the word but was a kind of nationalist agrarian reformer, thus strengthening Nehru's conviction that China was experiencing a nationalist revival and that there was a great similarity between himself and Mao (Panikkar, 1955, 82).

The Friendship Association with China was established in India in 1952. It flowered particularly after the 1954 agreement. It numbered tens of thousands of members in branches all over India. Indian delegations of intellectuals and writers flowed to China and on their return expressed their admiration for the Chinese model of society. Of course, most of these visitors did not know the Chinese language, saw what their hosts wished them to see,[18] and were utterly dependent on their hosts' explanations (Passin, 1961).

Nehru himself visited China in 1954 and was deeply impressed by the achievements of the regime. His visit, as he said, reinforced his preconceptions: "there is much in common in the tasks that confront them, and it is desirable for them to co-operate in as large a measure as possible" (Fisher and Bondurant, 1956a, 119).[19] It looked to him as though China had found the way to utilize efficiently its surplus of manpower. Consequently, Indian delegations were sent to China to study Chinese agricultural organization and methods (Hansen, 1968; 1967). Nehru and his colleagues were impressed by the workers' spirit of patriotism and motivation, by their self-discipline and self-criticism, and by the display of unity between the people and government.[20] Maoist philosophy seemed somewhat similar to Gandhi's doctrine in its emphasis on the rural sector, the sacrifice of private interests for the common good, and the transformation of the individual to the extent that he develops loyalty to that which is beyond his selfish interests (Fisher and Bondurant, 1956b, 262–264). And finally Nehru returned from China convinced, as he said, that China "wants peace, wants time for self-development and is thinking in terms of three or four five-year plans" (Fisher and Bondurant, 1956a, 108).[21] This concept went well with the assumption that a Socialist state would not tend to use violence against another state and especially not against a sister Socialist state. To the extent that China displayed militant policies, they were only the result of (a) the alienation and pressure brought to bear by the Western super power; (b) the refusal to recognize the legitimate standing of the Communist regime, which was a true nationalist government; and (c) the refusal on the part of the West to grant China its rightful place among the nations, that is, acceptance into the United Nations and a seat on the Security Council.

Nehru became a consistent supporter of Chinese efforts to gain admittance to the United Nations and to legitimize its claim of sovereignty over Taiwan. He assumed that, as China greatly desired to be accepted into the United Nations, India's support in this matter was of major significance. He also believed that stressing the idea of Asian solidarity would prevent China from becoming an integral part of the Communist bloc and, as such, totally dependent on the USSR. From this latter belief derived the importance of inviting China to Bandung. Furthermore, China's recognition of the principle of Asian solidarity seemed to Nehru a guarantee against the expansionist chauvinism that, in the past, had characterized periods of strong Chinese centralist government.

On the basis of all the reasons given for China's interest in continued Indian support, it was natural for Nehru to conclude that a 2,000-year-old Sino-Indian friendship would persist. This friendship was now based on a similarity of problems and basic interests: defense of the independence of both countries, which had just been liberated from the hands of the same enemy—colonialism; the need for both nations to avoid wasting resources on armies and to concentrate them on domestic economic development;[22] a joint struggle for the independence of the nations still under the colonial yoke; and the transformation of the international system from one of violence to one of solidarity and coexistence, as voiced in the Panch Sheel Agreement between China and India.[23] Furthermore, friendship with China was the "peg" on which Nehru hung Indian foreign policy in the broader sense.[24]

A confrontation between China and India would have meant a challenge to Nehru's oft-expressed warning that any local war would inevitably lead to global warfare. In addition, it would have flown in the face of Nehru's own request that every state employ self-restraint. It was therefore imperative to avoid war between China and India, especially as India was constantly urging Third World countries to avoid confrontations and to allow their common interests to overshadow their differences. Furthermore, special relations between India and China were seen as an expression of one of the basic premises underlying the establishment of the nonaligned bloc: the existence of a fundamental Asian solidarity that transcended differences. At the same time, friendly ties with the state considered by the United States to be its most hostile and dangerous enemy in Asia would serve as confirmation of India's political independence from the United States and proof that, despite U.S. economic aid, India was not a satellite of Washington. In short, such friendly ties provide one of the clearest expressions of nonalignment.

Even when the conflict between China and India became more intense, Nehru persisted in his belief that it was imperative to avoid a spill-over beyond a bilateral restrained and low-profile conflict. This explains his apprehension over the activities of various pressure groups within and without Parliament and his opposition to defining the conflict as rooted in the fact that China was a Communist country. It was not Communism that made China aggressive, Nehru argued: "It might be aggressive minus Communism or plus Communism" (*Par.,* I, 153). Had he acknowledged China's Communism to be the cause of its aggression, Sino-Indian antagonism would have been inevitable and insurmountable, due to the belief system of the Chinese regime, and India would have been compelled to take an anti-Communist stance not only against China. Finally, Nehru could not allow the Panch Sheel Agreement, which he esteemed as a moral ideal for all nations, to fail in the relations between India and its most important neighbor.

In order for all these conceptions to be valid, however, Nehru should have been certain that China held similar views, that it had an ideological, emotional, and practical interest in the same issues that Nehru saw as central to the bilateral, subsystemic, and global frameworks. And, indeed, even when the rift between the two countries worsened, Nehru took pains to emphasize that their basic interests were not in conflict. Even if differences of opinion could not be resolved in the immediate future, war was not a solution for either side. He attributed China's behavior to the abnormal conditions it was facing because of an economic crisis and isolation.[25] Nehru was convinced that, in the final analysis, war between China and India was mutually unfeasible. Therefore, if India persisted in its demands, which, he believed, it was militarily capable of supporting, time would work in its favor (*Par.,* II, 136). And even if hostilities should break out, India had a double line of defense: first, on the political level, its special relations with the two super powers, especially the Soviet Union, and its special status in the Third World, and second, its burgeoning military power (*Par.,* II, 114–115, 119). He was convinced that in time China would recognize the justice of India's demands and, moreover, that his political rivals would vindicate the general orientation of his foreign policy and more specifically his relations with China.

This is not how matters stood with China, however, nor was this how they developed in reality. Historically speaking, it was a mistake to think in terms of 2,000 years of friendship; indeed, the famed poet Tagore had erred in bequeathing this idea to Nehru. In actual fact, the 2,000 years had consisted mainly of lack of contact, or at best neutrality. The myth about Tagore's visit to China in 1924 having cemented the ties between the two nations was not anchored in reality. On the contrary, in terms of creating mutual appreciation between the elites of the two nations, the visit was a failure. Tagore's philosophy and world view met with disagreement from a large part of the radical and nationalistic press and intelligentsia, including

162   *The Bilateral Environment*

students, poets, and philosophers. On the political level, he was identified with the most conservative strata in contemporary Indian society. Radical elements in China held demonstrations against him carrying banners that depicted him as an elephant—a large, stupid, and ungainly animal, shameless and insensible to pain. The motto used was "Drive out the elephant" (Hay, 1970, 220–240).

The Chinese Communist leadership, which at the time formed part of these groups, and Mao in particular, could not but remember these events. Indian culture was never regarded as equal to that of China but was seen as inferior. Cultural ties among equals do not exist in Chinese-centered thinking.

Mao and Chou En-lai, who had deep cultural pride, obviously did not see eye to eye with Nehru on the comparison of the two cultures. A content analysis shows that although China never referred to India as a "great culture," Nehru in his speeches in Parliament called China a "great culture" in 17.3% of cases.[26] From an historical viewpoint, only in the seventh century had there been what could be called intensive ties between India and China. Hinduism was viewed by China as submissive, humbling, and regressive. So deeply did they reject the concept of the cultural similarity (emphasized by India mainly on the basis of the adoption of Buddhism in China) that Chinese thinkers tended to distinguish between India and Buddhism (Gupta, 1972a).

On the more concrete level of Sino-Indian relations, the Tibetan problem was regarded by the Chinese as far more serious than Nehru realized. His refusal to recognize China's full sovereignty over Tibet was viewed by China with great severity, especially against the background of Nehru's attempt to evade the issue by saying: "call it suzerainty, call it sovereignty—these things are fine distinctions and they are determined on the power of the State how far it goes" (*Par.,* I, 1). In other words, Nehru seemed to be implying that China's possession of Tibet was the outcome of the use of force rather than of legality. Moreover, the references to an autonomy within the framework of a Communist state (*Par.,* I, 6) recalled the policy of British Imperialism, which recognized Chinese suzerainty in Tibet and Tibetan autonomy at the same time. In that case, the British supported Tibet's de facto independence by the supply of weapons and the maintenance of diplomatic relations. What was the difference, then, between Nehru's policy and that of Lord Curzon?[27] In this regard, Nehru lost the credibility he had acquired by means of the 1954 agreement in giving up the rights inherited from Britain. Furthermore, China saw a later change in India's attitude to British policy in Tibet. Although in the past Nehru had described British policy in central Asia as a typical expression of British Imperialism, from 1961 onward he began to claim that the British had never had imperialist ambitions in Tibet (*P.R.,* May 4, 1962, 20).

This issue increased in significance for the Chinese government in light of the activities of the U.S. Central Intelligence Agency and Taiwanese agents in Tibet as well as the connections of some members of the Dalai Lama's family with the CIA, which dated back to the 1950s. The Chinese were of the opinion that the main base of these activities was the town of Kalimpong on the Tibetan-Indian border, which they defined as a spies' nest. Gyalo Thendup, the elder brother of the Dalai Lama, played a central role in the running of the spy ring in Tibet. He himself had close connections with the Indian representative in Sikkim and with B.N. Mullik, director of the Indian Intelligence Bureau. His activities were known to the Chinese government and caused it so much anxiety that in 1958 it demanded his extradition but was refused (Gupta, 1974, VII). The CIA activity, which had begun in 1956, grew to such an extent that it sent rebel groups to train in the United States, helped to organize the escape of the Dalai Lama, and assisted in the supply of arms and equipment to the rebels. The central figure in the organization of these operations was the CIA representative in New Delhi. The fact that the Indian government tolerated this connection must have disturbed the Chinese, especially after India gave political asylum and royal treatment to the Dalai Lama in New Delhi. From this viewpoint, it seemed to the Chinese government a verification of the thesis of conspiracy between reactionary elements in India, the CIA, and the regime of Chiang Kai-shek. This thesis took on more and more credibility as the dispute deepened. Thus it happened that what Nehru saw as minimal interference in the revolt, necessitated by public pressure in India, seemed to the Chinese to be grave meddling in their internal affairs. Nehru's attempt to assuage Chinese anger by forbidding the Dalai Lama to establish a government in exile on Indian territory and by refusing to raise the Tibetan problem at the United Nations did not convince the Chinese of his good intentions. It seemed to them that the subversive activities in Tibet were taking place with the full knowledge of the Indian government[28] and, moreover, because of imperialist intentions toward it.[29]

A second dimension injected into the dispute by China, probably without Nehru's awareness, was an ideological one: "If one agrees with Nehru's logic, not only the revolution in Tibet, but the whole Chinese revolution would be impermissible" (*P.R.,* May 12, 1959, 9). In principle, except for their scope, the Chinese and Tibetan revolutions were identical in that they freed the masses from the rule of a small feudal elite.

The third issue on which Nehru misjudged the Chinese position was the question of Chinese acceptance into the United Nations and the great value that he assumed China attached to India's support. From 1949 on, the Chinese attitude had undergone changes for which Nehru obviously did not account. Until June 1950 the Chinese did attach major significnce to their acceptance to the United Nations for reasons of status and legitimization. But afterward, until the end of the Korean War, in light of the UN position on the war, China displayed a far more reserved attitude and began distinguishing between the United Nations as it is portrayed in its charter and the United Nations as a U.S. tool. From 1954 to 1957, Peking adopted a policy of sitting on the fence, waiting to be invited to join, now that the representation of Third World nations in the organization had grown in number and influence. From 1958 on, it changed its policy again, realizing that status and recognition could be gained from joining .other, that is, Third World, organizations outside the United Nations. This approach gained a stronger hold after China was condemned at the United Nations on the question of Tibet in 1959, and after it was refused membership in the organization in December 1961 under U.S. pressure (62 for, 34 against, and 7 abstentions). This decision finally led the Chinese to see that power at the United Nations was controlled, via the secretariat, by the United States, the USSR, and India; as these countries were hostile to China, staying out of the organization and creating substitutes would give China greater political maneuverability (Weng, 1972, 69–132; 1966; Chiu and Edwards, 1968). At any rate, it was clear that over the years the importance attached by the Chinese leadership to joining the United Nations diminished, and with it diminished the value of Indian support.

A further error on Nehru's part was imagining that China accepted the Indian assessment of the international situation, on the global, subsystemic, and bilateral levels. Nehru did not understand that what for him were *strategic* goals on the international scene, such as detente, Asian solidarity, and support for nonalignment, were for Mao mere *tactical* goals. The identity of purpose, therefore, was of necessity (Shao, 1979) and not the result of an affinity of principles. It is doubtful whether Nehru really comprehended the basic elements in the Maoist world view. He ignored the ideological aspect and saw Maoism mainly in nationalist Marxist terms, and in Maoist terminology he saw a kind of payment of lip service only. To a certain extent, this perception resulted from the fact that insofar as Nehru saw a continuity between Imperial and Communist China, this continuity existed only in the realm of aggressive behavior and not in that of political-cultural traditions, which the Communist regime had inherited—traditions such as the belief that political-social order in China was based on ideological factors and that judgment of foreign leaders with whom China came into contact was made in terms of their acceptance of the inevitable results of that ideology (Fairbank, 1968, 8).

As he did not really understand the essence and implications of Maoist ideology and dialectic, he also did not see that from a Maoist point of view, unlike his own, war and peaceful coexistence were not opposing alternatives. Coexistence as Maoism regarded it was not an unchanging, positive ethical value. Rather, it was a tactical step in the class struggle. Once its usefulness was called into question, war could become the alternative in relations between Socialist and other states. India, then, was merely an object in Chinese foreign policy, the aims toward which would be decided in accordance with strategic goals of destroying U.S. Imperialism and initiating world-wide revolution. As such, Chinese foreign policy was dualistic in nature, containing, at once, elements of unity and struggle. In this context, China's diplomacy toward India was in fact a case of United Front diplomacy, defined as "a *limited* and *temporary* alignment between a Communist party or state and one or more non-Communist political units" (Armstrong, 1977, 13).

The possible use of war as a tool in relations with India was also related to another Maoist concept developed during the Yenan years, that is, flexible change from a violent to a nonviolent political struggle, without any contradiction between the two. As Mao put it: "War and peace transform themselves into each other because in a class society such contradictory things as war and peace are characterised by identity under certain circumstances" (quoted by Tsou and Halperin, 1965, 91). And so, in contrast to Nehru's philosophy, war was to be considered in terms of its utility and in rational terms of power relations,[30] and was not necessarily a negative phenomenon to be condemned and avoided.[31] It was an expression of what, in Maoist terminology, was called the *unity of contradictions.*

Another Maoist principle emphasized the need to see the connection between parts and the whole. Thus, the question of whether to stress the element of unity or that of struggle could not be decided only as a function of the direct relations between China and India but in the wider context of both the global-political situation and the Indian social system as a whole. In both areas, there was a basic difference between Chinese and Indian assessments the depth of which Nehru was unaware, and the Chinese assessment led to a complete reevaluation of Sino-Indian relations.

In short, Nehru did not comprehend the ideological foundations of the Chinese political evaluation of the situation, nor did he understand its dynamics or have any idea just how far his evaluations deviated from those of the Chinese. He explained Chinese militancy as a need to externalize internal difficulties in order to distract the public's attention from them. In this he made an additional error.[32] In a factor analysis of the Chinese leadership's perceptual system, the factor explaining the major part of the variance (50.9%) was the Chinese leadership's evaluation of the relations between the internal situation in China and the international system.[33] Thus, it seems reasonable to conclude that it was precisely the public evaluations made by policymakers of the West and India dealing with China's weakness following its internal crisis, as well as the cutting off of Soviet aid, that forced the Chinese to prove that their military strength had not been weakened. Indian military arrogance became a natural target.

Chinese history provides further support to our argument. Imperial dynasties in China had been known to collapse under the joint pressure of domestic unrest and external military threats (Fairbank, 1966, 15). It may be assumed that the contemporary Chinese leadership, acutely historically aware, would have learned the relevant lessons.

These same errors led Nehru to misjudge Chinese self-restraint in 1962 as weakness, while ignoring China's constant warnings against India's Forward Policy and its refusal to enter negotiations without preconditions (*W.P.*, VII, 10; 96–97; 105). Maoism in general did not see temporary retreats as weakness; it regarded infinite patience as a necessity, and hastiness and the taking of uncalculated risks as adventurous and unjustifiable (Powell, 1968b, 253). What seemed weakness to Nehru was really a Chinese attempt to reach at least a tacit agreement on maintaining the status quo, especially after the failure of the Nehru–Chou En-lai talks and the Indian rejection of a package deal consisting of Chinese recognition of the McMahon line and Indian acceptance of Chinese sovereignty in the crucial area of Aksai Chin.[34] Instead, the Chinese were confronted with the Forward Policy, which became increasingly provocative with time. From China's point of view, there was little to be done: "The present tense and grave situation along the Sino-Indian boundary is solely the creation of the Indian authorities" (*P.R.*, Aug. 17, 1962, 5).

In light of what has been said so far, it seems that from the Chinese vantage point, the use of force in the dispute with India became desirable and even essential. From an ideological point of view, the Indian leadership deserved a humbling lesson. Furthermore, such a step could have brought decisive results in the political and ideological struggle within the Communist world, in the Third World, and even in the West. Although on the bilateral level Indian stubbornness bordered on audacity in interpreting China's restraint as weakness, a realistic assessment of the balance of power by Chinese intelligence[35] must have shown that Indian power was nothing but a paper tiger and could easily and, for the most part, painlessly be revealed for what it was. It seems that in this matter, at least, there was a consensus among Chinese leaders in the months preceding the attack. If there were no choice, force would be used. An Indian refusal to negotiate without preconditions, India's attempts to cross the McMahon line to the north, the establishment of the Fourth Corps under the command of Kaul, a well-known hawk, Nehru's declaration of October 12, and the approaching winter—all contributed to making the use of force seem attractive, inevitable, and even worthwhile.

Because Indian activities in the area demanded an immediate response, and because climatic conditions would otherwise force the Chinese to wait until May 1963, the attack was planned for the months of October–November.

Nehru misread the Chinese evaluation of the situation on both the ideological-philosophical level, which placed India in a broader political-historical context and hence determined the attitude and degree of hostility or friendship of China toward India, as well as the practical level of bilateral relations, which concerned the outcome of immediate needs and interests as defined in each period by the conceptual-theoretical Maoist framework. These misperceptions account for Nehru's blindness concerning the military mistakes of the Forward Policy pursued against the warning of his own senior military men.[36] It took no less than a war between China and India to inject some dynamism into Nehru's static thinking on the issue.

Hostility, Threat, and Action Orientations: Comparative Aspects

The detailed perceptual systems just discussed were aptly reflected in the degree of hostility that India and China felt for each other, in the degree of threat each side attributed to the other, and in their behavioral dispositions. These three areas also served as points of reference for each side's anticipation of the other's future actions. In order to understand the reciprocity between these variables, we must examine them separately for each nation and comparatively in relation to the values of these factors at every point in time and to changes in them over time.

An examination of the graphs in Figures 6.1 through 6.5 presents an interesting picture of the dynamics of the above-mentioned concepts. The period under discussion is divided into six subperiods (the last day of each is marked on the graphs). The following seven central events, which mark the six periods, proved to be nodal points in the development of the conflict:

1. *March 17, 1959:* Escape of the Dalai Lama to India
2. *August 25, 1959:* Longju incident in the eastern sector
3. *April 19, 1960:* Commencement of Nehru–Chou En-lai talks
4. *February 14, 1961:* Publication of the Joint Committee Report
5. *December 5, 1961:* Instructions given to the army to execute the Forward Policy
6. *September 8, 1962:* Crossing of the Thag La Ridge by Chinese forces, a period ending with the Chinese attack on *October 20, 1962*
7. *November 21, 1962:* Declaration of ceasefire and unilateral ceasefire by the Chinese

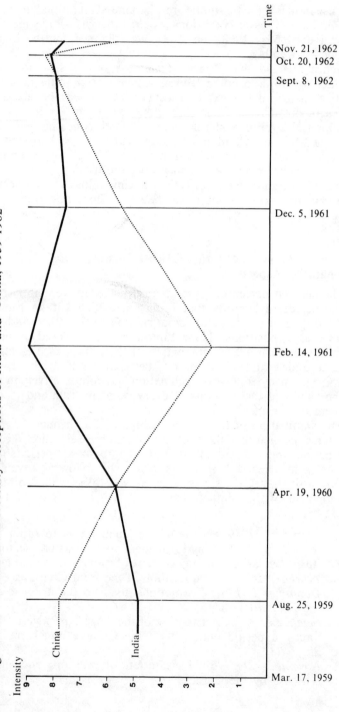

Figure 6.1.   Trends in the Hostility Perceptions of India and China, 1959-1962

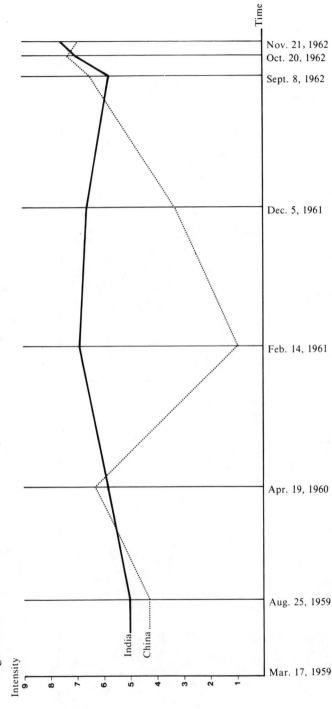

Figure 6.2.   Trends in the Threat Perceptions of India and China, 1959-1962

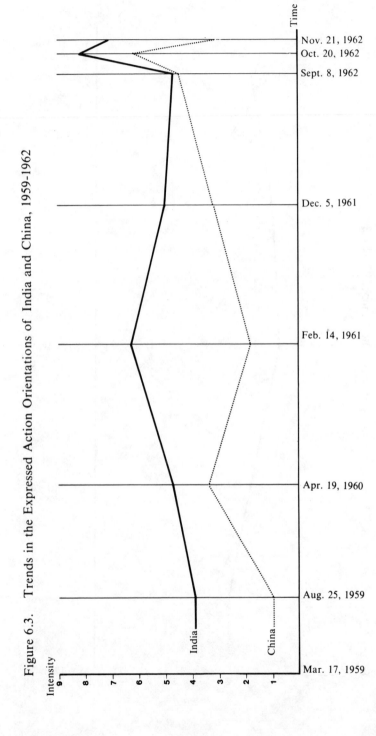

Figure 6.3.   Trends in the Expressed Action Orientations of India and China, 1959-1962

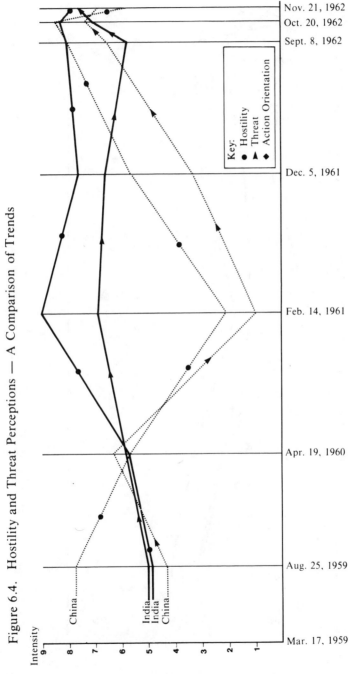

Figure 6.4. Hostility and Threat Perceptions — A Comparison of Trends

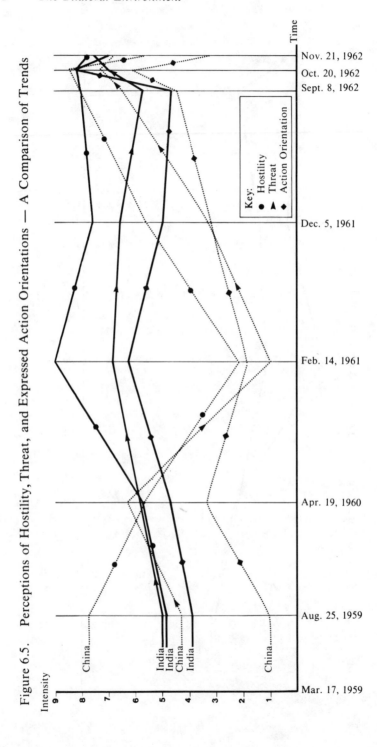

Figure 6.5.   Perceptions of Hostility, Threat, and Expressed Action Orientations — A Comparison of Trends

The graphs of threat, hostility, and action orientation are presented both separately and simultaneously for purposes of comparison. The detailed statistical data represented by the graphs can be found in the Statistical Appendix.[37]

It appears that Nehru's threat perception did not fluctuate to the same degree as that of the Chinese. Although his range of fluctuation was between 5.000 and 7.083, the Chinese showed much sharper fluctuations consisting of a steep rise, a sharp decline, and then a sharp rise again, and ending with an additional moderate rise, thus elevating the level of Chinese threat perception—generally lower than that of India—above the Indian threat at that time. It is noteworthy that after October 20 the Chinese threat perception dropped again. It seems, then, that Indian leadership was not sufficiently sensitive to fluctuations in the Chinese threat perception, nor did it attach enough importance to the intensity and meaning of this threat perception. Indeed, statistical analysis does not show a link between the change in India's threat level and the change in the level of the Chinese threat perception.[38] This finding might explain why India ignored China's signals and indications that it was willing to use war as a means of resolving the dispute. Nehru's approach probably resulted from his faith in the Indian army's ability to cope with any Chinese threat, his belief in the righteousness of his cause, and his notion that time was working in India's favor (*Par.,* II, 21; 85), and it inevitably led to a lack of sensitivity to the other side's reactions. In the existing balance of power, these trends were unjustified. Although until February 1962 the average Chinese perception of threat (4.769) was lower than the Indian average (5.881), during the period between February 1 and October 20, 1962 the situation reversed itself and the Indian average (6.243) was somewhat lower than that of the Chinese (6.417).[39]

The same insensitivity was present in *part* of the investigated period in India's perception of hostility. When broken down into subperiods, the Chinese and Indian hostility trends were asymmetrical, as were the threat trends. However, in the period beginning on December 5, 1961 a symmetry began to form in the trends of both countries' hostility perceptions. Until the eve of the Nehru-Chou En-lai talks, Indian hostility perception was lower than that of the Chinese, but following the talks it grew higher. At the same time, a survey of the entire period—during which time both sides tried to behave with self-restraint, that is, until the publication of the Joint Committee's report—shows that India's (5.749) and China's (5.654) average hostility levels were close. Similarly, during the entire period of the escalation, from the time of the publication of the report until the outbreak of war, there was little difference in the average level of hostility between India (8.037) and China (7.892).[40] Statistical analysis reveals that the *change* in Chinese hostility explains 51.4%

of the *change* in India's hostility toward China,[41] which confirms a positive and strong connection between the mutual reactions of hostility. In this sphere, then, over a period of time a tendency toward a compatability between the hostility levels of both sides was created. Indeed, it will be found that the Chinese hostility perception explains 34% of the Indian hostility perceptions and that the correlation between the two is .585.[42]

In a comparison of the relationship between the hostility and threat perception of China and those of India, two facts emerge. One is that the trends of the Chinese perceptions were more symmetrical than those of India and, beginning with the period following February 14, 1961, the gap between the height of China's and India's hostility and threat levels decreased and perceptions became interactive. This indicates that Nehru had a lesser tendency to link the level of India's hostility toward China to the level of threat to values but reacted to China's hostility. And, indeed, the absolute level of Indian hostility perception does not explain the perception of threat that India had for China. On the other hand, the Chinese leadership tended to relate the degree of hostility toward India to its level of conceived threat, and the perception of hostility explains 23% of the variance in the Chinese threat perception. We refer here to absolute levels of threat and hostility.[43] At the same time, we find that for both countries the levels of hostility perception are almost consistently higher than the levels of threat perception (see Figure 6.4).

We can thus conclude that for China, unlike India, the perception of hostility influenced the crystallization of the absolute threat level. The lack of awareness on India's part of the fact that China's perception of hostility was significant in the creation of its threat perception apparently brought about the underestimation of the *intention* factors. Because India had already underestimated Chinese *ability* and exaggerated its own, it seemed to legitimize the underestimation of the real, immediate Chinese threat even more so. The Indians misunderstood the influence of the perceptions of hostility on Chinese threat perceptions. Insofar as the Chinese leadership had formed a negative political-ideological evaluation of the Indian regime, society, and leadership, it was the hostility levels resulting from this evaluation and not from temporary fluctuations that influenced the crystallization of threat perceptions. This is probably the reason we do not find that the level of *change* in Chinese hostility levels is linked to the level of *change* in threat perception.[44]

An examination of the level of aggression expressed in verbal action orientation preferences shows that during the entire period Nehru maintained on the average a higher level of militance than did the Chinese leadership, which exercised self-restraint. Thus, we find that very aggressive action orientations are prominent in Chinese expressions only after the crossing of the Thag La Ridge by the

Chinese and especially in the days immediately preceding the attack,[45] when they reached the conclusion that the use of force was unavoidable.

The quantitative analysis points to an additional essential difference between the adversaries. With the Chinese we find that the action orientation was positively connected to their perception of threat, although its influence was relatively low and only about 14% of the variance is explained. On the other hand, we do not find Indian perception of hostility and threat definitely connected to the absolute level of aggression of India's action orientation.[46] This absence of connection strengthens the argument that, in the main, Nehru's action orientations were an outcome of internal political pressures and a belief in India's ability to cope with the problem and not of the threat from, or hostility toward, China that he felt—a conclusion compatible with the findings pointing to a relatively strong connection between the action orientations of both sides[47] and especially to the influence of changes in Chinese action orientations on Indian ones.[48]

The comparative analysis just described points to a generally asymmetrical trend in the behavior related to the threat perceptions, in contrast to the symmetry developing over time in the behavioral orientations and the hostility perceptions. It was precisely these trends that strengthened the erroneous conclusions of the Indian leadership concerning Chinese intentions toward India, encouraged a suspicious rejection of any Chinese suggestion of compromise, and pushed India toward an unrealistic policy, unsuitable to its power. The nonattribution of proper significance to the relevant Chinese threat perception, hostility, and action orientation led to a feeling of self-righteousness and invulnerability. In this sense, the patterns in these perceptual spheres are much the same as those already described.

Conclusions

Nehru's evaluations, calculations and expectations relating to Sino-Indian bilateral relations were based on misperceptions. These are summarized as follows:

1. Relating to the legal aspects of the dispute, Nehru failed to see that there was no basis in his assumption—at least as far as China was concerned—that the international legal system is an objective, universally acceptable phenomenon. This view did not change over the period in question and only fed his self-assurance that sooner or later China would have to accept India's position because there was no doubt about the fact that India was legally the wronged side. This was related to the exaggerated importance given to the legal aspects of the dispute by India and was at least in part a projection of the importance attached by Nehru to legalism. Over time this misperception became even worse and strengthened Nehru's determination not to budge, in the expectation that China would recognize that India was legally in the right.

2. As for the political aspects of the bilateral relations between the two countries, Nehru tended to underestimate the importance the Chinese attached to the Tibet issue and to overestimate the importance they attached to their acceptance into the United Nations, in which India was supposed to play a major role.

3. Nehru overestimated the degree and role of what was conceived by him as cultural kinship and a long history of Sino-Indian friendship. This misperception led to his belief in the inevitability of a peaceful solution to the conflict in line with the Indian position.

4. Nehru was unaware of the fundamental difference in long-term goals and interests between India and China and believed in a set of shared basic goals. He stuck to this misperception in the face of contradictory evidence until the war broke out.

5. The above-mentioned misperceptions served to support Nehru's evaluation that China and India had more or less comparable views on the contemporary international system and what its future shape should be. Only quite late in the dispute did Nehru begin to see that this was not so, at least as far as the evaluation of contemporary events was concerned, although only to a degree; that is, the adaptation process was only partial.

6. In light of the situation just previously noted, it is no wonder that Nehru irrelevantly linked Chinese hostility toward India to the repercussions of the internal political and economic problems in China that followed the failure of the Great Leap Forward. He held onto this rationalization even after the situation in China had stabilized.

7. These misperceptions had a spill-over effect on the perceptions of threat, hostility, and time. Nehru was unaware of the fluctuations in Chinese threat perception and so believed that this situation was not severe enough to bring about the use of large-scale military force. What is more, given his assumption that hostility was not related to threat, he came to disregard the implications of his *correct* evaluation of growing Chinese hostility.

Thus, Nehru retained his evaluation of a very low probability of war between India and China, seeing the growing number and intensity of border clashes as a manifestation of Chinese temporary hostility toward India but not as a warning to India to adopt a more cautious policy. This misperception only strengthened his growing belief in the fact that time was on India's side and that as India got stronger it was bound to have the last word in the dispute.

The Perceptual Framework:
An Overview and Some Puzzles

A detailed analysis of Nehru's concept of the China issue reveals a characteristic pattern that has significant implications for the dynamics of perceptual processes. On the spatial level, Nehru saw India as a "moral guide," a nation arousing and having interests far beyond its geographical boundaries, the obligations of which were primarily global and which certainly extended to subsystems other than Asia. Thus, relations with China were also regarded as conditioned by the role and the burden that India had undertaken.

In terms of the interaction between India and its environment, there was an aversion to the use of violence and a preference for peaceful coexistence. But in reality there was a combination of a reluctant acknowledgment of the unavoidability of instrumental violence on a *low* level and a sense of immunity from a sharp response from China. This dissonance created a feeling of discomfort, resulting from the contradiction between the aversion to violence and the feeling of its inevitability.

Time was seen as a factor of pressure on the tactical level because of the need to establish facts in the field before the adversary did so. On the strategic level, the dispute was seen as a low-intensity conflict of long duration. Existing simultaneously was the belief that time was in India's favor and in the long run would bring about a settlement of the dispute under terms favorable to India as a result of the anticipated growth in its prestige, economic power, and military might in the meantime.

The perceptions relating to the interaction between the two countries were based on Nehru's value system and his world view as to what was desirable in the relationships between nations and individuals. A number of these values, such as national honor, territorial integrity, and legal justice, aroused deep emotional reactions. At the same time, contradictions were often encountered in the system itself, not only between the ideal and the real but among values themselves. Thus, for example, the value of territorial integrity was an obstacle in reaching a settlement and in the realization of the value of peaceful coexistence. The value of coexistence with China during the Tibetan revolt collided with that of self-determination for the Tibetans. This collision, as will be shown later, had major psychological consequences.

Nehru's set of conceptions did not always appear compatible with those of the Indian public at large. The feelings of hostility and threat that were prevailing among the Indian public were much stronger than those of Nehru. As a result, the ensuing action orientations concerning such values as coexistence and the defense of national honor were also different. These contradictions between the concept of the leader and those of the public demanded resolution as quickly as possible, especially because the issues were emotionally charged. Thus, pressure was brought to bear on Nehru to act in a way that would give the impression that the contradictions did not exist.

Nehru showed over the years a great deal of self-assurance in evaluating situations concerning foreign policy. His confidence stemmed both from his self-esteem and from the support of his close circle of advisors, the media, and foreign leaders. Consequently, he was left with very little room for doubt from the time he adopted specific evaluations; dissonant information had to be dealt with decisively. In other words, he was vulnerable to uncertainty and had a constant need to overcome it, which in turn led him to be dogmatic and prevented him from reevaluating and updating his basic assumptions according to circumstances. The high assurance level of his "China policy" was expressed in his decisive and certain assessment of the low likelihood of a full-scale war, and the most extreme of possible violent developments between the two countries were seen as mere border incidents.

By extension, it appears that Nehru's perceptual system regarding the Chinese question was closely related to his own and India's national self-images. In order to protect these self-images, an ongoing resolution of contradictions was required; yet because of the degree of his self-assurance concerning basic assumptions, a thorough evaluation of the situation was never executed. The resulting misperceptions are summarized in Table 7.1.

In short, Nehru erred in evaluating the situation with regard to all dimensions comprising the environment.[1] He overestimated the limitation of other players in their interaction with India as a result of geographical and topographical conditions. He attributed importance to a nonrelevant factor from the Chinese point of view in the context of a massive attack against India—namely, the role of the United Nations and the Chinese interest in joining the organization. He misjudged the Chinese apprehension of the reaction of the Third World, and in particular the nonaligned bloc, just as he overestimated the support India could expect from the organization, and he drew the wrong conclusion as to the operational significance of the structure

Table 7.1. Misperceptions, Adaptation Processes, and Action Orientations

Issue Area	Misperceptions and Misconceptions	Type of Misperception	Type of Adaptation Process	Anticipation of Other Actors' Behavior	Indian Action Orientation
1. Definition of problem	1. Both sides defined problem as political; each side had a different world view, but Nehru was unaware of this fact.	Awareness gap	Nonadaptation	A common denominator can be found without India having to change its positions.	Nonconcessional policy can be continued; no danger in a risk-taking policy.
	2. Low evaluation of the strategic threat aspect	Evaluation gap	Very partial adaptation	No danger of war; no need for overcaution.	Nonconcessional policy can be continued.
2. The global system	3. A Sino-Indian war would lead to a world war. The super powers will prevent such a war.	Awareness gap	Nonadaptation	No danger of war; no need for overcaution with China.	Nonconcessional policy can be continued.
	4. Prestige in the international arena gives India immunity due to its deterrent aspect.	Evaluation gap	Nonadaptation	China will not risk war with India. Concessions are not necessary.	Nonconcessional policy can be continued.
	5. Prestige at the UN grants India immunity, as China needs Indian support on this matter.	Evaluation gap / Relevance gap	Nonadaptation / Nonadaptation	China will prevent relations with India from deteriorating. Concessions are not necessary.	Nonconcessional policy can be continued.

(Table continues)

Table 7.1 continued

Issue Area	Misperceptions and Misconceptions	Type of Misperception	Type of Adaptation Process	Anticipation of Other Actors' Behavior	Indian Action Orientation
	6. The Chinese problem is less important to India than are global problems.	Evaluation gap	Nonadaptation		Activities should be focused on global arena in the framework of nonalignment policy.
	7. All foreign policy successes are due to Nonalignment.	Awareness gap	Nonadaptation	Other actors wish to avoid a situation in which India would change non-alignment policy.	Nonalignment must be strictly pursued.
	8. In the existing global system, conflicts can be controlled only until violence erupts.	Awareness gap	Nonadaptation	China will prevent its relationship with India from deteriorating into war.	India can allow itself a firm stand on Chinese issues but must not lose control of the situation.
	9. India is the leader of the Third World, which will unanimously support India.	Evaluation gap	Nonadaptation	China cannot afford to confront Third World criticism.	India is granted "immunity" and can continue with a nonconcessional policy until China yields.
	10. The Third World and India as its leader have a balancing role in the global system.	Awareness gap	Nonadaptation	The super powers cannot afford to let the leader of the balancing force be humiliated or defeated.	India can, without fear, continue its firm attitude toward China.

(Table continues)

Table 7.1 continued

Issue Area	Misperceptions and Misconceptions	Type of Misperception	Type of Adaptation Process	Anticipation of Other Actors' Behavior	Indian Action Orientation
	11. India and China have similar evaluations of the global situation.	Awareness gap	Partial adaptation	China will draw the above appropriate conclusions; thus there is no threat to India.	India can take a firm and uncompromising position.
3. The Soviet position	12. The USSR remains the uncontested leader of the Communist bloc despite its rift with China.	Awareness gap	Nonadaptation		India can continue its nonconcessional policy and daring military policy.
	13. China is economically and militarily dependent on the USSR.	Awareness gap	Nonadaptation	China will not act over USSR objections.	India can continue its nonconcessional policy and daring military policy.
	14. The Sino-Soviet dispute exists but is not central to the Sino-Indian conflict.	Evaluation gap Relevance gap	Partial adaptation Nonadaptation	There is no necessary linkage between the Sino-USSR and Sino-Indian disputes.	It is not necessary to take this issue into consideration in evaluating possible Chinese reactions to Indian policies.
4. The U.S. position	15. The U.S. cannot agree to a military attack on India that might mean the rise of Chinese power in Asia.	Evaluation gap	Nonadaptation	The U.S. would intervene in a Sino-Indian war.	India can continue its nonconcessional policy.

(Table continues)

Table 7.1 continued

Issue Area	Misperceptions and Misconceptions	Type of Misperception	Type of Adaptation Process	Anticipation of Other Actors' Behavior	Indian Action Orientation
5. Subsystemic activities	16. Beyond any dispute, there exists Asian solidarity.	Awareness gap	Nonadaptation	A Sino-Indian war is impossible.	India can continue its non-concessional policy with no fear of war.
	17. India's status in the world, and especially in Asia, grants it immunity and political power.	Evaluation gap	Nonadaptation	Other actors would not dare to arouse Third World public opinion against them by a massive aggression.	India can continue its non-concessional policy with no fear of war.
	18. There exists a basically homogeneous Asian sub-system, with India at its core.	Awareness gap	Partial adaptation	India's neighbors would only reluctantly co-operate with China.	There is no need to change the policy toward the Hill States and Pakistan.
6. Geo-strategy	19. There is no chance of any war in the foreseeable future in this important geo-strategic area.	Awareness gap	Nonadaptation	China will not invade India, as the super powers will not agree to foreign control of the subcontinent.	India can continue its non-concessional policy.
	20. The topographical con-ditions permit only very limited fighting; thus India is protected.	Awareness gap	Nonadaptation	China will continue with its border-incidents policy and will not invade India.	India can continue its non-concessional and Forward Policy with no fear of war.

(Table continues)

Table 7.1 continued

Issue Area	Misperceptions and Misconceptions	Type of Misperception	Type of Adaptation Process	Anticipation of Other Actors' Behavior	Indian Action Orientation
	21. The double-defense-line thesis is still valid.	Relevance gap	Nonadaptation	China will respect Indian dominance in the Hill States.	India can continue to hold British strategic concepts, disregarding circumstances and without suitable military growth.
7. India and Pakistan	22. Pakistan poses the main threat to India.	Evaluation gap	Nonadaptation	Pakistan is preparing to invade Kashmir.	The main military effort must be to stop Pakistan. The dispute with China must be reduced so as not to open a second front.
	23. Pakistan and China have less in common than do China and India.	Awareness gap	Nonadaptation	A secular China will not cooperate with Muslim Pakistan.	The main military effort should be to contain Pakistan.
	24. Following the Sino-Pakistan agreement, Chinese support of Pakistan will encourage Pakistan to adopt an adventurous policy.	Awareness gap	Maladaptation	Pakistan is preparing a military attack against India.	The main military effort must be to defeat Pakistan.

(Table continues)

Table 7.1 continued

Issue Area	Misperceptions and Misconceptions	Type of Misperception	Type of Adaptation Process	Anticipation of Other Actors' Behavior	Indian Action Orientation
8. India and the Hill States	25. China unconditionally recognizes Indian dominance in the Hill States.	Evaluation gap	Adaptation	The Hill States have no alternative to India.	The double-defense-line strategy must be continued. (Following the adaptation process, Nehru understood that China was trying to create a buffer federation that would be independent of India.)
	26. Indian political presence guarantees India's military defense.	Awareness gap	Nonadaptation	China will not use force against the Hill States as a result of Indian deterrence.	Double-defense-line strategy must be continued. No significant change is needed in military planning.
	27. The Sino-Indian dispute has not changed the dependence on India of all the Hill States, regardless of size or status.	Evaluation gap	Nonadaptation	None of the Hill States would take steps that would threaten India strategically.	Policy of interference in their internal affairs can be continued. A display of daring and firmness must be made in the dispute with China so that India will not appear to be weak and thereby lose its dominant position with the Hill States.

(Table continues)

Table 7.1 continued

Issue Area	Misperceptions and Misconceptions	Type of Misperception	Type of Adaptation Process	Anticipation of Other Actors' Behavior	Indian Action Orientation
9. The balance of power	28. War between India and China is unlikely, as a decisive victory for one side is impossible.	Awareness gap	Nonadaptation	China will not invade India, although border incidents might occur.	The nonconcessional policy can be continued in spite of the secondary priority given to strengthening the Army.
	29. The Indian army is getting stronger in relation to the Chinese army.	Awareness gap	Maladaptation	China will not dare to invade India.	Forward Policy may be pursued.
	30. China is chiefly preoccupied with the U.S.-Taiwan threat.	Evaluation gap	Nonadaptation	China will not open a second front.	Chinese warnings may be ignored and the Forward Policy pursued. Secondary preference given to strengthening land forces may be continued.
10. Domestic politics	31. A coalition is possible between parts of Congress Party and opposition circles, endangering Nehru's political and personal status.	Evaluation gap	Nonadaptation		A firm stand on Chinese issue must be taken.

(Table continues)

Table 7.1 continued

Issue Area	Misperceptions and Misconceptions	Type of Misperception	Type of Adaptation Process	Anticipation of Other Actors' Behavior	Indian Action Orientation
	32. Concessions to the op-position can be made without losing control or freedom of decision.	Evaluation gap	Nonadaptation		A combination of uncom-promising firmness with a willingness to talk (as dis-tinguished from negotiation) best serves this purpose.
11. Legal aspects	33. The purely legal aspect of the affair is as important to China as it is to India.	Evaluation gap	Maladaptation	China will be convinced if India's legal right is proven.	India is legally right and should not give way.
	34. The legal system is universal.	Awareness gap	Nonadaptation	China accepts the prin-ciples of international law and sees it as auto-nomous, objective, and unconditional.	India should not give way, as China ultimately will accept India's positions.
12. China and India	35. There is a tradition of affinity and political friendship between China and India.	Evaluation gap	Nonadaptation	China would not allow the dispute to deteriorate beyond local conflicts. The dispute is a temporary matter, although a settle-ment may not be in sight.	India can take a firm stand without it leading to war.

(Table continues)

Table 7.1 continued

Issue Area	Misperceptions and Misconceptions	Type of Misperception	Type of Adaptation Process	Anticipation of Other Actors' Behavior	Indian Action Orientation
	36. China and India disagree on Tibet, but this is not a crucial issue.	Evaluation gap	Nonadaptation	A certain amount of Chinese hostility is to be expected.	A balance must be found between the Chinese position on Tibet and support of the Dalai Lama.
	37. China is very anxious to be accepted into the UN.	Evaluation gap	Nonadaptation	China needs India's support and will thus avoid taking extreme measures against it.	A nonconcessional policy and the Forward Policy may be continued.
	38. China basically accepts India's version of what the international system should be like and what it is like.	Evaluation Gap	Partial adaptation	China will avoid taking military (war) measures against India (see above).	India's uncompromising attitude is not leading to war.
	39. There is a unity of purpose between India and China that is independent of time and circumstances.	Awareness gap	Nonadaptation	China will avoid war.	India's uncompromising attitude is not leading to war.
	40. The hostility toward India is an externalization of Chinese internal economic and political problems.	Relevance gap	Nonadaptation	Limited externalization of violence and hostility is to be expected in the future due to the weakness of the Chinese regime. The self-restraint is a sign of weakness.	India's uncompromising attitude is not leading to war. Chinese warnings on the subject may be ignored.

(Table continues)

Table 7.1 continued

Issue Area	Misperceptions and Misconceptions	Type of Misperception	Type of Adaptation Process	Anticipation of Other Actors' Behavior	Indian Action Orientation
13. Threat	41. Insensitivity to swings in Chinese threat perceptions and their significance	Evaluation gap	Nonadaptation	China's threat perception is not strong enough for war to break out.	The uncompromising policy may be continued; the chances of war are slight.
14. Hostility	42. Asymmetry in hostility perceptions	Evaluation gap	Adaptation	China has temporarily become hostile to India and is unlikely to change in the near future.	India is justified in showing the same hostility toward China and suspicion of its suggestions.
	43. The Chinese hostility perception is not definitely linked to the level of threat.	Relevance gap	Nonadaptation	Chinese hostility perception does not necessarily mean a threat perception sufficiently high for war to break out.	An uncompromising policy may be continued.
15. Time	44. Time is in India's favor.	Awareness gap	Maladaptation	In the long run, China will have to accept India's demands.	India must pursue a relentless and uncompromising policy.

of the global system. These errors of judgment, of course, led to a mistaken evaluation of China's cost-benefit calculations in the event of an attack on India and consequently to an exaggeration of the deterrent power of these factors.

In his misunderstanding of the Chinese conceptual frame of reference, Nehru attributed values, norms, and beliefs to the Chinese leadership that it did not share. And even though China used terms that seemed to correspond to those values, a deeper probe would have revealed that the content behind the words was very different from what Nehru imagined.[2] Thus, his evaluation of the degree to which these values encouraged or prevented undesirable or dangerous behavior as far as India was concerned was mistaken. The same is true of his basic view of India and China as friendly nations with similar interests and with a 2,000-year tradition of friendship, a view that encouraged his belief in a Chinese action orientation of low violence.

Nehru also blundered over those issues that might appear to be more easily analyzable—the economic and military balance of power. As a result, he overestimated India's deterrent strength, thereby contributing to a perception of threat that excluded the possibility of war and was insensible to the adversary's threat perception. The final outcome of this misperceptual process was an acute failure in evaluating the relative capability and intentions of the enemy. The reasons for this failure will be discussed in the subsequent chapters.

Nehru's view of the Sino-Indian dispute raises a number of puzzles with regard to his "perceptual behavior" during this period, especially in light of the categorical conclusions he drew from information seeming to point elsewhere. It was on these conclusions that India's policy preferences were based; their operative application finally led to the Chinese attack at dawn on October 20, 1962.

From 1959 to 1962 we find that despite the significance of the Chinese issue to Indian foreign policy, and although a large number of other foreign policy matters did not bear on India's immediate interests as much, the Chinese issue was given only secondary importance relative to other internal and external problems occupying Nehru. Such neglect was characteristic of the entire period, even when tension was high. One example was Nehru's inexplicable trip to Ceylon one week before hostilities broke out, when a situation of extreme tension existed along India's northern borders.

Most of Nehru's misperceptions were of the evaluation-gap type. Some factors and variables were allowed to carry too small a weight in the situation evaluations, whereas others were overemphasized. In addition, as we noted earlier, there were some misconceptions of the awareness-gap type, but only a very few were of the relevance-gap type. How can these various types of misperception be explained, and how do we account for the dominance of nonadaptation or

maladaptation processes, especially in the crucial area of evaluation
of the power relations between India and China in which misperceptions grew steadily worse over time?

It emerges that, despite the significant change for the worse that
occurred in the mutual hostility conceptions, Nehru maintained an
almost mystical optimism, a belief that a solution to the problem,
and a favorable one to India at that, would finally be found. From
where did this optimism arise?

As for perceptions of threat, it appears that they remained on a
low level compared to the level of hostility perceptions. The evaluation
of threat also remained fairly constant. Nehru continued to underplay
the threat, to dismiss as unlikely the use of violence on a massive
scale by China, and to adhere to the belief that at most limited
military forays on the level of border incidents could be expected.

The puzzle increases in light of the fact that this optimistic
evaluation was maintained even following Chinese warnings to the
contrary that became progressively sharper in tone and content:[3] "The
Chinese Government warns the Indian Government, if the Indian
side does not immediately stop its armed attack and withdraw from
the Che Dong area but keeps on creating new incidents of bloodshed,
the Chinese side will surely act resolutely in self-defence and the
Indian Government must bear full responsibility" (*W.P.*, VII, 105).
India complacency continued despite the fact that Chinese preparations
for the possibility of a full-scale war were made quite openly. The
Chinese allowed Indian air reconnaissance over their military de-
ployments in Tibet (Dalvi, 1969, 153–154). In May 1962 Indian
intelligence came across a document that had been distributed by
the Chinese consulate in Calcutta, from which it was deduced that
a Chinese attack in the autumn was possible (Mullik, 1971, 330).
Smugness was so rampant in New Delhi in the days before the
outbreak of the war that the commander of the Fourth Corps,
Lieutenant General Kaul, was not in his sector—for health reasons—
and on the day the fighting broke out he was in New Delhi.[4]

Other perplexing questions arise: Why did Nehru attach so little
importance to the warnings of military men on the possibility of a
war for which India was not prepared and which would constitute
a national disaster? And how did it happen that, in spite of all the
evidence, such a deep and unshakable consensus was formed in
Nehru's close circle? The following chapters will attempt to discuss
and answer these questions and, on the basis of our theoretical
construct, perhaps throw some light on the puzzle.

Information: Type, Flow, and Handling

The Quality of the Information and Information Networks

The nature of the information dealing with China and the technical qualities of the network that gathered and processed this information contributed significantly to the rise of misperceptions. These factors encouraged the rejection of dissonant information or the belittling of its value, which in turn caused it to be interpreted in such a way that would not force Nehru and his associates to change their views and threat evaluations.

In the preceding chapters, we saw that India regarded itself as committed to political interactions on a global scale. This concept led to its simultaneous involvement in several arenas with various problems, from local conflicts in almost any part of the world to issues of disarmament and international organizations. Thus, the concentration and attention of the Indian leadership was often distracted from regional concerns; what was happening on India's borders seemed dwarfed in comparison to global affairs, a slight issue that would find its eventual solution.[1]

The central foreign policymaker, Nehru, was extremely active in all the other areas, too. He was at once prime minister, minister of External Affairs, head of the Atomic Energy Commission, head of the Planning Commission, leader of the Congress Party and, as such, a member of the various party bodies formal and informal, a member of Parliament, and a sort of Indian ambassador at large who was frequently away from home on missions of mediation and conciliation. In all these matters, he tended to see to the details himself without relying on others. The bureaucracy, too, accepted willingly that every matter was to be brought to Nehru for final approval. This centralist system of nondelegation of authority was so extreme that, as Nehru's biographer has rightly pointed out, "the bureaucracy functions only as rapidly as Nehru can handle the vast amount of paper that crosses his desk" (Brecher, 1959, 623).[2] The centralist system applied even more so in foreign policy, as this was the area in which Nehru was rarely challenged and in which he was considered by himself and others to be India's foremost expert. The tidal wave of information reaching his desk daily created such a great pressure on him that no single subject could receive his undivided attention, and he certainly did not have the strength to reevaluate issues or give them fresh thought. As he himself noted: "In Delhi our days are spent in rushing from one [person] to another or from one activity to another, and we do not have the advantage of leisurely thinking (*F.N.*, 5/59, May 28, 1959). Eventually the burden and his constant worrying damaged his health, and although no specific illness was diagnosed, in the first half of 1962 he felt constantly unwell: "It is true that I tend to overtax my system by putting too much of a burden on it. . . . Ultimately, however, the continuing strain brought about an accumulation of fatigue which led to my indisposition" (*F.N.*, 1/62, July 10, 1962). It seems that by the early 1960s Nehru was already past his prime physically and intellectually.[3]

In this state of affairs, the people Nehru relied upon and trusted were doubly important. The most prominent among them was Krishna Menon, who was perhaps closer to Nehru than any other person. As minister of defense, he enjoyed Nehru's complete confidence and almost a free reign in military matters. Menon was not interested in devoting time to the improvement of intelligence processing, which, as we shall see, was really deficient. He preferred dealing with the military industries and the diversity of current foreign policy involvements. Thus, important areas, such as the improvement of the intelligence system, army operations, and training were neglected. As Lieutenant General Kaul, a senior officer at army headquarters in New Delhi, put it: "If anyone made an effort to throw some light on them [these areas], Menon had little time for him" (Kaul, 1967, 205).

This subject was made even more problematic by its connection with India's domestic political system. Nehru was engaged in constant struggle over the nonalignment policy with the opposition in and out of his party, and here the interpretation of information relating to China was regarded as of prime importance. Thus, if and when he received interpretations, those formed either by the army or by the civil political opposition, unlike his own ideas, they were immediately rejected with the convenient claim that they expressed the dishonest intentions of his oppositionists. The army, for example, was out to get more money and more equipment by creating a false threat. To the intra-party and extra-party oppositions the intention was attributed of scheming to replace nonalignment with a pro-Western policy. Hence, it was possible to justify, with a minimum of intellectual and emotional discomfort, the rejection of interpretations that contradicted Nehru's prejudices.

An additional problem was posed by the fact that since China had turned Communist, it had become, for Western politicians and intelligence agencies, a mystifying entity. To gather information and especially to interpret what was happening behind the "bamboo curtain" was a complex and difficult task.[4] The fluctuations in its internal and external policies were not fully understood, and the exact balance of power and attitudes within the Chinese leadership had never been fully ascertained. Very little, indeed, was known about the more obscure central committee members. Knowledge of Chinese ideological terminology demanded expertise both in ideological writings and in Chinese language and culture.

For the Indian Intelligence Bureau these problems were doubly difficult because of objective conditions in India. Until the early 1950s, Chinese studies (language, culture, politics, and history) were notoriously neglected in the Indian academic system. A change for the better occurred in the mid-1950s following the thaw in relations between the two countries. The Chinese departments in Indian universities—particularly the School for International Studies in Delhi University and the School for Foreign Languages—were given something of a boost. But there was still a severe shortage of trained manpower in these areas, and only in 1958 were preparations begun on a Hindu-Chinese dictionary. It is estimated that during this period the number of people who could read and write Chinese in all of India was no more than half a dozen (Passin, 1961). Despite Nehru's instructions to Mullik, director of the Intelligence Bureau, right at the start of the 1950s, to begin intelligence activities and the collection of information on China (as part of handing over all intelligence activities abroad to the Intelligence Bureau),[5] this was apparently a very problematic assignment. The setting up of intelligence networks began from scratch both because of the lack of suitably trained people and because the British in their time had not trained Indians in intelligence activities, unlike other fields, and the Indians had no experience in this field. The director of the bureau maintained that until 1960 the organization managed to overcome these problems (Mullik, 1971, 134–135), but this is unlikely as even the U.S. intelligence community did not succeed in surmounting the obstacles of gathering information on China, despite the fact that, to begin with, its resources were much greater than those available to Indian intelligence.[6]

But these were not the only problems in the sphere of intelligence gathering and processing. The gathering system itself was deficient, and available material was improperly processed. The Joint Intelligence Committee of the armed forces, the Home Ministry, and the Ministry of External Affairs (MEA), established in 1948 and headed by an MEA official, functioned inadequately (Bandyopadhyaya, 1970, 197–198; Khera 1968, 215), and the military intelligence service deteriorated. Because of Mullik's personal status and key position as Nehru's confidant, the Intelligence Bureau, which was responsible both for internal security and intelligence abroad, became the central and authoritative source of situation evaluations in the area of strategic intelligence, that is, in the evaluation of capability and intentions of potential adversaries. The gathering of tactical intelligence, which was chiefly the responsibility of the military intelligence service, was deficient both in collection and interpretation, as the military service was downgraded,[7] lacking manpower and equipment; the post of chief of Military Intelligence was not sought after and was seen only as a stepping stone in the military hierarchy (Subrahamanyam, 1970a; Hoffmann, 1972).

Thus it happened that in both the MEA and the Ministry of Defense the subject of research and interpretation was neglected in favor of collecting material. Only a little attention was given to the establishment of suitable research teams; in the main, evaluations were made by agents whose expertise was the collection of information, but not political evaluations (Bandyopadhyaya, 1970, 200). Under the existing circumstances, the supreme body dealing with intelligence, the Joint Intelligence Committee, which should have performed an integrative and independent role in situation evaluation, became an ineffectual body that hardly functioned at all until 1963; hence, when divisions of opinion on evaluations occurred, compromises were generally accepted. For example, if the Intelligence Bureau talked of seven enemy divisions in Tibet and the Army claimed that there were only four, a compromise was reached on five and this figure was passed on to policymakers as an evaluation (Mullik, 1971, 305).

The chaos in the coordination of intelligence activities was aggravated by Mullik's intimacy with Nehru. Information on the Intelligence Bureau's activities and the material gathered often never reached those bodies whose business it was to know, such as the army. At times it was not even brought to the attention of those involved at the Home Ministry, to whom Mullik was subordinate. Matters were settled verbally and covertly between Nehru and Mullik for the sake of secrecy (Mullik, 1971, 192–193; Maxwell, 1972, 499). Under such conditions it is not farfetched to surmise that there may well have been some activities of which even Nehru was not aware and which he did not particularly care to know. Given his idealism and his ethical aversion to Machiavellianism in foreign policy, he had reservations about intelligence organizations and an aversion to their secretive methods (Bandyopadhyaya, 1970, 199). This situation probably left Mullik with a wide scope for independent action.

We might reasonably suppose that, although Nehru might not have been aware of it, there was a degree of truth in the Chinese claim of subversive and provocative Indian activities originating in Kalimpong, and that this made the Chinese perception of threat from Indian involvement in Tibet more acute.[8] Nehru's denials could be regarded from the Chinese point of view only as an expression of his untrustworthiness and insincerity, thus deepening the hostility of the Chinese leadership toward him and India. Nehru, unaware of the situation, continued to believe that Chou En-lai's information was erroneous or, as he put it, "the information they [the Chinese] get is not very correct—it is coloured information, that is, they see only one side of the picture, about the outside world I mean" (*Press.*, I, 89).

Nehru, as we have already pointed out, tried to keep the escalating conflict with China secret until 1959, confident that if it did not become an issue of public debate he would be able to solve it. This policy was carried so far that until 1959 the MEA avoided dealing with any information concerning Chinese infiltration into Indian territory. Nehru would get so angry over any reminder of the possibility of escalation of the dispute that it was immediately filed away. Thereafter in the Home Ministry, to put away something in the border file became a euphemistic phrase for any subject that nobody wanted to deal with (Nayar, 1969, 135). When the issue finally did become public, when it could no longer be ignored, Nehru underplayed its importance to justify his previous reluctance to deal with it openly.

The intense Chinese activity on the military and diplomatic fronts, such as the nonrecognition of the McMahon line and the ever-increasing border incidents, brought the matter to public attention. The strong reverberations it created in the domestic Indian political arena gave it ever greater significance. Nehru could not ignore information that concentrated on specific events such as military clashes in a certain place at a certain time, and that deviated so widely from his expectations. Later he would find rationalizations in claims, contradictory though they were, that China had always evinced expansionist tendencies in times of a strong centralist regime, or that this behavior was an expression of China's need to externalize its internal difficulties. These claims enabled him to accept the idea of a conflict without it posing a threat to his basic notions of the fundamental common interests of the two countries. Thus, he could cease to ignore the issue. What is more, some Chinese reactions were anticipated to a degree by Nehru, and thus such behavior caused neither undue alarm nor a reevaluation of dominant conceptions. Upon returning from his visit to China in 1954, Nehru told T.N. Kaul: "with the Chinese you never know and have to be prepared for unexpected reactions. This may be partly due to their isolation but it is mainly the Chinese character I think" (Kaul, 1979, 70).

At the same time, suitable circumstances allowed a special openness toward certain data, particularly data stressing the importance of global events in the relations between India and the super powers and, later on in the dispute, those details dealing with India's increasing power. These arrived at the proper time, so they could be used to gain support for Nehru's foreign policy and nonalignment orientation; Nehru could counter the criticism of his opponents with proof of super-power support, the growth of India's political might and military strength, and China's internal difficulties. It is significant that these concepts were not new and that Nehru already possessed the conceptual framework for absorbing this type of information.

The same concepts, however, made it easier for Nehru to ignore information indicating a growing Chinese threat. The sources of such information were military men such as General K.S. Thimayya, Chief of Army Staff (COAS); senior commanders in the eastern sector, such as Lieutenant General Umrao Singh; and Lieutenant General Daulat Singh in the western sector. By dismissing these sources as unimportant and branding the military as "warmongers,"[9] Nehru established a "first defense line" against dissonant information. The "second defense line" consisted of the assumptions of India's immunity as a result of super-power support, its special status in the Third World arena and in the global system, and its military strength. These two "defense lines" contributed to the feeling that even if there was a threat, India could deal with it effectively. Consequently, the threshold of penetration of threat information arose, and a series of Chinese warning signals (which will be discussed shortly) indicating that China would use force if necessary did not receive appropriate attention from Nehru.

An additional contributing factor was the fact that the information pointing to China's increasing willingness to resort to war did not arrive all at once but trickled in very slowly. This fact was partially due to China's attempts to try all other avenues first, although it seems that from the second half of 1961, the Chinese leadership was not adverse to the idea of a limited war with India (Khera, 1968, 36; *P.R.*, Dec. 15, 1961).

To all these factors we must add Nehru's inability to give threat signals an unequivocal interpretation. Pessimistic evaluations were always countered by less pessimistic ones. For example, the concentration of Chinese forces in Tibet was explained away by internal unrest there. And, of course, there was the situation in the Intelligence Bureau, which could not at that time fit the incoming information into a comprehensive picture, nor interpret it properly, nor present an alternative contradictory evaluation. A colleague of Mullik's, Kaul, testifies to this: "Mullik's assessments of their intentions and priorities were therefore mostly based on guesswork and seldom on reliable evidence" (Kaul, 1971, 291).

It should be emphasized that there was no lack of information. The problem lay in the area of the processing and evaluation of the raw material.[10] Additional factors magnified the confusion. The information pointing to a possible Chinese resort to war deviated so radically from the general image that even when it penetrated into Nehur's cognitive system it was given low value, and events that it predicted were given a low likelihood, and its general effect on the overall situation evaluation was negligible. Furthermore, in the past whenever the use of force was indicated and was put into effect, it had remained limited to border incidents; there seemed no reason to suppose that it would be different this time.

The tendency not to change existing beliefs was supported by Nehru's faith that even if he was underestimating the Chinese threat, India could successfully cope with any resulting scenario. He was also not worried by the existence of some dissonant information. As a veteran statesman, he probably knew that in international relations there is no unambiguous information, and he was aware of the game nations play of spreading false information or propaganda material that does not convey their real intentions. He did not, therefore, deem it necessary to change his positions and evaluations, even when some of his senior officers pointed out the inherent dangers in continuing the Forward Policy and warned against putting into action "Operation Leghorn," which was aimed at ousting Chinese forces that had penetrated south of the Thag La Ridge on September 8, 1962 (Maxwell, 1972, 329–330). Thus, despite the fact that this crisis caused the central policymaker at the time—Menon, as Nehru was away from India—to search frantically for information and to hold daily updating sessions in the Defense Ministry in the presence of military intelligence and MEA representatives, the option chosen was always military retaliation with no serious reexamination of alternatives. The director of the Intelligence Bureau, who was partner to those sessions from September 11 on, describes the situation in his reminiscences as follows: "the question was never raised whether the Chinese could or should be driven out. The only question was how soon this could be done and what more reinforcement was necessary" (Mullik, 1971, 341).

Moreover, when on October 10 it became clear to Kaul himself that Operation Leghorn was unfeasible and he presented New Delhi with different options, it was agreed to leave the decision about the operation to him, but he was categorically forbidden to retreat to defensible positions. He was told by Nehru that even if the worst were to happen he was to continue holding the strategically illogical defense line (Kaul, 1967, 386; Dalvi, 1969, 285). This was a continuation of the approach taken back in September in which, despite the general agreement on India's military weakness and against the optional defense plan proposed by the commander of the western sector, Lieutenant General Daulat Singh, a decision was taken on the basis of Mullik's decisive opinion, to stay on the existing line despite the difficulty in holding it (Mullik, 1971, 349).

As the problem was defined mainly as a political-diplomatic rather than a military-strategic one, the pessimistic situation evaluations made by the military staff were considered irrelevant, and great weight was given to the evaluations of the politicians and bureaucrats surrounding Nehru, such as Menon, Mullik, and the senior personnel of the Ministry of Defense and the MEA. The emphasis on the diplomatic-political dimension, which demanded that the problem be viewed in light of international events, Nehru's main interest, caused Chinese intentions to be judged in terms of the Indian analysis of the global situation.[11] From this point of view, the warnings of Indian field officers seemed unreliable and irrelevant, especially given that for Nehru to accept those opinions would have meant a distraction from his main preoccupation—the redesign of the international system as a means of dealing with secondary bilateral problems.

Nehru's principal advisor on intelligence matters, who by his own evidence received information on Chinese war preparations along the Sino-Indian border, preferred to keep his position and intimacy with Nehru and to supply him with evaluations similar to those he already held. This also guaranteed the prestige of the Intelligence Bureau (IB). It was Mullik who, in the debate on the Chinese reaction to the Forward Policy, insisted that they would avoid the use of force as long as Indian forces did not attack Chinese patrols (Maxwell, 1972, 234).

It is important to note that, considering the enormous burden of activity that lay on Nehru's shoulder, which prevented him from making a reassessment, no mechanism existed for such a reevaluation. And because Nehru's ideas about foreign policy in general and the Chinese problem in particular were fixed (*Par.*, I, 212), he did not like to "waste time" on new evaluations, even in response to dissonant information. Nehru preferred routinization or the absorption of data with the assumption that it could be left as it was. If information appeared that was particularly disturbing, he treated it by ignoring it, filtering it, or giving it a distorted interpretation supplied by aides and advisors appointed on the basis of the similarity of their views to his own, and who made sure that the information and interpretations reaching him would be acceptable to him under the given circumstances. Thus, they "saved" him time or encouraged him to maintain his assertion that the information did not require a reevaluation. The process was aided by Nehru's tendency to judge the information on the basis of its source. He usually surrounded himself with people on whom he relied and with whom he maintained personal friendly relations, so much so that he kept them in senior positions even if and when their incompetence had been proven (Brecher, 1959, 618; Kaul, 1967, 311). Naturally, Nehru developed a decided preference for information and situation evaluations coming from his inner circle of Menon, Kaul, Mullik, Gopal, and others. Opinions of other men who did not belong to this clique, no matter how talented or convincing, were rejected. In this way a vicious circle was created: acceptable evaluations came from a close group of advisors, but they were his advisors mainly because they supplied him with acceptable information. This situation was aggravated by a feature of the information gathering and processing system. The Intelligence Bureau did not follow the elementary rule, learned in other countries through past mistakes, of maintaining a separation between the collectors of information and its interpreters. It will further be seen that the same men who gathered the data were responsible for its processing and for bringing it to Nehru's attention. As there were no bodies to present alternative interpretations, it was not difficult to manipulate the material to suit Nehru's views.[12]

Nehru's tendency to judge information by its source probably contributed to his conclusion that China would be reluctant to go to war. The Chinese press, for example, was for him an unreliable source of information because of its manipulation by the authorities: "there has been rather an intense anti-Indian campaign in the Chinese Press. These campaigns there come on and go off as if one was turning a tap" (*Par.*, II, 76). As the press was faceless and it was never possible to pinpoint who was behind a particular article, it seems that Nehru tended to rely more on information for which the sources were clearer, and which came in face-to-face interaction, such as expressions of Chou En-lai or Ch'en Yi, China's foreign minister. However, these were diplomats who, under the circumstances, tended to downplay the possibility of war.

And, finally, it cannot escape our attention that because Nehru saw the China policy as expressing his world view, he felt responsible and highly personally involved. Any major change in his position or views would have meant the collapse of his special status both within and beyond India, as it would have proved his critics right. This situation pressured him into a selective preference of certain information, particularly in light of his personal lack of self-confidence, and greatly reduced his willingness to adopt new concepts, especially when the main sources of the dissonant information and interpretations were the military, the right wing of the Congress Party, and the opposition. Such being the case, Nehru was not surprised at the reactions of these groups. He attributed such reactions to the conceptual systems of the three groups and then flatly rejected their conceptual systems. Again, he was absolved from reexamining his own concepts.

A possibly significant factor in Nehru's lingering misconceptions was the asymmetry between the ways in which he came into contact with the political and military information. He gained his political information in direct talks with Chou En-lai, in his visit to China in 1954 with its lasting impact, and in the correspondence he held with the Chinese government. However, his military information came to him second hand (via officers, Menon, and Mullik), both because his knowledge of military matters was slight and because his interest in the subject was minor to begin with. As a result, if there appeared to be an incompatibility between the political and military information, he naturally tended to prefer the political point of view and to adapt the military information to it. This is what happened, for example, in September 1962 when the commander of the western sector warned against the Forward Policy and Nehru disregarded his warning (Mullik, 1971, 349).

The Sino-Indian Signaling System

The gathering and evaluating of information being as inefficient as it was, we shouldn't wonder that one of the major means of communication in the relations between the two countries, the signaling system, lost its effectiveness and even became, for both sides, a source of misleading information. The mutual lack of awareness caused moves made with a certain intention to be interpreted as pointing in the opposite direction and deepened both the misperceptions as well as the sense of hostility. The signaling system between the countries contained errors of both encoding and decoding.

I do not intend to present the reader with all the signals that were sent by the Chinese in their effort to urge the acuteness of the problem on the Indian consciousness in the three-and-a-half year period covered in this study. A number of examples concentrating mainly on the critical period in the months just preceding the war should suffice:

1. On April 30, 1962 China announced the renewal of patrols in the no-man's-land of the western sector, patrols that had been suspended since 1959. This announcement was meant to indicate that China would not sit by while the Forward Policy continued. Nehru, however, saw in it a verification of evaluations made during the policy debate, which had promised that the Chinese would react only diplomatically or symbolically and not in any massive military operation. The result was a further adherence to the Forward Policy (Maxwell, 1972, 251).

2. In May 1962, the Chinese began making use of the terminology that they had used on the eve of their involvement in the Korean War (Whiting, 1975, 58).[13] The Indian government was not aware of this, as the whole issue of Chinese terminology was foreign to Nehru and his advisors.

3. On July 10, a direct confrontation took place when the Chinese army, after repeated warnings, outflanked an Indian position in the Galwan Valley. The Indian unit received instructions not to retreat. The Chinese avoided a direct clash, probably only intending to show that it could easily surround and destroy the Indian position if need arose. Nehru, on the other hand, concluded that the Forward Policy was succeeding and that the evaluations indicating that the Chinese would not dare engage the Indian army in all-out war were proven correct.

4. In the same month, the Chinese ambassador returned to India with the intention of hinting that the diplomatic option was *also* still

open (Liao and Whiting, 1973). Nehru probably concluded that the Forward Policy was beginning to show results and that *only* the diplomatic option was felt by the Chinese government to be left open, thus making war unlikely.

5. In the Chinese press, there appeared explicit hints that India was going too far in its behavior and that it should not draw the wrong conclusions from Chinese restraint (*P.R.*, July 13, 1962, 10–11; July 27, 1962, 12–14). New Delhi did not attach significance to these hints. The same applied to the growing number of Chinese warnings in the correspondence with the Indian government (*W.P.*, VII, 96–98).[14]

6. On September 8, Chinese forces crossed the Thag La Ridge in the eastern sector as an indication to India that its provocations had gone too far. Nehru thought only that this Chinese arrogance called for a military reply—namely, the ousting of Chinese forces from Indian territory in the eastern sector; he therefore ordered the planning of Operation Leghorn.

7. On September 28, the first mass demonstration directly related to the Sino-Indian dispute was held in China. It occurred on the occasion of the funeral of five Chinese border guards who had fallen in border incidents and was broadcast over the all-China radio. The resolution taken at the end of the rally was in a way a preparation of the Chinese public for the possibility of large-scale fighting with India (Whiting, 1975, 104).

8. On October 10, Lieutenant General Kaul, under whose direction Operation Leghorn was to be carried out, sent a vanguard unit to capture a topographically dominant ridge overlooking the Thag La Ridge. The attempt met with strong Chinese resistence, and both sides suffered heavy casualties. This outcome should have been a clear signal to India that it could not be taken for granted that China would avoid military confrontations and be satisfied with diplomatic protests and certain symbolic moves. Neither was there room to assume that China would focus its moves on the western sector where it was in the superior position and would avoid the eastern sector where India had control.[15] Again, Nehru did not make the appropriate connections between events.

9. During the entire period China carried out its military preparations quite openly as a warning, but to no avail.

Based on the examples just presented, it would seem that the Chinese contributed to the misunderstanding of their own signals and were trapped by their own encoding errors, all of which resulted from a lack of understanding of the other side's frame of reference. As they could not understand how Nehru viewed Communist China, nor how he misjudged events in China, their signals and warnings lost effectiveness and were interpreted precisely in the opposite way from that intended:[16] warnings were seen as an expression of weakness and as an unwillingness on the part of China to go to extremes even if the occasion so warranted. The Chinese, on the other hand, saw in Indian reactions, which ignored their warnings, provocations calling for a strong retaliation. Otherwise, loss of face for the Chinese government and the army might be entailed. Due to the failure of the signaling system, a spiral of escalation was created. China itself had for years encouraged Nehru to think that war was not a viable possibility, despite the occurrence of border incidents, and now the Chinese expected the same signals to have a different effect. And, indeed, those involved in the decisionmaking process admitted that within the circle of those concerned with the Sino-Indian dispute, none of the actions taken by the Chinese since the Kongka Pass incident in October 1959 caused surprise or raised a demand for a reevaluation of existing concepts (Hoffmann, 1971, 240).

The Chinese leadership was probably not aware of how far its verbal warnings had lost effectiveness as a deterrent. Years of using a violent terminology as a style of expression against different targets in the international arena—such as Chiang Kai-shek and his government, the United States, Japan, and others in Southeast Asia—made the current warnings and signals appear much less threatening. Naturally, the Indian government did not suppose that India would be the first object since Korea on which China would choose to make effective its hitherto verbal warnings. Moreover, the ideological heavy-handedness of these warnings made it easier for India to ignore them. India's foreign secretary at the time later admitted that Chinese verbal threats were not regarded as containing a significant threat of war (Hoffmann, 1971, 674).[17]

Another matter of which the Chinese were most likely ignorant was the extent to which the continuing rebellion in Tibet had impressed the chief Indian policymakers. Consequently, the Indian policymakers were used to seeing any reinforcement of Chinese forces in Tibet as mere noise in the signaling system, and any movement of those forces as relating only to the upheaval in Tibet. Thus, the fact that the Chinese army did not take the trouble to conceal its growing strength in Tibet was not enough to act as a deterrent. Indian policymakers did not see that the noise was rapidly becoming a signal; they preferred to attribute to the presence of the Chinese army in Tibet reasons of law-and-order enforcement, even when the numbers grew beyond proportions reasonable for that purpose.

The misunderstanding of processes within the Indian political system also blinded the Chinese leadership to the degree to which Nehru was restricted and to the inevitable gap between his verbal commitments and what could be effected. China tended to see in impulsively uttered statements fully detailed, precise, and binding plans of action. Nehru on his part could neither clarify his statements, nor soften their impact, nor explain his true intentions. An example of such a statement was the one he made on October 12 upon leaving for Ceylon, in which he declared that he had ordered the army to evict the Chinese forces from Indian territory—a statement that had little relation to reality, as in actual fact Nehru had given the army all the time it needed to prepare for Operation Leghorn and this permission had effectively postponed action. But Nehru, as a participant in the domestic political game, could not admit to the Chinese leadership that he had permitted the army to postpone the operation, and it is doubtful whether the adversary, China, could have taken this fact into consideration. Again, the interpretations given to signals were incompatible with their content.

And finally, both sides had different cost-benefit considerations, although each camp attributed its own to the other side. Thus, the question of what a certain signal signified was a function of the question of the opponent's preferences, and because Nehru was convinced that it would not be worthwhile to China to risk a military conflict with India, as we saw in the previous chapters, Chinese caution in response to the Forward Policy was interpreted both as an expression of fear of a confrontation with India and as a justification of the situation evaluations that had led to the execution of the policy.

It appears, then, that *both sides* were to some degree responsible for the failure of the signaling system and for the fact that there was a misunderstanding of each opponent's thinking processes.[18] The system thus became counterproductive and contributed to the escalation of the dispute. This outcome, in turn, points up the particular acuteness of the mutual failures of encoding and decoding of information.

Conclusions

The characteristics concerning the nature of the information and the system that was supposed to manage it shed some light on the perceptual phenomena dealt with in the previous chapter. Now it is clearer why awareness gaps or the nonpenetration of information into the decisionmaker's cognitive system were relatively few, whereas the majority of relevant events became stimuli: the nature of the information was such that it had to be accounted for but did not prevent its manipulation, especially in light of the low quality of the evaluation process. Against this background, we can more easily comprehend why some information was overestimated and other information was underestimated; and why, after evaluations were made, they continued to predominate through inertia despite the penetration of dissonant information. Under these circumstances, the new stimuli were used only to reinforce the existing perceptual system. What is more, under the circumstances the failure of the signaling system was to be expected and, at least for this aspect of miscommunication, both sides share the blame.

The Impact of Cultural, Social, and National Attributes

The Sociocultural Background

It is difficult to establish the direct connection between social, cultural, and national attributes and specific actions and decisions made by political leaders. It is, however, easier to point out, at least in general terms, the possible implications of these factors for the perceptual process. In the case under study, the basic nature of Hindu society and culture and certain national axioms contributed to the distortion in information processing, both directly and through their influence on individual, group, and organizational patterns of behavior. The effect of these factors will be discussed and analyzed with reference to four main points: the general social conditions, the distant and recent historical heritage, the Hindu culture, and perceptions of the national role. Indeed, in trying to explain the factors that moulded his own personality and the face of India, Nehru said:

> India today is the outcome not only of the immediate past, but also of thousands of years of the long history of our country. Layer upon layer of thought, experience and action have conditioned us and made us what we are today. Those of my generation in India were specially moulded and conditioned by a series of events which are not likely to occur again. Not only did we come in contact with a great man and a mighty leader [Gandhi] who shook us up completely, upset our lives and drew us out of the normal routine of living, but we also witnessed and participated in events of historical importance. (Nehru, 1962, 2)

A number of basic sociocultural characteristics formed the background and framework for the perceptual behavior of Nehru and his associates. First was the fact that Nehru was acting in a developing country and that only a tiny proportion of the population played an active, everyday, and conscious role in political life at all, not to mention in foreign policy. He was challenged by the opposition in Parliament, but the impact of this opposition was minor. Thus, Nehru was free to externalize, through his political behavior and particularly via his foreign policy, his personal needs and preferences.

Second, although India was a country whose economic and social problems were practically insoluble, the leadership—endowed with developed egos and a sense of mission—was driven to create achievements by concentrating on foreign policy, in which headline success seemed more likely than the solving of socioeconomic problems.

Third, the social class from which Indian policymakers, bureaucrats, and politicians emerged was fairly homogeneous. This factor created in formal education and socialization a considerable uniformity of outlook and gave further momentum to the process, discussed further on, resulting from the tendency toward a lack of distinction in the relations between the social and political spheres that characterizes Hindu society.

Fourth, the regional linguistic, ethnic, and caste divisions in Indian society, existing for hundreds of years, created a constant problem of conflict of interests that was generally settled with caste interests taking precedence over the wider public ones. In other words, there was a tendency to judge and estimate matters in terms of their contribution to the narrow needs of the individual or group involved (Chudhury, 1965a, 11). The significance of this tendency, as far as the behavior of at least some of the leading figures is concerned, is clear. When these figures had to choose between interpretations of information that served their own narrow interests in terms of their status and intimacy with the chief policymaker—Nehru—and interpretations that contradicted Nehru's basic stance, they chose the former.

Fifth, India as a nation had a rich cultural and historical tradition that dictated the preference of personal, organizational, and certain national concepts and patterns of behavior, as we shall see later on. On the other hand, India, as an independent, resurrected, and young nation, was highly sensitive to threats against national symbols such as territory,[1] a sensitivity that created a cognitive closure and an inability to empathize with the opponent.[2] Such closure was maintained even in the face of dissonant information and was supported by situation evaluations that were probably rooted, as we shall see, in inaccurate historical analogies and comparisons. This phenomenon was even more apparent from the moment that public opinion, more than ever sensitive to anything resembling a threat to national honor, found expression. At that point, making decisions and forming perceptions that contradicted those of the public endangered Nehru's popularity, but "he loved to be admired and adored and nothing would induce him to risk his resplendent image to be tarnished" (Kulkarni, 1969, 548).[3]

If the social factors just mentioned were a kind of framework for the development of the cognitive systems of Nehru and his associates, then certain aspects of Hindu religion and culture serve to explain the specific perceptual dynamics that facilitated the creation of a psychological milieu supportive of the creation and maintenance of misconceptions. Hinduism is not merely a religion but a way of life (Radhakrishnan, 1949, 77), and it moulds and determines social patterns and infiltrates into every aspect of life. Nehru, although he described himself as an atheist, was deeply affected by his Hindu-Brahmin upbringing. As Dr. Rammanohar Lohia has noted: "Whatever Mr. Nehru might have written in his will, whatever he might have said about his attitude towards religion, the fact remains that Mr. Nehru was born a Hindu, he had his sacred thread ceremony performed in the Hindu way, he lived a Hindu, died a Hindu, and was cremated according to Hindu rites" (Edwards, 1973, 11).[4]

A number of aspects of Hindu culture and society are particularly pertinent to this study. The first is the element of continuity, which is one of the most important in Hindu political culture (Nandy, 1970, 61). This element explains the stubborn Indian adherence to the status quo as it was after the British left the subcontinent, as well as the refusal to revise and redesign the boundaries. It finds expression in the Hindu concept of time, which is basically very static (Nakamura, 1964, 73; 1966, 77) and thus views things as essentially unchanging, and it sheds light on the tendency to cling as far as possible to the existing conceptual system—namely, to a static set of images unlinked to the passing of time and the flow of events,[5] as the essence of things changes but little.

Culture had a hand in the intense emotional involvement of all concerned, an involvement that did not permit concessions and that reinforced the conviction that concession, in general, involved not only territory but the deepest essence of nationhood as well. The disputed territory in this case, the Himalayas, played a central role in Hindu and Buddhist cultures. They were the main source of Hindu mythology, the seat of the gods, and as such had a central role in Indian art, poetry, and philosophy. It is no wonder, then, that Nehru spoke of the cultural importance of the Himalayas as equal to their strategic importance, a point that found specific expression in November 1959 during a parliamentary debate: "they [the Himalayas] are something much more to us and more intimately tied up with India's history, tradition, faith, religion, beliefs, literature and culture, than, to my knowledge, any other mountain anywhere. . . . They are part of ourselves. And I want other people to realize how intimately *this question affects our innermost being*,[6] and quite apart even from a pure question of border" (*Par.*, I, 195). Two years later, in December 1961, while replying to the debate in the Lok Sabha, Nehru stressed this point again, saying:

One of the reasons I should like to state here which is a deeper reason because the Himalayas are not only a part of our territory but, if I may say so, they are part of our hearts and minds; and it is a deeper injury to us if anything happens to them. It has been associated with the thinking of our race, our forebears for thousands of years; and our whole cultural tradition is tied up with it; our literature is tied up with it; our mythology is tied up with it. So far it is an essential part of us, something deeper or greater and more important than merely some territorial claim. (*Par.*, II, 37)

Nehru's dilemma, then, consisted on the one hand of the need to make concessions in order to avoid a conflict with China, a confrontation he very much wished to avoid, and on the other hand the deep emotional involvement with the disputed area. To solve this problem it was necessary for Nehru to maintain self-deception,[7] to believe that there was no contradiction; in other words, he did not have to make territorial concessions, as a conflict would be avoided even without such concessions.

But the influence of Hindu cultural traditions went deeper than the individual sphere into the area of group dynamics and interorganizational relations, which, as we shall see, also contributed greatly to nonadaptation to the dissonant information coming in.

The most important factor in this context was the tendency of Hindu culture to create rigid hierarchical social structures with rigid conformity patterns. The family structure and traditional Hindu institutions, such as the caste system, demand conformity to an inflexible, well-defined, and regulated behavioral pattern, in which mobility is very restricted, allows for only limited individual choice, and, as such, encourages the development of a basically conformist and submissive personality. The adult in this culture would transfer his childhood loyalty from the head of the family to the one at the top of the social hierarchy in which he served. The result was, in addition to conformism, a dependence on authority, passivity, a lack of initiative, and a preference for what exists rather than a critical investigation into the social milieu and the expression of divergent opinions (Taylor, 1948; Narain, 1971; Dasgupta, 1972, 164).[8]

For the individual acting in the decisionmaking hierarchy of this culture, the above factors would probably have had a significance relevant to this study. The hierarchical structure and the tendency toward conformity caused interpretations of information, preferred by or decided upon by the head of the hierarchical ladder, to become a rigid framework with which one tended not to tamper. This description contributes to an explanation of the tendency of the group around Nehru to avoid presenting information and evaluations contrary to the basic principles of his world view and belief system, even in the face of strong dissonant information—a tendency just as true of the civil ranks and the senior army officers at New Delhi headquarters, especially given that we are speaking of criticism of the world view of the man who stood at the very pinnacle of the

Indian political ladder. Even the most prominent personalities preferred to support the world view of the central figure, Nehru, rather than risk a confrontation that would damage their status and positions,[9] in spite of, or rather because of, their seniority.[10]

Against this background, Menon's comment, "It is an Indian trait that when you respect a man you do not stand up to him," comes as no surprise (Gupta, 1973, 31). This trait surfaced even when it appeared that the previous definitions of the situation were erroneous. In Hindu culture, the submission to authority is often accompanied by moral cowardice that expresses itself in a reluctance to admit mistakes and bear the consequences, a symptom that seems to be more noticeable the higher one progresses in the formal hierarchical ladder (Chudhury, 1965a) and is probably associated with a strong preference for the security given by huddling under the protective wings of the senior policymaker, rather than confronting him.

Thus, we can readily understand why those who criticized Nehru's policies were either not hierarchically his underlings, like Pant and Patel, or had risen from a different political sphere, such as leaders of the opposition parties and the opposition press. Unfortunately, because of the great secrecy that shrouded all defense matters, these leaders and the opposition press were largely ineffective.

The symptoms described here actually encouraged the emergence of a charismatic leadership that was beyond criticism from the moment it took its place at the top of the ladder. Ironically, once such a leadership is shaped, it becomes vulnerable to the illusion of doing no wrong, an illusion it has foisted on other members of the society. The same factors that have created this leadership can prevent it from functioning adequately. The information fed to the leader is unidimensional and generally as harmonious as possible. The situation under discussion, then, was aggravated by the Hindu habit of secretiveness, even when the subject matter did not warrant it (Dasgupta, 1972, 203). Such secretiveness often prevented the effective flow and distribution of information outward to the relevant bodies and organizations.

The difficulties in keeping the existing conceptual system intact in the face of dissonant information was overcome with the help of an additional Hindu cultural characteristic: the predominance of words over actions. The gap between what is done in reality and the stated principles of the policymaker were not taken too seriously,[11] and when the problems were such that they could no longer be ignored, time was imbued with a mystical ability to settle all difficulties (Narain, 1971; Dasgupta, 1972, 211).

The aforementioned characteristics of words are particularly evident in Nehru's handling of foreign policy matters. For him, perhaps even more than for any other Indian figure, the spoken and written word was an aim and purpose in itself,[12] to which the many volumes of speeches and writings that he left will attest. Nehru the rationalist was intoxicated by his own words, so much so that he could not distinguish between verbal reality and concrete reality. The verbosity with which he described the steps taken to strengthen the army and its fitness to carry out assignments covered up what were really rather different facts. But Nehru and his associates believed in words, just as the faith that time would solve India's political and military problems was an outcome of the Hindu belief that time in itself was a problem-solving mechanism.[13]

Even when his China policy contradicted some of his principles, when reality and the ideal were not always compatible, Nehru found a way to ignore such inconsistencies, for in the culture in which he and his associates were brought up it was acceptable to pay lip service to principles while evading or even going against them in practice.[14]

Hence, societal-cultural attributes were instrumental in providing a fertile ground on which Nehru was able to base a mode of information processing that encouraged cognitive conservativism and facilitated the manipulation of deviant information.

The phenomenon of relating to information by its source—that is, judging and interpreting it as a function of its orginator—was strengthened by an additional characteristic of Indian society—the lack of distinction between political, personal, and social relations; as a consequence, an overlap between the personal appreciation of the source and the content of the information itself was created. Nehru, for this reason, preferred information given to him by his close associates, although this preference involved him in a vicious circle in that they gave it to him in a filtered form, that is, a form consistent with his preconceptions. With regard to leaders of other nations, Nehru failed to distinguish between his personal relations with them and their political behavior. In the specific case before us, his personal ties with Chou En-lai and his resultant impression that China would not invade India became his chief basis for evaluating information on China's intentions, despite changing circumstances[15] and the fact that Chou, who was Communist China's main negotiator with the outside world, was likely to underplay the military threat in his talks and to focus on a more subtle type of negotiation.

The Effect of Cultural Differences

An essential difference also exists between the Hindu and Confucian traditions and philosophies. Hinduism tends toward pluralism, in the sense that it recognizes the possibility and legitimacy of several world views coexisting in one society and lays emphasis on finding a common denominator among them. By contrast, the Sino-Centrist-Confucian world view admits only one truth (Nakamura, 1964, 168–172; Gupta, 1972a, 32–33). This tendency toward unidimensional truth gained even greater prominence with the adoption of modern nationalism and Marxist ideology (Mancall, 1963).

The differences between Hinduist pluralism and Confucian unidimensionalism partially explain Nehru's lack of insight into the Chinese view of the relationship between Maoist-Marxist and his own liberal-socialist world view. According to Nehru's Hindu philosophy,[16] several world views could coexist without confrontation.[17] But Nehru erred in constantly trying to find the common ground, such as nationalistic or Gandhian elements in Maoism, while ignoring the very real differences. Thus, he viewed the temporary reconciliation between the two countries as the true, unchanging, and substantive state of affairs, not realizing that for the Chinese this mutual acceptance was merely tactical. On the contrary, they regarded the coexistence of two opposing "truths" as an impossible situation that, in the long run, must result in victory of the "true and right"—Leninist-Marxist ideology—in the struggle.[18] And, indeed, as soon as the relationship between the two countries became hostile once again, the Chinese saw no reason to continue the tactic of military, political, or ideological peaceful coexistence. Nehru misunderstood this and tended to underestimate Chinese ideological pronouncements that stressed the political, ideological, and socioeconomic differences between the two nations and the operative conclusions resulting from it—in other words, that now there was no longer any tactical need for peaceful coexistence. War was not impossible even in the short term if the balance of military power should tip sufficiently in China's favor.

Nehru's misjudgment was aided by an additional difference between Hindu and Chinese cultures. Whereas Hinduism is a culture of pragmatic thinking that views each event in itself, that is, without inbuing it with a precedent value (Radhakrishnan, 1949), Chinese culture is one of associative thinking that stresses precedents and regards each event as part of a whole. This latter attitude was an important component of the Maoist world view (Tsou and Halperin, 1965).[19] It meant that India's refusal to reopen discussions on the question of colonially inherited borders was not interpreted by the Chinese pragmatically as Nehru anticipated, but instead was given the far-reaching interpretation of India's wish to join the hostile imperialist camp that wanted to turn back the clock (*P.R.*, Nov. 2, 1962, 14–19). Thus, the Chinese attributed much greater significance and higher threat values to Indian behavior than Nehru had estimated. The parameters of the cost-benefit equations that Nehru, as a rationalist, attributed to the Chinese were incorrect, as were his conclusions regarding what action they would take.

There is yet another basic difference between the two cultures. Indian philosophical schools tend to endow abstract concepts with substance, whereas the Chinese culture tends to value the concrete and the particular (Nakamura, 1964, 47–51, 177–199). This explains why abstract notions, such as Asian solidarity and the 2,000 years of friendship and brotherhood that played such a major role in Nehru's perception of India-China relations, were in fact only of minor importance, if that, in Chinese thinking.

In other instances, the problem of cultural influence became even more acute because, aside from the problem stemming from the gaps between the two cultures, a number of the leaders who participated in the process of interpreting information possessed the additional dilemma of being bicultural, having for so long been under the influence of the British. This was especially true of Nehru and Menon, given the long periods they had spent outside of India both before and after independence, in addition to their constant and prolonged contact with Western society. Nehru expressed this dilemma well when he said of himself: "I have become a queer mixture of the East and West, out of place everywhere, at home nowhere. Perhaps my thoughts and approach to life are more akin to what is called Western than Eastern, but India clings to me, as she does to all her children, in innumerable ways; and behind me lie, somewhere in the subconscious, racial memories of a hundred or whatever the number may be, generations of Brahmans. I cannot get rid of either that past inheritance or my recent acquisitions" (Nehru, 1941, 353).

This cultural factor seems to have had a two-fold influence. Like other Western socialist intellectuals, Nehru interpreted the content of Maoist ideology in terms and assumptions that, although accessible to Western thought, were in fact inaccurate. This thinking was also the source of the illusionary belief in the similarity between Indian and Chinese socialism that led to the view of the low probability of war between two Socialist states.

At the same time, Western rationalism and pragmatism were compatible with and supported the pragmatic Indian view of matters and indirectly contributed to the viewing of each event in isolation. Furthermore, they created a problem for a personality such as Nehru, torn between the two worlds as he was; for although rationalism demanded consistency between the components of a world view, the Hindu culture, as it was basically not a rationalistic culture, did not. In the resulting conflict, it was easier for Nehru to decide, where possible, that internal contradictions did not exist at all, thus forcing him to reject any information indicating otherwise—information that would have necessitated a choice between the dictums of the two cultures that handled inconsistency so differently. In short, Nehru preferred to avoid such a choice. This need to avoid philosophical and emotional contradictions stems from one of the central qualities of Hindu culture, namely, the need for harmony that stands out in ancient Hindu writings such as the Bahagavad Gita.[20] Further on, in the section dealing with Nehru's personality, we shall return to a more detailed discussion of this problem.

Another cultural dimension is the language problem, which was of importance in the interaction between the two nations (although it is difficult to assess the actual degree of importance). This factor had two dimensions: the verbal dimension and that of meaning and ideological connotation. Nehru was well versed in English and Hindi, two languages essentially different from the Chinese language, which was particularly hard to translate. The Chinese language was more than a verbal code; it was also a pattern of thought. The poet Tagore, who was one of the main influences on Nehru's view of the Chinese and who suffered from a good deal of discomfort during his visit to China because of an incident resulting from language difficulties, expressed it well in one of his poems:

You are veiled, my beloved
In a language unknown to me
Like a hill which seems a cloud
Behind its mask of mists.[21]

Early on, Nehru himself, in his contacts with the Chinese leadership, had learned from experience the difficulties of language barriers. In a televised interview in New York in 1961, he related that in 1954, on the eve of the Geneva talks, Chou En-lai came to New Delhi for talks. At the end of his visit, a joint statement was issued by the MEA. Chou, who approved of the text, asked his aides to translate it into Chinese. After it was translated, however, he refused to sign it, claiming that in Chinese it did not sound right: "That experience made me think how different was the genius of the Chinese language from not only English but all other languages, including the Indian languages. . . . The whole linguistic background of the Chinese is different and so they use words with different meaning. Their pictographs represent ideas, not words as in our language. That is why I think some trouble is caused by giving different interpretation to words" (Nehru, 1964, 380–381). He expressed himself similarly on the Sino-Indian dispute itself: "I often wonder if we, meaning the Government of India and the Government of China, speak quite the same language, if using the words or similar words we mean the same thing" (*Par.*, I, 129).

Despite Nehru's awareness of the existence of the problem, it is doubtful whether he fully realized its acuteness. And when he did realize it, the damage to mutual trust and reliability had usually been done already. Even a successful literal translation was not always sufficient to overcome the communication barrier, as Chinese and English often do not have equivalent words or connotations (Young, 1968a, 390). This discrepancy caused a serious breach of confidence between the two countries when India attributed to the Chinese presence in Tibet only the right of suzerainty. Specifically, a misunderstanding arose over the issue of whether China had sovereignty (the Chinese version) or suzerainty (the Indian version) over Tibet.

In fact, the Western concept of sovereignty was alien to the traditional Chinese approach to foreign policy. It gained acceptance only during the last decade of the Ching dynasty, which saw nationalism predominating. Thus, the two concepts—sovereignty and nationalism—were emotionally and cognitively tied to such a degree that "the most significant component of the new nationalist approach was that its basic goal was the retrieval and defense of full sovereignty for China . . . . the new policy was extremely broad, opposing not only those imperialist acts which threatened to introduce foreign control but all those which infringed, even theoretically, on China's sovereignty" (Schrecker, 1971, 251). Hence, for the nationalistic Chinese leadership this was no minor verbal or technical legal matter, but one of major affective and ideological importance, especially in light of the different connotations the two words have in Chinese. Suzerainty (*tsung chu ch'uan*) has imperialist connotations, as the words describe tribute relations that the words meaning sovereignty (*chu ch'uan*) do not have.[22] The Communist leadership, which rejected all connection with China's imperial past, could not agree to have modern China's relationship with Tibet defined by the concept of suzerainty. Although this point was clearly understood by the senior Indian diplomats in Peking in the 1950s (Kaul, 1979, 44), it was not the case with the MEA people in New Delhi, including Nehru himself (*Press*, II, 16).

The communications breakdown was intensified by a problem relating to the unique terminology of Maoist ideology, the understanding of which required a basic comprehension and acquaintance with the components and content of the ideology itself—and this Nehru lacked. Thus, when the leaders of both countries spoke of autonomy to Tibet, the term meant different things to each side.[23] The term *autonomy* in Chinese Communist terminology expressed mainly the fact that in a certain area an ethnic minority made up most of the population, whereas in Western terminology the term indicated a certain amount of independence. Similarly, in Nehru's terminology war and peace or peaceful coexistence were dichotomous alternatives. Peace was an alternative to war and preferable under any circumstances. In Maoist terminology, however, the word *war* itself did not necessarily carry a negative connotation.

In Mao's analysis of contradictions, conflict, competition, coexistence, and cooperation are all forms of a struggle that in itself is desirable, because struggle is one of the main vehicles of progress and, as such, is inevitable. Moreover, war and peace are not dichotomously different but constitute the unity of opposites.[24]

This information was crucial also because, in addition to the special content of Maoist terminology, it abounded in multiple meanings (Lall, 1968, 28). Thus the term *annihilation* could mean either the physical destruction of the enemy or its complete social change. During certain periods, the Chinese use of the word *Imperialism* was identical to Nehru's; that is, it indicated a relationship to the West. But from the beginning of the 1960s it also acquired anti-Soviet connotations;[25] thus, when Nehru thought that he and the Chinese had a common enemy—the United States—the Chinese were really also including Nehru's ally, the USSR.

It was therefore Maoist language and terminology that caused a failure of communication, without Nehru's knowledge and without his really grasping the other side's intentions. Consequently, when his perception of mutual understanding proved unfounded, his sense of having been betrayed became more pronounced.

History as a Point of Reference

Another influential factor in the national frameworks on the thinking of the central policymakers was their interpretation of ancient and modern national history. This matter was very important from Nehru's point of view, as he tended to evaluate developments in light of and as part of the wider historical background, according to his own conception of history. Nehru, despite his education in law and the natural sciences, saw himself first and foremost as a historian. This self-concept is expressed in his writings, both in *Glimpses of World History*, a survey of human history written in the 1930s, and in *The Discovery of India*, chiefly a historical survey of Indian national history written in the 1940s. In reality, however, Nehru had not been educated as a historian. He had acquired most of his knowledge on the subject in his long sojourns in British prisons, where he also wrote his books. As a result of the circumstances under which he acquired it, his knowledge of history was not professional. His readings on the subject were eclectic and arbitrary (Mehra, 1968, 20; Nanda, 1974b, 123), and, indeed, his writings contain mistakes of fact and argumentation. As a historian—that is, as one seeing events in their broad historical context—Nehru developed a deep commitment to claims based on historical evidence. And, of course, it is easy to understand the importance he attached to historical events that seemed to reflect on his immediate political situation. He himself stated in an interview: "The most important thing about our foreign policy is that it is part of our great historical tradition" (Karanjia, 1960, 24), thus expressing his view that India's foreign policy in the present should be regarded as a continuation of past policies.

Indian history abounds with both eras of greatness and periods of great humiliation. These contrasting memories were reflected in modern independent India. The tendency of the Indian leadership was to suppress the details connected with the humiliations and to stress and sanctify all that pertained to the period of national and cultural greatness under the great emperors, including, as outstanding among them, Emperor Asoka. Asoka ruled from 273–232 B.C. and expanded the empire's borders and influence north and south, until he concluded that a nation should live not by the sword but by brotherhood, peace, and coexistence with its neighbors.

One of the outstanding results of the internal contrasts in Indian history was the development of contradictory trends in Indian feelings of national inferiority on the one hand, and superiority on the other (Chudhury, 1965a). The feeling of superiority derived from faith in the cultural, religious, and moral values bequeathed by India to the civilized world in general and specifically to Asia. The influence of Buddhism, for instance, had extended beyond the Himalayas into China. But juxtaposed with this was the historical reality of years of Islamic conquest, followed by British Raj. The common explanation offered for the contradiction was that the barbarian conquerors had succeeded in overcoming India only by the use of the most scorned means—force. However, a comparison between British-Western culture and Hinduism could not fail to reveal some of the advantages of the former—hence, the ambivalent feelings toward foreigners and the mixture of arrogance and submission that resulted (Chudhury, 1965a). Violence as a means was regarded with mixed feelings: on the one hand, there was the need to reject the use of force on historical grounds, following the example of Emperor Asoka,[26] and yet the same historical experience taught Nehru that a nation insufficiently armed would eventually fall victim to invaders.[27] In the moral struggle between the boosting of national military strength and its rejection, there emerged a compromise: the development of an army with minimal investment, the creation of substitutes, such as the power and protection afforded by the influence of international bodies and international public opinion, and finally the rejection of information suggesting that the Indian army was not sufficiently strong to meet India's defense needs. Nehru was even less willing to confront a real situation that seemed historically analogous to the one in which foreign invaders conquered Indian territory because of military weakness. Thus, from the moment the situation began to resemble the past, Nehru could not agree to any concession to China deviating from his basic version of the historical facts; yet, at the same time, for the reasons just discussed, he was unwilling to make suitable military preparations.

The fact that Nehru tended to judge current events in the light of past ones,[28] ignoring specific facts and stressing the broader, more abstract context, made it easier for him to conclude that as India and China shared a past of colonialization they must also share a future of common interests and cooperation. To give this claim more substance he added that of basic Asian solidarity, which existed above and beyond temporary differences of opinion. More specifically, Nehru pointed to 2,000 years of Sino-Indian friendship (although they had in fact been years of passivity in relations) and to the contemporary historical tradition of alleged friendship supposedly expressed in Tagore's visit to China, which, as we saw, was in fact a failure.

In constructing his historical thesis, Nehru completely ignored the possibility that a historical event might be interpreted in more than one way and hence lead to different conclusions. Thus, according to the Chinese view, the colonialization of the past did indeed require solidarity in the present, but it did not indicate an automatic acceptance of the remnants of the past, which in this case were colonial boundaries. On the contrary, the past should be obliterated by reopening the boundary matter for discussion between the two independent states (*W.P.*, IV, 11), taking the present reality into consideration and without blindly adopting the historical status quo ante.

Nehru's relatively poor knowledge of the details of the national history of other countries,[29] specifically China, did not allow him to pay proper attention to the basic differences between the process by which India had gained its independence and the one by which the Chinese were liberated from the Japanese and the domestic reactionary forces (the Kuomintang). Although India had gained its freedom relatively easily and almost without bloodshed, so that it was almost possible to say that the two sides—the nationalists and the colonial power—had parted in mutual friendship and respect, China had had a different experience. Thus, Nehru could reject British colonialism as a general philosophy and yet adopt some of the trappings it had left behind, such as the political culture, borders, and geo-strategic thinking. From his point of view, a dual process of rejection and adoption was possible, whereas for the Chinese this approach was nothing but hyprocrisy and fraud. Nehru did not understand this.

The same lack in Nehru's historical understanding led to errors in his geo-strategic evaluations. He adopted British geo-strategic concepts, because for him there was a continuity between the past and present. And because these concepts had proven themselves in the past (insofar as no military force had ever attacked India from the north, but only from the northwest), the conclusion could be drawn that the Himalayas were impenetrable. This kind of generalization was fairly typical of Nehru's insensitivity to detail. In the case of the Himalayas, for example, he should have seen that their efficiency as a barrier in British Raj days was mainly due to China's lack of real interest in expanding southward, and to the strength of the British army no less than to the topographical conditions. He did not stop to think that there might be a contradiction between the 2,000-year-old friendship claim and the concept of the Himalayas as an impenetrable barrier. The supposition that they had not been crossed due to the ancient friendship in no way proved that they were militarily impassable. But such logical obstacles had not particularly disturbed Nehru.

In the same way, he was not concerned that his reservations about military force and armies in general coexisted with his fostering of typically military myths, meant to aggrandize the Indian army through stories of heroism and fighting of Indian troops in the world wars and border wars during British Raj times. These myths fed the faith that despite its quantitative inferiority, the Indian army could effectively deal with the Chinese forces.

Thus, we find Nehru using both macro-historical and micro-historical analogies to boost his own and the national self-confidence. His historical-philosophical sensibilities pushed him into attempting broad historical analogies relating to revived Asianism and to the renewal of the historical cooperation between nations having a common Eastern ethos and culture. These macro-historical analogies were supported by micro-historical analogies such as the impenetrability of the Himalayas in the present as in the past. From such analogies Nehru drew his conclusions as to what extent India could stand firm and demand a Chinese retreat to status quo ante positions without risking a full-scale war.

These analogies were supported by a contemporary historical analogy between Sino-Indian relations and those between the two super powers. This latter analogy maintained that coexistence was possible even within a basically hostile ideological framework, and that the worst result would be the continuation of the present status quo for an indefinite period (*Par.*, I, 355). In this view, small local incidents within the framework of the cold war were not impossible. The use of the term *cold war* was transferred from the super powers to Sino-Indian relations (*Press*, I, 10; *F.N.*, 10/59, Nov. 4, 1959; 1/62, July 10, 1962) and contributed consciously or unconsciously to the concept of the relationship between the two countries as a confrontation of low military intensity, in spite of intensifying hostility in the political realm. This transfer of images was highly natural in light of Nehru's preoccupation with the cold war in the global arena; yet, of course, it ignored the fact that the analogy was actually irrelevant if only because military confrontations between the super powers were always carried out by proxy so that they could more easily be controlled, whereas those between India and China were direct and, as such, much more difficult to restrain.

The central problem, overall, was that dissonant historical evidence had to be remoulded so as not to contradict what Nehru saw as the lessons of history, which for him were a means of reinforcing his general conceptual framework. This approach necessitated, at the same time, an ignoring or misunderstanding of the opponent's historical concepts, given Nehru's belief that only Nehru could interpret history correctly.[30]

Naturally, the Chinese view of history was quite different; dissimilar conclusions were drawn from the same events. And, as with India, when the resultant set of Chinese expectations were disappointed, hostility increased. The approach to the border question was clearly expressed by Chou En-lai in the early stages of the dispute in his letter of September 8, 1959 to Nehru:

> China and India are both countries which were long subjected to imperialist aggression. This common experience should have naturally caused China and India to hold an identical view of the above-said historical background and to adopt an attitude of mutual sympathy, mutual understanding and fairness and reasonableness in dealing with the boundary question. . . . Unexpectedly, to the Chinese Government, however, the Indian Government demanded that the Chinese Government give formal recognition to the situation created by the application of the British policy of aggression against China's Tibet region as the foundation for the settlement of the Sino-Indian boundary question." (*W.P.*, II, 27)[31]

The bilateral dialogue based on history was doomed to fail. History is multifaceted and ambiguous in its interpretation, depending on the viewpoint of the interpreter. In a situation in which there is no empathy between the sides, history does not contribute to an understanding; it only sharpens the mutual hostility and mistrust, precisely because the anticipation of the other side's actions is based on the belief that history can be seen only in one way. And the fact that the Chinese, too, were incorrect in their application of history to the definition of the situation could not have been a comfort to Nehru. On the contrary, it was because of this error that the effect of the historically based conclusions and analogies was so serious; it should have made Indian policymakers doubly wary such that they attempted, at least, to see matters from the Chinese point of view.

Role and Status Concepts

The last issue connected with national attributes as a basis for the definition of the situation was the perception of national status and role and the contradictions arising from role conflicts within each protagonist and in relation to the opponent. These conflicts necessitated, on the one hand, an instrumental relationship to the information as a verification that the country was fulfilling its designated role in the regional and international arenas and, on the other, a rigidity and a censorship of information indicating the impossibility of realizing the desired role. Conceptions of role and status were relatively difficult to change given their sources, namely, the cultural historical heritage, the national ideology, and perceived geographical determinism. As these variables were connected with intense personal and national commitments, they enhanced tendencies toward rigidity in perceptions and attitudes and a preference to manipulate dissonant information such that it protected national role concepts.

The concepts of India's role as adopted by Nehru were based on a number of factors that I shall mention only briefly: (1) ancient Indian history, in which India played a central role in Asia and also served as a cultural, political, and economic focus for regions beyond Asia; (2) later Indian history, in which India was subjugated to imperialist and colonial powers from beyond the subcontinent; (3) Gandhi's ideology and later Nehru's, which rejected power plays and violence among individuals and nations; and (4) the geographic location of the subcontinent at geo-political and geo-strategic cross-roads.

From these factors certain specific role conceptions naturally emerged. First, they gave India a position of leadership on two levels: a regional leadership in Asia in the geographical sphere and, in the realm of ideas, a leadership position among the neutralist and developing countries. Second, its colonial history committed India to a central role in the anti-imperialist struggle. Third, for ideological as well as pragmatic reasons, India conceived of two additional roles for itself: one as an international mediator and the other as a bridge between cultures and ideologies, that is, a link between East and West and between the Socialist and Capitalist worlds. All of these conceptions necessitated that India take on the role of active neutralism in international politics. Fourth, India saw itself as a political and economic model for other Third World nations.[32] All in all, Nehru conceived of six roles for India in the regional and international arenas, a conception that naturally indicated a perception of senior status for India on the international scene; this perception, in turn, implied a high degree of power and hence a perceived invulnerability.

What, on the other hand, were the role concepts of the Chinese leadership? Like India, China saw itself as a regional leader in Asia, in addition to its future role as a global leader. Two additional roles on the regional level were those of the stalwart of the world revolution, which called for support of change and the toppling of reactionary regimes, and the role of standing in the front line of anti-imperialist and anti-revisionist forces in the struggle against Imperialism. Finally, China, too, saw itself as a social, economic, and political model for all developing countries (*P.R.*, Apr. 26, 1960; Nov. 2, 1962; Tsou and Halperin, 1965; Schram, 1969, 372–414). China, then, conceived of five roles for itself, a conception that likewise indicated a perceived senior status in the regional and global hierarchies.

There were a number of inevitable conflicts between these two sets of role concepts. Both countries conceived of themselves as having leadership roles in the same region. A "zero sum game" was created as a division of leadership was not possible, especially in light of the fact that the Chinese view of world order was traditionally rigidly hierarchical, with China firmly at the top of the pyramid (Fairbank, 1966; Fitzgerald, 1969; Hinton, 1972, 31).[33]

So long as the relations between the two countries remained normal, it was still possible to soften the effect of the struggle for leadership somehow; but once relations deteriorated, the struggle for regional leadership became part and parcel of the border dispute and contributed to the Chinese cost-benefit analysis and its conclusion that military force would be of use in putting India in its place.

In addition, both countries saw themselves as models for other developing countries, and here the Indian leadership did not understand the significance of the struggle in relation to the differences between Hindu and Chinese cultures. According to the Hindu world view, in which there was not necessarily one truth, several truths could reside together, one complementing another. Thus, according to India, different socioeconomic models could coexist without incurring a confrontation between them. According to the traditional Chinese world view, however, as was true of Maoist doctrine based on Marxism, there was only one truth, which, at some point, when the opposing forces reached an irrevocable polarization, would necessarily impose itself and prove its superiority, even by force. Thus, once the behavior of the Indian leadership, by its treatment of the border conflict, established beyond doubt that the contradictions and conflicts could not be settled amicably, the contradiction between the Indian and Chinese models called for the use of force.

The possible use of force by China fit in with China's other role concepts: its standing in the front line in the struggle against Imperialism and Revisionism, in which India was seen as allied to both,[34] and that of supporting revolutionary change in the political status quo in countries defined as reactionary, as India was now.

For Nehru a complex problem was created. First, it was intolerable for him to admit that there was a regional leadership struggle between India and China. This was a struggle that completely contradicted his view of Asian solidarity, which applied especially to the two largest countries in Asia. Furthermore, admission of a Sino-Indian confrontation contradicted the concept of India as a bridge between East and West, North and South, Communism and Socialism; it would also have damaged Nehru's ability to act as a mediator and peacekeeper. At the same time, an admission that the Indian army was incapable of meeting the Chinese challenge would have demanded that India give up even its role as an independent nation, as massive foreign aid would have been required to cope with this situation.

Finally, the status that India had acquired in the international arena as a mediator and the leadership position it had earned among developing nations were based on a claimed moral righteousness rather than on material physical power—even though, for a pupil of Gandhi's, such moral and political strength was as important as the physical kind, if not more important. From the materialist Maoist position, the audacity of India, which seemed to be basing its behavior on the doubtful external political support of the United States and the USSR rather than on actual military strength, was difficult to swallow. To the Chinese it thus looked as if there would be no alternative but to demonstrate the real balance of power in the region as a basis for a renewal of negotiations in a realistic context (*P.R.*, Oct. 19, 1962). After all, as the saying goes, "power grows from the barrel of the gun."

The significance of the opposing role concepts escaped Nehru both because of his limited understanding of the Chinese world view and given his inability to cope with the disturbing conclusions that the relevant information forced on him. In order to continue holding onto the national role conceptions he attributed to India, especially insofar as they were part and parcel of the national self-image and ego that reflected the self-image of the man who was the embodiment of India in the eyes of the world and himself, he misinterpreted the available information.

Conclusions

Our analysis thus far points to the fact that social-national factors acted on two levels of perception formation: indirectly, by influencing the processing of information, and directly, by acting on the content of the information itself. The influence on the process of interpretation was exerted in such areas as attention to information relating to foreign policy and its uses; the motivation for an interorganizational and interpersonal consensus; the degree to which the leader's preconceptions were imposed on others as a rigid frame of reference; and the ability to weigh parochial needs against national interests— in short, the patterns of behavior of and relations between the individual, the small group, and the organization.

The direct influence on information content was exerted through the penetration of the emotional dimension that cultural national factors added to new information or to existing national images as well as through the evaluation of the degree to which national images would be endangered by the information (pointing either to irrelevance or to internal contradictions) and would necessitate making changes in the basic national image of self and others.

In the case before us, I have pointed to the existence and effects of such factors as social attributes, language, national history, and role and status conceptions. These cultural determinants have encouraged a treatment and manipulation of information that, in its turn, has encouraged cognitive conservativism and the lowering of the perception of threat even in face of dissonant information. At the same time, it should be noted that an analysis linking national-cultural characteristics with national behavior in the area of foreign policy must contain an element of speculation and should thus be regarded with a degree of caution.

10
Nehru's Personality

Personality Traits

Nehru was the dominant personality in Indian political life since the death of Patel in 1950, towering above every other political figure. In the area of foreign policy his control was absolute, for this was a subject on which he had been regarded as the expert even in the 1920s (as a result of the relative lack of interest in the subject shown by most other Indian leaders of the national movement at the time).

Moreover, in Nehru's mind foreign policy was his area of special contribution to India, given that the major contributions had already been made by Gandhi in the social area. He was proud of what he saw as his role in making every Indian, even the poorest and least educated, aware of the external world and foreign affairs (Mende, 1956, 126–127). This factor and the characteristics of the China problem made foreign policy (and this issue in particular) an inevitable but also a convenient stage for the externalization of Nehru's personality, for several reasons:

First, the new situation in Sino-Indian relations was for Nehru a complex and ambivalent one, in the sense that it contained an element of surprise. The Longju and Kongka incidents caught him completely unprepared. The situation was also multifaceted in that the policy on China had to be considered in the light of various types of variables, which led to differing, even contradictory, solutions such as the global system, the regional subsystem, the Indian internal political system, and others.

Second, Nehru knew that he was relied upon in every area of Indian life and especially in foreign policy, and that, as the process of decisionmaking was in the last account a personal one, in this sense those around him were not equal to him but meant only to "serve" him; he held the final responsibility. Thus, he was, perceptually speaking, his own "strategic intelligence officer," and his circle of aides were there only to provide him with information supporting his general frame for the definition of the situation. All this, together with his deep emotional involvement in the China question because of its political and moral significance, internal and external, and the fact that following the Thimayya affair he publicly took personal responsibility for the activities of the Indian defense apparatus, transformed the China issue into an arena for the expression of Nehru's personality.

Nehru was born in Kashmir on November 14, 1889, the only son of a Kashmiri Brahmin family of the most aristocratic strata of Indian society. The family was wealthy. The father had had a Western education and retained a modern world view as well as senior political standing in pre-independent Indian society. The members of the family looked up to the father with respect and admiration but also to a certain extent feared him, as he was hot tempered, authoritative, and at times even severe. The mother, on the other hand, managed the household and was a soft and submissive woman to whom the children felt close. They were much more likely to come to her with their experiences than to their father. She blatantly favored her son, spoiled him, protected him with her love, and approved of his every action.[1] The difference in his relationships with each of his parents is apparent in Nehru's autobiography: "I admired father tremendously. He seemed to me the embodiment of strength and courage and cleverness, far above all other men I saw, and I treasured the hope that when I grew up I would be rather like him. But much as I admired him and loved him I feared him also."

His relationship to his mother he describes as follows: "I had no fear of her, for I knew she would condone everything I did, and because of her excessive and indiscriminating love for me, I tried to dominate over her a little. I saw much more of her than I did of father, and she seemed nearer to me, so I would confide to her when I would not dream of doing so to father" (Nehru, 1941, 21–22).

Later on, the duality of Nehru's relationship to his parents was felt in his attitude toward power and its uses. He displayed a desire for autocratic power like his father; yet he also showed reservations and fear about the uses of power, which found expression in an indecisiveness similar to that of his mother. More specifically, his admiration of his father and his wish to be like him combined with the overprotection by his mother, which created some need for compensated masculinity, were probably instrumental in his need for power and in contributing to the formation of his authoritarian personality. At the same time, fear of his father's high-handedness, and dislike of it, created in him a reluctance toward power and its uses, which partly explains the contradictions between his authoritarianism in general and his inability to deal harshly with persons close to him, even when circumstances called for it.

Nehru was exposed to the direct influence of Western culture at a relatively early age, having been sent first to Harrow at 16 to study and then on to Cambridge (although he had already felt the Western influence before this through his private tutors). This influence deepened with his prolonged stay in Europe and at times even overshadowed his Hindu background; yet in later years, as is reflected in his writings, Nehru showed a strong tendency to return to his origins.[2]

A short while after Nehru returned to India from Europe, the Indian national movement, and especially its leader Gandhi, discovered his special talents and he quickly became one of its rising stars and a very close associate, if not the closest, of Gandhi. Nehru, with his charm and broad education, attracted the young intelligentsia to the movement. At the same time, he knew how to empathize with the masses, who followed him as a kind of father figure and teacher, especially after Gandhi's death. Indeed, it was with a paternal stance that he addressed them in his speeches.

Although during the years of struggle for independence sharp disagreements arose between Nehru and Gandhi on matters of strategy and tactics, Nehru's admiration of Gandhi never faltered. It also became apparent that Gandhi saw in Nehru the successor on whose shoulders his mantle was to fall. With the granting of independence, Nehru became the first prime minister of India. Until 1950, when Sardar Vallabhbhai Patel was still alive, the government was in fact run as a duumvirate. However, after 1950, with the death of Patel, Nehru stood head and shoulders above all the surviving generation of leaders who had taken part in the struggle for independence and became the focus of national adoration, remaining at the center of the Indian stage until his death in 1964.

Nehru the man had a number of outstanding personality traits that were both directly significant in the makeup of his perceptual dynamics and indirectly influential through their impact on his relations with his subordinates and in the choosing of his close circle of advisors and associates. These traits were in part a product of his early family environment and later the result of his education.

Nehru's outstanding characteristic, the one that set him apart from other figures in the Indian national movement, was his status as an aristocrat. As his biographer put it: "Nehru is a triple aristocrat, a Brahmin by birth, a gentleman by upbringing and education and the son of a Westernized lawyer of all-India renown" (Brecher, 1959, 389). This trait showed itself in the aloofness he maintained and the sense of superiority and condescension that he fostered in himself toward others. It was expressed in his belief that he could hardly go wrong and in his impatience with seemingly lesser intellects—in which light he regarded most of the politicians of the Congress Party. He displayed such self-confidence, even arrogance, that Chou En-lai, some months after Nehru's death, said of him that he had never met such an arrogant man.[3] Gandhi was aware of this fault and wrote him about it as early as 1936: "[Nehru's] colleagues dreaded you because of your irritability and impatience of them. They have chafed under your rebukes and magisterial manner and above all your arrogation of what has appeared to them your infallibility and superior knowledge."[4] Nehru, then, was the figure of an authoritative leader, prone to vanity, temperamental, given to anger, and in no small measure dogmatic and subborn (Shils, 1961, 36). Once he had made up his mind on a subject, it was very difficult to convince him otherwise. And, as we shall see further on, this was connected to another of his characteristics—his difficulty in making decisions. His stubbornness, arrogance, vanity, and self-confidence encouraged the reluctance to accept new evaluations—a convenience for Nehru, actually, as it enabled him to cut down to a minimum the need to change decisions already reached or to make new ones.

Side by side with these traits, Nehru developed a tendency toward centralization. He delegated responsibility only very reluctantly and to very few. The resulting overwork and anxiety this brought him caused him fatigue that finally resulted in illness in the first half of 1962.[5] Yet, despite and perhaps because he trusted only very few men, once an individual had earned a position close to him, he could not bring himself to fire that person, even upon discovering that he was incompetent or dishonest. Nehru excused his weakness by claiming that harsh judgment of people smacked of totalitarianism (Brecher, 1959, 628; Kaul, 1967, 311).[6] It also stemmed from his shrinking from unpleasantness and from his basic generosity. One result of his centralist ways was that, because people were afraid of his notorious temper,[7] inherited from his father, they brought every issue to him for approval.

However, despite his tendency toward centralization of authority as an outgrowth of his father's and Gandhi's paternalism, he developed dependencies on strong and decisive people older than himself (Brecher, 1959, 2). First there were his father and Gandhi, then Patel and later, though to a lesser degree, Pant. With Pant's death, Nehru no longer had a single figure to lean on except for his close circle of advisors.

This last detail is very important in light of Nehru's difficulties in making decisions and his need to reach a consensus before doing so. In the cases in which he did not get the support he needed, often no decision was taken at all, always with the reasoning that he did not want to be a dictator. In such cases, he preferred to be guided by stronger men, or to allow events to follow their own course until all options closed one by one. Thus, certain decisions were made for him (Kaul, 1967, 76; Edwards, 1973, 255).

On the intellectual level, Nehru was very able, open, lucid, quick-witted, able to concentrate, and analytical in his thinking (Crocker, 1966, 137). Ironically, these characteristics also contributed to his indecisiveness, in that he always saw all sides of a problem, and they reduced his decisionmaking ability considerably (Pandey, 1977, 684). On the other hand, his formal education, which had been in the sciences and law, fostered in him an almost extreme rationalistic and legalistic approach to problems.[8]

From an affective point of view, Nehru combined sentimentalism and intellectualism,[9] together with a tendency toward introversion and aloofness from other people except those closest to him.[10] This tendency, which grew more pronounced over the years and made him increasingly dependent on information coming from his close circle, explains at least in part his tendency to judge information by its source. His optimism was another outstanding trait despite occasional setbacks. In this area he testified about himself: "I am basically an optimist and I have never found any reason to be anything else" (Karanjia, 1960, 102).

What was the importance of these characteristics in the processing of information? The fact that Nehru was a broad-minded intellectual created a situation in which, on the one hand, he was open to and aware of new information in itself and could not ignore it even when it contradicted his basic notions. On the other hand, it was his very sharpness and intelligence that prompted him to distort dissonant information by relatively sophisticated means.

This last characteristic was supported by another of Nehru's qualities, his high self-esteem, which was notable even in moments of sober self-criticism (Nehru, 1941, 434). Abetted by the adoration of the masses, it contributed to his supreme self-confidence. It also explains why we find evaluation and relevance gaps in his thinking based chiefly on his interpretation of information rather than on the ignoring of information, and that once an evaluation was made it was difficult to bring about a change in his thinking.

Nehru's introversion led him to adapt reality to his psychological needs. These needs in Nehru's case called for minimal changes in his conceptual system. There were several reasons for this. First was his difficulty in decisionmaking, which had two aspects: a change in the conceptual system that he adopted in the Chinese context was an important decision in itself—the choosing between two essentially different approaches. Furthermore, a new decision about the conception of the Chinese issue had an operative significance; in other words, it would have necessitated additional difficult decisions concerning the allotment of resources or the willingness to make concessions, both of which for Nehru were most difficult. As he was aware of his limitations in the area of decisionmaking, Nehru developed a psychological need to handle a situation by defining it in such a way as to prevent changes that might demand new decisions.

Second, Nehru's dogmatism turned his conceptual framework into a relatively closed system and created a drive to distinguish sharply between his own beliefs and those that he rejected—the latter having been presented by the military—thus making the evaluations presented by the military even less acceptable.

A similar process was connected to Nehru's authoritativeness, which, while accepting incoming data, demanded only one interpretation of any given situation and the rejection of ambiguities, so that a choice among alternatives could be avoided or made self-evident. The certainty had to be such that his consistent system of beliefs and attitudes would not become unbalanced and contradictory. This approach was reinforced by Nehru's formal education in the sciences and law, both constructed on rational and consistent sets of assumptions. Finally, Nehru's self-esteem also channeled him in the direction of adopting those interpretations that supported former orientations and evaluations, since to retreat from them would have harmed his charisma and his special status, which were at the basis of his self-image.

Nehru's authoritativeness apparently also had implications in another area of information interpretation. A preference was created for evaluating Sino-Indian relations in simplistic stereotyped terms, such as 2,000 years of friendship, the Himalayan barrier, and so on, which were adopted with no real justification.

This trait is also related to the development of ethnocentrism, which was expressed in Nehru's ideas, in that he succeeded in convincing himself that India alone was right and acting fairly in the dispute, whereas China's claims had not a shred of justice. In other words, it led to a highly positive self-image and a negative view of the opponents' behavior, which, as discussed in the previous chapters, also contributed to Nehru's lack of empathy with, and understanding of, the behavior of the Chinese. Ethnocentrism in general is a phenomenon linked to the inability to distinguish between the ideal and the real, as was the case in the China issue.

An additional characteristic connected with Nehru's authoritativeness was his rigidity—that is, his non-linking of related cognitive factors, or the attribution of too limited a relevance to specific information. Thus, for example, the Chinese military reinforcement in Tibet was interpreted as linked only to the Tibet uprising and not to the Sino-Indian dispute.

Nehru's personal traits also affected his relations with his surroundings and moulded the reaction of the organizations and personalities with whom he maintained close connections.[11] His preference for evading difficult decisions except under conditions of a consensus, together with his natural authoritativeness, created in the circle of his close associates a tendency toward conformism, just as they created on his part a preference to surround himself as much as possible with people who did not object to conformism.

This quality of authoritativeness also explains Nehru's tendency to be dependent and to lean on people who displayed authority, such as his father and Patel, and when they disappeared from the scene, to trust people who, externally at least, displayed authority and self-confidence, such as Kaul, Mullik, and Menon, so that again the same orientation toward the source for the evaluation and interpretation of information was reinforced.

Values, Beliefs, and Attitudes

Nehru's political world view was rooted in a value system that was supposed to guide it. His ethical approach to politics was as much an outcome of his philosophy of history as of the influence of the Mahatma, who was his spiritual father. Mahatma Gandhi's world view called for the management of human interrelationships on the private and national levels not on a pragmatic basis but on a value basis, even if this meant that one had to pay a price for preserving one's values. But these two factors—the lessons of history[12] and the example of his teacher Gandhi—were actually two sides of the same coin. History taught Nehru that the individual's role was to serve collective humanity in the broadest sense. The role of the individual was to fight the existing negative trends in the world in the political sphere as well as in other spheres. In Nehru's eyes, it was Gandhi who embodied this lesson in his lifestyle and was the example by which Nehru had to live, even if his generation did not always understand it. Nehru illustrated his approach in a press conference held late in 1959: "You see, my difficulty is that I belong, if you will forgive my saying so, to an older generation than most of you. I belong to the Gandhi generation and I am not out of it" (*Press*, I, 54–55).[13] As such, Nehru was led to categorical conclusions concerning the choice between Machiavellianism and morality in foreign policy: "So far as I am concerned and so far as our Government is concerned, our foreign policy is as firm as a rock and it will remain so. It will be some other government that may change it. The present government will hold to non-alignment, because it is a matter of principle, not of opportunism or the convenience of the day" (*Par.*, I, 133). "Moreover right policy is right and rightness should not be judged by the wrongness of other peoples' action and that right conduct inevitably has right results" (*Par.*, I, 182). This emphasis on value-based orientation toward social relations was especially true since the solution of the problem by force seemed increasingly impossible in the twentieth century because of the potential danger of nuclear war. Thus, moral precepts remained the only real viable criteria of foreign policy.

It was precisely the field of foreign policy and the China issue in particular that brought out the importance, to Nehru, of the moral-ethical approach.[14] One reason was the significance attached to relations with China, which, in themselves, as we saw, touched on so many external and domestic issues; and another was that, in contrast to Pakistan or Portugal, toward whose governments it seemed correct to pursue a pragmatic, power-oriented, real-politik policy, China was a different matter. Nehru himself, despite his doubts about China, had described it as a socialist, anti-imperialist state, a pillar of Asian solidarity on which a new world was to be built, and a partner in the moral principles that he espoused. Thus, when Sino-Indian relations became a central arena that was to serve as a model for other nations, they immediately became an object for the externalization of Nehru's value system.

But, as we shall see, acute dilemmas quickly arose. Nehru, the rationalist, the indecisive man, was faced with conflicts: within his value system itself, between what was necessitated by different values in the Chinese context, and between values and political pressures and realities that dictated action orientations he considered unbefitting and illegitimate. Admitting the submission to pressures was unthinkable from the ethical, personal, and public viewpoints. Thus, Nehru stood in the midst of all these conflicts, having to settle them one way or another.

Within Nehru's value system, one needs to distinguish between values pertaining to the external-political world and those relating to the domestic one, and to note the reciprocity between the two systems. We shall find that both of these value networks influenced Nehru's China policy.

Perhaps Nehru's most cherished notion was that of independence. He saw himself as the appointed guardian of India's freedom in the broadest sense—territorially, but also politically and economically. He looked down on those countries that had won formal independence but had maintained dependent political, economic, or cultural ties with the colonial country. As a result, nonalignment became the realized expression of independence, to be preserved at all costs: "the policy of nonalignment and of having friendly relations is I believe basically a right policy under all circumstances, whatever happens" (*Par.*, I, 201). He firmly rejected the idea that this was his own definition only; rather he saw it as an "axiomatic truth" beyond Sino-Indian relations (*Par.*, I, 143–144).

Nehru's policy toward China was to him a characteristic expression of nonalignment that found its operative embodiment in the Panch Sheel Agreement. Nonalignment, according to Nehru, was not a policy of aloofness from all, but, on the contrary, the maintenance of friendly relations with all. Thus, he talked of nonalignment and the Panch Sheel Agreement in one breath, the latter to be an example to other nations of how foreign policy should be conducted, based on values of peace, friendship, and the recognition that "there is no reason why rival ideological and economic and social theories should not grow up and learn to live and let live" (quoted by Karanjia, 1960, 87). As a result, even when relations with China deteriorated, means that could be described by him as peaceful were preferred over any other (*Par.*, II, 101). This preference was also an outcome of the axiom that the means were no less important than, and must be as pure as, the ends, whatever they may be. Thus, as he stated in an interview, "ends were shaped by the means that led to them, and therefore the means had to be good, pure and truthful. That is what we learnt from him [from Gandhi] and it is well we did so" (Karanjia, 1960, 25).

Of all the negative means against which Nehru preached as irrelevant for gaining ends, none was worse than war: "my whole soul revolts against the idea of war anywhere. That is the training I have received throughout my life" (*Par.*, II, 37). This was at the very core of the *Satyagraha* (the power of truth) policy that Gandhi had employed in the struggle for independence, a policy that called for passive resistance using only the tactics of *ahimsa* (nonviolence).[15] That is, it contained an aversion to the main tools of violence—armies and militarism—in spite of the importance of the stakes involved.

It cannot be argued that Nehru rejected Gandhian principles on the subject of the non-use of violence and resigned himself realistically to the need for the use of military power, even though it can be testified that in this matter he often disagreed with Gandhi during the struggle for independence and did not hesitate to use force against Pakistan, or in Goa. As to the claims of disagreements between himself and Gandhi, Nehru himself stated that he changed from a critical disciple of Gandhi's to a close follower of his principles later in life. Or, as one scholar put it, Nehru rediscovered Gandhi (Nanda, 1979, 24). However, as Nehru said in an interview: "I don't know. It is difficult to analyse oneself. The atom bomb, of course, affected my mental outlook a great deal, but not in the particular aspect you mentioned. The transformation has been a gradual one" (Karanjia, 1960, 78). As for using violence against Portugal in Goa and Pakistan in Kashmir, it should be remembered that the fighting with Pakistan took place back in 1948 probably before the change in Nehru's values had taken shape and that, moreover, there were at the time many external and internal political pressures on him that necessitated the use of force. As a matter of fact, with regard to Goa, Nehru was more a follower than an initiator and actually objected strenuously to the use of force but was in fact led to it by his associates. Even then, he was clearly not happy with the means used to achieve this aim.[16] It was precisely those precedents that strengthened his reservations against war, and especially against using force on a state—China—that he defined in the most positive terms.[17]

But against these beliefs and values, which can be said to express an enlightened national interest, were those that represented the narrower national interest, to which Nehru also saw himself adhering.[18] These were the values of national honor and territorial integrity, and national security as defined in territorial terms: "Now let us be clear about certain basic factors, so that they need not be thought to be in doubt. We are committed, from every point of view, to defend our country, to preserve its integrity, to preserve its self-respect. That is not a matter of argument, I thought. Opinions may differ as to how to do it" (*Par.*, I, 278).[19]

To protect these values according to Nehru's conception, the leader in question must take all the consequences that a firm resolve involves: "it is obvious that no country worth its strain, and certainly not India, can submit to bullying tactics, can submit to force being used to take away its territory and otherwise to show that it can be treated casually, by another country. It is impossible, whatever the consequences might be" (*Par.*, II, 136).

These values expressed, and fit the other side of, the *Satyagraha* coin—namely, the unwillingness to compromise principles[20] and the firm standing on matters of principle before arriving at a practical arrangement (Range, 1961, 90; Ashe, 1969, 99–105), as expressed clearly by Nehru also in the Chinese context on August 16, 1961 in Parliament: "The main thing is that we must firmly hold to our position, our opinions, our views, and try to get them realized" (*Par.*, II, 3). Sometimes these values stood in contrast to those of restraint (*Par.*, I, 9, 273) and realism, which, according to Nehru, "any responsible person in authority, whether in the government or in the opposition must deal with" (*Par.*, II, 106). These values of restraint, realism, and avoidance of emotional reactions were in Nehru based actually on the central value of rationalism, which demanded poise and cool judgment in the process of defining a situation and reaction, as Nehru believed that the source of all conflicts was mutual fear and that release from fear was conditioned on composed rationalist thinking and behavior (Range, 1961, 24–28). Such rationalism, which would liberate mankind from violence, was the basic purpose expressed in the values of Gandhi's *Satyagraha* doctrine.[21] Values relating to domestic factors and social structure—the goal of transforming Indian society on Socialist Democratic lines—were also relevant to the dispute. Nehru believed in the basic goodness of mankind and insisted that symptoms of evil were a product of the social environment. Past wars, such as World War II, were the result of fascist political systems (Range, 1961, 5), as war between Socialist political systems could not occur. And as China and India were both Socialist societies, disagreements between them could thus not go beyond a local dispute.

According to Nehru's concept, Socialist states rejected war because they held economic development to be their primary goal. A strong economy was also the basis for the national power necessary in order to participate in changing the global system (*Par.*, I, 246). Thus, diverting resources away from economic development to an arms race was not only wrong; it was, in fact, counterproductive, as it damaged the long-term prospects of national security (*Par.*, I, 229; *Par.*, II, 57), which depends on economic development.

Political realities did not make things easier for Nehru the moralist. The actuality of Sino-Indian relations set his concepts into conflicts in which the realization of certain values perforce hurt others. Moreover, looking reality in the eyes threatened Nehru's self-image as a man of morals conducting an ethical foreign policy, essentially different from the foreign policies of other world leaders, and as one that could thus set an example to others, in itself an important Gandhian value.

The pain this conflict caused Nehru is evident in his verbal contortions in Parliament. Often those values representing the narrow national interest stood in contradiction to those expressing an enlightened one. For Nehru, the holder of a universalist approach, this created an embarrassing dilemma. The value of Indian national security opposed the universal values of equality among nations and of the non-interference of a strong country in the internal affairs of a weaker one. The deeper the Sino-Indian dispute went, the greater was India's need to interfere in the internal affairs of the Hill States— particularly Nepal, whose independent status had always been recognized *de jure*. This interference stood also in marked contrast to the Panch Sheel Agreement, the principles of which were regarded by India as universal.[22]

National security, territorial integrity, and the use of military means to maintain them stood in contradiction to the value of economic development, as in reality they required the diverting of funds from the economy to the defense budget. Independence and freedom, too, could be jeopardized, as, in the long run, any reduction of the development budget increased India's dependence on foreign aid. Moreover, keeping funds from being transferred from the economy to defense could be achieved only by accepting further outside military aid, the results of which were seen as a loss of face for India as an independent country. Thus it happened that in August 1962, when Sino-Indian relations were in a profound crisis and were taking on an increasingly military aspect, Nehru stated: "the few crores that we may save if we get [that] military equipment as a gift would be far outbalanced by the tremendous loss in prestige, in position and even in sympathy that we may have from the rest of the world" (*Par.*, II, 130).[23]

The need for a realistic evaluation and self-restraint contradicted the need for a display of firmness in favor of democracy and the national honor, which meant succumbing to the demands of public opinion. The outraged public in India categorically supported the rejection of any negotiations that might have resulted in mutual concessions. Nehru's dilemma was evinced in his calls for both restraint and firmness—for defense of national honor at all costs, but also for safeguarding the opponent's self-respect (*Par.*, I, 193). Moreover, the values of nonviolence and the use of peaceful means and negotiations to achieve goals, be they ever so righteous, in this case contradicted the right of democratic public opinion to influence matters; public opinion, in fact, rejected negotiations and forced Nehru to distinguish between them and talks, so that he had to claim that although he would never refuse to talk to any leader, negotiations were a different matter altogether (*Par.*, II, 115).

The values of restraint and rejection of war and violence stood in contradiction to the Forward Policy, especially when the latter ceased to be one of passive resistance and became either a means of using force at India's initiative, or so provocative that it made the use of force on both sides inevitable. This policy also contradicted the general ethical view of rejecting impure means to achieve even the highest goals.

It was thus necessary for Nehru to view the Forward Policy only in diplomatic terms, as a restrained tactic that guaranteed control of the situation and prevented its deterioration and yet at the same time satisfied public demands by standing firm. This is also why he flatly rejected any information indicating that the Chinese viewed it as a violent policy opposed to the Panch Sheel principles and as a policy that might lead to war.

Accepting information and evaluations indicating that a war between India and China was possible would have meant admitting that India had pursued a policy that had allowed the worst, ethically speaking, to come true. Even more damaging was the fact that China was that very nation with which relations were supposed to be the symbol of Panch Sheel and an expression of the effectiveness of nonalignment. In practice, war with China would have meant the admission that Nehru's was an irrational policy in the Chinese context, and that somewhere along the line a sharp deviation from the value system had occurred. Furthermore, the acceptance of information pointing to the possibility of war could lead only to one of two policies: either entry into an arms race, which contradicted India's economic and social goals and would have created conditions for the rise of reactionary social forces, or, alternatively, turning India into a state dependent on a super power for its military needs.

In any event, the immediate personal significance for Nehru was the need for a value trade-off—giving preference to certain values at the cost of others—a situation that would have hurt his image as a moralist towering over ordinary political leaders and would have downgraded India from a model nation into an ordinary one.

Such developments were an anathema to Nehru, both for reasons related to his self-perception and ego and for reasons connected to his overall world view. But even more serious on his part would have been an admission that inherent contradictions were possible among and within values of a sound moral policy, an assumption that clashed with his strong tendency toward scientific rationalism, of which consistency was a basic condition. It is no wonder, then, that he stated in an interview given in 1960: "Well, a good policy doesn't become bad because it runs into trouble with a restless or aggressive neighbour. It merely puts it to a test and we are sure it will overcome the challenge" (Karanjia, 1960, 81). Furthermore, an admission of conflicts would have forced Nehru to choose among values that were all more or less equally important to him in addition to being a crucial ingredient in the world view of a man who, as it was, had difficulty in making decisions. Such a choice, in an area where both his emotional and intellectual commitments were deeply involved, was what he wanted to prevent at all costs. The solution was to manipulate the "dangerous" information.

The manipulation of information and its evaluation was expressed, as we have seen, in Nehru's rejection of the notion that his policy was leading to war; in his ignoring of the possibility that his policy was seen by the Chinese as aggressive and uncontrolled; and in his deep feeling of personal and national self-righteousness. It was achieved through the lowering of the threshold of penetration for the kind of information that dealt with India's deterrent effectiveness and through the creation of illusory correlations between facts, such as India's status in the international arena and China's military options, or the nuclearization of the global system and the possibility that a war between China and India would break out. At times information was "created," either by Nehru himself, regarding China's intentions, for example, or by some other party,[24] as with the evaluation that the Indian army's strength was growing—an evaluation in which Nehru had serene faith, despite the objection of some of his senior military personnel.

Nehru can be seen as a typical example of a case in which a value system "imposes" on the policymaker a set of beliefs relating to his behavior, capabilities, and intentions and those of his opponents. This was so because the framework of his value system seemed so relevant to the China issue and because his ethical system was such an important part of his personality. Thus, it is no wonder that his dominant process regarding new information was one of nonadaptation; the main purpose of the information was to improve and add accuracy not to the policymaker's factual world but to his ethical code.

Against the background of Nehru's value system it is not difficult to comprehend the inner logic and symmetry in his attitudes toward, and evaluations of, Chinese intentions, as well as the great certainty that characterized his attitude toward his strategic estimates. Doubts only very rarely crept in, even when the dispute approached the surprise attack of autumn 1962, as his position on the Chinese issue was part of his total cognitive map, consisting as it did of his values and beliefs and an entire ensemble of issues in foreign and domestic policies. A strong verification of this detail emerges from the statistical analysis at the back of this book. The main factors emerging from the factor analysis are (a) the factor dealing with the connection between the China issue and domestic economic and political ones, which explains 29.4% of the variance, whereas (b) the factor second in importance, concerned mainly with happenings on the global level and within the different subsystems, explains 14.1% of the variance. In other words, these two factors, which express a linkage between the China problem and other domestic and foreign policy issues, together explain 43.5% of the variance. Together with the fourth and fifth factors dealing with the contribution, as Nehru saw it, of the influence of pressure groups and the super powers, and contributing together 18.7% to the explanation of the variance, it appears that factors not solely connected to the China issue per se contributed 62.2% to the explanation of the variance in Nehru's conception of the China problem.[25] Moreover, the attitudes pertaining to the China issue itself should be regarded as one structure composed of linked segments. In other words, each single attitude should be seen, on the one hand, as part of a sequence of attitudes on the China question; and, on the other hand, as an expression of Nehru's value system, hence, anchored in beliefs and basic assumptions, both implicit and explicit, relating to the above-mentioned sequences.

Nehru's attitudes on the China issue should therefore be seen in the context of his concept of the linkage between the real and the ideal—reality in the broad sense of the word as he conceived it, and the ideal as expressed in his system of values—that is, a connection characterized by the need to find consistency between the ideal and the real. This is one of the basic elements of Hinduism, which refused to recognize the gap between the spiritual world and the social, material world (Radhakrishnan, 1949, 79).

Table 10.1 enables us to examine the structure of the perceptual system and the action orientation related to it in the China context.

The qualities that characterized Nehru's attitudes in foreign policy facilitated the formation of misconceptions. First, we should remember that Nehru arrived on the foreign policy scene with his world view already generally outlined. India's position and role were predetermined, as were potential enemies and allies. In addition, Nehru's self-appreciation, his self-confidence in the righteousness of his position, made both his general world view and his specific attitudes on the China issue a fairly closed system, affording little chance of change.

Nehru's characterization of China, expressed in the adjectives with which he chose to describe it, concentrated chiefly (43.9%) on the positive friendly axis, with only a minority (17.3%) in the hostile and clearly negative category, and 38.8% neutral. Thus indicated is that Nehru tended to maintain his basic evaluations of China, and that on the strategic level this characterization decidedly influenced

Table 10.1. The Cognitive Map — Perception, Conclusions, and Action Orientations

Issue Area	Perceptions	Basic Assumptions		Conclusions	Action Orientation
		Explicit	Implicit		
1. Definition of the problem	1. The issue is mainly political.	Global politics are more important than local politics.		There is faith in the ability to cope with problem.	Preference given to moves in which the political aspect is dominant
	2. The issue is not a strategic defense one.			There is no strong sense of military threat.	Low investment in military growth
	3. The problems are political-legal.	Legal evidence is the basis for settling the disagreements.		There is an "objective" solution to the problem.	A legal airing of problem
2. The global system	4. There exists an arena of constant conflict and confrontation.	India's destiny is dependent on happenings in the global arena.		Local conflicts must not distract attention from the main problems.	Maximum attention must be given to the global arena, and nonalignment must be pursued.
	5. The conflict might deteriorate into nuclear war.	The nonaligned bloc has a role in preventing deterioration.	A local conflict might spark a general confrontation.	India, as leader of the bloc, has special status in the eyes of the super powers.	India can take daring steps against China thanks to the umbrella protection provided by the super powers.
		War between China and India will bring nuclear war.	Conflicts and crises become unmanageable as soon as they break out.	The super powers will not allow such a war.	India can maintain a daring policy, as full-scale war is unlikely.

(Table continues)

Table 10.1 continued

Issue Area	Perceptions	Basic Assumptions		Conclusions	Action Orientation
		Explicit	Implicit		
	6. The status of the Third World bloc is on the ascent.	India's prestige is at its height.	The Third World will act homogeneously and support India.	No actor will dare to rouse Third World wrath.	India can afford a daring nonyielding policy.
	7. The UN's status is on the ascent.	India's influence at the UN is at its height.		Power in the UN arena gives India deterrent power.	India can afford daring nonyielding policies.
3. Indo-USSR relations	8. USSR is India's natural ally against neocolonialism.	USSR is a peace-loving country.		India need not fear the USSR as British India did, nor give USSR reason to worry.	Nonalignment policy should be pursued.
		USSR is a source of unconditional aid.			Nonalignment policy should be pursued.
	9. USSR is leader of the Communist bloc.	Friendship with USSR is a condition for good relations with China.	Sino-Soviet rift is not important.	Sino-Soviet rift has not demaged Soviet ability to restrain China.	India can pursue noncon-cessional policy without fear.
	10. USSR is taking a pro-Indian stance in the conflict.			USSR will restrain China and force it to accept India's position.	India can pursue noncon-cessional policy without fear.

(Table continues)

Table 10.1 continued

Issue Area	Perceptions	Basic Assumptions Explicit	Basic Assumptions Implicit	Conclusions	Action Orientation
4. U.S.-India relations	11. U.S. has changed its hostile attitude to India.	U.S. recognize India's righteousness and importance.		U.S. cannot afford loss of Indian friendship and harm to its status.	India can pursue nonconcessional policy without fear.
	12. U.S. supports India in its dispute with China.	U.S. cannot afford a Chinese threat to India.		U.S. will come to India's aid when necessary, even without a formal treaty.	India can pursue nonconcessional policy without fear.
5. Subsystemic activity	13. Different subsystems have become main cold war arenas.	Local conflicts present penetration opportunities for the super powers.		There is a need to reduce areas of conflict by applying principles of peaceful coexistence.	India must be active in other subsystems and must set an example.
	14. Indian activity in various arenas has given it moral prestige.	Moral prestige is power.		The costs arising from attacking India are greater than the benefits, due to India's special status.	India can pursue nonconcessional policy without fear.
	15. Asia is a homogeneous and unified subsystem.	Shared colonial past gave a common denominator to all Asian countries.	Colonial past compensates for ideological and cultural differences.	Asia should be a model of peaceful competition based on solidarity. The failure of Asian coexistence will harm the essential solidarity needed even by China.	India can pursue continuously nonconcessional policy.

(Table continues)

Table 10.1 continued

Issue Area	Perceptions	Basic Assumptions Explicit	Basic Assumptions Implicit	Conclusions	Action Orientation
6. Geo-strategy	16. India's geo-strategic position is of crucial importance.	No super power can agree to the control of its rival over India.		India is protected by mutual deterrence.	India can pursue nonconcessional policy toward China.
		The main military threat is from the northwest.		The main threat is Pakistan.	India must concentrate its forces against Pakistan.
	17. India's security boundaries are the Himalayas.	Bhutan, Sikkim, and Nepal are India's defense line.		A threat against any of of them is a threat to India.	Indian dominance of the Hill States must be preserved.
	18. India's borders as defined by India are permanent and unchanging.			Concession on the border question constitutes loss of face and an expression of weakness.	The border question is not open to discussions of principles, but only to minor changes.
	19. The Himalayas are impenetrable to an invading army.	Technological changes have not changed that fact.		The threat from the north is negligible.	Indian can depend on topography and need not invest in military power. India can pursue nonconcessional policy toward China with no military fear.

(Table continues)

Table 10.1 continued

Issue Area	Perceptions	Basic Assumptions Explicit	Basic Assumptions Implicit	Conclusions	Action Orientation
	The difficult terrain does not permit large-scale fighting.			There is no danger of full-scale war.	India can follow a daring policy in this area without fear.
				There is no use of foreign military aid.	There is no practical use in giving up nonalignment to ensure foreign aid.
	20. The land features have prevented the ethnic minorities from being assimilated into India.			A foreign power could make use of ethnic unrest.	Hostilities between China and India must be kept to a minimum to preserve quiet in the area.
7. India-Pakistan relations	21. Pakistan is India's most dangerous enemy.	Pakistan never accepted India as a nation based on nonreligious principles, and is not happy with the *status quo*.		Pakistan might be provoked into military adventures.	Military attention must focus on Pakistan.
		Territorial concessions in Aksai Chin are dangerous as a precedent.			A double front must be avoided, but no concessions to China must be made.

(Table continues)

Table 10.1 continued

Issue Area	Perceptions	Basic Assumptions Explicit	Basic Assumptions Implicit	Conclusions	Action Orientation
		Pakistan is a tool in the hands of neo-colonialism.		Pakistan is also an ideological threat to India.	The USSR is an ally against that threat.
8. India and the Hill States	22. India must maintain its political dominance in the Hill States.	India's defense depends on the Hill States.		A Chinese penetration of those states would threaten India greatly.	India must try and reform them in its own image.
		China will recognize these states as an Indian sphere of influence. These states have no alternative to India.		Such a precedent of Chinese penetration in one of the states is dangerous.	The principalities must be prevented from having direct ties with China. India must not display weakness, which would encourage closeness to China and an imitation of Nepalese policy by Bhutan and Sikkim.
9. Balance of power	23. War between the two countries is unlikely.	A war between the two countries could not end in a decisive victory.		Relatively low sense of threat	Low investment in military power
	24. The Indian army can defeat any invasion.	Only limited Chinese penetrations were possible.		Low sense of threat; high confidence	India can continue the Forward Policy.

(Table continues)

Table 10.1 continued

Issue Area	Perceptions	Basic Assumptions		Conclusions	Action Orientation
		Explicit	Implicit		
	25. China is weak both militarily and econ-omically, due to internal factors.	Chinese aggressiveness is only an externaliz-ation of internal problems.		Chinese warnings need not be taken seriously.	Forward Policy may be continued.
	26. China cannot afford to open a second front.		In any situation, China's attention will remain on the U.S., Taiwan, and Japan.	Chinese hostility should not be interpreted as a threat.	India's demands must be pursued, and China will eventually succumb.
	27. Economic devel-opment is a con-dition for military might.			Too many resources must not be diverted to the military.	Low investment in the military
10. Indian internal arena	28. Opposition inside and outside of Congress Party expresses criti-cism on all domestic and foreign policy issues.	Opposition might spoil Sino-Indian relations.	Nehru might lose control of the situation.	Opposition must be disarmed.	Firm stands against China must be assumed so that internal and external policies will not suffer.

(Table continues)

Table 10.1 continued

Issue Area	Perceptions	Basic Assumptions Explicit	Basic Assumptions Implicit	Conclusions	Action Orientation
	29. A united front of all opposition factors could damage Nehru's special status.		The right wing of the Congress Party might co-operate with hawkish opposition parties.	Such a pact must be avoided and public opinion must be kept sympathetic to Nehru, so that his charisma is not diminished.	A firm policy should be continued, but proposals must be made from time to time to keep up the momentum of negotiations.
11. Legal aspects	30. The purely legal aspects of the dispute is important.	The legal aspect of the dispute can be separated from other aspects.		It is of crucial importance to convince China of India's legal rights.	It is desirable to invest great effort in the legal aspect of the dispute.
	31. India is undoubtedly in the right legally.	China is doing India a legal injustice.		Territory belonging legally to India must not be relinquished.	
	32. The legal system is universal.		Differences in regime and world view do not matter in the application of the legal rules.	Eventually China would have to accept India's concepts, as the Burmese and Nepalese precedents indicate.	No territorial concessions should be made.
12. China and India	33. China and India basically resemble one another.	There is a 2,000-year tradition of friendship.		Friendship and understanding with China	No need to invest too much in military defense of the northern border

(Table continues)

Table 10.1 continued

Issue Area	Perceptions	Basic Assumptions		Conclusions	Action Orientation
		Explicit	Implicit		
	34. China and India need each other.	Friendly ties between China and India are vital.		Unity of cause with China	No need to invest too much in military defense of the northern border.
	35. Policy toward China reflects India's foreign policy in general.			The failure of the policy toward China will be seen as failure of Nehru's entire foreign policy.	Such a failure must not be allowed or admitted.
	36. The policy toward China is also connected to domestic political power plays.			The failure of the policy will put arms in the hands of Nehru's rivals.	A firm policy must be pursued so as not to give weapons to Nehru's rivals.
	37. China wants to be accepted at the UN.			China cannot afford Indian antagonism.	A firm policy may be pursued with no fear of war.
	38. The Tibet problem is not a very serious issue in relations with China.			China will not react in an extreme way because of this problem.	Military investment on the northern border is not needed.
	39. China and India have basically the same evaluation of the global system.		The Maoist ideology need not be taken at face value.	China also understands that war with India is impossible.	India can continue its firm policy without fear.

(Table continues)

Table 10.1 continued

Issue Area	Perceptions	Basic Assumptions Explicit	Basic Assumptions Implicit	Conclusions	Action Orientation
	40. China's behavior is the outcome of its internal problems.			China will carry on its aggressive behavior only within limited boundaries, due to internal weakness.	India can ignore Chinese warnings and continue its firm policy.
13. Hostility and threat	41. Chinese feelings of hostility are not connected directly to a threat perception leading to war.		Verbal action orientations can be ignored, as they do not reflect China's actual intentions.	China is not willing to make massive use of force.	A daring nonyielding and firm policy may be continued.
14. Time	42. Time is working in India's favor.		China does not intend to realize its expressed intentions in the near future.	China will eventually have to accept Indian demands.	Compromises should not be made.

his evaluation of China's probable action orientation. The high percentage of neutral characteristics enabled Nehru to insert new information about China into the neutral categories without having to change the ratio between negative and positive characteristics. Moreover, the characteristics were of a banal nature in the sense that they did not contain uniquely Chinese elements such as Maoism or Sinocentrism. Instead, Nehru made use of generalized terms such as Communism or Socialism. Here we see Nehru's tendency to define and characterize protagonists in the international arena in macro-terms—a result of his broad concepts of historical processes—and to ignore the need to apply the general theories to specific cases. This is especially noticeable against the background of the Chinese leadership's characterization of India and the obvious lack of symmetry between both characterizations of each other, as the following table indicates.

Table 10.2. Comparative Presentation of the Characterization of the Rival

Type of Characterization	China by Nehru	India by Chinese Leadership
Friendly / Positive	43.9%	38.8%
Hostile / Negative	17.3%	61.2%
Neutral	38.8%	—
Total	100.0%	100.0%

Source: This table is based on the detailed analysis which appears in the Statistical Appendix, Tables A5 and A6.

This asymmetry has special significance in the context of assessing long-term developments, which in this case led to optimism. Nehru's unawareness of the fact that the main characteristics of Indian society and political culture were in China's view negative only deepened his tendency to assess information erroneously by anchoring it in a well-defined and rigid system.

Another dimension of India's set of attitudes was connected to its classification of its own actions. The action categories that were defined for India as passive or restrained included also typically violent actions. For this reason, Nehru could sincerely think of the Forward Policy as a controlled policy, whereas in relation to China, the action categories defined as negative and expressing ingratitude, hostility, and rigidity included every single Chinese action or proposal except Chinese withdrawal from its held positions to the status quo ante. The categories of power and success, too, from an Indian point of view, contained in the Chinese context every kind of Indian action that was not countered with an immediate violent Chinese reaction. Thus, it was possible to include hostile and violent Indian actions under conciliatory titles, and vice versa in terms of Chinese actions and expressions, all of which facilitated the manipulation of the information in question.

From an emotional viewpoint, Nehru's attitudes included a number of basic elements: a strong emotional commitment to generations-old Sino-Indian solidarity, strengthened by his visit to China in 1954 (Fisher and Bondurant, 1956a), a commitment that created a romantic attitude toward the Chinese revolution, state, and culture. At the same time, Nehru exhibited a strong emotional commitment toward the need to preserve India's national honor and the territorial integrity of the disputed area, due to its prominent place in Indian culture. This was accompanied by an almost sentimental-emotional commitment to other values reflected in Nehru's attitudes, which were sometimes contradictory. The emotional obligation, in turn, increased Nehru's need to explain information so as to avoid contradictions among his various emotional commitments, none of which he was able to reject.

If all this was not enough to turn the existing set of attitudes into a rigid one, the concept that his attitude was the only rational and right one—serving both the ethical, cultural-emotional, and national-instrumental interests—came into the picture. To Nehru the rationalist, this was another good reason to stick to these attitudes at all costs even in the face of dissonant information.

Under such conditions, when his attitudes in all areas were conditioned by the "proof" of his righteousness of positions on the China question, any change of attitudes on that subject became almost impossible, due to a conscious or unconscious fear of the collapse of other central attitudes and beliefs and, equally important, of a severe blow to the ego of a great but arrogant and vain man, who could not face what he intuitively grasped as a threat to the emotional and rational structure of his complex and sensitive world view.

Nehru's existing set of positions was balanced also in the sense that its conclusions seemed to support one other. As no inner contradictions were formed, there seemed to be no need for a reassessment or new decisions, or for a choice between attitudes that might have resulted from contradictory conclusions. The balance between attitudes, values, and beliefs led to so smug a feeling and such an insistent objection to change that ambivalent conformation, such as the lack of Chinese response to India's one-sided moves, was seen as having only one interpretation—that of supporting the existing set of beliefs with regard to India's deterrent power.

Thus, as what was acceptable and what was not had been predetermined, any unacceptable information or evaluation was flatly rejected. The information received was not used for assessing the system of beliefs. On the contrary, once the basis of the system of beliefs was decided on and conditioned by the emotional and ethical systems, the information was meant to serve the existing system or, if it could not fulfill that function, to be manipulated so that it would.

What further aggravated the situation was Nehru's wishful thinking, such that he delegated the situation to a secondary, ephemeral position. The basic assumption of Nehru's world view was that situations were passing and changing phenomena and as such should be accorded only secondary importance;[26] hence, his *aims* decided his attitudes and evaluations. His own characterization of an object as positive or negative was for Nehru the basis on which he determined a general strategic assessment. As China was defined and characterized positively,[27] the assumption that it could sink to such unthinkable depths as an invasion was unlikely. So, by defining the object, China, Nehru minimized the range of the change in assessment toward its intentions as a function of circumstances and specific situations that arose.[28] And as the definition of the object was sanctified, it could not be rediscussed even in light of a change in circumstances. Thus, information about situations that had changed but did not also simultaneously necessitate the acceptance of basic changes in attitude toward the object[29] did not require a change in the overall attitude itself; rather, it called for only minor changes such as an admission of the sort that recognized the possibility, not of war, but of a small local dispute with China.

Under these conditions, Nehru's system of attitudes fulfilled various functions: it expressed Nehru's value system; it protected his ego and prevented inner conflicts that would have been difficult for him to handle; and it gave a logical, rational, and consistent interpretation to the environment. It engendered order in that it based foreign policy on a set of consistent attitudes and prevented the development of cognitive dissonance. Furthermore, the existing attitudes seemed to be serving India's practical interests optimally, in the political, economic, and military spheres. Considering Nehru's deep personal involvement in the area of foreign policy in general and in China policy in particular, as well as the characteristics of his personality, it is no wonder that such a strong drive was created in him to preserve the existing system of beliefs and attitudes and to make only marginal changes in it.

I have already stated that because of his confidence in handling dissonant information and his intellectual sophistication, Nehru could not and did not always try to avoid dealing with dissonant information that threatened his cognitive balance. But that same intellectual sophistication also facilitated his coping with the information with a complete spectrum of "techniques," from the most banal and simplistic such as denial, to the most sophisticated such as transcendence.[30]

In the first stages of the dispute, Nehru made much use of the denial technique, beginning with its crudest forms such as keeping border incidents from the knowledge of his ministers and the public, justifying this to himself with the hope that they would be settled by diplomatic negotiations, and moving up to a more complex variety of attributing them to local initiative (*Par.*, I, 364).

As the dispute became public knowledge and Nehru could no longer delude himself or others with the notion that it had occurred at the initiative of the local Chinese command, he made use of more sophisticated techniques, such as the severing of cognitive links. Thus, when he was asked about the relevance of the Panch Sheel values to the events in Tibet, he could reply: "I don't think the question of Panch Sheel directly arises in this connection" (*Press*, I, 5). Later, he would ignore the connection between the Sino-Indian and the Sino-Soviet disputes, or the contradiction between the Forward Policy and his call for peaceful negotiations. An example of his use of the bolstering technique can be seen in his explanation of why it was not worthwhile to invest directly in the army; according to this thinking, economic developments, when realized, would automatically increase India's military strength.

But the greater the number of contradictions within and among his personal values and his publicly expressed attitudes, the more sophisticated were the techniques he required. Thus, we find an expression of the technique of differentiation in the famous distinction between negotiation, which he did not intend to hold, and talks, which he was always willing to have. On the other hand, when internal pressures increased he tended to use the transcendence technique: to claim that the dispute should be seen in its global context, to transcend the narrow views of local interests. This concept allowed Nehru to hold simultaneously opposing views: to claim that the global context gave immunity to India and naturally demanded a nonconcessional policy and, at the same time, to declare that within the global framework the border dispute would never actually assume more than marginal proportions. This double view should have yielded a more flexible orientation, but here the technique of severing cognitive links prevailed and Nehru ignored the connection as well as the contradictions in his assessments.

The use of these techniques enabled Nehru to confront dissonant information in a way that seemed to him convincing enough not to change his existing beliefs and attitudes. Not only were such changes avoided, but the techniques made changes seem unwise and irrational. In this light, even when change was unavoidable it was minimal. Thus, it was natural for Nehru to adopt the approach that although Chinese hostility toward India existed it was limited in time and place, and that it was an abnormal situation arising from internal unrest or a routine historical occurrence, repeating itself in times of a strong central regime in China. Again, Nehru was not aware of the inner contradiction between these two claims: if the regime was strong, internal unrest should not have been sufficient to necessitate aggressive externalization.

Thus far I have presented one side of the coin, in other words, the need for consistency or balance among the various factors in the cognitive system and the psychological limitations this need placed on Nehru in the formation of an accurate evaluation and handling of dissonant information. The other side of the coin is the relationship between attitudes and actions, or, how this relationship was perceived by Nehru both in the context of his self-image and in that relating to his evaluation of Chinese intentions. In this area, from the Chinese side, Nehru's fingers had been badly burned in the past, as his basic assumption since the early 1950s had been that the Chinese non-reaction to unilateral Indian moves expressed its acceptance of the Indian boundary definition. The outbreak of the border dispute and the fact that Chou En-lai denied this interpretation of the Chinese reaction (*W.P.*, II, 31) astonished Nehru. Instead of admitting that he had been mistaken, he preferred to adopt the view that the Chinese could not be relied upon, that their actions did not reflect their true positions. From there to the parallel attitude that Chinese positions were not indications of anticipated actions was but a step. Furthermore, this estimation of the relationship between attitudes and actions was consistent with Nehru's total set of beliefs, which insisted on the limitations of Chinese action potential. Such an approach put Nehru into a more desirable moral position, as the lack of compatibility between attitude and action was for Nehru the moralist an expression of a low moral level. As for his self-image, he saw himself as practicing what he preached, although this was not exactly so, as we have noted.

The fact that Nehru required the self-image of a man of action, acting in keeping with his expressed attitudes, made it difficult for him to choose a clear line of action, as he had to find one that would satisfy contradictory cognitive needs. The result was so twisted and oblique that it was difficult to assess its exact nature. It contained symbolic elements of each of the contradictory values in Nehru's cognitive system. But Nehru did not see his actions as symbolic; for him they expressed his true positions. As a consequence, he naturally could not accept the view that in the last account both his conciliatory actions—the proposals of negotiations on the basis of a return to the status quo ante (*W.P.*, VII, 37; *Par.*, II, 94)—and his violent ones—expressed in the hasty setting up of Indian positions as a symbol of Indian control of territory—were nothing but a source of confusion to the Chinese and to the Indian public. To the former, Nehru's position did not seem conciliatory, but more like paying lip service to the principle of negotiations as well as an expression of his hypocrisy. The cynical comment in the *Times of India*, on August 15, 1962, is appropriate: "Anyone reading the latest White Paper on Sino-Indian relations together with some of the recent speeches of the Prime Minister and Defence Minister on the subject might have been forgiven for feeling that the Government China Policy, like chop suey, contains a bit of everything—firmness and conciliation, bravado and caution, sweet reasonableness and defiance."[31]

But it must be remembered that Nehru perceived his symbolic actions as real actions whose contents were the same as their appearance. It was no wonder, then, that he could not understand or even realistically estimate the hollowness of his actions and the Chinese reaction to them. Nehru's recognition of this fact would have placed his ego and his self-image in an embarrassing state of humiliation. Clearly, the easy way out of all this was self-delusion as to the real value of his actions and the degree of their compatibility with his expressed positions. Nehru's behavior is also an interesting example of what is known as "identifying with the aggressor," an imitation of the latter's behavior and the acquiring of self-confidence by means of imitation. As Lieutenant General Kaul put it, Nehru created the Forward Policy "as a 'strategy' of beating the Chinese at their own game" (Kaul, 1967, 281).

The result of these psychological needs,[32] deriving from Nehru's personality traits and social, cultural, and personal values, was the creation of an inner drive to manipulate information in evaluation of the opponent's relative strength and intentions, as with India's ability to cope with the anticipated danger. Moreover, in Nehru there coexisted two contrasting senses—one being the motivation to control and dominate and the other being a reluctance to use power and authority—in other words, a reluctance to make the necessary difficult decisions. This duality created a clear preference for situations of certainty over those of uncertainty and ambivalence. The latter might have brought forward the latent tensions inherent in this dual approach to power, particularly when the making of a choice in an ambivalent context could lead to decisions demanding departure from existing routines of thinking and behavior. For this purpose, clear and unequivocal rules of prediction that facilitated the treatment of information leading to uncertainty were preferred. The "representativeness rule" formed an anticipation and estimation as to Chinese behavior that resembled and remained within the boundaries of Indian behavior, due to Nehru's perception of a basic similarity between India and China. But when the deterioration of relations diminished the reliability of this rule, Nehru was served by the "availability rule," according to which the likelihood he attributed to the realization of his optimistic anticipations increased with the greater effort he put into the process of convincing himself and others of India's invincibility. Such optimism made it easier to underestimate Chinese violence potential. Also deserving mention is the fact that the bureaucratic and organizational systems (as we shall see in the next chapter) helped to create information that served this rule. It is no wonder that in a reminiscence in November 1962, Nehru stated with almost pathetic naiveté: "We have taken it almost for granted that despite some lapses in recent years, as in the Suez affair—we had taken it for granted—that this type of aggression was almost a thing of the past" (*Par.*, II, 139).

Behind the two rules we have mentioned was the use of an anchoring point as a basis for the evaluation of information, in this case a detailed ethical, ideological system the existence of which somehow guaranteed the chance of its actual realization. The use of these simple prediction and attribution rules, although they reduced uncertainty, created an opening for the formation of the misperceptions discussed previously.

Conclusions

Nehru's personality traits directly influenced the interpretation of information in a biased way by creating a need for certainty as well as the avoidance of a reassessment of past decisions and conceptions. These same personality traits also had an indirect impact on information processing, in that they dictated the character of Nehru's personal relationships with other individuals in the information-processing community. Hence, they led to his inefficient handling of dissonant information and to the conservativeness of his attitudes.

These trends were supported and enhanced by the cognitive structure of the mind of this brilliant politician and statesman. Nehru, a complicated and sophisticated intellectual, adopted a personal operational code and value structure that colored and directed his perceptions of the world. This structure was a source of emotional and intellectual conflict when applied to the China issue. The conflict was the consequence of the need for trade-offs between values and beliefs, concerning both policies and the means used, which were all of high importance for a man whose self-image was so dependent on consistency and loyalty to convictions. His personality traits also supported his psychological motivation to avoid any kind of trade-off or inconsistency almost at any price, even that of manipulating the interpretation of both existing and new, incoming dissonant information.

In this way, cognitive and personality traits combined to work to prevent adaptation. Furthermore, although Nehru's sophistication usually made it difficult for him to completely disregard information or inconsistencies, it facilitated his search for the means, explanations, and rationalizations with which to handle such matters in what seemed to him a satisfactory manner.

11
Interpersonal and Interorganizational Relations

Thus far I have intimated that the information-processing system was influenced by interorganizational, intragroup, and interpersonal relationship patterns. These social relationships and interactions reflected deep-rooted cultural, societal, and traditional factors, as well as the personality traits of the individuals involved.

The Web of Bureaucratic-Organizational Relations

The point of departure for analyzing the patterns of the relationships on the organizational and personal levels and their interactions will be the classification of leading personalities involved in the China policy into the categories of politicians, bureaucrats, and military personnel, with a distinction being made within the last category between headquarters personnel and field commanders.

A note of caution should be added. Any categorization of this type is bound to be something of an approximation. There are exceptions to any general rule, such that certain individuals might be closer in their views to factions outside their own organization or group. However, in spite of the exceptions, the dominant factions can be defined and delimited quite clearly.

Table 11.1 will aid our analysis of the patterns of interrelationship. It maps out the relevant policymakers; their formal organizational origins; their group or groups of reference; their personal relationships with other policymakers, and especially with Nehru; and their importance in the hierarchical ladder within the framework to which they belong.

One of the underlying facts that emerges is the mutual distrust and even contempt between top civilians: between politicians and bureaucrats on the one hand and the military on the other, although, where Nehru personally is concerned, it is difficult to speak of contempt because of his special status. But there was undoubtedly a certain degree of mistrust even toward him, or at least a feeling that he did

Table 11.1. Hierarchy and Reciprocal Relations Among Involved Personalities

Personality	Role	Relevant Organization	Reference Group	Nature of Role	Relations with Nehru	Relations with Others	Centrality of Position*
POLITICIANS							
1. J. Nehru	Prime Minister, Minister of External Affairs	PM's office, MEA, cabinet committees on defense and foreign policy, parliament, Congress Party, Planning Commission	1. Indian public 2. Senior statesmen in international arena 3. Congress Party's left wing	Senior political decisionmaker and information processor		Very close relationship with Menon	1
2. V.K.K. Menon	Defense Minister	Defense Ministry, cabinet committees on defense and foreign policy, parliament	1. Military 2. MEA 3. Congress Party's left wing	Senior political decisionmaker, supplier and processor of information	Hierarchy dependence respect	Nehru: very good Desai: very bad Kaul: good Thapar: correct Indira: good Mullik: good	2
3. G.B. Pant (died in 1961)	Home Minister	Home ministry, cabinet committees on defense and foreign policy, Intelligence Bureau, parliament	Congress Party's right wing	Senior political decisionmaker, decision-ratifier, information processor	Hierarchy respect	Nehru: very good Menon: correct Mullik: good	2
4. M. Desai	Finance Minister	Finance Ministry, cabinet committees on defense and foreign policy, parliament	Congress Party's right wing	Senior political decisionmaker, decision-ratifier, information processor	Hierarchy respect	Nehru: correct Menon: very bad	3

*On a diminishing scale of 1–5 (relates to the China issue only). The scaling is intragroup but not intergroup.

(Table continues)

Table 11.1 continued

Personality	Role	Relevant Organization	Reference Group	Nature of Role	Relations with Nehru	Relations with Others	Centrality of Position*
5. L.B. Shastri	Home Minister (after Pant's death in 1961)	Home Ministry, cabinet committees on defense and foreign policy, Intelligence Bureau, parliament		Senior political decisionmaker, decision-ratifier, information processor	Hierarchy dependence respect	Nehru: good Menon: correct Mullik: good	3
6. J. Ram	Railways Minister	Parliament	Congress Party's right wing	Medium political decision-ratifier	Hierarchy respect	Nehru: good Menon: correct	4
7. S.K. Patil	Food and Agriculture Minister	Parliament	Congress Party'a right wing	Medium political decision-ratifier	Hierarchy respect	Nehru: cool Menon: bad	4
8. I. Gandhi	President of Congress Party		Congress Party's left wing	Medium political advisor	Hierarchy dependence respect	Nehru: very good Menon: good	4
9. A.K. Sen	Law Minister	Parliament, cabinet committee on defense and foreign policy		Medium political decision-ratifier	Hierarchy dependence respect	Nehru: good Menon: good	5
10. T.T. Krishna-machari	Minister without portfolio	Parliament, cabinet committee on foreign policy		Medium political decision-ratifier	Hierarchy dependence respect	Nehru: good Menon: good	5

(Table continues)

Table 11.1 continued

Personality	Role	Relevant Organization	Reference Group	Nature of Role	Relations with Nehru	Relations with Others	Centrality of Position*
11. S. Subbarayn	Transportation Minister	Parliament, cabinet committee on foreign policy		Medium political decision-ratifier	Hierarchy dependence respect	Nehru: good Menon: good	5
BUREAUCRATS							
12. B.N. Mullik	Director of Intelligence Bureau	Home Ministry	Defense Ministry, military, MEA	Senior bureaucratic advisor, executor, decisionmaker, supplier and processor of information	Hierarchy dependence respect	Nehru: very good Menon: correct	1
13. S. Dutt	Foreign Secretary	MEA		Senior bureaucratic advisor, executor, decisionmaker on minor matters, information processor	Hierarchy dependence respect	Nehru: very good Menon: correct	1
14. M.J. Desai	Foreign Secretary	MEA		Senior bureaucratic advisor, executor, information processor	Hierarchy dependence respect	Nehru: good Menon: cool	2

(Table continues)

Table 11.1 continued

Personality	Role	Relevant Organization	Reference Group	Nature of Role	Relations with Nehru	Relations with Others	Centrality of Position*
15. S. Gopal	Director of the Historical Division	MEA		Middle bureaucratic advisor, supplier and processor of information	Hierarchy dependence respect	Nehru: very good Menon: correct	2
16. J.S. Mehta	Director of China Section (later Northern Division)	MEA		Middle bureaucratic advisor, supplier and processor of information	Hierarchy dependence respect	Nehru: very good Menon: good	3
17. S. Sinha	Director of China Division	MEA		Middle bureaucratic advisor, supplier and processor of information	Hierarchy dependence respect	Nehru: correct	4
18. N.B. Menon	Director of China Division	MEA		Middle bureaucratic advisor, supplier and processor of information	Hierarchy dependence respect	Nehru: correct	4

(Table continues)

Table 11.1 continued

Personality	Role	Relevant Organization	Reference Group	Nature of Role	Relations with Nehru	Relations with Others	Centrality of Position*
19. G. Parthasarthi	India's ambassador to China	MEA		Middle bureaucratic advisor, supplier and information processor	Hierarchy dependence respect	Nehru: good	5
20. S.S. Khera	Cabinet Secretary	Prime Minister's Office		Senior bureaucratic advisor, information processor	Hierarchy dependence respect	Nehru: good Menon: correct	5
21. H.C. Sarin	Joint Secretary in the Defense Ministry	Defense Ministry		Middle bureaucratic executor, advisor	Hierarchy dependence respect	Kaul: good Nehru: correct Menon: correct Thapar: correct Mullik: correct Thimayya: cool	5
MILITARY							
22. B.M. Kaul (Lieutenant General)	1. C.G.S. 2. G.O.C. IV Corps	Army Headquarters, Defense Ministry	1. Senior political echelons 2. Senior officers in the army	Senior military (Headquarters) advisor, decision-maker, supplier and processor of information, executor	Hierarchy dependence respect	Nehru: very good Menon: good Thapar: good Thimayya: correct L.P. Sen: good Prasad: correct	1

(Table continues)

Table 11.1 continued

Personality	Role	Relevant Organization	Reference Group	Nature of Role	Relations with Nehru	Relations with Others	Centrality of Position*
23. K.S. Thimayya (General)	C.O.A.S.	Army Headquarters, Defense Ministry	1. Senior political echelons 2. Senior army officers	Senior military (Headquarters) advisor, executor, supplier and processor of information	Hierarchy dependence respect	Nehru: correct Menon: very bad	1
24. P.N. Thapar (General)	C.O.A.S.	Army Headquarters, Defense Ministry	1. Senior political echelons 2. Senior Army officers	Senior military (Headquarters) advisor, executor, supplier and processor of information	Hierarchy dependence, respect	Nehru: correct Menon: correct Kaul: good	2
25. L.P. Sen (Lieut. Gen.)	G.O.C.-in-Chief, Eastern Command	Army Headquarters, Defense Ministry	1. Senior political echelons 2. Senior army officers	Middle military (Headquarters) advisor, executor, supplier and processor of information	Hierarchy dependence respect	Nehru: correct Menon: correct Kaul: correct U. Singh: bad Thapar: correct	3
26. D. Singh (Lieut. Gen.)	G.O.C.-in-Chief, Western Command	Army Headquarters, Defense Ministry	Senior army officers	Middle military (Headquarters) advisor, executor, supplier and processor of information	Hierarchy dependence respect	Nehru: correct Menon: correct Kaul: correct Thapar: correct	3

(Table continues)

Table 11.1 continued

Personality	Role	Relevant Organization	Reference Group	Nature of Role	Relations with Nehru	Relations with Others	Centrality of Position*
27. U. Singh (Lieut. Gen.)	G.O.C. XXXIII Corps	Army		Middle military (field) executor, supplier of information	Hierarchy dependence respect	Menon: cool Kaul: cool L.P. Sen: bad Thapar: correct	4
28. N. Prasad (Major Gen.)	G.O.C. IV Division	Army		Junior military (field) executor, supplier of information	Hierarchy dependence respect	Menon: cool Kaul: cool Thapar: correct	5

not understand the needs of the armed forces and tended to identify with the civilian position on defense and strategy. This feeling was probably more dominant after 1957 when Krishna Menon was appointed minister of defense, given the long-standing intimacy between him and Nehru. If concrete evidence of this was needed, the Thimayya affair provided it.

General K.S. Thimayya was chief of army staff (COAS) when Menon took office. He had behind him a brilliant military career. Respected by all who knew him, he was a fearless man, likely to express his own opinions even to the most senior policymakers. He consistently sought to reduce the interference of the Ministry of Defense in purely military matters. Once Menon was appointed minister of defense, in light of his attitude toward senior military officers, it quickly became apparent that a clash between him and the general was inevitable. The military realized that their new defense minister was administratively efficient and, after many years of mediocre leadership resulting from the relatively low importance accorded this ministry by the politicians, they now had a minister who held a great deal of influence in the cabinet, thanks to Menon's close ties with Nehru. Menon's appointment in one sense came to the military as a breath of fresh air. But in a very short time, it became clear that the hopes and expectations of the military would founder on the personality of this highly educated, brilliant but difficult, dogmatic, and autocratic man.

Menon, who had a very inflated sense of his own intellectual superiority, saw himself as no less capable of running the army than any general (Rosenthal, 1957; George, 1964, 233), and as one who did not require aid or advice. He treated officers as though they were office boys, often with condescension and crudeness. Thus, for example: "If a General was speaking in a meeting and saying, for instance, 'I think . . .' he would snap: 'Soldiers are incapable of thinking'" (Kaul, 1967, 207). Only a very few dared to respond to his insults and sharp tongue. Moreover, to control the army, to further his own personal ambitions, and to reduce the influence of Thimayya, he did not hesitate to sow the seeds of friction in the ranks and the high command by publicly humiliating officers he disliked and did not want to promote; nor did he hesitate to play junior officers against their seniors, often ignoring the recommendations of the three service chiefs in the area of promotions and even military matters as well. The most striking appointment made against Thimayya's recommendation occurred in May 1959 when B.M. Kaul was made a lieutenant-general and was appointed army quartermaster-general, a post that was a stepping-stone to the highest positions in the Indian army and that guaranteed a voice on the appointments committee. Kaul was a distant relation of Nehru, a Kashmir Brahmin, a graduate of Sandhurst, energetic, smart, and impressive in appearance, who in the past had displayed physical bravery that had brought him into the limelight.[1] However, he had rather limited experience in commanding troops in battle. On the other hand, he excelled in his own public relations and, even in the formative years of the state, had become acquainted with Nehru, won his affection, and gained free access to him. These qualities of Kaul's convinced Nehru that he was a brilliant army man and blinded him to Kaul's faults. It was no wonder, then, that Menon supported this appointment despite the strong objections of the high command; the combination of Kaul's being Nehru's protégé, his administrative abilities, and, in particular, his disfavor with the high command were for Menon the best recommendations for appointing Kaul to a position ranking third in importance in the army.

Against the background of these relationship patterns, a severe crisis of confidence arose between the chiefs of the three services and the minister, such that the former, headed by the most senior and prestigious among them, General Thimayya, decided to force Nehru to take sides. The confrontation that took place a few days after the Longju Incident in August 1959 might have influenced the development of the dispute if it had ended differently. General Thimayya submitted his resignation on August 31, 1959 at a very inconvenient time for Nehru, as the opposition was attacking Menon for not doing enough for the defense of India. Nehru realized that these attacks were actually directed at him, and that the news of Thimayya's resignation could create a storm that would leave him no choice but to fire Menon, who had powerful enemies even within the Congress Party and no independent power base. He could not afford such a defeat, neither for political reasons (a victory for the conservative wing of the party) nor for personal ones, given his strong personal ties with Menon. He called General Thimayya to him and pressured him into taking back his letter of resignation. When the news leaked out to the press the following day, there was a public uproar, but Nehru handled it coolly, underplaying its importance and describing it as a storm in a teacup. He indirectly blamed Thimayya while praising Menon, but also promised to keep his eye personally on the Ministry of Defense (*Times of India*, September 3, 1959), assuring the public that the procedures for appointing senior officers would operate optimally. This affair increased Nehru's tendency to perceive military officers as hostile to his policies and to depend more and more on Menon and his group of protégés. On the other hand, "for the soldiers it carried the lesson that it did not pay to raise professional objections to the civilian handling of military matters" (Maxwell, 1972, 201).

These trends continued when, with the end of Thimayya's term of office early in 1961, Lieutenant-General P.N. Thapar—a mediocre officer who shied away from confrontations with politicians—rather than Lieutenant-General S.P. Thorat—GOC-in-Chief, Eastern Command, and recommended by Thimayya[2]—was appointed as COAS. Thapar was appointed thanks to the support of Menon and Kaul, an action that, of course, rendered him eternally grateful to them. His gratitude was immediately expressed in his appointing Lieutenant-General Kaul to the post of chief of general staff (CGS), despite his lack of qualifications for the job. These appointments aroused much resentment in military circles[3] and in Parliament, lulled only by Nehru's strong personal support of them. Now Kaul and Menon had a COAS after their own hearts. Kaul immediately set about appointing his loyalists to key posts in army headquarters,[4] such as Brigadier-General D.K. Palit as director of military operations and Major-General J.S. Dillon as his deputy. These officers became cynically known as "Kaul's boys."

In addition to manning key posts at headquarters with their people, Kaul and Menon made it clear that criticism would not be tolerated. A case in point was that of the commandant of the staff college, Major-General Sam Manekshaw, an officer with a distinguished record of active combat duty who looked down on Kaul and did not bother to hide it. Manekshaw, who had a sharp tongue, criticized the minister of defense and, on various occasions, Kaul, and this news reached Menon's ears. A military investigation committee was set up to look into the disciplinary and disloyalty charges against Manekshaw. Although the committee exonerated him, his advancement was frozen.[5] As a result, in top military circles, criticism was muted and "from watching one's words out of fear of informers it is only a step to choosing one's words to please superiors, military or civilians" (Maxwell, 1972, 205–206).

Another event that contributed to the same feelings at headquarters occurred a little earlier, at the beginning of 1961. Nehru had stated in Parliament that the situation in the western sector had improved in India's favor. Lieutenant-General S.D. Verma, commander of the Fifteenth Corps and in charge of the defense of the western sector, sent a letter to the GOC-in-Chief, Western Command refuting that claim and demanding that his letter be filed in army headquarters as proof that he did not share that optimistic outlook. A short while later he was forced to resign,[6] when officers junior to him were appointed as commanders of the Eastern and Western Commands. The lesson for the senior officers was loud and clear: politicians should be told what they wished to hear.

These events and the new appointments caused growing mistrust between the professional, critical military and the civilians. Officers in senior army posts were replaced either with men whose positions were dictated by their reference group—senior politicians and bureaucrats in the Ministry of Defense, the MEA, and the prime minister's office—or by officers who were afraid to stand up for their convictions. Two cases exemplify the process: Thimayya, in his time, had had no hesitation about confronting the minister of defense and the bureaucrats of the ministry. Moreover, when his objections were rejected because of the civilians' lack of understanding of the military balance, he at times ignored instructions, in cases where he felt they were potentially disastrous. Thus, when in May 1960 a memorandum was distributed, at Nehru's suggestion, by S. Dutt, the foreign secretary, demanding that the army take an active patrol policy and set up positions in the disputed area of the western sector (in other words, launch what was later called the Forward Policy), army headquarters ignored it and the instructions going out to the Western Command indicated only a maintenance of the status quo. And, indeed, the Forward Policy was put into effect only after the change in staff of the army command later in 1961. It may be that the civilian echelons were unaware of its instructions not being carried out in the field, or that they turned a blind eye to this fact because Nehru and his associates were wary of Thimayya's reaction and preferred to wait until his term in office was over. But either way, the difference in the behavior of army headquarters during Thimayya's term in office and afterwards is very noticeable. This difference has special significance in view of the fact that Nehru tended to accept the evaluations presented to him by the civilian echelons, even those concerning differences of opinion pertaining to strictly military matters. When in October 1962 Thapar tried, not too forcefully, to convince Nehru that the army could not carry out Operation Leghorn, the object of which was to oust Chinese forces that had crossed the Thag La Ridge, and was supported in his assessment by Lieutenant-General L.P. Sen, the GOC-in-Chief, Eastern Command, Nehru rejected the claim with a counterclaim that he had information indicating that the Chinese would not strike back. The sources of this information were Menon, the defense minister; the joint secretary in the Defense Ministry, H.C. Sarin; the director of the intelligence bureau, N.B. Mullik; and the senior officialdom of the MEA (Kaul, 1971, 292; Hoffmann, 1971, 651).

This growing situation, in which the majority of senior staff officers ceased to take into account the real military situation and insisted on its own evaluations, created a deepening gap between them and senior field officers, such as Major-General N. Prasad, commander of the Fourth Division, or Lieutenant-General Umrao Singh, commander of the Thirty-third Corps (Saigal, 1979, 21). These officers sensed that their men were being turned into cannon-fodder because of headquarters' unwillingness to challenge the civilian echelon, whereas in Thimayya's time they had at least thought that army headquarters in New Delhi understood their problems and fought their battles. Some field commanders, such as Lieutenant-General S.D. Verma and, later, Lieutenant-General Daulat Singh, tried to circumvent this problem by making sensible but tough logistic demands to prevent the implementation of what they viewed as a disastrous policy. The same strategy was adopted by Lieutenant-General Umrao Singh in his effort to avoid carrying out Operation Leghorn (Dalvi, 1969, 258–259). The demands were rejected by General Thapar and General Sen, as they remembered the fate and humiliation suffered by officers such as Thimayya and Verma, who had clashed with the civilians. They were also attentive to the clamor of public criticism, which claimed that the army had lost its fighting spirit after the long period of quiet (Maxwell, 1972, 347).

The field command, then, tried to delay for as long as possible the execution of what seemed like irrational orders. The result was that the civilian echelon in New Delhi was ignorant of the actual situation and the nonapplication—indeed, inapplicability—of its orders and instructions. Moreover, from the time it became clear to Thapar and Sen that there was no chance of changing the strategy dictated by the politicians without a challenge, and because they were unwilling to enter such a confrontation, the reservations and the detailed estimates and pessimistic evaluations of the field officers were not brought to the knowledge of the civilian ranks; it seems that some of these were not even brought by the commander of the eastern sector to the attention of headquarters in New Delhi. Against this background, Kaul was understandably surprised when, at the beginning of October 1962, he took command of the Fourth Corps and realized that the situation in the area with regard to the positioning of Indian troops was quite different from what Lieutenant-General Sen had reported to him only a few days earlier (Kaul, 1967, 370).

This unawareness also explains to some degree Nehru's peculiar declaration of October 12, 1962, which referred to the Indian army's intention of ousting the Chinese from Indian territory, when only one day before that he had allowed Kaul to postpone Operation Leghorn for as long as he felt necessary. Yet it seems that he was also optimistic, in spite of the new information from Kaul that contradicted his prior evaluations, as Nehru had no extensive first-hand knowledge of the area and of the military limitations involved.

In light of the dismal state of affairs and the subordination of military thinking to the needs of politicians, it is no wonder that an internal document of the Indian army, covering the work of head-quarters and the period in which Kaul was the chief of general staff, declared that its activities were based on "acting on whims and suppositions and then plugging holes, rather than deliberate military thought followed by planned action" (cited by Maxwell, 1972, 237).

What was the source of the mutual mistrust between the military and civilian echelons, and how did the communication short-circuit occur? The answer lies in the history of Indian public administration and in the system of values it fostered. The British, while encouraging the growth of a native public administration manned mainly by the native intelligentsia, did not do the same at the strategic-military level: this was an area in which the natives had no say whatsoever. The British alone dealt with this subject. Thus, with their departure, the leaders of the fledgling state were left with the burden of security and all matters pertaining to strategy without having the experience to cope with them.

At the same time, however, the new leaders, and especially Nehru, did not see the necessity of correcting the situation, because, in line with Gandhian thinking, the army had in principle no real place in the national liberation movement; it was perceived chiefly as a tool serving the imperialist powers. Another reason for Nehru's suspicion of the army was its excessive loyalty to the British almost up to the very moment of independence. Also from an ethical point of view, which espoused the achievement of goals through peaceful means, the military and militarism were rejected. Force was to be used only as the very last resort. In Nehru's opinion, India would, in any case, need only a small but mechanized and well-equipped army for its needs. Moreover, to his way of thinking, a military education was a dehumanizing process; he had an aversion to the army as an organization and considered soldiers to be mindless automatons carrying out orders. His stereotype of officers was one of a group of men intolerant of criticism and advice and unwilling to admit mistakes. The intellectual, liberal part of Nehru abhorred the military. Events in neighboring Pakistan, where the army began intervening in political life at an early stage, only deepened his convictions. As this perception was shared by politicians and bureaucrats alike, a combination of contempt and anxiety for the superiority of civilians over the military emerged[7] (Cohen, 1971b). Thus, in the period following independence, an alliance evolved between the bureaucrats and politicians against the officers, with the intention of reducing the army's part in decisionmaking as far as possible. This found formal expression in the rejection of the notion of an overall army commander-in-chief and in the division of the army into three services with federative relations among them, whereas on the organizational level the Ministry of Defense assumed the dominant role. The salary levels of senior army personnel were lower than those of the senior civil-service personnel, and the formal status of the COAS, as expressed at public functions, was not even as high as that of a high court justice or the cabinet secretary.

The mutual distrust was reinforced in Nehru's suspicion that the army, with its British traditions, did not fully support the basic principle of Indian foreign policy, that is, nonalignment, but rather wished India to join the Western alliance system. Any information passed on by the army was, as a result, examined in the light of the assumption that one of the underlying motives of the military was to bring about a change in Indian foreign policy. The suspicion was further strengthened by rumors as to the intentions of officers such as Thimayya, Verma, and Manekshaw to attempt a military coup. These rumors, though proven unfounded, nevertheless undercut the development of mutual trust between the two groups. The mood of the bureaucracy was so unsympathetic toward the army that its taking over control in the northeastern sector in November 1959, following the deterioration of relations with China, a sector that had been under MEA control until then, was received with utmost reluctance by both the civilian ranks and the semi-military units of the Assam Rifles, which were under the MEA's control (Dalvi, 1969, 57–58). Moreover, in the months preceding the war of 1962, Nehru and Menon personally intervened in the positioning and location of divisions and units down to the platoon level (Cohen, 1971a, 176), despite their ignorance of military matters. Over the years, because of the amateurish and contemptuous attitude toward military matters, the development of military science in India was much neglected. Until the 1962 crisis, there was not a single civilian institute dealing with or teaching such subjects or able to contribute to a constructive public debate, especially given, for reasons that will be discussed later, that neither Parliament nor the Indian press could freely and actively participate in such a discussion.[8]

Under such conditions of ignorance, it is no wonder that neither the politicians nor the bureaucrats in the prime minister's office, the MEA, or the Defense Ministry saw—or if they did see, understood— the military significance of what they regarded as basically a political-diplomatic move, and tended to treat warnings by the military as a sign of its reluctance to make an effort, or an excuse to evade its duty (Maxwell, 1972, 212–213). Naturally, the army's demand to deploy the concentration of forces on the likely three axes of invasion was ignored, and the political demand to distribute the forces along the McMahon line was given preference so that Nehru would be able to claim in Parliament that the army was positioned all along the McMahon line. As a result, air force headquarters was also under pressure to exaggerate its ability to provide the necessary logistic aid to the force thus spread out.

It is little wonder, then, that under such conditions the definition of the situation presented by the civilian Intelligence Bureau was given priority over that of military intelligence. The Intelligence Bureau was perceived to be that one body whose loyalty could be relied upon, as it was the "watchdog" of Indian democracy against the danger of a military coup. Understandably, the military intelligence service, as previously mentioned, slowly deteriorated, and inter-service intelligence coordinating committees failed to function. A vicious circle then began. The more pronounced the tendency to rely on the Intelligence Bureau, the less was the military intelligence needed at all; resources available to it were therefore reduced and the quality of its manpower declined. This, in turn, created a plausible reason to trust its estimates even less, and so on. Moreover, the Intelligence Bureau, which was in charge of internal security, probably viewed information arriving through the military intelligence as doubtful and gave it only secondary consideration in the final evaluations. Of course, it was absurd to expect trust to grow between two organizations, one of which had as part of its function the monitoring of the other in case it should attempt a military coup. This feeling was, of course, mutual. Military men looked askance at the Intelligence Bureau both on account of its provocative actions in border areas, which continued even after the area was put under the army's control, and because of its activities in the spheres of internal security such as when, in the years of 1959–1962, the Bureau was involved in a number of investigations against senior officers on charges of disloyalty (Subrahamanyam, 1970, 283).

Thus it happened that the army, which could have provided an alternative to the evaluations of the MEA, was intellectually castrated, both by the "stick and carrot" method and through the neutralization of its independent intelligence network and the "planting" of "suitable" officers in key positions. In fact, the only person in the army after 1961 who could have brought about the changes in the definition of the situation and action orientation, Lieutenant-General Kaul,[9] preferred not to do so both out of nonrealization of what was actually taking place and in order to advance his personal interests.

Kaul, as has already been pointed out, had been closely associated with Nehru in the days preceding independence. In contrast to other officers who seemed to Nehru to have retained some kind of loyalty to Britain in their hearts, Kaul did not bother to conceal the contempt and aversion he felt toward the remnants of British ways in the Indian army. To Nehru, he seemed a true nationalist. In addition, he had an impressive appearance and a good expressive ability. He was seen as an open-minded, wide-horizoned intellectual who had served abroad in semi-diplomatic posts: in Korea he had served as chief-of-staff to the chairman of the Neutral Nations Reparations Commission—General Thimayya; in 1947–1948 he filled the post of military attaché in Washington, D.C., and advisor to the Indian delegation to the United Nations; and later he toured China at the invitation of the Chinese government. While in Washington, D.C., he was sometimes assigned by Nehru to diplomatic or semi-diplomatic missions. In Nehru's eyes, he was the perfect diplomat-officer who viewed problems not only through the narrow military perspective but, as Nehru himself did, through the universal global prism. In the conditions created, Kaul was the only military man who had free access to Nehru. He himself used to boast of it and to point out that he had visited the prime minister at his home in the evenings (Khera, 1968, 221–222), a privilege not even accorded to the COAS.

It was clear all around that Kaul was the strong man of the army. Whereas Thapar, mediocre, passive, and afraid of confrontation, cared only to secure his own position; this he did by demanding his orders in writing, so as to be sure that no one could blame him in case things went wrong.

Clearly, Kaul was in line for the post of COAS some time in the future, and any officer anxious about his career took care not to ruffle his feathers. But Kaul's ambitions went even further. He saw himself as a potential successor even to Nehru, and it did indeed seem as if Nehru was grooming him for the job.[10] It was speculated in many circles that Kaul would be the one to take over Nehru's role (Kaul, 1967, 430; Hangen, 1963, 248). Kaul saw to it that his place in the race was kept secure by unequivocally supporting Nehru's foreign policy and the China policy with it. Realizing that Nehru was determined not to make concessions, he went out of his way to give him the military legitimacy he needed to justify his ideas, with ringing promises of the army's ability to withstand assault; moreover, keeping public opinion in mind, he displayed an even greater extremism late in 1960, when he demanded a firmer stand against China, suggesting the attack on Chinese patrols under tactical circumstances convenient to India. Thus, he would win laurels both from the public and the right wing of the Congress Party and strengthen his image as a daring and brilliant military leader and nationalist. In fact, Kaul was a politician who, by chance, was also an officer, or as one commentator remarked: "He is political to the end of his swagger stick" (Hangen, 1963, 247). The army for him was nothing but an instrument through which to further his political ambitions. To that end, although he saw in Menon a future rival, he was willing to cooperate with this man, who was Nehru's closest associate. Thus a love-hate relationship developed between the two (Mankekar, 1968, 33).

In the top echelons of the Ministry of Defense, there was not a single man willing to play devil's advocate, to present evaluations essentially different from those suggested by the MEA, headed by Nehru. In fact, Menon was also much involved in matters of foreign policy. It could be said that he was only a part-time minister of defense, the remainder of his time being devoted to deputizing Nehru on foreign policy matters.[11] He was the man who most effectively translated Nehru's abstract ideas, which were often clothed in vague language, into operative terms. This, together with Nehru's respect for his quick mind, was probably the explanation of the two men's intimacy ever since they had met in Europe in 1935 (Brecher, 1959, 573; Desai, 1974, 220).[12] Menon was the one who, over the years, came to resemble Nehru more and more in his world view and in the combination of theoretical, ideological, and practical concepts. He knew Nehru's views on the Sino-Indian dispute and identified with them both intellectually and emotionally, as a result of his feelings toward Nehru, which were very much a mixture of admiration and awe. He thus took care to supply Nehru with information that would support his views.[13]

The special relationship between Nehru and Menon suggests an additional explanation of a psychological nature that cannot be ruled out, although there is no direct evidence to support it. Nehru tried hard from 1952 on to bring Menon into the Cabinet. He succeeded only in overcoming resolute opposition from his associates in the Congress Party and the Cabinet in 1956. A later admission that Menon failed in the task of preparing the Indian army to defend India's territorial integrity against Chinese incursion would amount to bringing down the final curtain on Menon's political career and on his role as Nehru's principal advisor on foreign policy matters. This would please the right wing of the Congress Party and weaken the left, as well as have implications for the question: After Nehru, who? Also, Nehru was aware of and sensitive, on the basis of Menon's past behavior (Gopal, 1979, 142–144; 146–147), to Menon's potentially neurotic reaction to his removal from office and thereby from Nehru's immediate circle. Hence, emotional barriers to evaluations critical of Menon's performance as defense minister were further fortified.

Even worse, Nehru would then have had to admit that he had blundered seriously in assessing Menon, which, in light of his commitment to Menon, would have been a blow to Nehru's ego and prestige. This proved unacceptable to Nehru. Thus, assessments of the unpreparedness of the Indian army to challenge the People's Liberation Army (PLA) were not likely to be adopted, and became even less so with the growing number of occasions on which both men unequivocally declared that the opposite was true. Was Nehru consciously acting irresponsibly? Not necessarily; in his view, the probability of a large-scale Chinese attack was almost nil, so that even if Menon was wrong in his evaluation of the capabilities of the Indian army, there was no major risk to India involved.

Even if Menon had had any critics in the Defense Ministry, his authoritativeness and his display of superiority and disdain toward his subordinates undercut any attempt to disagree with him. But, as the dispute with China grew worse and became public, Menon's interests themselves demanded a selective attitude toward information about the scope of the Chinese threat. The repeated attacks in Parliament against him, as one not alert to the defense of India's national interests, and the 1962 elections in which he ran as a candidate in Bombay forced Menon, who lacked any basis of political support in the Congress Party, to take firm positions and to exaggerate the army's deterrent power. His impressive victory in the elections, with a platform of firmness toward China, also obligated him to continue to hold to this position even when receiving information indicating the wisdom of doing otherwise. Menon's victory increased Nehru's reliance on him. He believed that a hitherto popular support of Menon was evolving. An opportunistic officer such as Kaul was aware of these nuances and understood that it would be very difficult to convince Nehru to act against Menon's opinion (Kaul, 1967, 341). It was probably just as apparent to others, at all levels, that Menon's opinions echoed those of Nehru.

It is interesting to note that it was precisely in the MEA, which should have seen the aspects of the problem from a Chinese point of view, that the pace of erroneous evaluations was dictated. To understand this, we must take note of the human structure of that ministry. The bureaucracy in foreign service was composed of four main types: graduates of British India's civil service, who made up the majority; university intellectuals close in their world view to that of Nehru;[14] Nehru's relations; and former princes of Indian states. From this group, it could not be expected that a cadre of officials would emerge to challenge Nehru's evaluations (Bandyopadhyaya, 1970, 190). On the contrary, the general atmosphere was one of constant competition for Nehru's favor. This harmed the team spirit and led to an exaggerated tendency to satisfy and flatter Nehru at all costs (he himself knew personally only the senior officials and his favorites), to sycophancy, and to a subjective ad hoc approach to problems (Crocker, 1966, 87). In addition, the fact that the British civil-service graduates comprised the majority in the ministry contributed quite considerably to the fact that British geo-political and geo-strategic concepts, which were now irrelevant, were maintained and continued to serve as a basis for current policy.

It cannot be said that at any specific point in time there was complete homogeneity within Nehru's circle, but this was certainly true over time. Thus, for example, after the escape of such MEA officials as S. Dutt, foreign secretary, S. Gopal, director of the historical division, and J.S. Mehta, director of the China section, all presented the view that there was no immediate solution to the dispute and that Chinese hostility ran deep, whereas Nehru still thought that the problem was quite temporary (Hoffmann, 1971, 523). In this sense, the above-mentioned MEA officials were at first closer to Home Minister G.B. Pant and Finance Minister Morarji Desai than to Menon and Nehru. But gradually Nehru "fell into line." The shift started to emerge following the Kongka Pass incident of October 1959 and took form with the failure of Chou En-lai's visit in 1960, although Nehru was still more optimistic than Dutt, Gopal, and Mehta tended to be about the long-run prospects of Sino-Indian relations. Dutt, Gopal, and Mehta also made sure to support Nehru's assumption that there was a historical, traditional, and legal justification for India's position on the boundaries question. Gopal, in particular, was responsible for this: he supplied what he thought

Nehru wished in the area of documentation, and if he had thought that Nehru wanted testimonies to support Chinese claims in the western sector, he would have found them. Overall, as indicated, he supplied what Nehru wished to hear (Maxwell, 1972, 119; Gupta, 1974, 35). Among the main supporters of the thesis that China would not attack India, those who held that view even at the height of military escalation on both sides, beginning in July 1962, were Nehru, Menon, and MEA senior officials M.J. Desai, the then foreign secretary, and N.B. Menon, the director of the China division of the MEA. Undoubtedly, the MEA people adopted the values and beliefs that formed the basis for the policy of no concessions and for the faith in the need and ability to avoid large-scale military confrontation with China, together with the belief in China's inability or reluctance to strike at India (Hoffmann, 1971, 418–419; 654; 709). If there were disagreements among them or between them and Menon regarding the question of the degree of Chinese hostility, these never occurred over the degree of immediate threat; in other words, even when there was no complete conceptual consensus, there was an *operational* one as to what should be done. This fact reinforced Nehru's self-righteousness and his feeling that an "open debate" was continuing concerning the China policy. Actually, the debate dealt only with the legitimacy of the policy and not with its essence; that is, its conclusions were predetermined and different factions disagreed only as to the most efficient ways to arrive at the operational decisions already made by Nehru.

Thus far I have shown how in central organizations concerned with strategic situation evaluations—the MEA, the Ministry of Defense, and the army—there developed a situation of impotence and inability to examine information critically and to make the changes necessitated by new information. We will now try to examine why other bodies and organizations—such as the Cabinet, the Cabinet Committees on Foreign and Defense Affairs, Parliament, and the mass media—that could have presented an alternative or at least been restraining factors in the committing of errors did not function adequately.

On the surface, the Cabinet and its committees comprised an organization that should have tried and tested Nehru's hypotheses on the China issue. Furthermore, in contrast to the organizations we have discussed so far, the Cabinet did have a number of members who disagreed with Nehru, such as Pant, the home minister who enjoyed prestige and standing in the party, and who, from 1958, was Number Two in the Cabinet as well as de facto deputy prime minister; Desai, the minister of finance; and Patil, the minister of food and agriculture, who belonged to the right wing of the Congress Party.[15] Not only did these men object to Nehru's policies, but two of them at least—Desai and Patil—abhorred the second upholder of the

Chinese policy, namely, Menon (Hangen, 1963, 234). The most senior of the three, Pant, had, at least formally, a degree of control over the main intelligence organization, as the Intelligence Bureau was part of the Home Ministry. Pant also enjoyed an especially strong political status, having an independent power base in Uttar Pradesh. To a certain extent, Nehru was psychologically dependent on him as a result of his tendency, since adulthood, to lean on an older, more experienced man, such as his own father, then Gandhi, and then Sardar Patel[16] (Brecher, 1959, 2).

The Cabinet, although formally a body that could question Nehru's policies and evaluations, was not really able to do so, because of both its lack of power and its method of functioning. On the administrative-organizational level, despite the fact that formally the system of government was based on Cabinet decisions, Nehru tended to make his decisions after consulting with his close associates, depending on the subject in question, and then to bring it for formal ratification to the Cabinet. Cabinet meetings were not the scenes of fruitful or forceful discussions. Nehru or the minister involved would bring the foregone conclusions to the knowledge of the Cabinet members, who would then give their formal agreement. Consequently, the Cabinet did not meet at regular intervals. Rather, Nehru called meetings according to his needs. This approach was even more pronounced in the area of foreign and defense policies, in which Nehru, as external affairs minister, was directly responsible for decisions and kept information secret from almost everyone—just as detailed information on the China issue, especially on military matters, was never brought to the knowledge of Parliament and its committees. Although on the political side of the China issue Nehru had to lift the veil of secrecy from the exchange between India and China (see *White Papers*) as a result of public pressure as early as September 7, 1959, this did not apply to the other side of the coin, namely, India's relative military capabilities, detailed information about which was withheld from Cabinet, Parliament and the public at large. Nehru and Menon had to be taken at their word.

The Cabinet had two committees that purportedly dealt with foreign affairs and defense matters. These committees were the Foreign Affairs Committee and the Defense Committee.[17] But they, like the Cabinet, were not decisionmaking forums; at most, they were used for limited consultations or the presentation of issues with explanations. They did not set the stage for hammering out disagreements or for the analysis or examination of alternative evaluations. The Defense Committee, which met more frequently,[18] was a sort of mini-cabinet, and its decisions were binding and viewed as Cabinet decisions (Brecher, 1968, 249–251).

The Cabinet and its committees were, as Menon himself described it, only a formal forum in which no constructive debate took place.

The prime minister, with his domineering personality, was not interested in consultations,[19] although, according to Menon, the Cabinet members accepted this fact: "Somehow or other on account of his [Nehru's] big personality, on account of the fact that people trusted his wisdom or his ultimate judgement, debate in the accepted western sense did not take place" (Brecher, 1968, 246; Gopal, 1979, 303–304). Disagreements never reached the Cabinet floor, as they were usually settled previous to the meeting with the person in question. Those concerned with matters of foreign and defense policy were mainly Nehru, Menon, and, at times, Pant, particularly on the China issue, or Desai, the finance minister, if the topic had economic implications, such as enlarging the defense budget. Generally, however, consultations with Cabinet members were minimal, as Nehru, according to Menon, "was not a person who sought consultations, but you could 'force' consultation upon him" (Brecher, 1968, 241). After the death of Patel, it was difficult to see just who had the political clout that could have forced Nehru to consult, particularly on matters of foreign policy. Even Pant, a powerful member of the Cabinet, could not have done so.

It was natural, then, that the Cabinet and its committees could not provide a suitable framework for a challenge to Nehru's perceptions and evaluations.[20] Even strong personalities, such as Pant, could hardly contribute to it, as the only information given them through Mullik, who was formally under Pant, or through Menon or Kaul, pointed clearly only in one direction—that is, to India's ability to achieve its goals, even if it meant using the military, and to China's unwillingness and inability to meet India's challenge. The fact that these were the only sources of information in this area, and that they were acceptable even to Pant,[21] caused those inclined toward a hard line to become even more so. This is particularly true of those who could have tried to make Nehru accept a more realistic view. The result was that their pressure made Nehru's unrealistic concepts even less real, and thus Nehru fell into a trap of his own making.

Other sources of feedback that could have been useful were the two institutions that were the pride of independent India—the very active Parliament and the high-standard press. But these institutions, under the conditions of excessive secrecy that prevailed in India, were doomed to fail. The editors of the newspapers could publish only what was given them by the authorities, specifically, the Ministry of Defense. As a result, most journalists failed to develop the deeply critical faculty so necessary for reporting on matters of defense and security.[22] As for members of Parliament, only a handful had the knowledge and experience to analyze and investigate adequately the activities of the Indian army (Jones, 1975, 274). Even those few had neither the authority nor the ability nor the necessary means to do any of that: the major policymaker kept them utterly in the dark.

The annual report issued by the Ministry of Defense, for example, which was meant to describe the annual activities of that ministry, really provided only the scantiest, most insignificant information, whereas the parliamentary committee for defense affairs, attached to the Ministry of Defense, had no formal status and hence was "toothless." It had no access to the proper information and was not allowed to call on involved officials to testify before it. Thus, a noncritical attitude was maintained within and outside of the decisionmaking system, and a convenient background was created for the dominance of processes of nonadaptation to new information. In fact, criticism that was voiced by the parliamentary and extra-parliamentary opposition turned in the wrong direction; far from helping matters, this actually made them worse,[23] as it merely caused a toughening in Nehru's attitude on the China issue.

Under these conditions, the whole activity of gathering, processing, and evaluating data was concentrated in a small group of people who surrounded Nehru and enjoyed his personal confidence. This group included Menon, minister of defense; Mullik, director of the Intelligence Bureau; the two foreign secretaries, Dutt and his successor Sinha, as well as Mehta, in charge of the northern division at the foreign office;[24] Gopal, director of the history division of the MEA; and Kaul, chief of the general staff branch at army headquarters. From time to time, the voice of G. Parthasarathi, the ambassador to China, was also heard and, until his death, that of Pant, the home minister, as well.[25] In addition, it seemed that Nehru's daughter, Indira, must have been at least indirectly involved, although it is not clear to what extent because, as mentioned by one observer, "She has probably been involved in more top-level decisions than any other member of India's present ruling hierarchy, except her father" (Hangen, 1963, 159; Mehra, 1968). Menon, realizing her special position, did not miss a single opportunity to flatter her and win her favor. Her attitude on the China issue reflected, to some degree, her attitude to Menon (Hangen, 1963, 159) and, of course, the attitude of her father, whom she adored.

The Pattern and Impact of Social Relations

Within this group were nuances in the assessment of the future trend in Sino-Indian relations. There were optimists and pessimists. The optimists beleived that the dispute would finally be resolved in a manner favorable to India and that basically India and China had common interests. Nehru and Menon were the main representatives of this approach. The optimists also showed a great deal more willingness in the early stages of the dispute to make concessions.[26] The pessimists, on the other hand, already saw at the beginning of 1959 a long and protracted conflict in store and a divergence of interests between India and China. The main spokesmen for that camp were the two foreign secretaries of the MEA, and Mehta, the director of the northern division. But late in 1959, the members of the group agreed that concessions should not be made; that an active unyielding policy should be pursued; that for political, military, and economic reasons a major confrontation between India and China was unlikely; and that if the Chinese were to provoke a confrontation, they would suffer a humiliating defeat. In other words, within this group there was a full operational, if not conceptual, consensus. It should also be noted that the importance of Mullik and Kaul in this group rose as of September 1961, when the military aspects of the problems began to look more and more important.

From all that has been said so far, three relevant axes of analysis of the perceptual dynamics of those involved in the China issue emerge: (1) the reciprocal relations between Nehru and other participants regarding how they were chosen to serve in this group and the nature of their personal relations with him; (2) the interactions within the small circle around Nehru and the attitude toward the sources of information and evaluation outside that circle; and (3) the organizational behavior that occurred in relation to the problem.

The inner circle around and acceptable to Nehru had a number of common traits. Most of the permanent members of this group were intellectuals, very articulate, open-minded, or defined by Nehru as such, which gave them a sense of their own superiority. The group members were Hindu in their religion and background. At the same time, they were all British educated and some had long experience in the British Indian civil service. They had years of experience in working with Nehru, and all expressed in one way or another their complete identification with his *Weltanschauung* (world view). Most, if not all, revered him as a man and as a statesman, as the one and only representative of the true India. The group even had a kind of "whip" who kept members in line whenever necessary. This was, of course, the man closest to Nehru, personally and ideologically—Krishna Menon. None of the members of this group had an independent power base; that is, their power, whether political or bureaucratic, was dependent on Nehru, but this situation gave them more power than their formal role or position ever could. This power derived from the recognition by other organizations and people of their close contact with Nehru.

Thus, Mullik, director of the Intelligence Bureau, could ignore all the instructions and guidelines he received from different ministries or other government branches, in the knowledge that he could always rely on Nehru's support (Maxwell, 1972, 503). Thus, Kaul also became the Number One man in the army, and that is how Menon obtained his special status in the Congress Party and especially in the Cabinet. Similarly, the foreign secretary enjoyed a special status compared with other civil-service bureaucrats of the same rank, and often participated in the Cabinet's Foreign Affairs and Defense Committee meetings.

Correct personal relations existed among the member of the group, despite the rivalry for Nehru's attention that kept it cohesive. Furthermore, members kept in constant touch with each other. Menon frequently met with MEA men because of his informal, but strong, position there. In keeping with his post as defense minister, he, of course, frequently met with Kaul and Mullik. Close relations between Kaul and Mullik existed, and the two men were often in touch (Kaul, 1967, 273). However, at least some of the members had hostile rivals within the organization from which they had originated or in organizations outside the group. Thus, for example, hostility existed between Menon and the field officers, as well as other senior officers in the Indian army, and between himself and other members of the Cabinet. Kaul was on terms of enmity with some field personnel and some of the High Command. Mullik was also disliked by the military. Most MEA bureaucrats despised army men. Naturally the perception of the existence of personal "enemies" outside the group, a matter of waiting for them to trip up, increased the cohesion within the group. And finally, in its composition, the group included representatives of all branches of the political system—politicians, bureaucrats, and army personnel—as well as representatives of all the institutions relevant to the China issue—the prime minister's office, the MEA, the Defense Ministry, the Intelligence Bureau, and the army.

These characteristics of the group combined to create conditions of a biased, one-sided processing of information and the maintenance of irrelevant and outdated perceptions despite dissonant information. The fact that Nehru was surrounded by a group whose members had a similar background and world view, who all respected and admired him and his views, and who were dependent on him for their power within the general political framework and their own organizations, in particular, made the presentation of dissonant information either impossible or not worthwhile. The danger either of being rejected by the group or of being banished from it took on a high emotional and instrumental meaning, especially because membership in the group reinforced the elitism that already existed among some of its members as well as the "open-minded" intellectualism that contemptuously dismissed evaluations suggested by their "narrow-minded" rivals. Moreover, to its participants, this group seemed to have all the necessary ingredients and personnel for efficient evaluations both intellectual and functional. It even appeared to "debate" constructively, but, as we saw, all this was a thin disguise for a predetermined operational consensus. The consensus within the group made things so difficult that, even a short while before the crisis, when a major figure in the group, Kaul, who had been appointed commander of the Fourth Corps and assigned the execution of Operation Leghorn, discovered the real situation that showed all the previous evaluations to be erroneous, he did not dare to demand a full revision of policy but made do with requesting a temporary postponement. It is no wonder that even then Nehru continued to declare the operational maintenance of previous military goals in keeping with previous evaluations.

On the organizational level, the values of the organization that most members held were usually identical to those of the group. In the case of Kaul himself, in conflicts arising between the values of his peer group, the army, and this group, he gave obvious preference to the values and concepts of the latter, for the reasons stated above; these values were related to utilitarian considerations such as his belief that in the long run his place was with this group and that his real power lay in being a member of it. So the role he played in this group, and perceived himself as playing in the future, superseded his professional role obligations as CGS and later as commander of the Fourth Corps.

An additional factor that dictated the fixation of the images and process of nonadaptation was connected to the level of aspirations of the members of the group. The MEA people, including Nehru, identified deeply with the organization from which they had come, both because of its special status and because of the sense of mission it gave its members.[27] An admission that one's organization had been wrong all along on such a major issue as Indian policy toward China meant a serious blow to one's self-perception.[28] The need to prove methodically, all through the period in question, that the policy pursued had been the right one and that the level of aspirations had been realized made it necessary to ignore any information that contradicted these beliefs. This was also true of Mullik and the Intelligence Bureau, which supplied the information to support this policy, and of Menon and the Ministry of Defense.[29] Identification of the success of the organization with that of the individual at its head is especially relevant in the Indian context, because Indian culture and the Indian social framework have traditionally held a deep identification between leader and organization such that, in a sense, the organization becomes an expression of the leader and not vice versa. As a result, members of Nehru's group fed each other with assessments, descriptions, and optimistic estimations as to the quality of their organization's activity. The outcome was that, in the decisionmaking group, there existed an atmosphere of self-satisfaction and mutual backslapping that raised the threshold for penetration of dissonant information and created even greater self-confidence and hence a sense of invulnerability. This feeling led to an optimism and to a willingness to take risks that were expressed in the adoption of the Forward Policy, while placing exaggerated and unrealistic confidence in the ability of the concerned organizations to execute a policy containing such a high element of risk with success.

Another detail to be emphasized is that the China issue really became a struggle between two subcultures in the Indian political system. One was represented by Nehru and the other by the army officers[30] and politicians who rejected his views. Anyone who presented information or evaluations that conflicted with the existing ones was naturally seen to belong to the rival camp and, in Nehru's eyes, immediately suspected of distorting information in an attempt to achieve his goals.[31] This situation, in turn, was perceived to constitute a threat to the personal status of those identified with the opposite world view, with all the resulting implications.

As a consequence, "groupthink" evolved in Nehru's circle, with all its negative ramifications, including overoptimism, underestimation of the opponent, and a sense of self-righteousness. As we have seen, groupthink was strongly anchored in a multifaceted conformism related to the group members' functional relations with Nehru, arising from compliance and from a desire to reap its benefits—a conformism resulting from identification with Nehru, the charismatic leader, and from the internalization and acceptance of a system of values and beliefs dictated by Nehru. This multidimensional conformism led to a deep-seated perceptual conservatism and, under the conditions described, gave a feeling of security even in the face of possible failure, due to the umbrella protection afforded by those with the political responsibility—Nehru and Menon. Support of the military, on the other hand, and non-conformism did not generate such protection. Thus, conformism became, for members of the group, a no-risk gamble.

In a society where factional politics are an inherent part of the political culture, what emerged was, in fact, a tightly knit faction, which had most of the structural characteristics of a typical Indian political faction (Hoffmann, 1981, 233). The Nehru faction was bound together mainly by the personal ties between its leader and inner-core followers; it differentiated itself by drawing clear ideological boundaries between it and the other participants in the decisionmaking process; and the relationship between the members and Nehru were of the *guru-chela* (teacher-disciple) type. Nehru's followers depended on him; they drew power from his power and psychological support from their association with the great man. In the context of such a relationship, identification with and support of the leader's attitudes and conceptions comprised the only logical pattern; groupthink was almost inevitable. Hence, alternative perceptions and attitudes could effectively be introduced only by external rival factions that were equally as cohesive and as powerful. But such a rival faction never emerged. What faced the Nehru faction was a loose coalition of divided politicians and some army officers. There was no leader to bind this group together, and the power structure was clearly in favor of the Nehru faction, with no chance that the balance would tilt in the opposite direction. Thus, the outcome was a foregone conclusion: a dominance of Nehru's faction and an absence of effective articulation of dissonant conceptions.

An additional factor that detracted from the quality of performance was the stress factor. Within the Indian decisionmaking group, a few sources of stress could be discerned. First, the central personality in that group, Nehru, was under an immense pressure of work load. Eventually, given this state of affairs, which proved a psychological strain as much as a physical burden, he fell ill in mid-1962.

What further contributed to Nehru's physical stress was his perception of the Sino-Indian conflict as an ultimate test of India's— that is, *his*—external as well as domestic policies (*Par.*, I, 252). This sense of threat was shared by his close associates in the decisionmaking group who supported his policies and who identified with him and hence with his policies. The stress of the group was probably amplified by Nehru's moods, which communicated themselves to his close associates.

A third source of stress was the strong ongoing competition within Nehru's group for his attention and approval—a need and drive felt by the different group members to prove themselves to Nehru, so that their special status with him would remain intact. For the more senior among them, such as Menon or Kaul, this had implications for their long-run ambitions to inherit Nehru's mantle after he retired.

The fourth source of stress was of a more circumstantial nature. It arose after September 8, 1962, when the Chinese crossed the Thag La Ridge and decisionmakers perceived only a limited period of time available in which to take some form of action, due to public pressures. The time factor became even more significant because of weather conditions: the snow season began in mid-October, and after mid-November it would be impossible to carry out any major operation until the following May (Kaul, 1967, 263).

Conditions were thus formed under which the organizational system could not supply a cognitive or conceptual alternative to the existing one, while in the small group of Nehru's associates and advisors, due to bureaucratic politics and other factors, a group dynamic was created that did not allow the penetration of dissonant information and situation evaluations that might have injected a realistic note into Indian thinking. Consequently, Nehru's perceptions continued to travel in a vicious, self-reinforcing circle.

Conclusions

In this chapter I have analyzed the complex net of interpersonal, interorganizational, and intraorganizational relationships and discussed the evolving patterns and their significance for the biased processing of information and cognitive conservativeness. In the process, I have attempted to explain how it happened that, in a country proud of its truly democratic institutions and led by a man deeply committed to democratic values, a real debate and discussion of alternative definitions of the situation and remedies never really took place as far as the China policy was concerned.

Whether this pattern of relations was due mainly to Nehru's personality (see Chapter 10) or to cultural traditions (see Chapter 9), or resulted from the way in which the organizational and personal content of the different social institutions had evolved since independence, is beyond the scope of this study. What we should note is the pattern of social interaction conducive to a biased interpretation of data and cognitive conservativeness in the face of dissonant information. This pattern once again indicates that even within a democratic and open society, the human factor is strong enough to overcome any institutional, built-in guarantees for the open discussion of foreign policy issues. In the absence of such discussion, and given the introduction of over-secrecy into political-military matters, disaster is a probable result.

12
Theory and the Case Study

This book has had two interrelated objectives. The first was to present a theory that explains misperception in international relations. The second was to relate this theory to the perceptual framework that guided Nehru's China policy in the critical period between the outbreak of the revolt in Tibet in 1959 and the Chinese invasion of India in 1962 (the latter having been the nadir of this man's brilliant political career). The case study analyzed serves the purpose of a "crucial case study," to use H. Eckstein's term for a single case study that tests a theory. As such, the case history in question "*must closely fit* a theory if one is to have confidence in the theory's validity" (Eckstein, 1975, 118).

This methodology is problematic in terms of external validity for reasons that come easily to mind and need not be elaborated here. However, it has its compensations and merits, not the least of them being: "if we conduct crucial case studies, we are far more likely to develop theories logically and imaginatively" (Eckstein, 1975, 123). Hence, in "cost-benefit" terms, this particular methodology is justified as a viable and worthwhile method for testing theories and for drawing the relevant conclusions, although with some caution.

Nehru's perceptual process in relation to his China policy seems indeed to "fit closely" the theory presented in the first chapter, as has been shown in some detail in the subsequent chapters. Moreover, this theory proved powerful in explaining most of the relevant and complex details of the case in an overall coherent, consistent, and what seems logical, almost deterministic, explanation. Nevertheless, we should keep in mind that "one swallow does not make a summer." Thus, a successful application of the theory to additional case studies would undoubtedly be advantageous for the sake of external validity.

The case history provides not only a validation of the theory. Due to the centrality of the China issue for Nehru, in both moral-ideological and functional terms, it highlights the wider region of the mind and world view of the man who shaped modern India's stance in world politics, not only in his time but also for years to come. Moreover, it affords us a closer look into the social and cultural background of information processing and decisionmaking in India. These factors are by nature rather inflexible to major adjustments in the short run, and as such are bound to be of continuing impact on the decision-making process in India for some time to come.

Having stated these caveats, I can proceed with some concluding comments related both to the suggested theoretical propositions and to the case history itself.

The present case study indicates that, in this instance, the preferred pattern of confrontation between the decisionmaker Nehru and his environment determined his specific "perceptual reaction" patterns. The pattern of confrontation with the international environment that Nehru chose was *change*. Preference for this pattern stemmed from Nehru's *Weltanschauung*. He realized the need for change in the character of relations between the new states in the international system, and believed in their capacity to effect this change and to serve as an example and catalyst for other actors in the system. Although at its source this approach discerned the limitations imposed by the international environment, it failed to give them due weight and laid more stress on the capacity of men and nations to effect fundamental change—the realization of which would necessitate basic alterations in the structure of power relations and in the accepted values of the international system, and could not possibly come about in a relatively short space of time.

This approach gave preference to efforts invested in the global arena to the relative neglect of the regional one, out of a belief that transformation of the former would automatically bring about trans-formation of the latter. The fallacy here was two-fold: first, the envisaged change in the global arena did not necessarily fall within realistic bounds, and second, even if it were to happen, its full consequences for the "grey" regions could not be predicted; a regional actor such as China, endowed with sufficient power and willing to challenge the super powers, could in certain circumstances isolate the regional arena from major transformational trends in the global one. More than this, Nehru's logic, which seemed to him so convincing and irrefutable, was not accepted as such by others, often leading other actors to form their own conclusions and direct their own actions in a manner very different from that foreseen and predicted by Nehru.[1] As a result, he failed to evaluate the situation with regard to all the major dimensions that comprise the interaction between an actor and the international environment. He overestimated India's deterrent power, which contributed to a concept of threat that did not take a war into account and was insensitive to the other side's concept of threat. The final outcome of this process was a very serious failure to correctly assess both the relative capacity of the adversary and its intention.

For any leader—particularly for a man larger than life such as Nehru, beloved and admired by his countrymen, respected and held in awe by his political opponents, and listened to by world leaders from East and West, from developed and underdeveloped nations—self-esteem and the esteem of others is a powerful motive. This is so especially for a personality torn between weakness and strength of character, between the need for power and the rejection of its consequences. Under such circumstances, having to admit and face what he considered a catastrophic failure of his whole world view and vision, as symbolized in the deteriorating dispute with China,[2] became almost unbearable for Nehru in terms of the possible consequences to both his self-esteem and the esteem of others on which it fed. As a result, he developed a need to cling to outdated images, concepts, and expectations, while at the same time fleeing from reality through "convenient" interpretations of the dissonant information flowing from the environment. This escape from reality was caused and reinforced by Nehru's personality needs, and gained momentum as a result of the structure of the organizational and information screening and processing systems, as well as through national-cultural factors encouraging certain patterns of thought on the one hand, and on the other promoting the creation of social relationship patterns within the decisionmaking group that nurtured unimaginative and purblinded collective thinking. Thus, the effectiveness of the dissonant information in the feedback processes was very much reduced, and these processes came in fact to be of very little value in changing erroneous conceptions and making up-to-date assessments.

The findings presented in the preceding chapters strongly support the "channelling proposition," which states that the degree of accuracy of stimuli-perception at any point in time, as well as the effectiveness of the feedback processes, is liable to be "channeled" by the interaction of the structure of the information-screening and evaluating system, the national culture, the organizational structure, the decisionmaking group dynamics and structure, and the personality of the policymaker. This is true almost without regard to the quantity, quality, and content of the data reaching the policymaker.

In the case of Nehru, as discussed in Chapter 10, we have dwelled on the fact that his complicated personality and his beliefs and attitudes were the dominant factors underlying his inaccurate processing of information. Possible corrections of biases, mistakes, and erroneous evaluations were prevented as a result of the nature of the information-managing procedures, which were also influenced by cultural and social factors and by the structure of the organizational system that had to deal with the China question. To this were added the combined effects of interorganizational relations along with the impotence of organizations that were supposed to fill the role of "devil's advocate" by presenting alternative interpretations of the information, but which could not or would not fulfill this potential function, for one reason or another. This phenomenon was also discerned among Nehru's faithful friends, advisors, and supporters in the inner circle of decisionmakers, who did not wish and were perhaps unable to persuade him to correct his perceptions and evaluations, but preferred to support them. This stemmed largely from the web of their mutual relations, those between themselves and Nehru, and between them and the people outside this circle. An atmosphere was created that discouraged an honest coping with dissonant information and the presentation of interpretations unacceptable to the leader. This phenomenon also rested on cultural norms, national, and societal characteristics and on the related organizational structure. As postulated by our hypothesis, preference was given under these conditions only to one definition of the situation. This definition resisted proper adjustment and generally took the form of stalemated, petrified thinking and the absolute dominance of the process of nonadaptation.

The impact that these variables brought to bear on the definition of the situation was extremely effective, because conditions existed in the dispute that amplified the relevance of the variables contributing to channeling perceptions in specific directions not necessarily in line with the real content of the information, as suggested by our "arousal perconditions" proposition.

In the first place, ever since the rising in Tibet and the growing dispute over the Sino-Indian borders, which up to then the Indian leadership had thought was acceptable to the Chinese, the behavior of the Chinese was seen as baffling, in that it introduced an element that contradicted existing Indian perceptions and expectations and aroused uncertainty as to Chinese intentions. This uncertainty was not to Nehru's liking, sure as he was of his own qualifications, conceptions, and infallibility in foreign policy matters. In any event, a way had to be found to cope with this uncertainty.

Second, uncertainty was particularly troublesome because of the importance attached to the question of China as a symbol of Nehru's system of values and attitudes in the sphere of foreign policy and his policy of nonalignment. To confess to failure in his conceptions and his policy on the China question was perceived by Nehru as involving very serious consequences, indeed, for India's foreign policy and for domestic politics as well.

Third, the considerations explained in the two preceding paragraphs carried special weight with Nehru because his China Policy, perhaps more than any other issue, was identified with him personally, both in other people's eyes and in his own. Thus, a situation arose in which Nehru was personally very deeply committed, politically and emotionally, to the concepts directing Indian policy toward China.

Fourth, this matter involved coping with the psychological stress stemming from the considerations noted in the preceding paragraphs. This condition was aggravated by Nehru's own attitudes and personality traits, and by a shortage of time due both to the many matters he had to deal with in a limited period and to environmental, seasonal factors.[3] In the same way, pressures also arose from relations within the groups and among the organizations in the consultative and decisionmaking system. All these pressures added to Nehru's stress and anxiety and prevented any fresh reappraisal of the situation.

These background conditions—the *uncertainty*, the *importance* attached to this issue, the feeling of *personal commitment* and *responsibility*, and the *stress*, both psychological and physical, on the policymaker—combined to produce a compelling need to manipulate the information on this sensitive question so as to reduce the pressures and the psychological burden. Manipulating the information made it possible to cope by producing a definition of the situation that would be "suitable" from Nehru's point of view. It was these background conditions and the existence of such compelling needs that made the variables referred to earlier so influential in channeling political thinking in a convenient and desirable, though disastrous, direction.

There is also strong support for the "ripple" proposition, which states that misperceptions in one sphere will bring others in their wake in other spheres. Chapter 7 sums up the connection between misperceptions in various spheres of foreign policy, beginning with Nehru's judgments of the significance of the structure of the global system, its interaction with what took place in other subsystems and in the Asian subsystem in particular, and the judgment implicitly following from this as to bilateral relations with China and the super powers. Hence, Nehru attached relatively low importance to the military element as compared with the political. However, this hypothesis should be accompanied by the caveat that it would appear to apply more particularly to policymakers with an integrative, all-embracing *Weltanschauung*, who are inclined to combine the components of their perceptions into a unified conceptual system.[4]

One might have expected the correction of biases and fallacies to be more probable in a well-integrated perceptual system. The multiple issues related and integrated in the analysis of any single issue will raise the chances of exposing fallacies through the analysis of different though related issues, serving as a kind of warning signal that an alternative interpretation is both available and possibly more proper. It turns out that this is not the case. The power of the biasing personal and societal factors is stronger than that of self-correcting processes, and that is true even for leaders such as Nehru, who are aware, and stress the importance, of rationality.[5]

The analysis also supports a related proposition, namely, the "cumulative" proposition, which suggests that the longer misconceptions remain uncorrected the more difficult it becomes to correct them because of their cumulative effect. In the cumulative process, dependence on existing concepts increases, further enhancing their centrality and hence their rigidity. This proposition, too, contradicts what might have been expected, that the longer the time an individual holds to a misperception the greater the probability that he will encounter feedbacks that will bring about a correction of his perceptual fallacies. The process does not necessarily occur in this way; the factors mentioned in this study, for instance, eliminate the impact of feedback. A circular process follows, such that the longer a misperception persists the more difficult it becomes to correct and to adjust.

What happened over time in the case of India was that no significant change occurred in basic conceptions, as has been clearly noted in the preceding chapters. As a result, Nehru's belief in the appropriateness of his policy was preserved, and the tendency increased to underestimate the importance to be attached to Chinese warnings and signals, even on the eve of the Chinese attack, despite the clear information that was in the hands of the Intelligence Bureau and despite the warnings of some senior army officers. This tendency found concrete expression in soothing statements and assessments by the director of the Indian Intelligence Bureau, the minister of defense, and Nehru himself, who declared that there was no prospect of an all-out Chinese attack.

The failure to draw on and learn from feedback has a counterpart that is exactly the opposite but just as wrong. This is expressed by what we have called the "pendulum" proposition, which is also supported by the findings in the preceding chapters. As the reader may recall, this proposition suggests that when misperceptions lead to policy failures the consequence is not necessarily correction of the misperceptions by feedback. Instead of a *balanced* reevaluation of prior perceptions, preference may be given to those views *diametrically* opposed to the original views. The case we are studying displays this phenomenon in that, when Nehru realized that India's actions and attitudes on the boundary and Tibet issues were meeting with hostility and repeated anti-Indian Chinese actions, his conception of China—which had hitherto been almost purely idyllic—changed to one of a society "gone crazy" and not interested in peaceful settlement, without attempting to understand Chinese motives in a more balanced way. This phenomenon appeared in its most striking fashion immediately after the Chinese attack, when instead of self-criticism there was bitter disappointment felt by Nehru over China's behavior. Nehru called it a stab in the back and he put the whole burden of blame on China, without trying to understand where India had gone wrong in its judgments and perceptions.

Finally, we came to test the "point of departure" proposition, which suggested that there might be a relationship between the type of misperception and the ensuing process of adaptation. The analysis in Chapters 2 through 7 indicates that most of the instances in which it was found that Nehru was in the process of adapting or partly adapting on the basis of information from the environment were instances in which the point of departure was an evaluation gap— the lowest level of perceptual distortion. Not even one instance was found in which a process of complete positive adaptation followed on the heels of a complete awareness gap. Moreover, most of the instances in which we found maladaptation, that is, aggravated perceptual distortion, were instances in which the point of departure was an awareness gap—the highest level of perceptual failure.

However, we found nothing in the empirical analysis to substantiate the other contention that the process of adaptation goes through stages—in other words, that an awareness gap becomes a relevance gap, and a relevance gap becomes an evaluation gap. Our research findings, therefore, only partially confirm the "point of departure" hypothesis, although they do not actually refute any of it.

Thus far we have dealt only with the proposed general attributes of misperception. However, as misperception in international politics is often related to threat and hostility, it is worthwhile to mark some points of importance in this connection, flowing from the empirical data of the case in question.

It is possible to put forward the three following hypotheses based on the findings of this study: (1) There is a greater tendency toward symmetry between changes in reciprocal perceptions of hostility than there is between changes in reciprocal perceptions of threat. In the Sino-Indian dispute, we found a correlation between changes in the two sides' perceptions of hostility (.717) but no clear connection over time between changes in the Indian and Chinese reciprocal perceptions of threat.[6]

The reason for this could be that it is mainly a changed threat perception that might lead to a major change in policy. Thus, when policymakers do not want or are not able to change policy, they will tend to react and be aware of the rival's hostility perception rather than his threat perception. Related to this is the following hypothesis: (2) It is not the *absolute* level of threat that determines the reaction, but the *rate of change* in the level of threat. The sharper the fluctuations in the level of threat, the more vivid is the awareness of, and sensitivity to, the problems created by the threat. A comparison between the average periodic levels of perceived threat of India and China shows that the fluctuations in these levels of threat were decisively smaller with India than with China. This may explain India's lack of sensitivity to China's signals and warnings of intentions to act as well as China's increasing sensitivity to India's behavior, a sensitivity that was finally expressed in the large-scale military blow. The next point relates to the preferred behavioral reaction to threat and hostility: (3) If no symmetry exists between the levels of aggressiveness expressed in the action orientation of the two rival actors, there will be a tendency for such a symmetry to be formed over time. This influence can be traced in the graphs (Figures 6.3 and 6.5) showing the trends of development of the action orientations of India and China in the period from 1959 to 1962. This "balance" is created even when the declared intention of both sides is to prevent the situation's deterioration, regardless of how committed to this purpose both sides may be. One could say that the process has a dynamic of its own.

A study of the sources and processes of misperception cannot avoid the question of determinism or, to put it more clearly, the question of whether this process is basically a deterministic process or not. Regarding the case at hand, one may ask: Was Nehru a victim of his own mistakes and should he carry the burden of blame? Or was he an innocent victim of the inevitable? The answers to these questions are not only of philosophical importance, but they are also relevant to policymaking and as a future focus of research.

Both the theoretical and the empirical analyses in this book point to a strong element of determinism in the formation and preservation of misperceptions. It is quite clear that beyond a certain stage there is a point of no return—where misperceptions become inevitable—although we must still take into account both the nature and the interaction of the suggested explanatory variables. At least some of these variables are by nature deterministic. National style and culture, which cannot be changed or manipulated in the short or even the long run, have a direct impact on the thinking process and an indirect impact on other variables, such as group and organizational dynamics, as already pointed out. The personality attributes of any given leader at any given point in time cannot be transformed, except through a change of leadership, which often cannot be effected, at least in the short run. But even if such a change were to take place, under the processes of choice existing now both in democratic and nondemocratic societies, it can hardly guarantee that the next incumbent leadership would be better equipped to handle information, as the related qualifications for effective and accurate information processing are not necessarily identical to those needed in order to achieve a leadership position.

The relatively easier variables to manipulate are group and organizational structure and behavior, as well as information-processing procedures. However, even these variables are not completely manipulable, in that change often requires overcoming difficult bureaucratic obstacles, powerful personality needs (such as for a supportive human group), and national style forms such as consensual decisionmaking. Still, they are *relatively* easier to change and adjust to the needs of proper information processing than the former.

At any rate, the nature of the problem and the variables affecting information processing demand that the policymaker be aware of the possible pitfalls pointed out in this study, and that he be willing to confront the related difficulties in avoiding the above-mentioned stumbling blocks. Moreover, even an honest effort by a conscious and aware policymaker cannot guarantee success, as some of these biased processes happen unconsciously. What is more, the human mind finds ways to subdue awareness, to forget and look the other way, while at the same time being fully convinced that no self-delusion is taking place.

Fighting this deterministic trend is an uphill struggle for the individual involved. He must keep permanently in mind the factors that might bias his information processing. This type of continuous soul and mind searching, as well as trying to take into account the motives of other relevant actors, is costly in terms of the time and intellectual and emotional effort involved. Consequently, role overload, under which political leaders usually find themselves, either out of choice or otherwise, inhibits them from going through the process, no matter how willing they are to do so. Moreover, given that such leaders are often inadequately qualified and trained to perform this particularly demanding task, the probability that it will be done properly, consistently, and systematically is quite slim.

One more point that should be considered is the interaction between the variables. If all variables work in the same direction, there is little chance of preventing misperceptions from occurring, because they tend to enhance the impact of each other in an almost self-perpetuating momentum. The chances are better, however, when the variables do not all work in the same direction. In this case, the question becomes: Which are the more potent in the specific situation? For example, in a personalistic decisionmaking system, even if all other variables are tuned to produce the best possible definition of the situation, personality needs will nevertheless tend to decide the outcome and make for a biased interpretation of information.

As for the case of Nehru, there is no simple, clear-cut answer to the question of whether he was merely a victim of a deterministic process or should carry the full blame for the eventual turn of events. On the one hand, there is strong evidence that the interaction of the relevant variables led inevitably to an incorrect interpretation of the information. It would be somewhat unfair to blame Nehru for his personality attributes and needs, and for the cultural and societal frames of reference that encouraged the evolution and preservation of his misperceptions. On the other hand, he carries at least some of the blame for enhancing this negative characteristic of the system by choosing and relying on the wrong individuals to serve as his aides, for making foreign policy a one-man show, for letting his ego overcome his intelligence and self-criticism, and for letting his arrogance get the better of his judgment.

If this gloomy prognosis about the high probability of misperception occurring and even being, to some extent, unavoidable has merit, then much more effort should be dedicated to the preparation of decisionmaking systems designed to manage misperception *after* it has had its impact; meanwhile, we should avoid concentrating only on the almost impossible task of its complete prevention. More specifically, we must concentrate our efforts on dealing with the *outcomes* of misperception. This would necessitate, for example, preplanning for emergencies on vital issues under the most extreme assumptions—namely, that *all or most* core beliefs and expectations may prove to be *wrong*.

Although decisionmaking systems often plan for alternative futures, as a matter of course, the possibility of being completely wrong is often overlooked. Even pessimists find it difficult to admit that they could be involved in and responsible for such major failures in matters of momentous importance to the national interest and, by implication, to their own personal interests and values. Few top-ranking political leaders have characters that would admit such failure. Individuals who might have this kind of doubt about their performance are usually not the kind who aspire to leadership positions in the first place.

It is true that planning and preparing for the worst-case scenario might carry the seeds of self-fulfilling prophecies. However, this seems a small price to pay compared with the benefits of being ready for emergencies of major proportions and avoiding the consequences, both physical and psychological, of being caught in the middle of a crumbling *Weltanschauung*, with the related confusion of fear and anxiety that hamper proper reaction, especially when no immediate remedy exists at hand. There is an abundance of literary and historical evidence describing the horrible impact of the lack of preplanned reactions at critical junctures in terms of complete disruption of command, control, and communication; the related waste of human life and resources; and the long-term political consequences. One has only to read the descriptions of the stunned reactions in the immediate aftermath of surprise in Washington, D.C., after the Japanese attack on Pearl Harbor, in Stalin's headquartes in Moscow after Hitler launched Barbarosa, in New Delhi after the Chinese invasion in 1962, or in Tel Aviv and Jerusalem after the outbreak of the Yom Kippur War.

At this point, a final note of caution should be sounded. When a book focuses on the analysis of a single major blunder committed by a political leader, the reader's overall perspective may be distorted and final judgment may be unambiguously harsh. but it should be kept in mind that this study does not presume to deal with the whole range of decisions and issues in which Nehru played the central role during the years he dominated the Indian political scene. Thus, the purpose of this book is not to shatter Nehru's image as an exceptional man and great leader, nor to challenge his foreign policy in all its aspects. On the contrary, if one looks at Nehru's record from an overall perspective of achievements versus failures, the balance sheet will indicate that he was one of the greatest leaders in the world arena in the period following World War II. However, even giants commit mistakes; because of the power they hold over the destinies of their nations, their mistakes are often as great as they are.

Nehru was no fool; he had, according to an observer who knew him well, "an ardent yet philosophic mind" but "was not capable of deep or original thought" (Gopal, 1979, 316), nor was he free of faults. Indeed, his faults, combined with other factors, played a causal role in a chain of errors that led to disastrous consequences. The results of his China policy do not negate his achievements in other areas, in spite of the proven relationship between most aspects of foreign policy and the China debacle—even if paradoxically these achievements contributed to the making of erroneous assessments and to the inference of inappropriate interpretations from the information available to him. The final outcomes were misperceptions, which led to certain policy decisions, which led in turn to a defeat of magnitude never before imagined. This defeat sent shock waves through India's psyche and political structure, and its mark on Sino-Indian relations remains to this day.

Statistical Appendix

This appendix contains the detailed statistical tables to which we have referred in the preceding chapters. It also includes some details relating to the coding procedures, according to which the data was processed, as well as the sources used in the content analysis.

About 430,000 words were coded. These included (1) *Prime Minister on Sino-Indian Relations: In Parliament*—about 200,000 words; (2) *White Papers*, Volumes I–VIII—about 145,000 words (75,000 for China and 70,000 for India); and (3) *Peking Review*—about 85,000 words (for a list of articles, see bibliography).

Analysis of the Perceptions of
Internal and External Environments

The correlation and factor-analysis tables are the result of the analysis of the *Peking Review* and Nehru's speeches and statements in Parliament. The *White Papers* were not used here because, by their nature, they were meant to focus in particular on the geographical and bilateral aspects. As such, they do not reflect fully the comprehensive psychological environment of the parties to the conflict, but rather highlight only these two components. In the other two sources mentioned, we find a full reflection of the cognitive frameworks of the adversaries.

The components coded were those presented in Chapter 1, with one exception: the legal component was often woven into the bilateral and geographical components so that it was not coded separately. Below is the list of the components coded and their symbols as used in Tables A1–A4.

GS - Global system
 S - South Asian subsystem
SO - Other subsystems
 B - Bilateral relations between India and China
DB - Dominant bilateral relations, i.e., relations with the two super powers
BO - Bilateral relations with other states, such as Bhutan, Pakistan, etc.
 G - Geographical/topographical aspects
 M - Military power
 E - Economic power

299

PS - Structure of the political system
IG - Interest groups
CE - Competing elites

It should be noted that for India the material coded consists of those verbal expressions produced by a specific individual, namely, Nehru, who is the object of our inquiry, whereas this is not the case with the Chinese material. I was generally not able to identify clearly the specific Chinese leader who was responsible for this or that view expressed in the *Peking Review* articles, which were the object of our quantitative analysis. This being an inherent difficulty in dealing with this kind of source material, I refer instead to the psychological environment of the "Chinese leadership," a somewhat general term though sufficient for the purposes of our analysis. Further justifying this usage, where China's India policy is concerned, is the fact that there were no serious cleavages within the top Chinese leadership. For this reason, the reader will not find any references pointing to the existence of competing elites on this issue in the *Peking Review* articles included in the quantitative analysis.

Definition of the Adversary

Tables A5–A6 present the adjectives used by each of the two sides to describe the other's regime, society, or state. Here again, the *White Papers* were not coded. Given the diplomatic exchange of messages involved, both sides used diplomatic language; hence, the adjectives are not fully representative of the way India and China thought of each other. The preferred sources were those in which both sides expressed themselves more freely.

Perceptions of Threat Hostility and Action Orientation

I performed the quantitative analysis of the perceptions of hostility, threat, and expressed preferred action orientation by coding the themes represented in the following ordinal scales. These scales of themes are arranged on a rising order of intensity from 1 to 9. They were built by using typical themes and sentences from the texts analyzed, although the texts' language was rephrased rather than quoted directly. The texts analyzed were as follows: *Prime Minister on Sino-Indian Relations: In Parliament, White Papers*, and *Peking Review*.

This approach enabled me not only to count the *frequency* of appearance but also to take into account their *intensity*, giving every daily observation a weighted average. This was done for each observed day by using the following equation:

$$\text{daily weighted average} = \frac{(\text{frequency} \times \text{intensity})}{\text{frequency}}$$

These daily weighted averages could then be used for monthly or periodic averages, as will be seen in the subsequent tables.

As there might be an element of subjective judgment involved in assessing intensity, I checked the coded material for reliability. This was done by picking a random sample of a *third* of the statements coded, recoding them by a second coder, and then checking for intercoder reliability. The equation used for this was as follows (Holsti, 1969, 140):

$$C.R. = \frac{2M}{N_1 + N_2}$$

This equation expresses the ratio between the number of agreements between the two coders and the number of themes coded. The findings of this intercoder reliability test for hostility, threat, and action orientation for each source used are reported hereafter with each of the relevant scales.

Regression Analysis

Given that there was no comparable regularity in the appearances of the daily observations (daily weighted averages), I used monthly aggregates in the regression equations. A month for that purpose was defined as a calendric month. This means that for all practical purposes the first month in the analysis (March 1959), although coding was begun on the 17th day, is considered a full month. This is also true for the last month in the analysis—October 1962—for coding was stopped on the 20th, the day of the Chinese invasion.

The type of regression technique used is a step-wise regression. This permitted the addition of one more variable, in a controlled fashion, at each step and hence the testing of alternative models explaining the relationship between perceptions of hostility, threat, and expressed action orientations. However, the following tables usually include information only for those models that were acceptable according to two criteria: level of significance and explained variance (R^2).

The sources coded were as follows: (1) For India, a combination of Nehru's speeches and statements in Parliament and the *White Papers*; and (2) For China a combination of the *Peking Review* and the *White Papers*.

These combinations made possible an analysis based on documents expressing different nuances: direct diplomatic correspondence with the other side and indirect communication through some intermediary means, such as public statements in Parliament and the government's new media.

The key to the symbols used in Tables A11–A21 follows:

H_I — Indian hostility perceptions
ΔH_I — Change in Indian hostility perceptions
T_I — Indian threat perceptions
ΔT_I — Change in Indian threat perceptions
A_I — Indian preferred action orientations
ΔA_I — Change in Indian preferred action orientations
H_C — Chinese hostility perceptions
ΔH_C — Change in Chinese hostility perceptions
T_C — Chinese threat perceptions
ΔT_C — Change in Chinese threat perceptions
A_C — Chinese preferred action orientations
ΔA_C — Change in Chinese preferred action orientations

Table A1. Correlation Matrix of Nehru's Psychological Environment

Components	GS	S	SO	B	DB	G	M	E	PS	IG	CE	BO
GS	1.000	.475*	.411*	.515*	.032	-.046	-.053	.416*	.416*	.296*	.560*	.167
S		1.000	.677*	.100	.210**	-.054	-.050	.229**	.180	.133	.284*	.320*
SO			1.000	.118	.126	-.022	-.006	-.009	.004	-.086	.253**	.194
B				1.000	.123	.177	.076	.243**	.409*	.231**	.559*	.283*
DB					1.000	-.079	.063	-.054	.153	-.055	.330*	.045
G						1.000	.514*	.034	.006	.018	.037	-.056
M							1.000	.034	-.070	-.056	.193	-.023
E								1.000	.494*	.302*	.400*	.331*
PS									1.000	.155	.553*	.373*
IG										1.000	.176	-.109
CE											1.000	.414*
BO												1.000

Source: Prime Minister on Sino-Indian Relations: In Parliament   *P ≤ .01   **P ≤ .05

Table A2. Correlation Matrix of the Chinese Leadership's Psychological Environment

Components	GS	S	SO	B	DB	G	M	E	PS	IG	CE	BO
GS	1.000	-.068	.752*	.451**	.756*	-.213	-.168	.947*	.997*	.947*	—	.216
S		1.000	-.090	-.133	-.147	-.140	-.164	-.053	-.065	-.053	—	-.072
SO			1.000	.419***	.619*	-.240	-.080	.810*	.773*	.810*	—	-.123
B				1.000	.487**	.388**	-.199	.472**	.461**	.472**	—	.039
DB					1.000	.082	-.257*	.758*	.764*	.758*	—	.212
G						1.000	-.233	-.241	-.222	-.164	—	.174
M							1.000	-.164	-.168	-.164	—	-.102
E								1.000	.969*	1.000*	—	-.072
PS									1.000	.969*	—	.148
IG										1.000	—	-.072
CE											1.000	—
BO												1.000

Source: Peking Review, 1959–1962 (for list of articles see bibliography).   *P ≤ .01   **P ≤ .05

Table A3. Factor Analysis of Nehru's Psychological Environment

	Factor 1	Factor 2	Factor 3	Factor 4	Factor 5	h²
GS	.364	−.504	−.035	.434	.034	.744
S	.027	−.884	−.062	.025	−.005	.802
SO	−.173	−.950	.043	−.083	.034	.860
B	.542	−.020	.199	.265	.232	.566
DB	.014	−.035	−.070	−.065	.914	.846
G	−.007	.012	.869	.027	−.149	.762
M	−.015	.009	.861	−.095	.074	.756
E	.712	−.012	.009	.166	−.306	.637
PS	.829	.120	−.096	.026	.120	.687
IG	.066	−.007	−.058	.848	−.097	.749
CE	.663	−.155	.141	.075	.378	.782
BO	.735	−.165	−.047	−.549	−.120	.777
% of explained variance	29.4	14.1	12.5	10.0	8.7	74.8
% of cumulative explained variance	29.4	43.5	56.0	66.1	74.8	74.8
% of common variance	39.3	18.9	16.7	13.4	11.7	100.0

F_1 = Linkage Politics Factor (Bilateral-Internal).
F_2 = Systemic Factor
F_3 = Geo-strategic Factor
F_4 = Interest Groups Factor
F_5 = Super Powers Factor

Source: Prime Minister on Sino-Indian Relations: In Parliament
Note: Oblique Factor Analysis: δ = 0

Table A4. Factor Analysis of Chinese Leadership's Psychological Environment

	Factor 1	Factor 2	Factor 3	Factor 4	h²
GS	.972	−.084	.000	.191	.970
S	−.049	−.296	−.837	.021	.777
SO	.858	−.031	.054	−.214	.776
B	.445	.692	.046	−.147	.742
DB	.785	.226	.017	.202	.770
G	−.317	.887	.011	.091	.851
M	−.140	−.380	.671	−.198	.690
E	.990	−.041	−.029	−.092	.979
PS	.986	−.075	−.007	.123	.976
IG	.990	−.041	−.029	−.092	.979
CE	−	−	−	−	−
BO	.027	−.024	.072	.975	.959
% of explained variance	50.9	15.2	10.5	9.5	86.1
% of cumulative explained variance	50.9	66.0	76.6	86.1	86.1
% of common variance	59.1	17.7	12.2	11.0	100.0

F_1 = Linkage Politics Factor (Global-Internal)
F_2 = Territorial Conflict Factor
F_3 = Subsystemic Power Factor
F_4 = Influence in Neighboring States Factor

Source: Peking Review, 1959–1962 (for list of articles see bibliography).
Note: Oblique Factor Analysis: δ = 0

Table A5. Nehru's Definitions of Chinese Society, Regime, and State

	N	%
Aggressive	6	6.12
Expansionist	7	7.14
Unreasonable	3	3.06
Unfriendly	1	1.02
Great Country	21	21.43
Great Culture	17	17.35
Big	16	16.33
Responsible	1	1.02
Powerful	17	17.35
Advanced	1	1.02
Not Mean	3	3.06
Communist/Socialist	2	2.04
Friendly	3	3.06
Total	98	100.0

Source: Prime Minister on Sino-Indian Relations: In Parliament

Table A6. Chinese Definitions of Indian Society, Regime, and State

	N	%
Unfriendly	2	4.59
Aggressive	4	9.10
Expansionist	1	2.27
Reactionary (Ruling circles)	12	27.27
Imperialist	7	15.91
Capitalist	1	2.27
Friendly	7	15.91
Great	5	11.36
Peaceloving	1	2.27
Defender of peace	4	9.10
Total	44	100.0

Source: Peking Review, 1959–1962 (for list of articles see bibliography).

Table A7. Friendship-Hostility Perceptions Scale

1. We want to cooperate with them on all matters.
2. We want a peaceful solution to the border problem.
3. We are neighbors (and we should live side by side).
4. It is difficult to feel friendly toward them.
5. They have not treated us fairly.
6. They are unreasonable.
7. They cannot be trusted.
8. They are hostile (in language or attitude).
9. They are aggressive or provocative (in deeds).

Notes:
1. This scale expresses the spectrum of feelings between friendship and hostility in Sino-Indian relations.
2. C.R. for this scale is as follows:
   a. Nehru in Parliament   85%
   b. Letters from the Indian to the Chinese government   94%
   c. *Peking Review*   90%
   d. Letters from the Chinese to the Indian government   88%

Table A8. Threat Perception Scale

1. They try to impose their claims on us.
2. They interfere in our internal affairs.
3. They try to isolate us.
4. Our international status is threatened.
5. Our national honor is at stake.
6. Our future economic development is endangered.
7. Our territorial integrity is in danger.
8. Major hostilities are imminent (even though full-scale war is not at hand).
9. War and invasion are in the air.

Notes:
1. This scale presents the perceived threatened values.
2. C.R. for this scale is as follows:

a.	Nehru in Parliament	94%
b.	Letters from the Indian to the Chinese government	91%
c.	*Peking Review*	89%
d.	Letters from the Chinese to the Indian government	88%

Table A9. Action Orientation Scale

1. We should continue to seek friendship.
2. We should seek a peaceful settlement.
3. We have to sit down and talk.
4. We must be tolerant.
5. We should adopt realistic attitudes.
6. We must hold firmly to our positions, views, and ideas.
7. We should stick to the status quo (ante).*
8. We must prepare for war (to defend our borders).
9. We should fight.

Notes:
1. This scale expresses the preferred action orientations at different stages of the conflict.
2. C.R. for this scale is as follows:

a.	Nehru in Parliament	90%
b.	Letters from the Indian to the Chinese government	90%
c.	*Peking Review*	94%
d.	Letters from the Chinese to the Indian government	93%

* The Indians demanded return to the status quo ante as a precondition for negotiation. The Chinese insisted on the existing status quo as the point of departure.

Table A10. Average Scores for Levels of Threat, Hostility, and Action Orientation by Periods

Period	India			China		
	Threat	Hostility	Action Orientation	Threat	Hostility	Action Orientation
Mar. 17, 1959 to Aug. 24, 1959	5.000	4.857	3.917	4.273	7.741	1.000
Aug. 25, 1959 to Apr. 18, 1960	5.779	5.671	4.697	6.270	5.714	3.327
Apr. 19, 1960 to Feb. 13, 1961	6.840 (5.881)	9.000 (5.749)	6.250 (4.599)	1.000 (4.769)	2.100 (5.654)	1.813 (2.992)
Feb. 14, 1961 to Dec. 4, 1961	6.561	7.635	5.019	3.292	5.625	3.167
Dec. 5, 1961 to Sept. 7, 1962	5.938	8.047	4.737	6.511	8.024	4.443
Sept. 8, 1962 to Oct. 19, 1962	7.083 (6.243)	8.327 (8.037)	8.200 (5.357)	7.332 (6.417)	8.414 (7.892)	6.205 (4.827)
Oct. 20, 1962 to Nov. 21, 1962	7.583	7.725	7.081	6.843	5.752	3.180

Sources:
India: *Prime Minister on Sino-Indian Relations: In Parliament; White Papers,* vols. I–VIII
China: *Peking Review,* 1959–1962; *White Papers,* vols. I–VIII

Note: The numbers within brackets in line 4 represent the overall average score for the whole period in which both sides tried to prevent escalation, i.e., March 17, 1959 to February 13, 1961. The numbers within brackets in line 7 represent the overall average score for the escalation period, i.e., February 14, 1961 to October 19, 1962.

Table A11. Nehru's Hostility Perception

Parameter	Dependent Variable	Independent Variable	Constant
	H_I	H_C	
b		.522	
β		.585	
F		9.400	
p		.007	.003
R^2		.343	
R		.585	
a			3.749
N	20		

Equation: $H_I = a + bH_C$

Note: The information in the column *constant* in tables A11–A21 refers to *a* in the regression equation.

Table A12. Change in Nehru's Hostility Perception

Parameter	Dependent Variable	Independent Variable	Constant
	ΔH_I	ΔH_C	
b		.938	
β		.717	
F		17.998	
p		.001	.820
R^2		.514	
R		.717	
a			.117
N	19		

Equation: $\Delta H_I = a + b\Delta H_C$

Table A13. Nehru's Threat Perception

Parameter	Dependent Variable	Independent Variable	Constant
	T_I	H_I	
b		.129	
β		.201	
F		1.189	
p		.285	.000
R^2		.040	
R		.201	
a			4.905
N	30		

Equation: $T_I = a + bH_I$

Table A14. Change in Nehru's Threat Perception

Parameter	Dependent Variable	Independent Variable	Constant
	ΔT_I	ΔT_C	
b		.629	
β		.140	
F		.320	
p		.579	.918
R^2		.019	
R		.140	
a			.030
N	18		

Equation: $\Delta T_I = a + b\Delta T_C$

Table A15. Change in Nehru's Threat Perception

Parameter	Dependent Variable	Independent Variable	Constant
	ΔT_I	ΔH_I	
b		−.060	
β		−.105	
F		.303	
p		.586	.599
R^2		.011	
R		.105	
a			.225
N	29		

Equation: $\Delta T_I = a + b\Delta H_I$

Table A16. Chinese Threat Perception

Parameter	Dependent Variable	Independent Variable	Constant
	T_C	H_C	
b		.460	
β		.479	
F		6.562	
p		.018	.083
R^2		.229	
R		.479	
a			2.019
N	24		

Equation: $T_C = a + bH_C$

Table A17. Change in Chinese Threat Perception

Parameter	Dependent Variable	Independent Variable	Constant
	ΔT_C	ΔH_C	
b		.182	
β		.123	
F		.326	
p		.574	.759
R^2		.015	
R		.123	
a			.216
N	23		

Equation: $\Delta T_C = a + b\Delta H_C$

Table A18. Nehru's Action Orientations

Parameter	Dependent Variable	Independent Variable	Independent Variable	Constant
	A_I	T_I	H_I	
b		−.118		
β		−.138		
F		.602	n.s.	
p		.443		.000
R^2		.019		
R		−.138		
a				4.106
N	33			

Equations: $A_I = a + b_1 T_I$
$A_I = a + b_1 T_I + b_2 H_I$

Table A19. Nehru's Action Orientations

Parameter	Dependent Variable	Independent Variable	Constant
	A_I	A_C	
b		4.656	
β		.452	
F		3.859	
p		.068	.021
R^2		.204	
R		.452	
a			2.509
N	17		

Equation: $A_I = a + bA_C$

Table A20. Change in Nehru's Action Orientations

Parameter	Dependent Variable	Independent Variable	Constant
	ΔA_I	ΔA_C	
b		.552	
β		.535	
F		5.622	
p		.033	.973
R^2		.286	
R		.535	
a			−.013
N	16		

Equation: $\Delta A_I = a + b\Delta A_C$

Table A21. Chinese Action Orientations

Parameter	Dependent Variable	Independent Variable	Constant
	A_C	T_C	
b		.271	
β		.378	
F		3.841	
p		.062	.009
R^2		.143	
R		.378	
a			2.045
N	25		

Equation: $A_C = a + bT_C$

Notes

Preface

1. I prefer the term *management* because it better conveys the possibility of a conscious distorting of information, of which—as will be seen later—the distorter himself or herself might become a victim.

2. A fully detailed theoretical treatment of the problem entitled *Information Processing and Misperception: The Case of Foreign Policy* is in preparation.

3. And so avoids the pitfall of what is defined by Alexander George as theories "not well-grounded in historical experience" (George, 1978a, 11).

4. On the advantages and disadvantages of a single case-study analysis, see H. Eckstein, 1975; George, 1978a.

5. The term *disciplined-configurative* was coined by Verba (1967, 114). The value of this kind of analysis is discussed in detail by H. Eckstein (1975). See also Lipjhart, 1971.

6. That it was a problem of misperception was made clear both by accounts of some of the major actors in the case as well as by Nehru himself. See, for example, Dalvi, 1969; Mullik, 1971; Kaul, 1967; 1971, 282–297; and Menon's reflections on the case as expressed in an interview with Brecher (1968, 137–179).

7. A typical expression of Nehru's preoccupation with the subject in pre-independence days can be found in his wide-ranging book, *The Discovery of India*, first published in 1946 and written in prison during the five months between April and September 1944.

8. Although we shall be concerned, to some extent, with political military and civil service figures, such as V.K. Krishna Menon, B.M. Kaul, B.N. Mullik, and others, their contributions will be considered only in terms of how they influenced Nehru's perceptual dynamics.

9. This was the case with many of India's scholars writing on the case.

10. This was not the first military incident, however.

11. The most distinguished among these leaders was J.P. Narayan.

12. See, for example, Khera, 1968; Dalvi, 1969; Mullik, 1971; Kaul, 1967; 1971, 282–297.

13. For examples, see Menon, 1963; Bhat, 1967; Woodman, 1970; Mullik, 1971.

14. It is interesting to note that the title of the book by Mullik, who was the director of India's Intelligence Bureau in the period under discussion, is *The Chinese Betrayal*, whereas "My Years with Nehru" appears only as the subtitle.

15. For examples of this kind of literature, see Lamb, 1964; 1966; 1973; Maxwell, 1972; Whiting, 1972; 1975. Maxwell's book earned both wide acclaim and intense criticism, especially from Indian writers (see Kaul, 1971, 268–281) as well as from scholars (see Subrahamanyam, 1970a).

16. For literature supporting the Indian version, see Caroe, 1963; Sharma, 1965; 1971; Singh, 1967; Sen, 1971. For literature supporting the Chinese version, see Maxwell, 1972; Lamb, 1966 (eastern sector); Lamb, 1973 (western sector). For attempts to present a more balanced view, see Rubin, 1960. For a presentation of legal claims by the parties to the dispute, see the report of the Joint Committee set up in April 1960 in a meeting between Nehru and Chou En-lai in New Delhi, the findings of which were published in February 1961: Government of India (1961) *Report of the Officials of the Government of India and the People's Republic of China on the Boundary Question*, New Delhi.

17. Two of the best studies in this category are Rowland, 1967 and Van Eckelen, 1964.

Chapter 1

1. In the discussion following, the term *conception* will be used to describe a system of interconnected images.

2. For elaboration and explanation of this approach and some case studies, see, for example, Sprout and Sprout, 1956; 1969; Snyder *et al.*, 1962; Boulding, 1956; 1965; Zinnes *et al.*, 1961; Holsti, 1965; Brecher *et al.*, 1969; Brecher 1972; 1974. For criticism and evaluation of this approach, see Zinnes, 1972; Gold, 1978.

3. Various aspects of this point can be found in Verba, 1969; Jervis, 1969; Kissinger, 1969; Neustadt, 1970; Allison, 1969; 1971.

4. See, for example, Betts' pessimistic evaluation (1978) of the ability of intelligence organizations to avoid failures.

5. This category includes both the situation in which there is very little or no relevant information and that in which there is mainly false and misleading information fed into the system by the rival actor.

6. For comparison, see Moose, 1973.

7. This discussion was crucially influenced by the pioneering work of Boulding (1956, 47–48).

8. This factor is linked to a large extent to the "philosophic code" (George, 1969; Holsti, 1977).

9. What is more, "value, whether positive or negative, leads to perceptual accentuation" (Bruner and Postman, 1948, 206).

10. This factor plays an important role in connection with the social pressures exerted on the policymaker.

11. This factor sometimes encourages the fixity of existing images and makes adjustment difficult. See Pruitt, 1965.

12. See the application of this framework in exhaustive studies of Israel's foreign policy (Brecher, 1972; 1974).

13. This item does not appear as an independent variable in the original framework, but only in the limited context of its contribution to the state's military power or deterrent ability. We think this variable deserves an independent status, as it contributes not only to military power but also to (a) economic power (the influence of climate and topography on the possibility

of developing certain essential crops or on the transportation system); (b) the social structure (for example, the influence of size on social cohesiveness); and (c) geo-political orientations.

14. In contrast to pressure groups that preach specific concepts and decisions in narrowly defined issue areas only.

15. Opposing or unidentical directions of adaptation patterns reflect a situation in which there is no connection in the perceiver's mind between the relevant variables. It is difficult to determine in advance to what extent the final conception, in the case of opposing processes, will be more accurate than the one preceding, and it is conditional on the relative importance (in relation to an accurate definition of the situation) of the variables contained in the opposing processes.

16. This issue fits the distinction between two kinds of learning: (a) learning as a result of feedback, which is accepted as the dominant learning process by the cybernetic school (Steinbruner, 1974) and is more frequent when the relevant variables in both periods are identical, and (b) learning that includes the recognition of new, unfamiliar phenomena and is more frequent when the relevant variables in the second period are essentially different from those in the preceding period (see also Kilpatrick, 1970).

17. For comparison, see Scott, 1966.

18. The exception would be only those cases in which the processors of information reject a correct interpretation without adopting any other, due to the anticipation of additional information or inability to reach a decision consensus on a particular interpretation that should be adopted.

19. A secondary actor gathers or encounters information connected to the behavior of rival secondary actors.

20. A noise, then, is an event that is not a message but is regarded as such by one of the actors.

21. For possibilities in this area and detailed discussion with examples, see Jervis, 1970.

22. It happens quite often that certain "sensitive" information is not absolutely essential, but the mere fact of its lack makes it seem crucial for making a decision or for delaying it.

23. Secrecy and uncertainty in issues important to the actor on the international scene are usually fertile ground for the creation of rumors (Allport and Postman, 1972, 33), which are noises that interfere with an accurate interpretation of information.

24. The actual need for certain information increases the individual's willingness to be exposed to it and to absorb it (Triandis, 1971, 98).

25. This does not mean that if he has all the relevant information his images will necessarily be accurate, although the probability that they will be is higher.

26. One study defined this situation well by indicating: "to some extent the audience is the message" (Miller and Siegelman, 1978, 79).

27. A detailed discussion of fifteen characteristics and possible situations in this context is presented in my forthcoming study dealing with information processing.

28. This resembles the question that preoccupies journalists as to what makes an "event" news. See Galtung and Ruge, 1965; Smith, 1969.

29. Timing is relevant on two levels. On the broader level, the question is whether the issue or problem is one of interest to the policymaker at the

time. On the more specific level, the question is whether the policymaker at that stage of decisionmaking requires information. (For an analysis of the stages of decisionmaking and their relationship to the need for information, see Janis and Mann, 1977, 180–183.)

30. See Slovic and Lichtenstein, 1971.

31. The following facts should be noted: (a) The definition of what is abundant information is relative, as different information processors have different coping and absorption abilities. (b) *Quantity* does not necessarily presuppose *quality* in its contribution to accurate evaluations.

32. For a detailed analysis of techniques for handling information overload, see also Miller, 1965.

33. See Wiegele (1973) for a detailed discussion on this problem as it relates to decisionmakers' behavior in international crises.

34. This statement is not equally true in all cases. The phenomenon is especially noticeable in individuals with low self-esteem (Clarke and James, 1967).

35. We find, for example, that an engineer appears to be more reliable than a dishwasher even in relation to information that does not pertain to his or her qualifications or education as an engineer (Aronson and Golden, 1962). Ironically, a message coming from a low-prestige source creates only a low probability of distortion (Minis, 1961), as the sender's low prestige prevents dissonant information from being conceived as a threat to the existing system of images and hence to the self-image.

36. It has been found that strangers whose positions come close to those of the individual are accepted by that individual as wiser, as more moral, and as having more knowledge than strangers whose positions he knows to differ from his own (Byrne, 1961).

37. External in the sense that it uses not the intrinsic specific content of the message to evaluate the information but other criteria such as source, target, and so on.

38. The role of categorization is in line with the cybernetic paradigm (Steinbruner, 1974, 47–87). The paradigm claims that policymakers, on both the individual and the group levels, tend to simplify complex problems involving a significant element of uncertainty. One way to achieve this is to break down the problem into a series of simple problems that can easily be handled by dividing them among several policymakers or organizations.

39. The two most outstanding studies dealing with the analysis of signaling systems, their advantages, disadvantages, and failures are Wohlstetter, 1962 and Jervis, 1970.

40. (a) Encoding errors are possible only for *initiated* signals, whose sender is fully aware of, and intends them to serve as, signals. Decoding errors, on the other hand, may occur even when signals are not preplanned, such that their source is not aware that they are being interpreted as signals. This distinction is an obvious result of the difference between the definition of the two types of failures. (b) An interesting encoding error is created when actor A sends a signal meant to mislead actor B, but actor B makes a mistake other than the one intended for him by actor A.

41. The writer is aware of the difficulty in locating who is "to blame," due to the problematics of the question of whether the decoding error

stemmed from an encoding error or whether it was independent of the encoding process.

42. For a detailed and extensive analysis of the issue of changing meaning, or of introducing new signals and indices, see Jervis, 1970, 142–145; 179–190.

43. The research sample chosen by Snyder and Diesing points to the fact that most of the errors (51%) connected to the transmission of messages were in decoding, whereas encoding errors comprised only 9% of the total sample (Snyder and Diesing, 1977, 316).

44. For discussion of the tendency of intelligence communities to think that information (insofar as it is "clear") has only one categorical meaning and to assume that facts have an inner "truth," see Hilsman, 1956; 1961; Wasserman, 1960.

45. Research by scholars of the Bayesian school indicates that intuitive cost-benefit calculations do not necessarily lead to rational decisionmaking in terms of maximum utility, or even in terms of the system of preferences and values of the decisionmaker himself (Slovic and Lichtenstein, 1971).

46. For a detailed discussion on the power of words in international politics, see Franck and Weisband, 1972.

47. Further on we shall see that this need for a system of criteria proceeds not only from the characteristics of the information but also from the needs and drives connected with the individual's personality and his relations with his social environment.

48. An attempt to suggest a typology of operational codes can be found in Holsti, 1977.

49. There is a connection between the individual's personal values and the ideologies that he adopts in relations among nations (Scott, 1960). For example, an individual who regards personal status as important will emphasize the importance of national prestige, whereas one who sees loyalty as important will tend toward chauvinism.

50. The difference between an attitude and a value is that an attitude relates to a specific situation or object, whereas a value relates not to a specific object or situation but to broader categories of objects and situations.

51. It has been found that an individual having values and orientations indicating preference for cooperation in the management of conflicts tends to see his attitudes closer to those of his opponent than they are (Judd, 1978).

52. For example, an individual who is not a spendthrift can be described as either frugal (positive) or miserly (negative).

53. Or to make unitary actor assumptions.

54. There is in this definition an attempt to combine both a dynamic and a static aspect, in contrast to other definitions that have either only a static aspect (see, for example, Triandis, 1971, 2) or a dynamic one that relates chiefly to the judgmental-evaluative process (see Lee, 1966, 88).

55. On the other hand, the more sophisticated the cognitive structure, the more sophisticated will be the ways used to ignore stimuli; the more simplistic it is, however, the greater the use will be made of simplistic means such as denial and repression, which do not require the ability to differentiate (Witkin, 1974, 101).

56. It appears that the tendency of the individual to create broad or narrow categories is not specific to a certain issue-area but is part of the total cognitive style (Pittigrew, 1958).

57. For futher details, see Abelson, 1959 and Vertzberger, in progress. Techniques of coping with imbalance through manipulation of information are different in terms of the degree of cognitive sophistication that they require.

58. There might also be a manipulation of causal connections as a means of protecting the balance. When this possibility does not exist, there may be a manipulation of the motive for action or behavior as a means of protecting the balance (Rosenberg and Wolfsfeld, 1977).

59. The first is more serious as mistrust is more difficult to change, given that it is generally connected with the policymaker's most important beliefs about the nature of his opponent.

60. Only paranoid policymakers will adopt model 2 totally and without distinction, and only totally naive policymakers will adopt model 1 without distinction.

61. See also Rosenberg and Wolfsfeld, 1977.

62. In this context, one must distinguish between expressed attitudes known to the public and nonexpressed ones. For the committing power of expressed attitudes, see Graber, 1976, 195–198.

63. See also Festinger, 1964, 151.

64. The term causality in this context includes two aspects: the first in the sense of *essence*, that is, the determination of the independent and the dependent variables, and the second in the sense of *order*, that is, ordering the events in time. Naturally the two are interrelated, as the independent variable, whether event or behavior, always comes before the dependent variable.

65. We shall present only a number of main misconceptions involved. For a detailed discussion of misconceptions, see Vertzberger (forthcoming). See also Nisbett and Ross, 1980.

66. From a probabilistic point of view, the likelihood of a plan succeeding grows smaller in reverse proportion to the number of steps in the chain of actions needed for its success.

67. For a survey and discussion of the intervening variable that determines the potential relative importance of personality trait variables in determining the definition of the situation, see Greenstein, 1967, 1969, 46–57; Verba, 1969; Hermann, 1974; 1978.

68. One of the more popular explanations in the literature for the development of personality traits characterized by these kinds of cognitive patterns is the one relating to the socialization process undergone by the individual from childhood, particularly in his relationships with his parents and as a consequence of the parents' interrelationship (see, for example, Rokeach, 1960, 365; Harvey, 1966; Dixon, 1976; Friedlander and Cohen, 1975).

69. For criticism of the usage of personality traits as variables that explain human behavior, see Mischel, 1968, 73–148.

70. Most of the symptoms related to authoritativeness were already noted in the classical study by Adorno *et al.* (1950).

71. Organization and group pressures. (See the following section entitled "The Group and Organization as Sources of Misperception.")

72. The acuteness of these problems varies from one decisionmaking group to another and is a function of the leader's leadership power, the

nature of the mutual relations among the group members and their tolerance of each other, leadership style, the mutual relations between the leader and the group members, the resulting atmosphere, and so on. See: White and Lippit, 1968; Gibb, 1974.

73. Different studies have pointed to the fact that the connection between role and attitude formation is so strong that a change of role might cause a change in attitude (Greenwald, 1969; Lieberman, 1956; Culbertson, 1957).

74. The group dynamics might create the concept that the majority is right not only because it is the majority but because it really is right. Such a process of rationalization depends on background variables such as the degree of ambivalence in the information (see Deutsch and Gerard, 1955, 629–630).

75. A further complication in this context is one of inconsistency between the roleholder's concept of his role and how he acts in reality, as earlier discussed.

76. Status is defined in terms of the ability to deviate from group norms and expectations (Hollander, 1965).

77. The terms *compliance, identification,* and *internalization* were suggested by Kelman (1958), but were adapted to the needs of this subject by the present author.

78. The degree to which the individual identifies himself with the decisionmaking group is dependent to a large extent on his status within it. The more central his role, the more he will tend to identify the quality of performance with his own efficiency (Zander, 1971, 196).

79. The extent to which preference or equal status is granted to the value system of the subculture (of foreign ministers) versus the national value and belief system is a function of the foreign ministers' personal beliefs and values. The more internationalistic they are in their concepts, the more importance they will grant to values that pertain to the outcome of their partnership in the world elite, rather than to values and beliefs arising from their partnership in the national elite (see Modelski, 1970, 166–168; Lutzker, 1960).

80. The national culture tends toward stereotyped conceptions as it is directed at a broad public, the mass nature of which requires simplicity and lack of sophistication in order to be easily assimilated. The degree to which stereotypes are used varies in proportion to the level of the intellectual sophistication of the society. The more primitive the society, the greater the need for stereotypes in addressing the masses in order to gain legitimation for the leadership's definition of the situation.

81. Studies by East (1972) and Wallace (1973) dealing with the gap between the actual status and that which a state perceives itself to deserve indicate that such a gap might lead to an externalization of conflictual behavior, to remedy the status gap.

82. Compare Bennet (1975) with Rosenau (1970).

Chapter 2

1. Detailed descriptions can be found in Chakravarti, 1961, 1971; Arora, 1961; Van Eckelen, 1964; Rowland, 1967; Rao, 1968; Sen Gupta, 1970; Maxwell, 1972; Gupta, 1974; Jetly, 1979.

2. The letter is quoted in full in Das, 1974, 335–341.

3. See letters of the Indian government of October 26 and October 31, 1950 in The International Commission of Jurists (1959), *The Question of Tibet and the Rule of Law*, Geneva, Document No. 9.

4. For the text of the agreement, see The International Commission of Jurists (1959), *The Question of Tibet and the Rule of Law*, Geneva, Document No. 10.

5. For the full text, see *W.P.*, I, 98–101.

6. The first border incident took place as early as June 1954, when an Indian military unit penetrated Bara Hoti and the Chinese government protested to India about it in the following month (*W.P.*, I, 1).

7. A detailed analysis of interorganizational and personal bickering can be found in Chapter 11.

8. A content analysis of fourteen of Nehru's speeches in the period 1949–1961 shows that China is third only to India and the United Nations in the number of times it was mentioned. It is interesting to note that most of the references to India itself are in connection with China (159) even more than with Pakistan and Kashmir (114). In public opinion, too, China occupied a central position second only to Goa (Stein, 1968, 171a–179).

9. Such differences may occur even when there is agreement as to the essence of the problem.

10. For an example of the argument on the Indian side, see the discussion in the Rajya Sabha of September 4, 1959 (*Par.*, I, 119–120). For a similar example on the Chinese side, see the letter by Chou En-lai of September 1959 (*W.P.*, II, 27–33).

11. Later, as, for example, in April 1961, Nehru said in a Rajya Sabha debate, referring to the Longju incident: "Longju has no importance" (*Par.*, I, 396).

12. See Statistical Appendix, Table A3.

13. That is why, when the military aspect did become important, late in 1961, it was Lieutenant-General Kaul, considered by Nehru to be a soldier-diplomat, who gained prominence (see Chapter 11).

14. Though mistakenly so.

15. For a detailed analysis of this point, see Chapter 6.

16. See Statistical Appendix Table A4.

17. In analyzing the cognitive systems of both sides, no definite correlation was found between the geographical and the military-defense factors for China, whereas for India it was found that the geographical factor was conceived as having prominent defense implications, showing a correlation of .514 (see Statistical Appendix Tables A1 and A2). However, India's unjustified confidence in its capacity to deal with defense problems led to carelessness.

Chapter 3

1. This thesis was echoed in the Indian press immediately following the signing of the 1954 agreement. On May 1, 1954 the *Times of India* declared: "The unobtrusiveness of the talks and their reward were in significant contrast to the importunateness of cold war diplomacy with its endless frustrations."

2. This combination of optimism with a touch of pessimism was a regular feature of Nehru's makeup.

3. But he never really tried to find out what the substance of those obligations was, partly out of his hesitation to breach his policy of nonalignment and partly out of his conviction that war with China was improbable (*Par.*, II, 119).

4. This was an error of judgment, as we shall see later on.

5. Nehru objected, despite the events in Tibet, to demands that, in order to penalize China, India should stop its activities on its behalf at the United Nations (*Par.*, I, 211–212). During the 1960 New Delhi talks, Chou En-lai was told that China was ungrateful to India after all it had done for it (Desai, 1974, 186–187).

6. See Statistical Appendix, Table A1.

7. See Chapter 5.

8. During one of the most tense periods on the Sino-Indian border, Nehru wrote, when analyzing the foreign policy issues facing India, "Meanwhile it should be remembered that the problem most important of all is that of disarmament" (*F.N.*, 1/62, July 10, 1962).

9. See *Par.*, I, 279.

10. Only such assumptions give a measure of rationality to the naive immunity concept presented earlier.

11. Thus exchanging reality for wishful thinking and what is for what ought to be.

12. Deterrence can be achieved only if the enemy perceives the rationale for being deterred.

13. The discussion of these basic differences between China and India has been presented here in brief, as a detailed discussion occurs further on.

14. The need to reevaluate the negative appreciation of Gandhi led Soviet Orientalist scholars to produce some apologetic literature in which the main motif was the claim that the past negative view of Gandhi's nonviolence strategy was the result of a misunderstanding of the relevant historical background (Ray, 1969, 99–102).

15. Up to the beginning of the 1960s, Soviet economic aid to India had reached $800 million as against $450 million to China. As for military aid, the first agreement was signed in 1960 and included the supply of Antonov-12 transports and helicopters suitable for logistic activity in Ladakh.

16. Although at a certain point he expressed doubt whether even the USSR could do so.

17. In this statement, the West was accused of attempting to provoke a quarrel between China and India, and the USSR made it clear that it was taking a neutral position (for the full text, see Prasad, 1973, 186). When the East German prime minister condemned India, he was scolded by Khrushchev, and the Soviet ambassador to China was recalled after having taken a pro-Chinese stand (Ray, 1965).

18. For the full text of Khrushchev's speech before the Indian Parliament in February 1960, see Prasad, 1973, 191–201.

19. Of the ten nations in South and Southeast Asia with which the Soviets exchanged high-ranking delegations, the exchange of delegates with India comprised 33% in 1959 and 1960, and 20% in 1961–1962. The details of exchange delegations with India by area are as follows:

	Political/ Military Delegations	Economic Delegations	Cultural Delegations
1959		4	
1960	1	6	1
1961	1	3	1
1962	1	8	1
Total	3	21	3

Data based on McLane, 1973, 64–67; 143.

20. According to Soviet statistics, throughout the years 1959–1962 (excluding 1960) there was a surplus in India's balance of payments with the USSR. According to Indian statistics, throughout the same years there was a deficit in its balance of payments with the USSR. The difference is probably the result of different accounting methods (Datar, 1972, 20).

21. See also Datar, 1972.

22. The Chinese saw this as hypocrisy, as the USSR had used force more than once in territorial conflicts—for example, in its dispute with Turkey in 1921 (*P.R.*, Nov. 8, 1963).

23. There were a number of deviations from this optimistic picture of relations, such as the publication of a Soviet map in the spring of 1962 in which parts of India were shown as belonging to China; the USSR did not respond to an Indian complaint on the matter. In addition, according to the Chinese, Khrushchev informed the Chinese ambassador in Moscow on October 14, 1962 that he had information about a possible Indian attack on China, and promised him the USSR's support (*P.R.*, Nov. 8, 1963).

24. This matter brings to mind the situation previous to the Yom Kippur War, when the Israeli and U.S. intelligence agencies reinforced each others' misevaluations of the Arab threat.

25. Two Soviet scholars accuse the Chinese of having broken the 1950 agreement about consultation and notification in advance of such moves (Borrisov and Koloskov, 1975, 157).

26. A reliable Indian observer also expressed the opinion that until 1962 the importance of the Sino-Soviet conflict for the defense of India was not fully understood (Subrahamanyam, 1970b). Nehru's understanding of the nature of the ideological rift was unidimensional; he tended to relate it mainly to the issue of peaceful coexistence between East and West (*Par.*, I, 371).

27. For a detailed description of those contacts, see *P.R.*, Nov. 8, 1963.

28. For a description of Chinese activities, see Siegel, 1968.

29. For a detailed polemic on Soviet attitude toward India, see *P.R.*, Nov. 8, 1963.

30. On the ideological debate, see, for example, Zagoria, 1962, Ch. 10.

31. In that article, Sinkiang and Tibet are mentioned in the same breath.

32. This was also the year in which the Soviets ceased economic and technical aid to China.

33. An analogy between Sinkiang and Tibet can be found as early as May 1959 (*P.R.*, May 12, 1959, 14). It is interesting to note that the Aksai Chin area is defined as Chinese Sinkiang (*P.R.*, Nov. 30, 1963).

34. We shall not elaborate on Tibetan history here, as it has been mentioned several times and will be again. As for Sinkiang, a detailed discussion can be found in Whiting and Sheng Shin-ts'ai (1958).

35. For the internal situation in Sinkiang during this period, see details in Whiting, 1975, 28–40. Between May and June 1962, thousands escaped from Sinkiang to the USSR, among them General Zunum Taibov, Deputy Chief of Staff of the Sinkiang Military Region (Whitson, 1973, 488).

36. See also *P.R.*, Nov. 8, 1963, 24.

37. According to the director of the Indian Intelligence Bureau, Indian intelligence began to be aware of the acuteness of the Sino-Soviet rift after the 22nd Communist Party of the Soviet Union (CPSU) Congress in October 1961.

38. How little Nehru understood of Sino-Soviet differences can be learned from the testimony of the director of the Indian Intelligence Bureau, who claimed that Nehru thought that "there was very little ideology in it" (Mullik, 1971, 303). Nehru admitted: "I do not pretend to understand fully these ideological conflicts" (*F.N.*, 6/58, June 30, 1958).

39. On his visit to the Soviet Union in 1955, Nehru was the first non-Communist leader who was allowed to speak before a Soviet audience. He was convinced that tolerance toward the Soviet regime yielded more openness.

40. Choudhury, 1975, 95.

41. See Mullik, 1971, 285–286.

42. Not including food aid.

43. In a conversation with the Indian ambassador in Washington, D.C., Kennedy stated his position on Goa by saying: "The reason why people are criticizing you is because they have seen a minister coming out of a brothel" (Nayar, 1973, 148).

44. As for the Soviet Union, see the remark of the then Indian defense minister quoted in Brecher, 1968, 169. As for the United States, this can be deduced from the fact that Washington, D.C. was no less surprised than New Delhi, as is obvious from Kenneth Galbraith's reminiscences (Galbraith, 1969).

45. A similar claim was made again in August 1962 (*P.R.*, Aug. 17, 1962, 7).

46. See Statistical Appendix, Tables A1 and A2.

47. In an appearance before the Indian Parliament in April 1961, Nehru championed the fact that China's position in the Sino-Indian dispute was rejected and criticized in Asia and other subsystems, a fact that proved a severe blow to its prestige and acted as a serious deterrent (*Par.*, I, 398–399). See also: *Par.* II, 118, a debate held in the Rajya Sabha on August 14, 1962.

48. These words were spoken in 1952 to the first official goodwill delegation, led by Nehru's sister, on its departure to China.

49. Canada and Poland were the other members of that committee.

50. Signs of a change were evident in 1956 when New Delhi recognized the governments of both North and South Vietnam, gave up its insistence on the unification of the two, and ceased criticizing the dependence on South Vietnam on SEATO's protection.

51. They were probably thinking of the Korean lesson.

Chapter 4

1. "Memorandum on the correspondence relating to the proposed Agreement between Great Britain and Russia on the Subject of Thibet" (8926), Foreign Office, April 18, 1907. The agreement was ratified on September 23, 1907. (For the full text of the memorandum, see Gooch and Temperley, 1929, 336–349.)

2. At the beginning of the twentieth century the British adopted the attitude that Aksai Chin was a part of Tibet, in order to prevent Russian claims over it. The situation would have been different if the British had recognized Aksai Chin to be part of Sinkiang (Maxwell, 1972, 20).

3. Later on, this led to a situation in which the Indians were not aware of the building of the road in Aksai Chin connecting Tibet with Sinkiang until September 1957, although it had actually been started two years earlier.

4. The Himalayas are the transition point between the southern slopes of the Plateau of Tibet and the Plains of India, and in the eastern area there is no clear watershed line. Thus, even when both sides accepted the watershed principle in determining the boundary line, opinion remained divided as to where it ran (Lamb, 1970). The watershed line was more obvious in the western part of the Himalayan range and the length of the Karakoram range to the Wakhan range in Afghanistan. Indeed, that line serves as a border between China and Pakistani Kashmir.

5. For a short but inclusive survey of the physical features on the northern border and their significance in Sino-Indian relations, see Dutt, 1966.

6. Nehru inherited this concept, too, from the British, and it was Patel, in his letter of November 1950, who firmly but vainly demanded a reevaluation of it.

7. This he did according to the advice of Panikkar, India's ambassador to China (Dutt, 1977, 87).

8. Most of India's press agreed with Nehru's idea on the subject at the time. The *Hindustan Times* of May 4, 1954 declared that India "made Red China agree to respect the territorial integrity of India which is based on the McMahon Line." A similar view was taken by the *Indian Express*, the *National Herald*, and the *Times of India*. A stand supporting Bajpai's view was taken by *Amrita Bazar, Pioneer*, and others (Fisher and Bondurant, 1956a, 27–28).

9. For the full text of the letter, see *The Sino-Indian Border Question* (enlarged ed.), Peking, Foreign Language Press, 1962, 6–38.

10. The Chinese controlled the dominating features in both the western and the eastern sectors and had considerably more convenient access routes in both. It was for this reason that the Chinese suggestion that both sides retreat 20 km from the disputed line was rejected: the Chinese would have found it much easier to recapture the line if they had wished to do so (Hoffmann, 1971, 562; *Times of India*, Nov. 21, 1959).

11. India's leaders had little understanding of these subjects, as we shall see in Chapter 11, due to their lack of any chance to gain experience on defense and strategy issues during the British Raj.

12. Ayub Khan claimed as early as 1959 that a territorial arrangement in Ladakh was impossible without the agreement of Pakistan, and the Pakistani press expressed doubt as to whether India had any right to demand the

evacuation of an "Indian" territory by the Chinese without reaching an understanding with Pakistan on Kashmir (Rajan, 1962).

13. For the full text of the agreement, see Muni, 1973, Appendix V.

14. The aim being to transform the subcontinent politically in India's image (Muni, 1975).

15. There were early signs of the doctrine as early as 1950, however. See, for example, Nehru's budget speech in March 1950 (Nehru, 1954, 147).

16. For a fuller description of the significance of the "special relations" in the economic and political spheres, see Muni, 1973, 67–96; Jha, 1973, 18–52; Shaha, 1975, 114–121.

17. Although in July 1955 an agreement was reached on diplomatic relations between China and Nepal, the latter at India's request avoided giving a permit for the establishment of a Chinese consulate in Katmandu.

18. The scope of Chinese foreign aid in the years from 1955/1956 to 1962/1963 (excluding 1961/1962) was 35.335 million rupees, as compared to 165.698 million from India (Muni, 1973, 216).

19. The government of Nepal decided to increase its defense expenditure for 1959/1960 by 100%.

20. For example, during most of the years from 1958/1959 to 1962/1963, more than 95% of Nepal's exports and imports went to or came from India, whereas 1% or less of exports and imports went to or came from China (see table in Muni, 1973, 221).

21. It is interesting to note that a considerable part of Indian aid to Nepal was used to build roads, not only for economic reasons but for logistic-strategic ones as well. In the years 1952–1967 a major part of Indian aid, about 35.6%, was invested in land and air transportation. A number of these projects were carried out by Indian army engineers and were completed in record time (Ayoob, 1970, 129; Muni, 1973, 188). The aid program failed in some areas; the most successful projects were those that had strategic goals, such as the geographical mapping of Nepal, the building of the road connecting Nepal to India, and the construction of an airport in Katmandu. The Nepalese themselves were ambivalent about Indian aid, which they saw as serving Indian interests. On the other hand, Chinese aid enjoyed greater political success even though it was much smaller in scope. It was seen as unconditional and not designed to limit Nepal's independence. The terms of this aid were also far more dignified: for example, the Chinese experts came at least partly under Nepalese supervision (Mihaly, 1965, 140–156). Chinese correct and reasonable treatment of Nepal stood out compared with India's paternalistic treatment of Nepal. This had a decisive impact on the Nepalese elite's attitude toward India and China, as made clear by Shaha, a member of the Nepalese Cabinet at the time (1975, 123–128).

22. See also Jha, 1973, 113–118.

23. One can observe Mahendra's attempt to preserve a facade of balance and neutrality between India and China (as opposed to real content, which shows a definite bias toward China) as reflected by the almost identical numbers of days spent by important visitors and delegations from Nepal in India and from India in Nepal, and from China in Nepal and from Nepal in China; 34 and 39 respectively. But only in 50% of exchange visits with India were joint declarations issued, whereas joint declarations were issued on every occasion in the case of Chinese exchange visits.

24. For the full text of the agreements, see Lok Sabha Secretariat (1959), *Foreign Policy of India: Text of Documents*, 2nd ed. New Delhi: Government of India Press.

25. The Sikkim-Tibet border was delimited, whereas along the Bhutan-Tibet border there was a dispute over an area of 200 square miles. Another issue concerned eight enclaves in western Tibet that had been administered by Bhutanese officials. These enclaves were seized by the Chinese in 1959 (Rose, 1977, 80).

26. This was one of the factors underlying the decision of Nehru and Pant to grant political asylum to the Dalai Lama upon his escape from Tibet in 1959, so as not to anger part of the population and leadership of the two principalities (Mullik, 1971, 225).

27. See also *Times of India*, Oct. 15, 1959.

28. The Chinese offered economic aid and assured Bhutan that it had nothing to fear from China (Rose, 1977, 79).

29. Indian policymakers considered Bhutan to be one of the more vulnerable points along India's northern front.

30. Even in 1960 Bhutan had agreed to receive Indian aid for its first five-year plan. In the same year Bhutan closed its border with Tibet, thus damaging its trade, as, due to the lack of convenient routes to India, Tibet was Bhutan's main market. Only in 1963 was the road between Bhutan and India completed, which gave Bhutan easy access to the Indian market.

31. In March 1960 diplomatic relations between Nepal and Pakistan were established, and King Mahendra visited Pakistan in September 1961.

32. Such a hostile alliance could, for example, control most of India's river sources.

33. At the end of 1959 Nepal's foreign minister promptly responded to Nehru's statement that aggression against Nepal would be considered by India as aggression against itself: "In the event of any aggression on Nepal, it is Nepal who will decide if there has been any aggression" (quoted by Sinha, 1970, 477).

34. This situation was aggravated by the behavior of some of India's diplomatic representatives in Nepal who, according to a senior Indian official, did not have "proper appreciation of the history and culture of the countries in which they were to serve" (Dutt, 1977, 286).

Chapter 5

1. His confidence never waivered during the entire period. See also his statement of August 14, 1962, in which the Indian army and air force were enthusiastically appraised (*Par.*, II, 111).

2. Italics are mine. The same confidence in the capabilities of the Indian army is expressed in his letter of October 12, 1962 (*F.N.*, 3/62).

3. This referred to China's dependence on imported oil and its by-products from the USSR and Rumania.

4. "To the last moment we did not expect this invasion in overwhelming numbers" (*Par.*, II, 176). See also Nehru's letters of September and October 1962, in which he predicts only tension and petty conflicts (*F.N.*, 2/62, Sept. 3, 1962; 3/62, Oct. 12, 1962).

5. For a description of the chaos in China following the Great Leap Forward, see A. Eckstein, 1975, 279–291; Karnow, 1972, 92–109.

6. For an important collection of documents on this affair, including the defense minister's critical letter to Mao, see Union Research Institute (1969), *The Case of P'eng Te-huai 1959–1968*, Hong Kong. For an analysis and detailed description of the leadership struggle, see Joffe, 1975, 8–20; Karnow, 1972, 110–126; Bridgham, 1970, 212–220.

7. Alsop's article summarized what he had argued in his columns in the U.S. daily press.

8. This view was widespread in the West. The Chinese leadership was aware of that and its possible consequences (see Note 34, Chapter 5).

9. It consisted of twenty-nine issues of the secret military journal *Bulletin of Activities* (Kung-tso T'ung-hsün), published by the political department of the army and distributed only to regimental commanders and higher-ranking officers.

10. The Tibetan rebels were supported by the CIA and Taiwan. See Mullin, 1975; Wise, 1973.

11. India regularly received intelligence information from the West, including the United States (Kaul, 1971, 291).

12. In the First Five-Year Plan, 12% of all public investments came from foreign aid. In the Second Five-Year Plan, by contrast, 37% of the total investment came from foreign aid (Kothari, 1970, 412).

13. In contrast to the Chinese opinion, the matter of foreign economic aid was only of minor importance to most Indian parties except the Communists. A content analysis of the parties' resolutions in the years 1949–1964 shows that the Congress Party referred to foreign aid in only 2% of its resolutions, the PSP in 3%, and the Jana Sangh and Swatantra not at all. The Communist Party, on the other hand, referred to it in 12% of its resolutions decisions (Ilchman, 1967, 682).

14. He repeated this thesis throughout the conflict. See, for example, *Par.*, I, 345; *Par.*, II, 57.

15. For an evaluation of the problems and achievements of India's first three Five-Year Plans, see Frankel, 1978, 113–245.

16. The lack of foreign exchange was paralyzing part of the industry because spare parts could not be purchased.

17. The demands for a greater investment in military power were most fiercely supported by the Jana Sangh. See Jhangiani, 1967, 69–73.

18. This type of policy was demanded in the media. Thus, the *Times of India* stated in an editorial of December 7, 1961: "To rule out any kind of positive measure, since we are not prepared for the extreme measure of war, is in effect to restrict the possibility of permissible action for an indefinite period."

19. The establishment of an aircraft industry to manufacture the Migs was to guarantee political independence via military self-reliance.

20. The basis for the Forward Policy had been laid in May 1960 after the visit of Chou En-lai, but the army did not begin to carry it out until November 2, 1961.

21. This is a quotation from the original guidelines issued by the political echelon, as quoted by Maxwell, 1972, 234.

22. The assumption of the Indian army's ability to stand up to the Chinese army was not limited to India's policymakers, but was prevalent in the Indian press except for a small number of critical journalists. Western experts such as Leo Rose and Margaret Fisher, in an article published at the beginning

of 1962, wrote optimistically about Indian military activity in the area of Ladakh (Fisher and Rose, 1962). An article published in the U.S. *Military Review* in January 1962 made the following assessment: "To make any impact Red China would have to assemble a gigantic expeditionary force, with all its necessary services, and maintain a conventional line of communication over the massive obstacle of the Himalayan ranges. It is doubtful whether China could do this because her army is static and guerrilla minded" (O'Ballance, 1962, 35).

23. Another Indian battalion served in Gaza since 1957 as part of the UN peacekeeping force.

24. The Cabinet's Defense Committee approved only about a tenth of the army's budget demands (Kavic, 1967, 97).

25. In 1959 the Indian army had, along the northern border, 38 posts with 1,334 soldiers. At the end of 1962 there were 77 posts with 1,590 soldiers, about 20 soldiers per position (Kaul, 1971, 288).

26. In an exercise performed in January 1961, the aim of which was to rehearse the defense of the sector, the Chinese attack was envisioned to begin with a three-spearhead penetration, as indeed it did in reality (Kavic, 1967, 89).

27. This topic will be further discussed in Chapter 11.

28. Indian operational plans were based on the intelligence evaluation that for actual combat purposes the Chinese would be able to allow only one regiment equal to an Indian brigade. In fact, during the fighting in October, they used two divisions. The Intelligence Bureau had reported in mid-September that there were ten Chinese divisions in Tibet, of which two or three were facing the northeastern sector from Walong to Tawang.

29. Hundreds of ponies and Tibetan coolies were assembled to carry supplies through untraversable routes. A road suitable for trucks up to seven tons was built up to Maramang only a few hours away from Thag-La Ridge, and even prison camps were organized in readiness.

30. According to the report of Brigadier Dalvi, one of the commanders of the Chinese forces in Tibet was a former commander of Chinese forces in Korea. According to Whitson (1973, 489), two Chinese Corps, the 54th and the 18th, were immediately deployed as the war broke out. The 54th took part in the Korean war as well. Later on, Lin Piao dispatched elements of the 46th Corps from Manchuria. The 46th had been Lin Piao's own corps in Korea.

31. An alternative, if less flattering, explanation of Chinese tolerance is that it was caused by Chinese reluctance to enter into war before September, as May through August are months of monsoon rains coming from the Bay of Bengal. However, even according to this explanation, it was not the power of the Indian army that deterred Chinese reaction, as was proven in October 1962.

32. He was taken prisoner in this war as commander of the Seventh Brigade.

33. This is especially true of the hard-liners in the Ministry of External Affairs, the CGS and the director of the Intelligence Bureau.

34. The Chinese foreign minister emphasized this in an interview he gave to Canadian Television in July 1961, in which he said that, although there had been economic difficulties in China as a result of natural disasters, they should not be exaggerated: "Yet some people in the West are using this

situation to trump up all sorts of stories. This is done with ulterior motives. I hope you will not be taken in by them" (*P.R.*, July 14, 1961, 10). In addition, in a factor analysis done on the psychological environment of the Chinese leadership in the Sino-Indian dispute, it was found that the most important factor (which explains about 50.9% of the variance) was the perception of the linkage between events on the internal Chinese scene and those on the global system (see Statistical Appendix, Table A4). Conceptually, this connection can also be found in the high correlations between the perception of China's relations with the super powers and that of China's economy and the nature of its political system—correlations of .758 and .764, respectively (see Statistical Appendix, Table A2).

35. This was, indeed, the style of the blow delivered by the Chinese against India in October 1962.

36. The anxiety over having to fight on two fronts was manifested as early as May 1959, when the Chinese ambassador expressed his opinion that neither China nor India could afford to open a second front (*W.P.*, I, 76).

37. This evaluation is based on the comparison of graphs presented by Liao, 1974, 69; 71; 81; 84. For a plausible analysis of the change from a diplomatic to a militant line, see Gurtov and Hwang, 1980, 134–142.

38. So deeply rooted was this conception that even in November 1962, after reality had proven different, Nehru continued to hold the lame notions that militarily everything was satisfactory; that the COAS and the CGS were talented officers; and that the defeat was not a result of the lack of appropriate weapons and equipment but due to the human-wave tactics of the Chinese (*Par.*, II, 148; 176–181).

39. For example, leading personalities such as Rajagopalachari, Acharya Kripalani, and Jayaprakash Narayan.

40. For a detailed discussion of the development of the Indian political system from the nineteenth century onwards, see Kothari, 1970; Palmer, 1961.

41. Nehru was deeply worried by Narayan's activities and speeches on the subject (*Press*, I, 32). He was unwilling to make the Tibet issue an Afro-Asian block issue, as called for by Narayan in an all-India/Tibet convention that was held in May 1959 (Jetly, 1969, 72).

42. So much so that members of the opposition, such as Kripalani, accused the government of treason (*Par.*, I, 301).

43. Nehru defended Menon warmly and praised his work and qualifications. See, for example, *Par.*, II, 133.

44. For a detailed profile of the party, see Jhangiani, 1967, 106–132; Erdman, 1967.

45. This fear is clearly expressed in an interview given by Nehru to an Indian reporter (Karanjia, 1960, 60–61).

46. For a detailed profile of the party's ideology, organization, and strength, see Baxter, 1967; Jhangiani, 1967, 44–105. It is of interest to note that the Jana Sangh did not criticize nonalignment as such but, rather, the way it was implemented.

47. This differed from the Chinese approach, as we have seen.

48. For a detailed discussion of the positions and changes of attitude and supporters of each trend, see Stern, 1965.

49. In Nehru's cognitive system a correlation of .559 was found between Sino-Indian bilateral relations and his controversy with other political leaders (see Statistical Appendix, Table A1).

50. In our analysis we found a correlation of .553 between his image of his disagreement with political rivals and the structure of the Indian political system in general (see Statistical Appendix, Table A1).

51. The two behaved with such vehemence toward the visitor that Nehru was obliged to ask Swaran Singh to meet Chou En-lai to soften the impression that he had received from Pant and Desai.

52. It did not do any good. He was accused of fraud throughout the entire period. Asoka Mehta, a Socialist leader in Parliament, said in 1961 that "you have been consistent in your attitude of understating the facts by using words which did not really express the real position" (*Par.*, II, 43).

53. No elections were held in Kashmir and Jammu, which also border on China.

54. The Tibetan market was dependent on the Indian. The Chinese, in their vision of transforming the feudal Tibetan economy, could not agree to this. They wanted India to supply Tibet only with those provisions that they themselves could not carry over long supply routes. Northern India supplied Tibet with products such as sugar and textiles in return for Tibetan wool. This wool was crucial for the economy of Northern India, which was based on the cottage industry. The supply of wool ceased to exist in 1959 (Polat, 1968).

55. Nehru was convinced that the Indian army could stop a Chinese invasion, and although he admitted that the army could not initiate an attack (*Par.*, II, 111), he at times discarded even that caution and expressed his confidence in the army's ability to attack, as was shown in the "Leghorn" operation plan.

56. For a more detailed survey of the individual makeup and organizational origin of members of these pressure groups, see Chapter 11.

57. It is interesting to note that it was the same worry over the behavior of the northeast border ethnic group that served as a consideration in giving the Dalai Lama political asylum, as he was their religious leader (Mullik, 1971, 225). According to Dutt (1977, 34) the Naga issue worried the MEA no less than did the China issue.

58. As soon as India won independence in 1947, Naga leaders raised separatist demands. After 1953 their campaign for their demands involved the use of violence, which became intensive after 1956. Disquiet among the Mizos started in 1959, but separatist demands were raised for the first time by their leader, Laldenga, in 1962. (For details, see Marwah, 1977.)

59. Tables 5.2 and 5.3 indicate precisely this dominance. The control of the political system was such that it enabled Nehru to overcome a problem that might have arisen from a decision of the Indian Supreme Court of March 14, 1960 in a matter concerning the territorial conflict between India and Pakistan. The decision stated that, according to the Indian constitution, any international treaty involving the relinquishment of Indian territory had to involve a change in the constitution, as Indian borders were defined in the constitution. To avoid this problem it was necessary to win a majority of two-thirds in the federal Parliament and a simple majority in over half of the state assemblies.

60. An example is Nehru's statement on October 12, 1962 to the effect that he had instructed the army to evict the Chinese from Indian territory. What is more, because Nehru used to speak in Parliament at length without consulting any written notes, he sometimes made mistakes in his facts and

details. These imprecisions were later exploited by the Chinese (Dutt, 1977, 30–31).

61. India's ambassador to the USSR until 1961.

62. In the original, this sentence is italicized.

63. A detailed analysis of the results appeared in the Chinese press (*P.R.*, Mar. 23, 1962).

64. The importance of the Indian internal political structure in China's negative perception is evident in a content analysis of Indian characteristics in the eyes of the Chinese. About 50% of the total negative definitions and about 30% of the total definitions related to the subject of society and government (see Statistical Appendix, Table A6).

65. These two dimensions—moral and cognitive legitimacy—were suggested by George (1979).

66. He may have overestimated the actual militancy of the public. A public opinion survey conducted in August 1962 by the Indian Institute of Public Opinion indicated that there seemed to have been strong support for settling the border dispute by peaceful means (45.2%) such as mobilizing world public opinion or asking the USSR to apply pressure on China. There was a significant minority (37.5%) that felt otherwise, but even among them a majority (54.5%) did not support a policy precipitating war (Monthly Public Opinion Survey, October–November, 1962, 49–50).

Chapter 6

1. For literature dealing with the legal aspects of the problem, see Lamb 1960; 1964; 1966; 1973; Mehra, 1974; Rubin, 1960; 1968; Sharma, 1965; 1971; Singh, 1967; Stahanke, 1970; and, especially, Government of India (1961), *Report of the Officials of the Governments of India and the People's Republic of China on the Boundary Question.*

2. With the establishment of the Joint Committee, instructions were given to withdraw all the material that contradicted Indian claims. The official reason was to prevent it from falling into Chinese hands (Nayar, 1969, 137–138).

3. The main agreements used by the Indians as evidence were as follows: in the eastern sector, the treaty signed at the Simla Conference and the 1914 correspondence between China and Britain; in the western and central sectors, the Tibet-Ladakh Agreement of 1684, the ratification of the same agreement in 1842, a further reinforcement in an exchange of letters between the Chinese and British governments in 1852, and the fixing of the Aksai Chin border in a letter by the government of British India in 1899.

4. Although the Indian maps showed the McMahon line as the border in the eastern sector as early as 1950, the western sector boundary was indicated on Indian maps only after 1954. In 1959 Nehru still admitted that the border delimitation in that area was problematic (*Par.*, I, 104). It was only later that he was persuaded by Gopal that Indian rights to the western sector were undisputed.

5. For the presentation of the legal claims by each side, see Chou En-lai's letter of September 8, 1959 (*W.P.*, II, 27–33) and Nehru's reply, as well as the appendix to his letter of September 26, 1959 (*W.P.*, II, 34–52). A very detailed presentation of both sides' claims can be found in the report of the Joint Committee.

332   Notes to Chapter 6

6. These rights include realization of rights belonging to every nation, even in a system basically capitalist, such as representation at the United Nations. But in this matter, too, India retreated to a more passive position than in the past, specifically since the beginning of the 1960s (Sinha, 1971, 391–393).

7. See Statistical Appendix, Table A6.

8. According to Nehru, Chou En-lai, on his visit to India in 1956, stated that "they did not consider Tibet as a province of China. The people were different from the people of China proper. . . . He told me further that it was absurd for anyone to imagine that China was going to force Communism on Tibet. Communism could not be enforced in this way on a very backward country" (*Par.*, I, 36).

9. Article 51 of the 1954 Constitution of the PRC states vaguely that "Regional autonomy shall be exercised in areas where national minorities are concentrated and various kinds of autonomy organisations of different nationalities shall be set up according to the size of the respective populations and regions." On the other hand, K.P.S. Menon, a high official in the MEA at the time, states in his autobiography that "The British government of India had undertaken to support the independence of Tibet subject to the suzerainty of China. Independent India had, in a sense, inherited this commitment" (Menon, 1965, 270). For a detailed discussion of China's policy toward minorities in the autonomous regions, and Tibet in particular, see Dreyer, 1976 (of which Chapters 6, 7, and 10 are especially relevant).

10. For a discussion of the absolute nature of state sovereignty in the Chinese view, see also Ogden, 1976, 31–36.

11. Quoted from a Chinese legal journal of April 1958 by Chiu, 1972b, 259.

12. See Chapter 5.

13. For a detailed discussion of the Sino-Burmese negotiations, see Ghatate, 1968; Whittam, 1961.

14. Describing a meeting between the Chinese foreign minister and Swaran Singh in April 1960, Dutt, then a senior official in the MEA, stated that "Burma, according to Chen Yi, conceded that China would not accept the McMahon Line and this made it possible to bring about a settlement which was reasonable and practical" (Dutt, 1977, 127).

15. Bajpai, as early as 1952, had expressed his concern that China would not recognize the McMahon line and raise the issue when it suited its interests, as a formal agreement on the matter had never been signed (letter to India's ambassador to Peking, from Maxwell, 1972; 70–71). He therefore demanded that suitable military preparations be taken and that the matter be negotiated explicitly with the Chinese (Dutt, 1977, 87).

16. For a description and analysis of Nehru's earlier (pre-Communist) encounter with China and its impact on him, see Yang, 1974. See also Sheikh's (1973) content analysis of Chapter 9 of the *Discovery of India*, which points out that all references to possible strategies toward China fall under the category of cooperation.

17. He was a close associate of Nehru for many years.

18. There were rare exceptions such as Frank Moraes and Raja Hutheesing, who wrote more balanced and skeptical reports upon their return.

19. Nehru was impressed by the reception given to him by a million Chinese when he arrived for a state visit in 1954: "It appeared to him almost

an emotional upheaval and represented the basic urge of the people for friendship with India" (Dutt, 1977, 95). He seemed never to have forgotten this reception.

20. The absence of democracy was explained in terms of success in creating a consensus and national unity of the highest order.

21. This state of affairs suited Nehru, as he estimated that India, too, needed at least twenty years of peace, an opinion that he confided to the director of India's Intelligence Bureau (Mullik, 1971, 180–181).

22. And according to Nehru's evaluation, as we have seen, China was supposed to be almost wholly preoccupied with economic issues for the next fifteen to twenty years, or at least until the end of the 1960s.

23. Against this background it is easier to understand the rejection, as early as 1955, of information about the construction of a road in Aksai Chin, given to the Indian ambassador in China and to the Indian foreign ministry in New Delhi, as information concocted by war-mongers (Nayar, 1973, 150).

24. I shall discuss the significance of this phenomenon in Chapter 10, in the context of the dynamics of misperception.

25. Speaking in Parliament, Nehru made the following observation: "Now China is very, very far from normality, and that is our misfortune, and the world's misfortune" (*Par.*, I, 214).

26. See Statistical Appendix, Table A5.

27. For a concise discussion of Lord Curzon's policy in Tibet, see Christi, 1976. For a detailed discussion of the Tibet issue from a Chinese point of view, see Li, 1960. For an explanation of the character of the relationship between the Chinese Empire and Tibet, see, for example, Suzuki, 1968.

28. This is clear from the accusations made by the Indian Communist Party that the Indian representative in Sikkim was the one responsible for subversive activities in Tibet (*Press*, I, 14). As for India itself, it is not certain how aware the government was of the extent of CIA operations. There are those who claim that New Delhi did not know of much of the activities, and that even if the Indian Intelligence Bureau did receive information, it did not pass it on to Nehru. Mullik, the director of the Intelligence Bureau, in describing its activities, said: "It was always my practice only to take up policy matters with the Prime Minister or the Home Minister and never bother them about administrative details" (Mullik, 1971, 241). For a detailed description of the revolt and activities of the CIA in Tibet, see Mullin, 1975; Wise, 1973; Peissel, 1972; Richardson, 1972. For an interpretation of the Chinese view of the affair, see Norbu, 1979; Gurtov and Hwang, 1980.

29. Menon, the minister of defense, admitted a few years later that he had erred in not making it absolutely clear to China that India was not interested in Tibet. The Dalai Lama, he said, could have been treated like an ordinary refugee; the special treatment he received gave rise to the thought that India had not relinquished the idea of a buffer state in Tibet (Brecher, 1968, 146–147; see also Dutt, 1977, 133).

30. And this is why China, in the first stages of the dispute, did try to stress the absurdity and irrationality of deterioration in relations: "It is impossible for the two sides to change the geographical reality of their being neighbours or to break off all contacts along the lengthy boundary line. It is particularly impossible to entertain the absurd idea that our two great friendly neighbours with a combined population of more than one thousand million might start a war over such temporary and local disputes" (*W.P.*,

III, 78). Only when it seemed to the Chinese that there was no more hope, and that force was the only alternative and not a really dangerous one, did they turn to it as a means. By then the contradictions between India and China that were only secondary to the main contradictions—those between China and the United States and the USSR—had become part of the main contradiction as India became closely linked to its sources of support.

31. Against states defined as imperialist, war was ideologically justified.

32. Further support for this argument can be found in Liao, 1974. Liao did not find a correlation between the externalization of internal political problems in China and its attitude toward India, and he points out that the variable explaining most of China's attitude toward India in the years 1960–1961 was India's military activity. Further evidence of this can be seen in the fact that during the entire dispute, including the period September–November 1962, there was not a single mass campaign held against New Delhi as there had been against the United States, Taiwan, and Japan, indicating that the Chinese continued to exercise toward India a state-to-state diplomacy and not a people's diplomacy, and did not use the issue for internal purposes. For another approach claiming that the Sino-Indian dispute was used for internal purposes, see Simmonds, 1972, 96.

33. See Statistical Appendix, Table A4.

34. For details on the proposal, see Maxwell, 1972, 163–166.

35. See Dalvi's (1969, 152) evaluation of its effectiveness in collecting information in the border areas. Of the same opinion is Lieutenant-Colonel Saigal, who served in the area at the time (1979, 42–43).

36. In August 1962 the commander of the western sector, in a letter to New Delhi, warned that the Forward Policy was a disaster. In September he received the answer that the policy had proved itself.

37. See Statistical Appendix, Table A10.

38. See Statistical Appendix, Table A14.

39. See Statistical Appendix, Table A10.

40. See Statistical Appendix, Table A10.

41. See Statistical Appendix, Table A12.

42. See Statistical Appendix, Table A11.

43. See Statistical Appendix, Tables A13 and A16.

44. See Statistical Appendix, Table A17.

45. See Statistical Appendix, Table A10; Gurtov and Hwang, 1980, 139–141.

46. Compare Tables A18 and A21 in the Statistical Appendix.

47. In contrast to the lack of connection that we saw earlier between action orientations and perceptions of threat and hostility.

48. See Statistical Appendix, Tables A19 and A20.

Chapter 7

1. See Chapter 1.

2. This will be discussed at length in the following chapters.

3. It was especially noticeable in the letters of the Chinese government to the Indian government after July 1962 (*W.P.*, VII, 10; 64; 88; 72; 92).

4. Even though he had pneumonia, he would probably not have left his post in anticipation of a state of emergency, most likely continuing instead to carry the supreme military responsibility for the North-East Frontier Agency (NEFA).

Chapter 8

1. Krishna Menon, the Indian minister of defense at that time, is quoted as saying: "We were all the time either because of lack of knowledge of these matters, or because the regions concerned were far away, or for other reasons, trying not to look upon it as a major conflict but as something we could resolve eventually" (Dalvi, 1969, 42).

2. See also Kulkarni, 1969, 547.

3. See also the comments of a family friend on the subject of Nehru's health (Seton, 1967, 325). On the occasion of Nehru's visit to the United States in 1961, he gave the impression of "an old man, his energies depleted, who heard things as at a great distance and answered most questions with indifference" (Schlesinger, 1965, 485).

4. The difficulty can be seen in the description of the problems of gathering information even in Tibet, which was a relatively convenient intelligence target, being nearby and easy to penetrate due to topographical conditions (Mullik, 1971, 195).

5. This happened following a serious failure of the military intelligence. The Intelligence Bureau belonged to the Home Ministry but its director reported chiefly to the prime minister, and it seems that the bureau was not very keen on taking upon itself the additional burden (Subrahamanyam, 1970a, 282).

6. This unrealistic self-appraisal, on the part of the man responsible to a large degree for the mistakes of Nehru and his associates, gives us a glimpse into the failure of the Intelligence Bureau that Mullik headed since its establishment.

7. In 1956 an additional body called the Joint Intelligence Organization was established. Its job was to aid the Ministry of Defense in gathering nonsecret material. It was divided into two units: the eastern branch, which concentrated on China, and the western branch, which dealt with Pakistan. The organization had a very modest research team, and it was meant to receive material from the various intelligence agencies. Its function, however, was very minor.

8. A further verification of this claim can be found in the words of Mullik himself, according to whom military commanders were bothered by the overindependence of the Intelligence Bureau and its activities in the border area, claiming that its provocativeness would drag China into war. See Mullik, 1971, 244 for a description of the meeting held by the prime minister on September 23, 1959.

9. For a detailed discussion of Nehru's attitude toward military personnel, see Chapter 11.

10. See also Subrahamanyam, 1976 and the testimony of Brigadier Dalvi, who stressed that the Chinese did not even try to interfere with Indian reconnaissance planes flying over their installations in Tibet (Dalvi, 1969, 153–154). Thus, there was no lack of information about Chinese forces, their size, and their layout in Tibet. Indeed, a report by Lieutenant-General Henderson-Brooks, which examined the background to the Indian defeat, came to the same conclusions (see Nayar, 1969, 225–226).

11. According to T.N. Kaul, a senior diplomat who worked closely with Nehru for many years: "His [Nehru's] method was to look at a problem in

a world perspective, as it affected India's own national interests, India's relations with other countries and world peace" (1979, 83).

12. This shows Mullik's claim—namely, that both the MEA and the army command in New Delhi received both the raw material and the evaluations (Mullik, 1971, 195)—to be irrelevant. It was Mullik who decided which intelligence material and which evaluations these organizations would receive. In addition, it should be remembered that the senior officials of the MEA and, after General Thimayya's retirement, the senior personnel at army headquarters were either close in their views to Nehru's own or did not dare disagree with him, as we shall see shortly. Thus, provision of intelligence material to these men created only the illusion of a consensus. Indeed, it actually increased reliance on Mullik's one-sided evaluations and hence prevented the possibility of constructive criticism.

13. Whiting claims that on the practical level, too, the Chinese acted as they had in Korea. There was a week between each tactical move and a month between major moves. For example, on September 13 the Chinese suggested reopening the negotiations, on September 20 they initiated a massive incident, and on October 20 the war broke out (Whiting, 1972, 59). This elaborate signaling was meant to enable the Indian opponent to weigh his steps and respond as desired.

14. See, for example, *P.R.*, Sept. 28, 1962. On October 14 an article appeared in the *Renmin Ribao* entitled: "Mr. Nehru Should Pull Back from the Brink." It was republished on October 19—a day before the Chinese attack—in the *Peking Review*. It should also be noted that until then the Chinese press had used the term "Frontier Guards," whereas in this article they referred to "Comrades, commanders and fighters of the PLA."

15. That, at least, is what the Indians thought.

16. This happened also in other conflicts in which China was involved and in which efforts at conflict management failed, as in Korea. For a detailed analysis of conflict management by China, see Chan, 1978; Bobrow *et al.*, 1979, 71–75.

17. It is possible that when the Chinese leadership realized it had lost its deterrent effectiveness following the Indian government's ignoring of its warnings, it saw a potential bonus in a short war with India—namely, the regaining of its credibility and the improvement of its bargaining powers in the international arena on subjects close to home, such as Indochina and Taiwan.

18. A further verification of this analysis can be found in a study that showed, on the basis of a quantitative analysis of the correspondence between the two countries, that to a certain extent they both operated as closed systems. In other words, in the period $t + 1$, the behavior of China was more closely connected to its own behavior than with that of India—and likewise in the case of India (Duncan and Siverson, 1975, 371).

Chapter 9

1. Thus, the British border policy had pragmatic political significance that could be adapted when needed. But when Nehru adopted a certain territorial policy, he became bound to it by his national feelings; national territory had become part and parcel of his concept of self-determination.

2. A case in point was Nehru's inability to accept the fact that the Chinese leadership, which had formed both on the military and political levels a centralist social and organizational system, had difficulty in regarding the anti-Chinese activity in India following the revolt in Tibet as private acts dissociated from Nehru's government. Nehru's denials of the claim that the Indian government had initiated these incidents were flatly rejected, as were his claims that he could not force the activists to stop their activity.

3. Morarji Desai, a member of Nehru's Cabinet, mentions that Nehru "used at times to give up a correct position in order to please the crowd . . . he was always afraid of being unpopular" (Desai, 1974, 217).

4. See also Kulkarni, 1969, 345, and the words spoken by Nehru in an interview given in 1960, in which he admitted that he had changed in this respect and had come back to religion in one way or another (Karanjia, 1960, 32–33).

5. It is interesting to note that in Hindi the word *kol* means both today and tomorrow.

6. Italics are mine.

7. For a discussion of Nehru's need for a consistent conceptual system, see Chapter 10.

8. This is part of a tradition of consensual politics at the intra-state level. See Rana, 1976, 170 for further analysis.

9. Although some of them, at least, adopted Nehru's world view because of their similar education and background.

10. Especially insofar as Nehru, according to a close associate "was not able to reconcile himself to any opposition in any matter where he wanted to act in a particular manner" (Desai, 1974, 147).

11. One prominent scholar describes it as "[a tendency] not to differentiate too sharply between the actual and the ideal or between fact and imagination or fantasy" (Nakamura, 1964, 136).

12. Nehru was described as "a man who treasured words as a courtesan treasures jewels" (Collins and Lapierre, 1976, 103).

13. Hindu thought deals extensively with the idea that man has repeated chances (Radhakrishnan, 1949, 126). This is also the source of the notion that time tends to work in the individual's favor, thus leading to an optimistic frame of mind.

14. Nehru's biographer emphasized the fact that with Nehru in particular, the gap between words and actions was prominent (Brecher, 1959, 624).

15. This point is related to the view mentioned earlier concerning the substance of things changing slightly.

16. This, too, fit the Western political liberal culture that he absorbed at a later stage when living in Europe.

17. This concept was also at the root of nonalignment, according to Nehru: "Now what is this co-existence? It is a mental or spiritual attitude which synthesizes difference and contradiction, tries to understand and accommodate different religions, ideologies, political, social and economic systems, and refuses to think in terms of conflict or military solutions" (Karanjia, 1960, 89).

18. For example, while talking to an enlarged Central Workers Conference on January 30, 1962, Mao declared: "Marxism-Leninism is truth, it cannot be resisted" (Schram, 1974, 181).

19. But it is also a component of traditional Chinese thinking (Nakamura, 1964, 204).

20. An excellent and comprehensive discussion of this point can be found in Rana, 1976, 161–171.

21. The lines are quoted in Hay, 1970, 146.

22. I am grateful to Mr. Roy Tsung from Stanford University for pointing out to me this differentiation in the connotations of the two words.

23. Nehru discovered that this was indeed the situation of late. In May 1959 he said in Parliament: "we talk of autonomy to Tibet. So do the Chinese, but a doubt creeps into my mind as to whether the meaning I attach to it is the same as they attach to it" (*Par.*, I, 53–54).

24. Peace might be a "facade" on which the structure of an unjust and exploitative social and economic order relies. See Kim, 1979, 55–66; Bobrow *et al.*, 1979, 110.

25. Now referred to as social-imperialism.

26. Asoka, who was smitten by remorse at the thought of all the blood he had shed in his wars, yielded up the use of arms and, under the influence of Buddhism, turned to adventures and victories in other spheres, even giving up the conquest of the southern tip of the subcontinent, which he could easily have achieved (Nehru, 1951, 112–115).

27. For a detailed discussion of Nehru's attitude toward violence, see Chapter 10.

28. This approach is evident in Nehru's writings (Nehru, 1941; 1951).

29. As opposed to his macro-historical understanding.

30. For example, the lack of understanding that Chinese passivity at the beginning of the 1950s in face of one-sided Indian moves to delimit the boundary was not an expression of China's acceptance of these moves, but an expression of the Chinese historical experience. In the nineteenth century, Imperial China lost enormous territories because it had negotiated with Russia from a weak bargaining position.

31. See also *W.P.*, IV, 11. India, of course, flatly rejected this claim and counterclaimed that actually the borders of the Chinese Empire were at the time fixed through imperialist expansion (*W.P.*, V, 37). As a result of the discomfort caused India by this Chinese claim, Nehru claimed in the early stages of the dispute that he would prefer that the term *McMahon line* not be used, as it connoted an external imposition (*Press*, I, 50).

32. See, for example, an interview Nehru gave in 1960 in which he expressed these role conditions most clearly (Karanjia, 1960, 100–101).

33. In the past this had led to military confrontations between the two cultures in Southeast Asia.

34. A document distributed in 1961 in Chinese embassies abroad stated: "The Chinese would unite with all forces which were available and would deal with American Imperialism as the main enemy. Within this broad framework, the country against which the Chinese would have to struggle chiefly was India" (quoted by Khera, 1968, 136).

Chapter 10

1. "As often happened in Indian families of those days, the lack of companionship between husband and wife led to the mother building her life and her affection round her son" (Gopal, 1975, 16).

2. Nehru picked up much of the Hindu culture and tradition in his childhood, through the women of the house (Gopal, 1975, 16; Mende, 1956, 9).

3. Carlos Romulo, the foreign minister of the Phillipines, in describing the Bandung Conference, said that although Nehru impressed the delegates with his intellect, he was arrogant and rigid (Romulo, 1956, 11). Eisenhower said of Nehru that he tended to think everyone in the wrong except himself.

4. Quoted by Burke, 1974, 91–92.

5. See Chapter 8.

6. This tendency carried special weight, given that Nehru did not excel in his judgment of people (Kaul, 1967, 312–313).

7. He used this to manipulate other people. As Desai notes, "seven or eight times out of ten he used to feign anger in order to make other men submit to him" (1974, 215).

8. See also Subhan, 1968, 132.

9. Azad, one of his colleagues, said about him that "he is at times apt to be carried away by his feelings. Not only so, but sometimes he is so impressed by theoretical considerations that he is apt to underestimate the realities of the situation" (quoted in Gopal, 1975, 327).

10. Nehru was isolated from his peers since childhood and as a young man was quite lonely. This lack of intimacy in his life was compensated by his close attachment to the masses. "It was in this context that Nehru received the emotional support generally lacking in his private life" (Wood, 1974, 111).

11. This topic will be discussed at length in Chapter 11.

12. He was especially influenced by the behavior of the Emperor Asoka, one of the great Buddhist emperors of India who gave up personal and national power for moral principles (Nehru, 1942, 61–65). The moral precepts of Buddhism so impressed him that, already in the 1950s, he said to one of his associates: "No orthodox religion attracts me, but if I had to choose, it would certainly be Buddhism" (quoted in: Brecher, 1959, 606).

13. This motif is repeated time and again by Nehru. See *Press*, I, 58; 78.

14. In Nehru's mind, foreign policy was his area of special contribution to India, or in his own words: "Where I come in is rather in regard to external affairs" (Mende, 1956, 127).

15. The two terms are basic to the values of Gandhi's doctrine, which were taken from Buddhist and Hindu philosophy.

16. M. Seton (1967, 315–317), a close friend of the Nehru family, describes how very unhappy and reluctant Nehru was about the issue of the use of force to liberate Goa.

17. See Statistical Appendix, Table A5.

18. The problem stemmed from the fact that Nehru saw himself belonging concurrently to two cultures—the Indian national culture, which committed him to an emphasis on egoistic nationalist values, and the universal international culture, the values of which were expressed in organizations such as the United Nations and which emphasized altruism. Nehru believed that in the final analysis a partnership between the two was possible. However, as we shall see, this is not how it worked out.

19. See also *Par.*, I, 135; 280; *Par.*, II, 98; 118.

20. According to Nehru: "He [Gandhi] did not give up any essentials, but he would compromise on the non-essentials" (Mende, 1956, 22).

21. But it should be stressed that, however close his views came to those of Gandhi, he was never a carbon copy of his great teacher (see also Lal, 1970, 256).

22. Consequently, Nehru attempted to explain that India's involvement in Nepal was established only in order to protect it and was not connected with any attempt to change the face of the Nepalese political system.

23. A similar opinion was expressed in later stages of the dispute when Nehru flatly rejected the possibility of receiving military aid and demanded that India be satisfied with its own resources.

24. For example, the defense minister or the director of the Intelligence Bureau.

25. See Statistical Appendix, Table A3.

26. This approach was in line with both the traditional Hindu view, which stressed the primacy of long-range cycles, as well as the influence of Marx, Engels, and Lasky on Nehru's thinking.

27. See Table 10.2.

28. Similarly, because the United States was defined as capitalist and imperialist, Nehru adopted toward it an attitude of suspicion and distrust, despite the fact that it gave India economic aid on a large scale and supported India in its dispute with China.

29. We can see in the preference for a certain position toward an object also a possible source of the preference for information coming from objects close and acceptable to Nehru, even in situations demanding that greater attention be paid to information coming from less popular but more relevant sources, such as the evaluations and warnings from field commanders with the worsening of the dispute.

30. For a theoretical analysis of most of these techniques, see Abelson, 1959.

31. The Chinese accepted this assessment in full, and the editorial was quoted in *P.R.*, Sept. 14, 1962, 10. As can be observed in *P.R.*, July 27, 1962, 12, the Chinese carefully followed Indian verbalizations on the dispute appearing in the press and in Parliament.

32. An interesting expression of the need for consistency among and within values, positions, and actions can be found in Nehru's autobiography, in which he devoted a chapter to explaining what seemed to him similar inconsistencies and contradictions in Gandhi's thinking (Nehru, 1941, 318–325).

Chapter 11

1. As in 1954, in the rescue mission of a number of soldiers trapped in difficult mountainous terrain in the northeastern sector during a blizzard (see Kaul, 1967, 160–169).

2. Consequently, this talented officer resigned from the army. It should be remembered, however, that Menon was appointed to his position to prevent the politicization of the Indian army; although his policy did weaken India militarily, it served well Nehru's political objectives. However, in his speech in Parliament, Nehru assured the public that the procedure for appointing senior officers operated optimally, and he wished he could say the same about the civil service.

3. In a letter to one of the newspapers published by a group of officers, it was alleged that Menon was attempting to surround himself with officers

personally loyal to him. The letter was signed "Demoralized Army Officers" (Maxwell, 1972, 197).

4. Kaul, as part of his duties as CGS, was in charge of coordination, planning, operations, training, intelligence, and weapons acquisition. Both the director of military intelligence and the director of military operations were under him. His job was thus one of the key positions in the Indian army, and he himself became a key figure in the information-processing apparatus.

5. Following the defeat of 1962, he was "remembered" by the Defense Ministry and was appointed to the post of commander of the Fourth Corps. Later, he commanded the eastern sector, and in 1969 he was nominated army chief of staff. At present, following his retirement from the Indian army, he carries the highest rank ever accorded an Indian officer, that of field marshall.

6. At the same time, a whispering campaign against him, similar to that against Thimayya, was started regarding his intention to plan a military coup. The Intelligence Bureau investigated the matter but found no evidence to support it. Nevertheless, his pension was suspended for a year and returned to him only after he protested directly to Nehru.

7. The suspicious approach of officialdom to the military finds expression in the accusations of the ex-Cabinet Secretary, who claimed that in Thimayya's time leading army figures tried to make direct contact with the minister of defense over the heads of the civilian bureaucracy, whom they regarded with contempt in the Kitchner tradition. This tradition saw the civilian bureaucracy only as a rubber stamp for military decisions (Khera, 1968, 75).

8. The one academic institute that dealt extensively at the time with foreign policy issues was the Indian Council on World Affairs, which was led by H.N. Kunzru. It had very little, if any, influence on and access to decisionmaking and decisionmakers in this field. Moreover, its scholars had no more information about military affairs than was made available to other segments of the public. (Only after the 1962 war was an Institute for Strategic Studies and Analyses established; this institute also began to issue a journal on the problems of defense and strategy.)

9. Proof of Kaul's ability to bring about changes of policy can be seen in the fact that he was the only one able to have Operation Leghorn postponed on October 11, after being appointed commander of the Fourth Corps. Dalvi says of Kaul's special status: "In 1962 only Kaul's advice mattered" (Dalvi, 1969, 245).

10. Although Nehru never referred to it explicitly, he was careful to avoid any step that would indicate clearly who his successor would be. When he left the country, he avoided appointing a deputy for just that reason. While Pant was alive he filled Nehru's place, but after his death in 1961, when Nehru went on one of his frequent trips abroad, a vacuum was created in the decisionmaking process.

11. When Menon was appointed minister of defense, he remained informally responsible for certain foreign affairs matters, such as Kashmir, Goa, and UN affairs (Reid, 1981, 187).

12. This was the result of two factors: (a) a major part of his public career was in diplomacy, and (b) as Nehru's many preoccupations prevented him from dealing with all aspects of foreign policy, he tended to leave some to his most ardent loyalist, Menon.

13. "It was my experience that Jawaharlalji could make Shri Krishna Menon accept his point of view whenever he thought it necessary, and Shri Menon always agreed to do what he was asked by Jawaharlalji" (Desai, 1974, 145). An episode that illustrates just how much Menon held Nehru in awe is recalled by Seton. Menon was not happy about Nehru's departure for Ceylon on October 12, 1962, when tension on the border was at its height. Up to the last moment, he tried to summon the courage to ask Nehru to stay, but he did not manage to do so (Seton, 1967, 331). Menon had demonstrated more than once an almost hysterical fear of losing Nehru's affection and esteem. (See, for example, his letters to M.O. Matahi of August 7, 1951 and to Nehru of February 12, 1953, quoted in Gopal, 1979, 142; 146.)

14. Such were, for example, Panikkar, India's first ambassador to China, and Gopal, the director of the historical division at the MEA as well as a noted historian and the son of Professor Radhakrishan, a noted philosopher.

15. Morarji Desai considered himself a potential successor to Nehru. Nehru, however, had reservations because of his political views, and in 1962 he prevented his election to the post of deputy party president. On the other hand, he supported the appointment of J. Ram, the minister of railways, to the post. Menon also had a hand in this move, which increased the hatred between the two—so much so that they stopped greeting each other altogether. This made things difficult for the army given that, because of the personal rivalry between the two, there were sometimes delays in budgetary transfers involved in the financing of defense expenditures. Patil also hated Menon and was hostile toward his pro-Soviet and anti-U.S. orientation. He was also politically independent of Nehru; moreover, as the party leader in Bombay, he had a strong and independent power base.

16. Interestingly enough, he had serious political disagreements, often with those he needed to lean on. Such was the case with Mahatma Ghandi, his father, and Patel.

17. Members of both committees were appointed by Nehru; in the years of the dispute with China, he used to bring to the meetings of the Foreign Affairs Committee some of the MEA officials to whom he was close, such as S. Gopal, S. Dutt, J.S. Mehta, and M.J. Desai.

18. Nehru's letters to the Chinese government were brought for formal approval to the Foreign Affairs Committee.

19. Nehru not only did not consult with Cabinet members, but at times he made decisions that they became aware of only through reading about them in the press.

20. The Cabinet committee's inability to serve at such a forum was expressed by the fact that, after Pant's death, they never met when Nehru was away from the country, including September 1962 when tensions were high.

21. Mullik enjoyed Pant's full confidence (Mullik, 1971, 192–193).

22. Thus, for example, in one of India's most important newspapers, a military evaluation was published in which India's fire power was described as greater than that of the Chinese along the entire border. The Indian army's logistic situation was estimated to be equal to that of the Chinese, and generally it was thought that Chinese troops in the Himalaya area would not be able to challenge the Indian forces (*Times of India,* May 5, 1961).

23. Some evidence of the effect that proper information might have had on the opposition's stand can be found in the words of Vajpayee, who was in his time one of the chief spokesmen of the Parliamentary opposition, as a member of Parliament for the Jana Sangh, and one of the most extreme hawks on the China question. In an interview in October 1977, he said: "Sometimes one wonders whether the Forward Policy of Nehru was correct when we were not ready or able to push out the aggressor" (*Far Eastern Economic Review*, October 7, 1977, 32).

24. Until May 1961. His successor, Sinha, was much less intimate with Nehru.

25. Pant also participated in the formulation of the Indian government's letters to China. The letters were written by Dutt (and afterwards by M.J. Desai), checked by Nehru and Pant, and approved by the Committee.

26. Menon objected vehemently to Gopal's historical approach and once told him to go to hell with his historical evidence (Hoffmann, 1971, 784). The optimistic camp included a number of diplomats not counted among Nehru's intimate circle, such as R.K. Nehru, India's ambassador to China in the mid-1950s; K.P.S. Menon, India's ambassador to the USSR (Menon, 1963, 320); and T.N. Kaul, one of India's representatives to the 1954 talks. These men saw themselves as the architects of friendship with China.

27. For a critical view on the sense of elitism that prevailed in the MEA, see the recollections of one of its most senior members, Kaul (1979, 85).

28. It should be remembered that until 1959 NEFA was administered by the MEA and, following the Longju incident, was brought under army responsibility (despite the civilian echelon's reluctance); after the Kongka Pass Incident in October 1959, the western sector was also brought under army control.

29. Thus it happened that with the infiltration of the Chinese beyond the Thag La Ridge, "the Thagla incursion was gradually allowed to become the battle for the survival of those responsible for India's China policy" (Dalvi, 1969, 184).

30. The first was considered universal, idealistic, and open-minded, whereas the second was considered narrow, materialistic, and, of course, anachronistic and erroneous.

31. For example, the increase of defense expenditures or joining a Western pact.

Chapter 12

1. For a leader who had such clearcut convictions, ideology, and certainty as to what the future should, could, and would be, hindsight and foresight often blended into one. Insofar as the future was no more difficult to predict and seemed almost no less certain than the past, factors that might have contributed to the emergence of different futures than the one foreseen were underestimated.

2. Given that the China issue was perceived as related to and touching on most of the core values and other issue-areas. See also Seton, 1967, 332.

3. These factors refer principally to the crisis that preceded the outbreak of war, that is, the Chinese crossing of the Thag La Ridge.

4. In the correlation matrix of Nehru's psychological environment, we find relatively many interrelated components. See Statistical Appendix, Table A1.

5. This phenomenon clearly contradicts Verba's (1969) hypothesis, which suggests that individuals who attach greater value to rationality are less bound to fall prey to the consequences of nonrational personality needs and motives.

6. See Statistical Appendix, Tables A12 and A13.

Bibliography

Official Publications and Documents

Das, D. (Ed.) (1974), *Sardar Patels Correspondence 1945–50,* Vol. X, Phmedabad: Navajivan Publishing House.

Gooch, G.P., and Temperley, H. (Eds.) (1929), *British Documents on the Origins of the War,* 1898–1914, Vol. IV, London: H.M. Stationery Office.

India, Government of, Ministry of External Affairs (1959–1963), *Notes, Memoranda and Letters Exchanged and Agreements Signed Between the Government of India and China: White Paper,* Vols. I–VIII, New Delhi: Government of India, Ministry of External Affairs. [Referred to in text and notes as *W.P.*]

India, Government of, Ministry of External Affairs (1961–1962), *Prime Minister on Sino-Indian Relations: In Parliament,* New Delhi: Government of India Press (2 parts). [Referred to in text and notes as *Par.*]

India, Government of, Ministry of External Affairs (1961–1962), *Prime Minister on Sino-Indian Relations: In Press Conferences,* New Delhi: Government of India Press (2 Parts). [Referred to in text and notes as *Press*]

India, Government of (1961), *Report of the Officials of the Governments of India and the People's Republic of China on the Boundary Question,* New Delhi: Government of India.

International Commission of Jurists (1960), *Tibet and the Chinese People's Republic,* Geneva.

International Commission of Jurists (1959), *Tibet and the Role of Law,* Geneva.

Lok Sabha Secretariat (1959), *Foreign Policy of India: Text of Documents* (2nd ed.), New Delhi: Government of India.

Nehru J. (1964), *Jawaharlal Nehru's Speeches September 1957–April 1963,* New Delhi: Government of India, Publications Division.

——— (1958), *Jawaharlal Nehru's Speeches: March 1953–August 1957,* New Delhi: Government of India, Publications Division.

——— (1954), *Jawaharlal Nehru's Speeches: August 1949–February 1953,* New Delhi: Government of India, Publications Division.

——— (1949), *Jawaharlal Nehru's Speeches: September 1946–May 1949,* New Delhi: Government of India, Publications Division.

——— (1957–1962), *Fortnightly Letters* (not previously published). [Referred to in text and notes as *F.N.*]

————— (1962) *The Sino-Indian Boundary Question* (enlarged ed.), Peking: Foreign Language Press.

Newspapers and Magazines

New York Times, 1959–1962.

Peking Review [P.R.], in chronological order:

Renmin Ribao (*People's Daily*), editorial (1959), "The Revolution in Tibet and Nehru's Philosphy," *P.R.,* Vol. II, May 12, No. 19, pp. 6–15.

Editorial (1959), "The Crux of the Boundary Question," *P.R.,* Vol. II, Sept. 15, No. 37, p. 3.

Renmin Ribao, editorial (1959), "The Truth of the Matter," *P.R.,* Vol. II, Sept. 15, No. 37, pp. 9–12.

(1959), "Vice Premier Chen Yi's Speech to Standing Committee of the National People's Congress," *P.R.,* Vol. II, Sept. 15, No. 37, pp. 14–15.

(1959), "Chinese Foreign Ministry Statement," *P.R.,* Vol. II, Nov. 3, No. 44, pp. 7–9.

(1960), "Premier Chou En-lai's Written Statement," *P.R.,* Vol. III, May 3, No. 18, pp. 18–19.

(1960), "Chou's Press Conference in New Delhi," *P.R.,* Vol. III, May 3, No. 18, pp. 19–22.

Renmin Ribao, editorial (1960), "Common Aspirations of 1,000 Million People," *P.R.,* Vol. III, May 3, No. 18, pp. 23–25.

Hongqi, editorial department of (1960), "Long Live Leninism!" *P.R.,* Vol. III, April 26, No. 17, pp. 6–23.

Renmin Ribao (1961), "The Truth About the Nehru-Instigated Anti-Chinese Campaign in India," *P.R.,* Vol. IV, Dec. 15, No. 50, pp. 11–14.

(1961), "Chen Yi's Television Interview with Canadian Newsmen," *P.R.,* Vol. IV, July 14, No. 28, pp. 8–11.

Hsiao Leng (1962), "What the Results of India's General Elections Show," *P.R.,* Vol. V, March 23, No. 12, pp. 10–12.

(1962), "Statement of Information Department of China's Foreign Ministry, *P.R.,* Vol. V, April 20, No. 16, p. 10.

Hsinhau (1962), "Summary of the Report of Chinese and Indian Officials," *P.R.,* Vol. V., May 4, No. 18, pp. 18–20.

Chou Chun-li (1962), "New Delhi's Dangerous Game," *P.R.,* Vol. V, June 8, No. 23, pp. 8–10.

(1962), "Indian Government Should Rein-In on the Brink of the Precipice," *P.R.,* Vol. V, July 13, No. 28, pp. 10–11.

Chou Chun-li (1962), "Sino-Indian Situation Worsens," *P.R.,* Vol. V, July 20, No. 29, pp. 14–16.

Renmin Ribao, Observer (1962), "The Indian Authorities Must Not Miscalculate," *P.R.,* Vol. V, July 27, No. 30, pp. 12–14.

(1962), "India's Deliberate Military Provocations," *P.R.,* Vol. V, July 27, No. 30, p. 14.

Chang Chi (1962), "Sino-Indian Boundary Question," *P.R.,* Vol. V, August 17, No. 33, pp. 5–7.

Chou Chun-li (1962), "Peaceful Settlement New Delhi Style," *P.R.,* Vol. V, Sept. 14, No. 37, pp. 9–11.

Chou Chun-li (1962), "New Delhi's Latest Dangerous Move," *P.R.,* Vol. V, Sept. 28, No. 39, pp. 13–14.

Renmin Ribao, editorial (1962), "Some Questions to the Indian Authorities," *P.R.,* Vol. V, Oct. 12, No. 41, pp. 7–9.

Renmin Ribao, editorial (1962), "Mr. Nehru Should Pull Back from the Brink," *P.R.,* Vol. V, Oct. 19, No. 42, pp. 6–7.

Renmin Ribao, Observer (1962), "It Is Nehru Who Refused to Negotiate; It Is Also Nehru Who Gives the Order to Fight," *P.R.,* Vol. V, Oct. 26, No. 43, pp. 8–11.

(1962), "U.S. 'Aid' and India's Anti-Chinese Campaign," *P.R.,* Vol. V, Oct. 26, No. 43, p. 15.

Renmin Ribao, editorial (1962), "Fair and Reasonable Proposals," *P.R.,* Vol. V, Nov. 2, No. 22, pp. 8–10.

Renmin Ribao, editorial (1962), "More on Nehru's Philosophy in Light of the Sino-Indian Boundary Question," *P.R.,* Vol. V, Nov. 2, No. 44, pp. 10–22.

Chu Pao-ju (1962), "New Delhi Prepares Further Attacks on China," *P.R.,* Vol. V, Nov. 9, No. 45, pp. 20–22.

Renmin Ribao, Observer (1962), "The Pretense of Nonalignment Falls Away," *P.R.,* Vol. V, Nov. 16, No. 46, pp. 5–7.

Chou En-lai (1962), "Letter to Leaders of Asian and African Countries," *P.R.,* Vol. V, Nov. 30, Nos. 47–48, pp. 7–15.

Hongqi, editorial (1962), "Why is the Nehru Government Still Rejecting Peaceful Negotiations?" *P.R.,* Vol. V, Nov. 30, Nos. 47–48, pp. 16–19.

Renmin Ribao, editorial department of (1963), "The Truth About How the CPSU Leaders Ally with India Against China," *P.R.,* Vol. VI, Nov. 8, No. 45, pp. 18–27.

Times of India, 1959–1962.

Secondary Sources

Abelson, R.P. (1959), "Modes of Resolution of Belief Dilemmas," *Journal of Conflict Resolution,* 3:343–352.

Adelman, M.L. (1973), "Crisis Decision-Making and Cognitive Balance," *Sage Professional Papers in International Studies,* 1:02–002, Beverly Hills, Calif.: Sage Publications, pp. 61–94.

Adie, W.A.C. (1972), *Chinese Strategic Thinking Under Mao Tse-Tung,* Canberra Papers on Strategy and Defence, No. 13.

――――― (1962), "China, Russia and the Third World," *China Quarterly,* 16:86–98.

Adorno, T.W., Frenkel-Brunswick, E., Levinson, D.N., and Sanford, R.N. (1950), *The Authoritarian Personality,* New York: Harper & Row.

Allison, G.T. (1971), *The Essence of Decision,* Boston: Little, Brown & Company.

――――― (1969), "Conceptual Models and the Cuban Missile Crisis," *American Political Science Review,* 64:689–718.

Allison, G.T., and Halperin, M.H. (1972) "Bureaucratic Politics," *World Politics,* 24; supplement edited by Tanter, R., and Ullman, R.H., *On Theory and Policy in International Relations,* pp. 40–79.

Allport, G.W., and Postman, L. (1972), *The Psychology of Rumor,* New York: Russell & Russell.

Alsop, J. (1962), "On China's Descending Spiral," *China Quarterly,* 12:21–37.

Apsler, R., and Sears, D.O. (1968), "Warning Personal Involvement and Attitude Change," *Journal of Personality and Social Psychology*, 9:162–166.

Armstrong, J.D. (1977), *Revolutionary Diplomacy*, Berkeley: University of California Press.

Aronson, E., and Golden, B.W. (1962), "The Effect of Relevant and Irrelevant Aspects of Communication Credibility on Opinion Change," *Journal of Personality*, 30:135–146.

Arora, R.S. (1961), "The Sino-Indian Conflict: A Study of Diplomatic Manoeuvres," *International Spectator*, 19:1605–1628.

Arora, S.K., and Lasswell, H.D. (1969), *Political Communication*, New York: Holt, Rinehart & Winston.

Ashe, G. (1969), *Gandhi*, New York: Stein and Day.

Atkins, A.L., Deaux, K.K., and Bieri, J. (1967), "Latitude of Acceptance and Attitude Change," *Journal of Personality and Social Psychology*, 6:47–54.

Axelrod, R. (1976), *Structure of Decision*, Princeton, N.J.: Princeton University Press.

———— (1973), "Schema Theory: An Information Processing Model of Perception and Cognition," *American Political Science Review*, 67:1248–1266.

Ayoob, M. (1970), "India and Nepal: Politics of Aid and Trade," *Institute for Defense Studies and Analyses Journal*, 2:127–156.

———— (1968), "India as a Factor in Sino-Pakistani Relations," *International Studies*, 3:279–300.

Ayub, A.S. (1963), "Reflections on the Chinese Invasion: The Silver Lining," *Quest*, 36:46–52.

Bandyopadhyaya, J. (1970), *The Making of India's Foreign Policy*, New Delhi: Allied Publishers.

———— (1962), "China, India and Tibet," *India Quarterly*, 18:382–393.

Baxter, C. (1967), *The Jana Sangh*, Philadelphia: University of Pennsylvania Press.

Belfiglio, V.J. (1972), "India's Economic and Political Relations with Bhutan," *Asian Survey*, 12:676–685.

Bennett, J.P. (1975), "Foreign Policy as Maladaptive Behavior: Operationalizing Some Implications," *Papers of the Peace Science Society (International)*, 25:85–104.

Betts, R.K. (1978), "Analysis, War and Decision: Why Intelligence Failures Are Inevitable," *World Politics*, 31:61–89.

Bhambhri, C.P. (1971), *Bureaucracy and Politics in India*, New Delhi: Vikas.

———— (1968), "The Indian Foreign Service," *Journal of Administration Overseas*, 7:528–537.

Bhargava, G.S. (1964), *The Battle of NEFA; The Undeclared War*, Bombay: Allied Publishers.

Bhat, S. (1967), *India and China*, New Delhi: Popular Book Service.

Bhattacharya, D. (1974), "India and China: Contrast and Comparison 1950–72," *Journal of Contemporary Asia*, 4:339–360.

Bieri, J. (1966), "Cognitive Complexity and Personality Development," in Harvey, O.J. (Ed.), *Experience, Structure and Adaptability*, New York: Springer Publishing Company, pp. 13–37.

Blinkenberg, L. (1972), *India-Pakistan: The History of Unsolved Conflicts*, Copenhagen: Danks Underigspolitisk Institus.

Block, J., and Petersen, B. (1955), "Some Personality Correlates of Confidence, Caution and Speed in Decision Situation," *Journal of Abnormal Social Psychology*, 51:34–41.

Bobrow, D.B. (1966), "The Chinese Communist Conflict System," *Orbis*, 9:930–952.

———— (1964), "Peking's Military Calculus," *World Politics*, 16:287–301.

Bobrow, D.B., Chan, S., and Kringen, J.A. (1979), *Understanding Foreign Policy Decisions: The Chinese Case*, New York: The Free Press.

Bolaraman, K. (1956), "The Indian Press and Foreign Policy," *Journal of International Affairs*, 10:178–184.

Boorman, S.A. (1972), "Deception in Chinese Strategy," in Whitson, W.W. (Ed.), *The Military and Political Power in China in the 1970s*, New York: Praeger, pp. 313–338.

Borisov, O.B., and Koloskov, B.T. (1975), *Sino-Soviet Relations 1945–1970*, Bloomington: Indiana University Press.

Boulding, K.E. (1965), "The Learning and Reality-Testing Process in the International System," in Farrell, J.C., and Smith, A.P. (Eds.), *Image and Reality in World Politics*, New York: Columbia University Press, pp. 1–15.

———— (1956), *The Image*, Ann Arbor: University of Michigan Press.

Brecher, M. (1974), *Decisions in Israel's Foreign Policy*, London: Oxford University Press.

———— (1972), *The Foreign Policy System of Israel*, London: Oxford University Press.

———— (1968), *India and World Politics: Krishna Menon's View of the World*, New York: Praeger.

———— (1967), "Elite Images and Foreign Policy Choices: Krishna Menon's View of the World," *Pacific Affairs*, 40:60–92.

———— (1966), *Nehru's Mantle*, New York: Praeger.

———— (1959), *Nehru: A Political Biography*, London: Oxford University Press.

Brecher, M., Steinberg, B., and Stein, J. (1969), "A Framework for Research on Foreign Policy Behavior," *Journal of Conflict Resolution*, 13:75–101.

Bridgham, P. (1970), "Factionalism in the Central Committee," in Lewis, J.W. (Ed.), *Party Leadership and Revolutionary Power in China*, Cambridge: Cambridge University Press, pp. 203–235.

Brines, R. (1968), *The Indo-Pakistani Conflict*, London: Pall Mall Press.

Brown, M. (1971), "The Diplomatic Development of Nepal," *Asian Survey*, 11:661–676.

Bruner, J.S., and Postman, L. (1948), "Symbolic Value as an Organizing Factor in Perception," *Journal of Social Psychology*, 27:203–208.

Budner, S. (1962), "Intolerance of Ambiguity as a Personality Factor," *Journal of Personality*, 30:29–50.

Burke, S.M. (1974), *Mainsprings of Indian and Pakistani Foreign Policies*, Minneapolis: University of Minnesota Press.

———— (1973), *Pakistan's Foreign Policy*, London: Oxford University Press.

Burnstein, E. (1967), "Source of Cognitive Bias in the Representation of Simple Social Structures," *Journal of Personality and Social Psychology*, 7:36–48.

Byrne, D. (1961), "Interpersonal Attraction and Attitude Similarity," *Journal of Abnormal and Social Psychology*, 62:713–715.

C.S. (1967), "China and the Asian Triangle: An Appraisal of the Sino-Indian Border War," *India Quarterly,* 23:87–105.

Caroe, O. (Sir) (1963), "The Sino-Indian Frontier Dispute," *Asian Review,* 59:67–81.

———— (1961), "The Indian-Chinese Boundary Dispute," *Geographical Journal,* 77:345–346.

Chakravarti, P.C. (1971), *The Evolution of India's Northern Borders,* New York: Asia Publishing House.

———— (1969), "India and the Tibetan Question," *International Studies,* 10:446–463.

———— (1961), *Indian-China Relations,* Calcutta: K.C. Mukhpadhyay.

Chan, S. (1978), "Chinese Conflict Calculus and Behavior: Assessment from a Perspective of Conflict Management," *World Politics,* 30:391–410.

Chari, P.R. (1977), "Civil-Military Relations in India," *Armed Forces and Society,* 4:3–28.

Cheng, C.J. (Ed.), (1966), *The Politics of the Chinese Red Army,* Stanford: Hoover Institution.

———— (1964), "Problems of Chinese Communist Leadership as Seen in the Secret Military Papers," *Asian Survey,* 4:861–872.

Chiu, H. (1972a), "The Nature of International Law and the Problem of a Universal System," in Leng, S.C., and Chiu, H. (Eds.), *Law in Chinese Foreign Policy,* New York: Oceana Publications, pp. 1–35.

———— (1972b), "Comparison of the Nationalist and Communist Views of Unequal Treaties," in Cohen, J.A. (Ed.), *China's Practice of International Law: Some Case Studies,* Cambridge, Mass.: Harvard University Press, pp. 239–267.

———— (1966), "Communist China's Attitude Toward International Law," *American Journal of International Law,* 60:245–267.

Chiu, H., and Edwards, R.R. (1968), "Communist China's Attitude Toward the United Nations," *American Journal of International Law,* 62:20–50.

Chopra, M.K. (1969), *India: The Search for Power,* Bombay: Lalvani Publishing House.

———— (1963), "The Himalayan Border War: An Indian Military View," *Military Review* (May), 43:8–16.

Choudhury, G.W. (1975), *India, Pakistan, Bangladesh and the Major Powers,* New York: The Free Press.

Christi, C. (1976), "Great Britain, China and the Status of Tibet," *Modern Asian Studies,* 10:481–508.

Christol, C.Q. (1968), "Communist China and International Law: Strategy and Tactics," *Western Political Quarterly,* 21:456–467.

Chucri, N. (1969), "The Perceptual Base of Non-alignment," *Journal of Conflict Resolution,* 13:57–74.

Chudhury, N.C. (1965a), "Dichotomy in Hindu Life and Its Impact on India's External Relations," *Quest,* 45:9–16.

———— (1965b) "Dichotomy in Hindu Life: Courage and Intelligence," *Quest,* 46:20–28.

Clarke, P., and James, J. (1967), "The Effects of Situation, Attitude and Intensity and Personality on Information-Seeking," *Sociometry,* 30:235–245.

Class, D.C. (1968), "Theories of Consistency and the Study of Personality," in Borgatta, E.F., and Lambert, W.W. (Eds.), *Handbook of Personality Theory and Research,* Chicago: Rand McNally, pp. 788–854.

Clubb, O.E. (1971), *China and Russia: The "Great Game,"* New York: Columbia University Press.

Cohen, J.A. (1970), "Chinese Attitude to International Law—and Our Own," in Cohen, J.A. (Ed.), *Contemporary Chinese Law: Research Problems and Perspectives,* Cambridge, Mass.: Harvard University Press, pp. 282–293.

Cohen, S.P. (1974), "The Security Policymaking Process in India," in Horton, F.B., III, Rogerson, A.C., and Warner, E.L., III (Eds.), *Comparative Defense Analysis,* Baltimore: The Johns Hopkins University Press, pp. 156–168.

———— (1971a), *The Indian Army: Its Contributions to the Development of a Nation,* Berkeley: University of California Press.

———— (1971b), "India's China War and After," *Journal of Asian Studies,* 30:847–857.

Collins, L., and Lapierre, D. (1976), *Freedom at Midnight,* New York: Avon.

Crabb, C.V. (1968), *Nations in a Multipolar World,* New York: Harper & Row.

Crane, R.D. (1964), "The Sino-Soviet Dispute on War and the Cuban Crisis," *Orbis,* 8:537–549.

Crocker, W. (1966), *Nehru: A Contemporary's Estimate,* London: George Allen and Unwin.

Culbertson, F.M. (1957), "The Modification of an Emotionally Held Attitude Through Role Playing," *Journal of Abnormal and Social Psychology,* 54:30–33.

Dai, S. (1963), "Peking, Katmandu and New Delhi," *China Quarterly,* 16:86–98.

Dalai Lama (1962), *My Land and My People,* New York: McGraw-Hill.

Dalvi, J.S. (Brigadier) (1969), *Himalayan Blunder,* Bombay: Thacker & Co.

Das, M.N. (1961), *The Political Philosophy of Jawaharhal Nehru,* London: George Allen and Unwin.

Das, P.K. (1969), "The Indo-Chinese Crisis and India's Efforts Toward Peacemaking 1959–1966," *International Studies,* 10:303–318.

Dasgupta, S. (1972), *Hindu Ethos and the Challenge of Change,* Calcutta: The Minerva Association.

Datar, A.L. (1972), *India's Economic Relations with the USSR and Eastern Europe 1953 to 1959,* Cambridge: Cambridge University Press.

Desai, M. (1974), *The Story of My Life,* Vol. 2, New Delhi: Macmillan India.

Deutsch, M., and Gerard, H.B. (1955), "A Study of Normative and Informational Social Influence upon Individual Judgment," *Journal of Abnormal and Social Psychology,* 51:629–635.

Dhirendra, N. (1967), "Indian National Character in the 20th Century," *Annals of the American Academy of Political and Social Science,* 370: 124–132.

Diesing, P. (1971), *Patterns of Discovery in the Social Sciences,* Chicago: Aldine.

Dixon, N.R. (1976), *On the Psychology of Military Incompetence,* London: Jonathan Cape.

Dreyer, J.T. (1976), *China's Forty Millions,* Cambridge, Mass.: Harvard University Press.

Duncan, G.T., and Siverson, R. (1975), "Markov Chain Models for Conflict Resolution: Results from Sino-Indian Relations 1959–1964," *International Studies Quarterly,* 19:344–374.

Dutt, S. (1977), *With Nehru in the Foreign Office*, New Delhi: Minerva Publications.

Dutt, D.S. (Major General, retired) (1966), "The Defence of India's Northern Borders," *Adelphi Papers*, No. 25.

Eagly, A.H. (1969), "Responses to Attitude—Discrepant Information as a Function of Intolerance of Inconsistency and Category Width," *Journal of Personality*, 37:601–617.

East, M.A. (1972), "Status Discrepancy and Violence in the International System," in Rosenau, J.N., Davis V., and East, M.A. (Eds.), *The Analysis of International Politics*, New York: The Free Press, pp. 299–310.

Eckstein, A. (1975), *China's Economic Development*, Ann Arbor: The University of Michigan Press.

————— (1972), "Economic Development: Prospect and Problems," *Annals of the American Academy of Political and Social Science*, 402:107–116.

————— (1962), "Comment: On China's Descending Spiral," *China Quarterly*, 12:19–25.

Eckstein, H. (1975), "Case Study and Theory in Political Science," in Greenstein, F.I., and Polsby, N.W. (Eds.), *Handbook of Political Science*, Vol. 7, Reading, Mass.: Addison-Wesley, pp. 79–138.

Edwards, M. (1973), *Nehru: A Political Biography*, Harmondsworth: Pelican Books.

————— (1965), "Illusion and Reality in India's Foreign Policy," *International Affairs*, 41:48–58.

Erdman, H.L. (1967), *The Swatantra Party and Indian Conservatism*, Cambridge: Cambridge University Press.

————— (1966), "The Foreign Policy Views of the Indian Right," *Pacific Affairs*, 39:5–18.

Eysenck, H.J. (1954), *The Psychology of Politics*, London: Routledge & Kegan Paul.

Fairbank, J.K. (1968), "A Preliminary Framework," in Fairbank, J.K. (Ed.), *The Chinese World Order*, Cambridge, Mass.: Harvard University Press, pp. 1–19.

————— (1966), "China's World Order," *Encounter*, 27:14–20.

Fall, B.B. (1962), "Red China's Aims in South Asia," *Current History*, 43:136–141.

Festinger, L. (1964), *Conflict, Decision and Dissonance*, Stanford, Calif.: Stanford University Press.

————— (1957), *A Theory of Cognitive Dissonance*, Evanston, Ill.: Row Peterson.

Field, J.O. (1972), "The Sino-Indian Border Conflict: An Exploratory Analysis of Action and Perception," *Sage Professional Papers in International Studies*, 1:02–002, Beverly Hills: Sage Publications, pp. 31–59.

Fisher, M.W., Rose, L.E., and Huttenback, R.A. (1963), *Himalayan Battleground: Sino-Indian Rivalry in Ladakh*, New York: Praeger.

Fisher, M.W., and Rose, L.E. (1962), "Ladakh and the Sino-Indian Border Crisis," *Asian Survey*, 2:27–37.

Fisher, M.W., and Bondurant, J.V. (1956a), *Indian Views of Sino-Indian Relations*, Berkeley: Institute of International Studies, University of California.

————— (1956b), "The Impact of Communist China on Visitors from India," *Far Eastern Quarterly*, 15:249–265.

Fitzgerald, C.P. (1969), *The Chinese View of Their Place in the World,* London: Oxford University Press.

Floyd, D. (1964), *Mao Against Khrushchev,* London: Pall Mall.

Franck, M.T., and Weisband, E. (1972), *World Politics,* New York: Oxford University Press.

Frankel, F.R. (1978), *India's Political Economy, 1947–1977,* Princeton, N.J.: Princeton University Press.

Friedlander, S., and Cohen, R. (1975), "The Personality Correlates of Belligerence in International Politics: A Comparative Analysis of Historical Case Studies," *Comparative Politics,* 7:155–186.

Friedman, E. (1975), "Some Political Constraints on a Political Science: Quantitative Content Analysis and the Indo-Chinese Border Crisis of 1962," *China Quarterly,* 63:528–538.

Galbraith, J.K. (1969), *Ambassador's Journal,* Boston: Houghton Mifflin.

Galtung, J., and Ruge, M. (1965), "The Structure of Foreign News," *Journal of Peace Research,* 2:64–91.

George, A.L. (1979), *Domestic Constraints on Regime Change in U.S. Foreign Policy: The Need for Policy Legitimacy,* Stanford: Stanford University (mimeo).

———— (1978a), "Case Studies and Theory Development: The Method of Structured, Focussed Comparison," Stanford: Stanford University (mimeo).

———— (1978b), "The Causal Nexus Between Cognitive Beliefs and Decision-Making Behavior: The 'Operational Code' Belief System," Stanford: Stanford University (mimeo).

———— (1969), "The 'Operational Code': A Neglected Approach to the Study of Political Leaders and Decision-Making," *International Studies Quarterly,* 13:190–222.

George, A.L., and Associates (1975), *Towards a More Soundly Based Foreign Policy: Making Better Use of Information,* Vol. II, Appendix D., Washington, D.C.: U.S. Government Printing Office.

George, T.J.S. (1964), *Krishna Menon: A Biography,* London: Jonathan Cape.

Ghatate, N.M. (1968), "The Sino-Burmese Border Settlement," *India Quarterly,* 23:87–105.

Gibb, G.R. (1974), "Defensive Communication," in Cathcart, R.S., and Samovar, L.A. (Eds.), *Small Group Communication* (2nd ed.), Iowa: Web.

Gittings, J. (1968), *Survey of the Sino-Soviet Dispute,* London: Oxford University Press.

Glenn, E.S., Johnson, R.H., Kimmel, P.R., and Wedge, B. (1970), "A Cognitive Interaction Model to Analyze Culture Conflict in International Relations," *Journal of Conflict Resolution,* 14:35–48.

Gokhale, G.B. (1976), "Nehru and Asia," *The South Atlantic Quarterly,* 75:98–114.

Gold, H. (1978), "Foreign Policy Decision-Making and the Environment: The Claims of Snyder, Brecher and the Sprouts," *International Studies Quarterly,* 22:545–568.

Gopal, S. (1975), *Jawaharlal Nehru: A Biography, Vol. I, 1889–1947,* London: Jonathan Cape.

———— (1979), *Jawaharlal Nehru: A Biography, Vol. II, 1947–1956,* London: Jonathan Cape.

Graber, D.A. (1976), *Verbal Behavior and Politics,* Urbana: University of Illinois Press.

Graham, I.C.C. (1964), "The Indo-Soviet Mig Deal and Its International Repercussions," *Asian Survey,* 4:823–832.

Greaser, C. (1966), *Sino-Indian Border Dispute, 1954–1962,* unpublished master's thesis, University of California, Berkeley 1966.

Greenstein, F.I. (1969), *Personality and Politics: Problems of Evidence Influence and Conceptualization,* Chicago: Markham Publishing Company.

―――― (1967), "The Impact of Personality on Politics: An Attempt to Clear the Underbrush," *American Political Science Review,* 41:629–641.

Greenwald, A.G. (1969), "The Open-Mindedness of the Counterattitudinal Role Player," *Journal of Experimental Social Psychology,* 5:375–388.

Griffith, W.E. (1964), *The Sino-Soviet Rift,* Cambridge, Mass.: M.I.T. Press.

Grossman, B. (1969), *The PLA-Economic Aspects,* Sonderdruck Nr. 18, Hamburg: Institue Fur Asienkunde.

Gupta, K.P. (1972a), "Indian Approaches to Modern China—I: A Socio-historical Analysis," *China Report* (July–August), 8:29–51.

―――― (1972b), "Indian Approaches to Modern China—II: A Socio-historical Analysis," *China Report* (September–October), 8:38–58.

Gupta, R.A. (1973), *V.K. Krishna Menon: An Appraisal of the Man and His Rhetoric,* Dehra Dun: Vanguard Press.

Gupta, S.K. (1974), *The Hidden History of the Sino-Indian Frontier,* Calcutta: Minerva.

Gurtov, M., and Hwang, B.M. (1980), *China Under Threat,* Baltimore: Johns Hopkins University Press.

Halperin, M.H. (1974), *Bureaucratic Politics and Foreign Policy,* Washington, D.C.: The Brookings Institution.

Halpern, A.M. (1961), "The Chinese Communist Line on Neutralism," *China Quarterly,* 5:90–115.

Hangen, W. (1963), *After Nehru, Who?* London: Ruper Hart-Davis.

Hansen, G.E. (1968), "Indian Perception of the Chinese Communist Regime and Revolution," *Orbis,* 12:268–293.

―――― (1967), "The Impact of the Border War on Indian Perceptions of China," *Pacific Affairs,* 40:235–249.

Hart, H.C. (1964), "India After the Chinese Attack," *Annals of the American Academy of Political and Social Sciences,* 351:50–57.

Harvey, O.J. (1966), "System Structure, Flexibility and Creativity," in Harvey, O.J. (ed.), *Experience Structure and Adaptability,* New York: Springer Publishing Company, pp. 39–65.

Hay, S.N. (1970), *Asian Ideas of East and West,* Cambridge, Mass.: Harvard University Press.

Heider, F. (1958), *The Psychology of Interpersonal Relations,* New York: John Wiley.

Heimsath, C.H., and Mansingh, S. (1971), *A Diplomatic History of Modern India,* Calcutta: Allied Publishers.

Hermann, M.G. (1978), "Effects of Personal Characteristics of Political Leaders on Foreign Policy," in East, M.A., Salmore, S.A., and Hermann, C.F. (eds.), *Why Nations Act?* Beverly Hills: Sage Publications, pp. 49–68.

―――― (1974), "Leader Personality and Foreign Policy Behavior," in Rosenau, J.N. (Ed.), *Comparing Foreign Policies,* Beverly Hills: Sage Publications, pp. 201–234.

Hilsman, R., Jr. (1961), "Intelligence and Policy Making in Foreign Affairs," in Rosenau, J.N., *International Politics and Foreign Policy,* New York: The Free Press, pp. 209–221.

_____ (1956), *Strategic Intelligence and National Decisions,* Illinois: The Free Press.

Himmelstrand, U. (1960), "Verbal Attitudes and Behaviour," *Public Opinion Quarterly,* 23:224–250.

Hinton, H.C. (1972), *China's Turbulent Quest* (enlarged ed.), New York: Macmillan.

_____ (1966), *Communist China in World Politics,* Boston: Houghton Mifflin.

_____ (1962), "Communist China's Military Posture," *Current History,* 43:149–155.

Hoffmann, S. (1968), *Gulliver's Troubles,* New York: McGraw Hill.

Hoffmann, S.A. (1981), "Faction Behavior and Cultural Codes: India and Japan," *Journal of Asian Studies,* 40:231–254.

_____ (1973), "Perceived Hostility and the Indian Reaction to China," *India Quarterly,* 26:283–399.

_____ (1972), "Anticipation, Disaster and Victory: India, 1962–1971," *Asian Survey,* 12:960–979.

_____ (1971), *The China Decisions of the Indian Government: 1959–1962,* unpublished Ph.D. dissertation, University of Pennsylvania.

Hollander, E.P. (1965), "Conformity Status and Idiosyncrasy Credit," in Singer, D.J. (Ed.), *Human Behavior and International Politics,* Chicago: Rand McNally, pp. 169–176.

Holsti, K.J. (1970), "National Role Conception in the Study of Foreign Policy," *International Studies Quarterly,* 14:233–309.

Holsti, O.R. (1977), "The 'Operational Code' as an Approach to the Analysis of Beliefs Systems," Final Report to the National Science Foundation, Grant No. SOC 75-15368, Durham, N.C.: Duke University.

_____ (1969), *Content Analysis for the Social Sciences and Humanities,* Reading, Mass.: Addison-Wesley.

_____ (1965), "The 1914 Case," *American Political Science Review,* 59:365–378.

Holsti, O.R., and George, A.L. (1975), "The Effect of Stress on the Performance of Foreign Policy Makers," in Cotter, C.P. (Ed.), *Political Science Annual: Individual Decision Making,* Indianapolis: Bobbs-Merrill, pp. 255–319.

Houn, F.W. (1967), "The Principles and Operational Code of China's International Conduct," *Journal of Asian Studies,* 27:21–40.

Hsiung, J.C. (1972a), *Law and Policy in China's Foreign Relations: A Study of Attitudes and Practice,* New York: Columbia University Press.

_____ (1972b), "Peaceful Coexistence and Its Correlations with Proletarian Internationalism," in Leng, S.C., and Chiu, H. (Eds.), *Law in Chinese Foreign Policy,* New York: Oceana Publications, pp. 36–79.

Hudson, G.F. (1962), "The Frontier of China and Assam," *China Quarterly,* 12:203–206.

Hussain, K. (1962), "China's Image of India's Foreign Policy of Non-Alignment," *Indian Journal of Political Science,* 23:242–251.

Huttenback, R.A.A. (1964), "Historical Note on the Sino-Indian Dispute over the Aksai Chin," *China Quarterly,* 18:201–207.

Ilchman, W.F. (1967), "Political Economy of Foreign Aid: The Case of India," *Asian Survey,* 7:667–688.

_____ (1966), "Political Development and Foreign Policy: The Case of India," *Journal of Commonwealth Political Studies,* 4:216–230.

Indian Institute of Public Opinion (1962), *Monthly Public Opinion Survey,* Vol. 8, Nos. 1 and 2, October–November.

Insko, C.A., and Schapler, J. (1971), "Triadic Consistency: A Statement of Affective-Cognitive-Conative Consistency," in Thomas, K. (Ed.), *Attitude and Behaviour,* Harmondsworth: Penguin, pp. 22–33.

Jacobson, E., Kumata, H., and Gullahorn, J.E. (1960), "Cross Cultural Contributions to Attitude Research," *Public Opinion Quarterly,* 24:205–223.

Jain, G. (1969), "Indo-Soviet Relations," *Institute for Defense Studies and Analyses Journal,* 2:30–39.

———— (1961), *Panchsheella and After,* New York: Asian Publishing House.

Janis, I.L. (1972), *Victims of Groupthink,* Boston: Houghton Mifflin.

———— (1962), "Psychological Effects of Warning," in Baker, G.W., and Champan, D.W. (Eds.), *Man and Society in Disaster,* New York: Basic Books, pp. 55–92.

———— (1954), "Personality Correlates of Susceptibility to Persuasion," *Journal of Personality,* 22:504–518.

Janis, I.L., and Mann, L. (1977), *Decision Making: A Psychological Analysis of Conflict, Choice and Commitment,* New York: The Free Press.

Jayaux, F. (1968), "Les Raisons Interieures Chinoises au Conflict Sino-Indian de 1962," in Centre d'Etude du Sud-Est Asiatique et de l'Extreme Orient, *Foreign Policy Making in India and China,* Proceedings, 3rd Working Session, Nov. 5–6, pp. 43–48.

Jervis, R. (1976), *Perception and Misperception in International Politics,* Princeton, N.J.: Princeton University Press.

———— (1970), *The Logic of Images in International Relations,* Princeton, N.J.: Princeton University Press.

———— (1969), "Hypotheses of Misperception," in Rosenau, J.N. (Ed.), *International Politics and Foreign Policy* (revised ed.), New York: The Free Press, pp. 239–254.

Jetly, N. (1979), *India China Relations 1947–1977,* New Delhi: Radiant.

———— (1976), "Parliament and India's China Policy, 1959–1963," *International Studies,* 15:229–260.

———— (1969), "Indian Opinion on the Tibetan Question," *International Studies,* 10:564–583.

Jha, B.K. (1973), *Indo-Nepalese Relations,* Bombay: Vora.

Jhangiani, M.A. (1967), *Jana Sangh and Swatantra,* Bombay: Manktalas.

Joffe, E. (1975), *Between Two Plenums: China's Intraleadership Conflict, 1959–1962,* Michigan Papers on Chinese Studies, No. 22.

Johnson, H.H., and Scileppi, J.A. (1969), "Effects of Ego-Involvement Conditions on Attitude Change to High and Low Credibility Communicators," *Journal of Personality and Social Psychology,* 13:31–36.

Johnston, D.M., and Chiu, H. (1968), *Agreements of the People's Republic of China, 1949–1967,* Cambridge, Mass.: Harvard University Press.

Jones, C. (1975), *How the Indian Lok Sabha Handles Defense Matters—An Institutional Study,* unpublished Ph.D. dissertation, American University, Washington, D.C.

Jones, E.E., and Decharms, R. (1957), "Changes in Social Perceptions as a Function of the Personal Relevance of Behavior," *Sociometry,* 20:75–85.

Judd, C.M. (1978), "Cognitive Effects of Attitude Conflict Resolution," *Journal of Conflict Resolution,* 22:483–498.

Kahin, G.M. (1955), *The Asian-African Conference, Bandung, Indonesia, April 1955,* Ithaca, N.Y.: Cornell University Press.

Kahn, R.L., Wolfe, D.M., Quinn, R.P., Snoek, J.D., and Rosenthal, R.A. (1964), *Organizational Stress,* New York: John Wiley.

Kao, T. (1963), "A Chinese View of the McMahon Line," *Eastern World* (February), 17:13–14.

Karanjia, R.K. (1960), *The Mind of Mr. Nehru: An Interview,* London: George Allen & Unwin.

Karnow, S. (1972), *Mao and China: From Revolution to Revolution,* New York: The Viking Press.

Katz, D. (1960), "The Functional Approach to the Study of Attitudes," *Public Opinion Quarterly,* 24:163–204.

Katz, D., and Kahn, R.L. (1966), *The Social Psychology of Organisations,* New York: Wiley.

Kaul, B.M. (Lt. Gen.) (1971), *Confrontation with Pakistan,* New Delhi: Vikas.

————— (1967), *The Untold Story,* Bombay: Allied Publishers.

Kaul, T.N. (1979), *Diplomacy in Peace and War: Recollection and Reflections,* New Delhi: Vikas.

Kavic, L.J. (1967), *India's Quest for Security: Defense Policies, 1947–1965,* Berkeley, Calif.: University of California.

Kelley, H.H. (1967), "Attribution Theory in Social Psychology," in Levine, D. (Ed.), *Nebraska Symposium on Motivation,* Lincoln: University of Nebraska Press, pp. 192–246.

Kelley, H.H. (1965), "Two Functions of Reference Groups," in Proshansky, H.M., and Seidenberg, B. (Eds), *Basic Studies in Social Psychology,* New York: Holt, Rinehart & Winston, pp. 210–215.

Kelman, H.C. (1975), "International Interchanges: Some Contributions from Theories of Attitude Change," *Comparative International Development,* 10:83–99.

————— (1958), "Compliance, Identification and Internalization: Three Processes of Attitude Change, *Journal of Conflict Resolution,* 2:51–60.

Kelman, H.C., and Eagly, A.H. (1974), "Attitude Toward the Communicator Perception of Communication Content and Attitude Change," in Himmelfarb, S., and Eagly, A.H. (Eds.), *Readings in Attitude Change,* New York: John Wiley, pp. 173–190.

Khera, S.S. (1968), *India's Defence Problem,* New Delhi: Orient Longmans.

Kilpatrick, F.P. (1970), "Two Processes in Perceptual Learning," in Proshansky, H.M., Ittelson, W.H., and Rivlin, L.G. (Eds.), *Environmental Psychology,* New York: Holt, Rinehart & Winston, pp. 104–112.

Kim, S.S. (1979), *China, The United Nations and World Order,* Princeton, N.J.: Princeton University Press.

Kishore, M.A. (1969), *Jana Sangh and India's Foreign Policy,* New Delhi: Associated Publishing House.

Kissinger, H.A. (1969), "Domestic Structure and Foreign Policy," in Rosenau, J.N. (Ed.), *International Politics and Foreign Policy* (revised ed.), New York: The Free Press, pp. 261–275.

Kleck, R.A., and Wheaton, J. (1967), "Dogmatism and Responses to Opinion-Consistent and Opinion-Inconsistent Information," *Journal of Personality and Social Psychology,* 5:249–252.

Kothari, R. (1970), *Politics in India,* Boston: Little, Brown.

Krech, D., and Crutchfield, R.S. (1971), "Perceiving the World," in Schramm, W., and Roberts, D.F. (Eds.), *The Process and Effect of Mass Communication* (revised ed.), Urbana: University of Illinois Press, pp. 235–264.

Krishnan, Kunhi, T.V. (1973), *Chavan and the Troubled Decade,* New Delhi: Hind Pocket Books.

Kulkarni, V.B. (1969), *The Indian Triumvirate,* Bombay: Baharatiya Vidya Bhavan.

Lal, K. (1970), *Jawaharlal Nehru: Promise and Performance,* New Delhi: Art & Letters.

Lall, A. (1968), *How Communist China Negotiates,* New York: Columbia University Press.

Lamb, A. (1973), *The Sino-Indian Border in Ladakh,* Canberra: Australian National University Press.

———— (1971), "War in the Himalayas," *Modern Asian Studies,* 5:389–397.

———— (1970), "The Sino-Indian and the Sino-Russian Borders: Some Comparisons and Contrasts," in Chien, J., and Tarling, N. (Eds.), *Studies in Social History of China and South-East Asia,* Cambridge: Cambridge University Press, pp., 135–152.

———— (1968), *Asian Frontiers,* London: Pall Mall

———— (1966), *The McMahon Line,* London: Routledge and Kegan Paul (2 vols.).

———— (1964), *The China-India Border,* London: Oxford University Press.

———— (1960), "The Indo-Tibetan Border," *Australian Journal of Politics and History,* 6:28–40.

Lazarus, R.S. (1966), *Psychological Stress and Coping Process,* New York: McGraw Hill.

Lee, D.H.K. (1966), "The Role of Attitude in Response to Environment," *Journal of Social Issues,* 22:83–91.

Lee, L.T. (1969), *China and International Agreements,* Durham, N.C.: Rule of Law Press.

———— (1967), "Treaty Relations of the People's Republic of China: A Study of Compliance," *University of Pennsylvania Law Review,* 116:244–314.

Levi, W. (1968), *The Challenge of World Politics in South and Southeast Asia,* Englewood Cliffs, N.J.: Prentice-Hall.

———— (1964), "Indian Neutralism Reconsidered," *Pacific Affairs,* 37: 137–147.

———— (1963), "Necrology on Indian Neutralism," *Eastern World* (February), 17:9–11.

Levinson, T.J. (1959), "Role, Personality and Social Structure in the Organizational Setting," *Journal of Abnormal and Social Psychology,* 58:170–180.

Li, T.T. (1960), *Tibet Today and Yesterdaay,* New York: Bookman Associates.

Liao, K. (1974), *Internal Mobilization and External Hostility in the Peoples Republic of China, 1960–1962 and 1967–1969,* unpublished Ph.D. dissertation, University of Michigan.

Liao, K., and Whiting, A.S. (1973), "Chinese Press Perception on Threat: The U.S. and India, 1962," *China Quarterly,* 53:80–97.

Lieberman, S. (1956), "The Effects of Changes in Roles on the Attitudes of Role Occupants," *Human Relations,* 9:385–402.

Lipjhart, A. (1971), "Comparative Politics and the Comparative Method," *American Political Science Review,* 63:682–693.

Longer, V. (1974), *Red Coats to Olive Green,* Bombay: Allied Publishers.

Lutzker, D.R. (1960), "Internationalism as a Predictor of Cooperative Behaviour," *Journal of Conflict Resolution*, 4:426–430.

Macmillan, M. (1969), "The Indian Army Since Independence," *South Asian Review*, 3:45–58.

Mammen, P.M. (1971), "Content Analysis and a Case Study in Nehru's Value-Profile," *Indian Political Science Review*, 5:159–176.

Mancall, M. (1963), "The Persistence of Tradition in Chinese Foreign Policy," *Annals of the American Academy of Political and Social Science*, 349:14–26.

Mankekar, D.R. (1968), *The Guilty Men of 1962*, Bombay: Tulsi Shah Enterprises.

Marwah, O. (1977), "Northeastern India: New Delhi Confronts the Insurgents," *Orbis*, 21:353–374.

Marwah, O.S. (1974), "Change and Modernization in India and China," *Institute for Defense Studies and Analyses Journal*, 7:131–301.

Mason, P. (1974), *A Matter of Honour: An Account of the Indian Army, Its Officers and Men*, London: Jonathan Cape.

Maxwell, N. (1972), *India's China War*, Harmondsworth: Pelican Books.

McClosky, H. (1967), "Personality and Attitude Correlates of Foreign Policy Orientation," in Rosenau, N.J. (Ed.), *Domestic Sources of Foreign Policy*, New York: The Free Press, pp. 51–110.

McLane, C.B. (1973), *Soviet-Asian Relations*, London: Central Asian Research Center.

Mehra, P. (1974), *The McMahon Line and After*, New Delhi: Macmillan.

———— (1968), "The Institutions at Work During the 1962 Conflict," in Centre d'Etude du Sud-Est Asiatique et de l'Extreme Orient, *Foreign Policy-Making in India and China*, Proceedings, 3rd Working Session, Nov. 5–6, pp. 1–26.

Mende, T. (1956), *Nehru: Conversations on India and World Affairs*, New York: Braziller.

Menon, K.P.S. (1968), *China, Past and Present*, Bombay: Asia Publishing House.

———— (1965), *Many Worlds: An Autobiography*, London: Oxford University Press.

———— (1963), *The Flying Troika*, London: Oxford University Press.

Mihaly, E.B. (1965), *Foreign Aid and Politics in Nepal*, London: Oxford University Press.

Miller, J.G. (1965), "The Individual as an Information Processing System," in Singer, D.J. (Ed.), *Human Behavior and International Politics*, Chicago: Rand McNally, pp. 202–212.

Miller, L.W., and Siegelman, L. (1978), "Is the Audience the Message? A Note on LBJ's Vietnam Statements," *Public Opinion Quarterly*, 42:71–80.

Minis, M. (1961), "The Interpretation of Opinion Statements as a Function of Recipients' Attitude and Source Prestige," *Journal of Abnormal and Social Psychology*, 63:82–86.

Mischel, W. (1968), *Personality and Assessment*, New York: John Wiley.

Misra, K.P. (1970), "Foreign Policy Planning Efforts in India," *Institute for Defense Studies and Analyses Journal*, 2:379–406.

Modelski, G. (1970), "The World's Foreign Ministers: A Political Elite," *Journal of Conflict Resolution*, 17:135–175.

———— (1964), "Kautilya: Foreign Policy and International System in the Ancient Hindu World," *American Political Science Review*, 58:549–560.

Moorthy, K.K.P. (1961), "South Asian Image of India," *Economic Weekly* (Bombay) (July), 13:1043–1045.

Moose, R. (1973), "Conceptualization of Human Environments," *American Psychologist*, 28:652–665.

Moraes, F. (1973), *Witness to an Era*, London: Weidenfeld & Nicolson.

—————— (1964), *Nehru, Sunlight and Shadow*, Bombay: Jaico Publishing House.

—————— (1956), *Jawaharlal Nehru: A Biography*, New York: Macmillan.

Mullik, B.N. (1971), *The Chinese Betrayal*, Bombay: Allied Publishers.

Mullin, C. (1975), "Tibetan Conspiracy," *Far Eastern Economic Review* (September 5), 89:30–34.

Muni, S.D. (1975), "India's Political Preferences in South Asia," *India Quarterly*, 31:23–35.

—————— (1973), *The Foreign Policy of Nepal*, New Delhi: National.

—————— (1968), "Sino-Nepalese Relations: Two Troubled Years—1959–1960," *South Asian Studies*, 3:33–46.

Murty, T.S. (1969), "India's Himalayan Frontier," *International Studies*, 10:464–485.

Myrdal, G. (1968), *Asian Drama*, Vol. I, New York: The Twentieth Century Fund.

Nakamura, H. (1966), "Time in Indian and Japanese Thought," in Fraser, J.T. (Ed.), *The Voice of Time*, New York: Braziller, pp. 77–91.

—————— (1964), *Ways of Thinking of Eastern Peoples: India-China-Tibet-Japan*, Honolulu: East-West Center Press.

Nanda, B.R. (1979), "Gandhi and Jawaharlal Nehru," in Nanda, B.R., Joshi, P.C., and Krishna, R. (Eds.), *Gandhi and Nehru*, New Delhi: Oxford University Press, pp. 1–32.

—————— (1974a), *The Nehrus: Motilal and Jawaharlal*, Chicago: The University of Chicago Press.

—————— (1974b), "Jawaharlal Nehru as a Writer," in Nanda, B.R. (Ed.), *Gokhale, Gandhi and the Nehrues*, London: George Allen & Unwin, pp. 120–129.

Nandy, A. (1970), "The Culture of Indian Politics," *Journal of Asian Studies*, 30:57–80.

Narain, I. (1971), "India's Quest for Security and the Philosophical Postulates of the Political System: An Analysis in the Context of Nehru's Approach," *Indian Journal of Political Science*, 32:261–273.

Nayar, K. (1973), *India: The Critical Years*, New Delhi: Vikas.

—————— (1969), *Between the Lines*, Bombay: Allied Publishers.

Nehru, J. (1962), "India Today and Tomorrow," in Nehru, J. *et al., India and The World*, New Delhi: Allied Publishers, pp. 1–46.

—————— (1951), *The Discovery of India* (3rd ed.), London: Meridian Books.

—————— (1942), *Glimpses of World History*, New York: John Day Company.

—————— (1941), *Toward Freedom: An Autobiography of Jawaharlal Nehru*, New York: John Day Company.

Neustadt, R.E. (1970), *Alliance Politics*, New York: Columbia University Press.

Nisbett, R., and Ross, L. (1980), *Human Inference: Strategies and Shortcomings of Social Judgement*, Englewood Cliffs, N.J.: Prentice-Hall.

Nizami, T.A. (1971), *The Communist Party and India's Foreign Policy*, New York: Barnes & Noble.

Norbu, D. (1979), "The 1959 Tibetan Rebellion: An Interpretation," *China Quarterly,* 77:74–93.

O'Ballance, E. (1962), "The Strength of India," *Military Review* (January), 42:25–35.

Ogden, C.K., and Richards, I.A. (1972), *The Meaning of Meaning* 10th ed.), London: Routledge and Kegan Paul.

Ogden, S. (1976), "China and International Law: Implication for Foreign Policy," *Pacific Affairs,* 49:28–48.

Osgood, C.E. (1960), "Cognitive Dynamics in the Conduct of Human Affairs," *Public Opinion Quarterly,* 24:341–365.

Palmer, N.D. (1975), *Election and Political Development: The South Asian Experience,* Durham, N.C.: Duke University Press.

———— (1961), *The Indian Political System,* Boston: Houghton Mifflin.

Pandey, B.N. (1977), "Jawaharlal Nehru: The Emergence of a Leader," in Pandey, B.N. (Ed.), *Leadership in South Asia,* New Delhi: Vikas, pp. 667–691.

———— (1976), *Nehru,* London: Macmillan.

Panikkar, K.M. (1963), *Studies in Indian History,* New York: Asia Publishing House.

———— (1957), *India and China,* Bombay: Asia Publishing House.

———— (1955), *In Two Chinas,* London: Allen & Unwin.

Passin, H. (1961), "Sino-Indian Cultural Relations" *China Quarterly,* 7:85–100.

Patterson, G.N. (1964), *Peking Versus Delhi,* New York: Praeger.

———— (1962), "Recent Chinese Policies in Tibet and Towards the Himalayan Border States," *China Quarterly,* 12:191–202.

Peissel, M. (1972), *Cavaliers of Kham: The Secret War in Tibet,* London: Heinemann.

Pittigrew, T.F. (1958), "The Measurement and Correlates of Category Width as a Cognitive Variable," *Journal of Personality,* 26:532–544.

Polat, A. (1968), "Tibet as a Mirror in Policy Making in the Field of Sino-Indian Relations," in Centre d'Etude du Sud-Est Asiatique et de l'Extreme Orient, *Foreign Policy Making in India and China,* Proceedings, 3rd Working Session, Nov. 5–6, pp. 27–42.

Postman, L., and Bruner, J.S. (1948), "Perception Under Stress," *Psychological Review,* 55:314–323.

Poulouse, T.T. (1971), "Bhutan's External Relations with China," *International and Comparative Law Quarterly,* 20:195–212.

Powell, R.L. (1968a), "The Increasing Power of Lin Piao and the Party Soldiers, 1959–1966," *China Quarterly,* 24:38–65.

———— (1968b), "Maoist Military Doctrines," *Asian Survey,* 8:239–262.

Prasad, B. (1977), "Jawaharlal Nehru as Prime Minister," in Pandey, B.N. (Ed.), *Leadership in South Asia,* New Delhi: Vikas, pp. 692–715.

———— (1973), *Indo-Soviet Relations, 1947–1972: A Documentary Study,* Bombay: Allied Publishers.

———— (1965), *Our Foreign Policy Legacy,* New Delhi: Peoples Publishing House.

Pruitt, D.G. (1965), "Definition of the Situation as a Determinant of International Action," in Kelman, H.C. (Ed.), *International Behavior,* New York: Holt, Rinehart & Winston, pp. 392–432.

Pye, L.W. (1961), "The Non-Western Political Process," in Rosenau, J.N. (Ed.), *International Politics and Foreign Policy,* New York: The Free Press, pp. 286–294.

Radhakrishnan, S. (1949), *The Hindu View of Life,* London: Allen & Unwin.
Rajan, M.S. (1962), "India and Pakistan as Factors in Each Other's Foreign Policy," *International Studies,* 3:349–394.
Rana, A.P. (1976), *The Imperative of Non-alignment,* New Delhi: Macmillan.
Range, W. (1961), *Jawaharlal Nehru's World View,* Atlanta: University of Georgia Press.
Rao, G.N. (1968), *The India-China Border,* London: Asia Publishing House.
Rao, P.V.R. (1970), *Defence Without Drift,* Bombay: Popular Prokoshan.
Ray, H. (1973), *Indo-Soviet Relations, 1955–1971,* Bombay: Jaico Publishing House.
———— (1969), "Changing Soviet Views on Mahatma Gandhi," *Journal of Asian Studies,* 29:85–106.
———— (1965), "The Policy of Russia Towards the Sino-Indian Conflict," *Political Quarterly,* 36:92–104.
Ray, S. (1963), "Reflections on the Chinese Invasion: Anguished Awakening," *Quest,* 36:40–45.
Reed, S.M. (1973), *Psychological Processes in Pattern Recognition,* New York: Academic Press.
Reid, E. (1981), *Envoy to Nehru,* New Delhi: Oxford University Press.
Retzlaff, R. (1969), "Revisionists and Sectarians: India's Two Communist Parties," in Scalapino, R.A. (Ed.), *The Communist Revolution in Asia,* Englewood Cliffs, N.J.: Prentice-Hall, pp. 329–362.
Richardson, H.E. (1972), *Tibet and Its History,* London: Oxford University Press.
Robinson, T.W. (1971), *Lin Piao as an Elite Type,* Santa Monica, Calif.: The Rand Corporation.
———— (1970), "Chou En-lai's Political Style: Comparison with Mao and Lin Piao," *Asian Survey,* 10:1101–116.
Rokeach, M. (1973), *The Nature of Human Values,* New York: The Free Press.
———— (1968), *Beliefs, Attitudes and Values,* San Francisco: Jossey-Bass.
———— (1966), "Attitude Change and Behavioral Change," *Public Opinion Quarterly,* 30:529–550.
———— (1960), *The Open and Closed Mind,* New York: Basic Books.
———— (1956), "On the Unity of Thought and Belief," *Journal of Personality,* 25:224–250.
———— (1954), "The Nature and Meaning of Dogmatism," *Psychological Review,* 61:194–204.
Romulo, C.P. (1956), *The Meaning of Bandung,* Chapel Hill: University of North Carolina Press.
Rose, L.E. (1977), *The Politics of Bhutan,* Ithaca, N.Y.: Cornell University Press.
———— (1974), "Bhutan's External Relations," *Pacific Affairs,* 47:192–208.
———— (1971), *Nepal: Strategy for Survival,* Berkeley: University of California Press.
———— (1963), "The Himalayan Border States: Buffers in Transition," *Asian Survey,* 3:116–122.
———— (1961), "Sino-Indian Rivalry and the Himalayan Border States," *Orbis,* 5:198–215.
Rosenau, J.N. (1970), "Foreign Policy as an Adaptive Behavior," *Comparative Politics,* 2:365–387.

Rosenberg, M.J. (1960), "A Structural Theory of Attitude Dynamics," *Public Opinion Quarterly,* 24:319–340.
Rosenberg, S.W., and Wolfsfeld, G. (1977), "International Conflict and the Problem of Attribution," *Journal of Conflict Resolution,* 21:75–104.
Rosenthal, A.M. (1957), "Krishna Menon," *New York Times Magazine,* April 7.
Rowland, J. (1967), *A History of Sino-Indian Relations,* Princeton, N.J.: D. Van Nostrand.
Rubin, A.P. (1968), "The Position of Tibet in International Law," *China Quarterly,* 35:110–154.
———— (1960), "The Sino-Indian Border Dispute," *International and Comparative Law Quarterly,* 9:96–125.
Rubinoff, A.G. (1971), *India's Use of Force in Goa,* Bombay: Popular Prokoshan.
Rudolph, L.I., and Rudolph, S.H. (1966), "Generals and Politicians in India," *Pacific Affairs,* 37:5–19.
Saigal, J.R. (Lt. Col.) (1979), *The Unfought War of 1962: The NEFA Debacle,* Bombay: Allied Publishers.
Sardesai, D.R. (1968), *Indian Foreign Policy in Cambodia, Laos and Vietnam, 1947–1964,* Berkeley: University of California Press.
Sawhny, R. (1969), "China's Control of Tibet and Its Implication," *International Studies,* 10:486–494.
Schelling, T.C. (1970), *The Strategy of Conflict,* London: Oxford University Press.
Schlesinger, A.M. (1965), *A Thousand Days,* Greenwich, Conn.: Fawcett Publications.
Schram, S.R. (1974) (Ed.), *Chairman Mao Talks to the People: Talks and Letters 1956–1971,* New York: Pantheon Books.
———— (1969), *The Political Thought of Mao Tse-tung,* New York: Praeger.
Schrecker, J.E. (1971), *Imperialism and Chinese Nationalism,* Cambridge, Mass.: Harvard University Press.
Schwartz, B.I. (1968), "The Chinese Perception of World Order, Past and Present," in Fairbank, J.K. (Ed.), *The Chinese World Order,* Cambridge, Mass.: Harvard University Press, pp. 276–290.
Scott, G.L. (1975), *Chinese Treaties,* New York: Oceana Publications.
Scott, W.A. (1969), "Structures of Natural Cognitions," *Journal of Personality and Social Psychology* 12:261–278.
———— (1966), "Flexibility, Rigidity and Adaptation: Toward Clarification of a Concept," in Harvey, O.J. (Ed.), *Experience Structure and Adaptability,* New York: Springer Publishing Company, pp. 369–400.
———— (1965), "Psychological and Social Correlates of International Images," in Kelman, H.C. (Ed.) *International Behavior,* New York: Holt, Rinehart & Winston, pp. 71–103.
———— (1963), "Cognitive Complexity and Cognitive Flexibility," *Sociometry,* 26:66–74.
———— (1960), "International Ideology and Interpersonal Ideology," *Public Opinion Quarterly,* 27:719–735.
———— (1959), "Cognitive Consistency Response Reinforcement and Attitude Change," *Sociometry,* 22:219–229.
———— (1958), "Rationality and Non-Rationality of International Attitudes," *Journal of Conflict Resolution,* 2:8–16.

Sebastian, M.S. (1975), *Soviet Economic Aid to India*, New Delhi: N.V. Publications.

Sen, B. (1966), "Himalayas and Their Occupation Patterns," *Eastern Anthropologist*, 19:177–189.

Sen, C. (1969), "Tibet and the Sino-Indian Impasse," *International Studies*, 10:523–541.

Sen Gupta, B. (1970), *The Fulcrum of Asia*, New York: Pegasus.

Sen, S.P. (1971) (Ed.), *The Sino-Indian Border Question: A Historical Review*, Calcutta: Institute of Historical Studies.

Seton, M. (1967), *Panditji: A Portrait of Jawaharlal Nehru*, London: Dennis Dobson.

Shao, K.K. (1979), "Chou En-lai's Diplomatic Approach to Non-Aligned States in Asia," *China Quarterly*, 78:324–338.

Shah, A.B. (1966), *India's Defence and Foreign Policies*, Bombay: Manaktolas.

Shaha, R. (1975), *Nepali Politics: Retrospect and Prospect*, New Delhi: Oxford University Press.

Sharma, S.P. (1971), *India's Boundary and Territorial Dispute*, New Delhi: Vikas.

———— (1965), "The India-China Border Dispute: An Indian Perspective," *American Journal of International Law*, 59:16–47.

Sheikh, F. (1973), "Nehru's Images of the International Environment: A Content Analysis," *Pakistan Horizon*, 26:43–49.

Shelvankar, K.S. (1962), "China's Himalayan Frontiers, I: India's Attitude," *International Affairs*, 38:472–478.

Sherif, M., and Sherif, C.W. (1967), "Attitude as the Individual's Own Categories: The Social Judgment–Involvement Approach to Attitude and Attitude Change," in Sherif, C.W., and Sherif, M. (Eds.), *Attitude, Ego-Involvement and Change*, New York: John Wiley, pp. 105–139.

Shils, E. (1961), "Influence and Withdrawal: The Intellectual in Indian Political Development," in Marvic, D. (Ed.), *Political Decision-Makers*, New York: The Free Press, pp. 29–56.

Sidonius, J. (1978), "Intolerance to Ambiguity and Socio-politico Ideology: A Multidimensional Analysis," *European Journal of Social Psychology* 8:215–236.

Siegel, R.L. (1968), "Chinese Efforts to Influence Soviet Policy to India," *India Quarterly*, 24:213–238.

Simmonds, J.D. (1972), "The New Gun-Barrel Elite," in Whitson, W.W. (Ed), *The Military and Political Power in China in the 1970s*, New York: Praeger, pp. 93–114.

———— (1969), "P'eng Te-huai: A Chronological Re-examination," *China Quarterly*, 37:120–138.

Simon, H.A. (1976), *Administrative Behavior*, 3rd ed., New York: The Free Press.

Singh, B. (1967), "The Legality of the McMahon Line: An Indian Perspective," *Orbis*, 11:271–284.

Sinha, M. (1971), "The Maoist World System and India's Place in It," *Institute for Defence Studies and Analyses Journal*, 3:353–406.

———— (1970), "Nepal's Role in Sino-Indian Relations: 1949–1969," *Institute for Defence Studies and Analyses Journal*, 2:456–486.

Slovic, P., and Lichtenstein, S. (1971), "Comparison of Bayesian and Regression Approaches to the Study of Information Processing in Judgment," *Organizational Behavior and Human Performance*, 6:649–744.

Smith, R.F. (1969), "On the Structure of Foreign News: A Comparison of the *New York Times* and the *Indian White Papers," Journal of Peace Research*, 6:23–36.

Smoker, P. (1969), "A Time Series Analysis of Sino-Indian Relations, *Journal of Conflict Resolution*, 13:172–188.

—— (1964), "Sino-Indian Relations: A Study of Trade Communication and Defense," *Journal of Peace Research*, 2:65–76.

Snyder, G.H., and Diesing, P. (1977), *Conflict Among Nations: Bargaining Decision Making and System Structure in International Crises*, Princeton, N.J.: Princeton University Press.

Snyder, J. (1978), "Rationality at the Brink: The Role of Cognitive Processes in Failure of Deterrence," *World Politics*, 30:345–365.

Snyder, R.C., Bruck, H.W., and Sapin, B. (1962), *Foreign Policy Decision Making*, New York: The Free Press.

Sprout, H., and Sprout, M. (1969), "Environmental Factors in the Study of International Politics," in Rosenau, J.N. (Ed.), *International Politics and Foreign Policy* (Revised ed.), New York: The Free Press, pp. 41–56.

—— (1956), *Man-Milieu Relationship Hypotheses in Context of International Politics*, Princeton, N.J.: Center of International Studies, Princeton University.

Stahnke, A.A. (1970), "The Place of International Law in Chinese Strategy and Tactics: The Case of the Sino-Indian Dispute," *Journal of Asian Studies*, 30:95–120.

Stein, A.B. (1969), *India and the Soviet Union: The Nehru Era*, Chicago: University of Chicago Press.

Stein-Gross, J., and Tanter, R. (1980), *Rational Decision-Making: Israel's Security Choices 1967*, Columbus: Ohio State University Press.

Stein-Gross, J. (1968), *Elite Images and Foreign Policy: Nehru, Menon and India's Policies*, unpublished Ph.D. dissertation, McGill University.

Steinbruner, J.D. (1974), *The Cybernetic Theory of Decision*, Princeton, N.J.: Princeton University Press.

Stern, R.W. (1965), "The Sino-Indian Border Controversy and the Communist Party of India," *Journal of Politics*, 27:66–86.

Subhan, M. (1968), "Sino-Indian Relations," in Centre D'Etude du Sud-Est Asiatique et de L'Extreme Orient, *The Cultural Revolution and China's Foreign Policy*, Proceedings, 2nd Working Session, June 26–27, Bruxelles, pp. 128–142.

Subrahamanyam, K. (1976), "Nehru and the India-China Conflict," in Nanda, B.R. (Ed.), *Indian Foreign Policy: The Nehru Years*, New Delhi: Vikas, pp. 102–130.

—— (1970a), "Neville Maxwell's War," *Institute for Defence Studies and Analyses Journal*, 3:268–291.

—— (1970b), "Decision Making in Defence," *Institute for Defence Studies and Analyses Journal*, 2:424–444.

Suedfeld, P., and Tetlock, P. (1977), "Integrative Complexity of Communication in International Crisis," *International Studies Quarterly*, 21:169–184.

Suzuki, C. (1968), "China's Relations with Inner Asia: The Hsiung-Nu, Tibet," in Fairbank, J.K. (Ed.), *The Chinese World Order*, Cambridge, Mass.: Harvard University Press, pp. 180–197.

Taylor, W.S. (1948), "Basic Personality in Orthodox Hindu Culture Patterns," *Journal of Abnormal and Social Psychology*, 43:3–12.

Thomas, A.E. (1956), "Indo-Sino Cultural Relations," *Far Eastern Economic Review* (November 1), 21:551–553.

Thomas, E.J. (1968), "Role Theory, Personality and the Individual," in Borgatta, E.F., and Lambert, W.W. (Eds.), *Handbook of Personality Theory and Research,* Chicago: Rand McNally, pp. 694–727.

Thompson, J.D., and McEwen, W.J. (1969), "Organizational Goals and Environment," in Etzioni, A. (Ed.), *A Sociological Reader on Complex Organizations* (2nd ed.), New York: Holt, Rinehart & Winston, pp. 187–198.

Triandis, H.C. (1971), *Attitudes and Attitude Change,* New York: John Wiley.

———— (1964), "Cultural Influence upon Cognitive Processes," in Berkowitz, L. (Ed.), *Advances in Experimental Social Psychology,* Vol 1, New York: Academic Press, pp. 2–48.

Triandis, H.C., Vassiliou, V., and Nassiakou, M. (1968), "The Cross-Cultural Studies of Subjective Culture," *Journal of Personality and Social Psychology,* monograph supplement, Part 2, 8:1–42.

Triandis, H.C., and Vassiliou, V. (1967), "Frequency of Contact and Stereotyping," *Journal of Personality and Social Psychology,* 7:316–328.

Tsou, T. (1964), "Mao Tse-tung and Peaceful Coexistence," *Orbis,* 8:35–61.

Tsou, T., and Halperin, M.H. (1965), "Mao Tse-tung's Revolutionary Strategy and Peking's International Behavior," *American Political Science Review,* 59:80–99.

Tversky, A., and Kahneman, D. (1974), "Judgment Under Uncertainty: Heuristics and Biases," *Science,* 185:1124–1131.

Union Research Institute (1969), *The Case of P'eng Teh-huai, 1959–1968,* Hong Kong.

Van Eckelen, W.F. (1968), "Analysis of the Decision Process," in Centre d'Etude du Sud-Est Asiatique et de l'Extreme Orient, *Foreign Policy Making in India and China,* Proceedings, 3rd Working Session, Nov. 5–6, pp. 64–77.

———— (1964), *Indian Foreign Policy and the Border Dispute with China,* The Hague: Martinus Nijhoff.

Varkey, O. (1974), *At the Crossroads,* Calcutta: Minerva.

Venkatewaran, A.L. (1967), *Defence Organization in India,* New Delhi: Government of India, Ministry of Information and Broadcasting.

Verba, S. (1967), "Some Dilemmas in Comparative Research," *World Politics,* 20:111–127.

———— (1969), "Assumptions of Rationality and Non-Rationality in Models of the International System," in Rosenau, J.N. (Ed.), *International Politics and Foreign Policy* (revised ed.), New York: The Free Press, pp. 217–231.

Vertzberger, Y. (forthcoming), *Information Processing and Misperception: The Case of Foreign Policy.*

———— (1978), "India's Border Crisis with China, 1962," *Jerusalem Journal of International Relations,* 3:117–142.

Wallace, M.D. (1973), *War and Rank Among Nations,* Lexington, Mass.: Lexington Books.

Wasserman, B. (1960), "The Failure of Intelligence Prediction," *Political Studies,* 8:156–169.

Weng, B.S. (1972), *Peking's U.N. Policy,* New York: Praeger.

———— (1966), "Communist China's Changing Attitudes Toward the United Nations," *International Organization,* 20:677–704.

White, R.K., and Lippit, R. (1968), "Leader Behavior and Member Reaction in Three Social Climates," in Cartwright, D., and Sander, A. (Eds.), *Group Dynamics* (3rd ed.), New York: Tavistock Publications, pp. 318–335.

Whiting, A.S. (1975), *The Chinese Calculus of Deterrence,* Ann Arbor, Mich.: Michigan University Press.

———— (1972), "The Use of Force in Foreign Policy by the People's Republic of China," *Annals of the American Academy of Political and Social Science,* 402:55–66.

Whiting, A.S., and Sheng, S. (1958), *Sinkiang: Pawn or Pivot,* East Lansing: Michigan University Press.

Whitson, W.W. (1973), *The Chinese High Command: A History of Communist Military Politics 1927-71,* London: Macmillan.

Whittam, D.C. (1961), "The Sino-Burmese Boundary Treaty," *Pacific Affairs,* 34:174–183.

Whorfe, B.L. (1956), *Language Thought and Reality,* Cambridge, Mass.: M.I.T. Press.

Wicker, A.W. (1971), "Attitude versus Action: The Relationship of Verbal and Overt Behavioural Responses to Attitude Change," in Thomas, K. (Ed.), *Attitudes and Behaviour,* Harmondsworth: Penguin, pp. 135–178.

Wiegele, T.C. (1973), "Decision Making in an International Crisis: Some Biological Factors," *International Studies Quarterly,* 17:295–335.

Wilcox, W.A. (1968), "China's Strategic Alternatives in South Asia," in Tsou, T. (Ed.), *China in Crisis,* Vol. 2, Chicago: University of Chicago Press, pp. 395–440.

———— (1964), *India, Pakistan and the Rise of China,* New York: Walker and Company.

Williams, R.L.F. (1962), *The State of Pakistan,* London: Faber and Faber.

Wise, D. (1973), *The Politics of Lying,* New York: Random House.

Witkin, H.A. (1974), "Cognitive Styles Across Cultures," in Berry, J.W., and Dasen, P.R. (Eds.), *Culture and Cognition,* London: Methuen, pp. 99–118.

Wohlstetter, R. (1962), *Pearl Harbor: Warning and Decision,* Stanford: Stanford University Press.

Wood, G.L. (1974), "Nehru: Authority, Intimacy and Vocational in the Life of a Revolutionary," *Indian Journal of Political Science,* 35:105–121.

Woodman, D. (1970), *Himalayan Frontiers,* New York: Barrie and Jenkins.

Yang, Yan-Yuan (1974), *Nehru and China 1927-1949,* unpublished Ph.D. dissertation, The University of Virginia.

Young, K.T. (1968a), *Negotiating with the Chinese Communists: The U.S. Experience 1953-1967.* New York: McGraw-Hill.

———— (1968b), "The Hidden Problems in Negotiating with Asia's Reds," *Look* (March 5), 32:17–19.

Zagoria, D.S. (1962), *The Sino-Soviet Conflict, 1956-1961,* Princeton, N.J.: Princeton University Press.

Zajonc, R.B. (1960), "The Concepts of Balance, Congruity and Dissonance," *Public Opinion Quarterly,* 24:280–296.

Zander, A. (1971), *Motives and Goals in Groups,* New York: Academic Press.

Zinkin, T. (1961), "Sikkim: India's Achilles Heel," *New Commonwealth* (January), 39:12–14.

———— (1955), "Indian Foreign Policy: An Interpretation of Attitudes," *World Politics,* 7:179–208.

Zinnes, D.A., Zinnes, J.L., and McClure, R.D. (1972), "Hostility in Diplomatic Communication," in Hermann, C.F. (Ed.), *International Crises,* New York: The Free Press, pp. 139–164.

Zinnes, D.A., North, R.C., and Koch, H.E., Jr. (1961), "Capability, Threat and the Outbreak of War," in Rosenau, J.N. (Ed.), *International Politics and Foreign Policy,* New York: The Free Press, pp. 468–482.

Index